CAMBRIDGE GREEK AND LATIN CLASSICS

GENERAL EDITORS

E. J. KENNEY
Emeritus Kennedy Professor of Latin, University of Cambridge

AND

P. E. EASTERLING
Regius Professor of Greek, University of Cambridge

HORACE
EPODES

EDITED BY
DAVID MANKIN
Associate Professor of Classics, Cornell University

 CAMBRIDGE
UNIVERSITY PRESS

Published by the Press Syndicate of the University of Cambridge
The Pitt Building, Trumpington Street, Cambridge CB2 1RP
40 West 20th Street, New York, NY 10011-4211, USA
10 Stamford Road, Oakleigh, Melbourne 3166, Australia

© Cambridge University Press 1995

First published 1995

A catalogue record for this book is available from the British Library

Library of Congress cataloguing in publication data

Horace.
[Epodi. English]
Epodes / Horace ; edited by David Mankin.
p.   cm. – (Cambridge Greek and Latin classics)
Includes bibliographical references and index.
ISBN 0 521 39469 4 (hardback) – ISBN 0 521 39774 X (paperback)
1. Political poetry, Latin – Translations into English.   2. Verse
satire, Latin – Translations into English.   3. Rome – Poetry.
1. Mankin, David.   11. Title.   111. Series.
PA6396.A1   1995
871′.01–dc20   94-38675
CIP

ISBN 0 521 39469 4 hardback
ISBN 0 521 39774 X paperback
Transferred to digital printing 2002

CONTENTS

'Who goes there?' 'A friend,' he said. The two in the back, who doubtless considered the answer to be a stock reply to a stock question, were climbing over the side reluctantly slowly. They were covering him with pistols. 'Advance, friend, and be recognized,' said the bigger one squeakily. Then he cleared his throat. And he, Prewitt that is, the unrecognized friend, came toward them slowly.

James Jones
From Here to Eternity

PREFACE

The purpose of this book is to provide students of Latin poetry with the means for attempting to understand the *Epodes*. To this end the editor has provided what he believes to be the necessary grammatical and linguistic material, historical context, and literary background, and also offered both his own interpretations and those of his predecessors for the reader to accept, reject, or ignore.

The *Epodes* have received less attention than Horace's other works, and the editor imagines, at least, that some of what is included here is original. But his debt to his predecessors, especially Lambinus, Bentley, L. Mueller, Kiessling, Heinze, and Giarratano, is large even when, for reasons of space, unacknowledged, and the bibliography should indicate how much is owed to more recent scholarship, particularly that published before 1993.

The editor also gratefully acknowledges the assistance of many people, among them F. M. Ahl, Barbara Bennett, Victoria Borus, J. S. Clay, Steffi Green, Vanessa Karahalios, Shelley Kaufhold, Jane Krupp, Grace Ledbetter, all the Mankins (including Marmalade), Rosamund Miles, J. F. Miller, Piero Pucci, and especially the editors at Cambridge, P. E. Easterling, P. Hire, S. Moore, and most of all E. J. Kenney. Finally, he wishes to dedicate this work to the memory of J. P. Elder, teacher and scholar *de Horatio optime meritus*, and of Harold Pinkney, best of grandfathers and last of 'the boys up our way'.

Ithaca, NY   David Mankin
November 1994

INTRODUCTION

1. HORACE

The main sources for information on Quintus Horatius Flaccus (H.)[1] are his own works and a short biography transmitted with his text that probably came from the *De uiris illustribus* of Suetonius (time of Trajan).[2] H. was born at the town of Venusia in Calabria close to Apulia on 8 December 65 BC (13.6n.),[3] the son of an ex-slave who had become an auction agent (*S.* 1.6).[4] This father had H. educated at Rome and then Athens as would befit the son of an equestrian or a senator (*S.* 1.6.76–7, *Ep.* 2.1.69–71, 2.41–5).

While H. was at Athens he joined the army of the 'liberator' M. Brutus (Intro. 2), rising to the high rank of *tribunus militum* (4.20n.). He fought in the battle of Philippi (42 BC), and, when his side was defeated, eventually returned to Italy. There he found himself deprived of his father's estate (*Ep.* 2.2.50–1), possibly as a result of its confiscation and assignment to a discharged soldier of the victors.[5]

Later in life H. would claim that he was completely impoverished, and that this is why he took up 'writing verses' (*Ep.* 2.2.51–4). But he could not have been entirely without resources. He was able somehow to purchase a 'living' as a *scriba quaestorius* and, even more significant, he remained an equestrian in status with the possibility, if he had so chosen, of advancing to senatorial rank.[6]

Around this time (early thirties BC) H. became friends with the poets Virgil and Varius, which suggests that he was already writing and showing his works to others. It seems likely that he was concen-

---

[1] For H.'s full name, cf. *S.* 2.6.37 (Quintus), *C.* 4.6.44, *Ep.* 1.14.5 (Horatius), *Epodes* 15.12, *S.* 2.1.18 (Flaccus), and *ILS* 5050 (commemorating the Secular games of 17 BC) *carmen composuit Q. Hor[at]ius Flaccus*.

[2] Fraenkel (1957) 1–2.

[3] H. mentions the year and month (13.6, *C.* 3.21.1, *Ep.* 1.20.26–7), Suetonius the day (*natus est VI idus Decembris L. Cotta et L. Torquato consulibus*).

[4] Cf. Fraenkel (1957) 4–5. Nothing is known about H.'s mother, but he does mention a nurse named Pullia (*C.* 3.4.10; cf. Fraenkel (1957) 274).

[5] H. does not say this, but it has been inferred from the knowledge of such confiscations that he shows in his Ofellus poem (*S.* 2.2).

[6] Cf. *S.* 1.6 with the interpretation of Armstrong (1986) and (1989) 18–19.

trating on the hexameter poems that would make up his first book of
Satires,[7] although some would date certain *Epodes* to this period
(Intro. 4). In 39 or 38 BC Virgil and Varius introduced H. to Maece-
nas, who 'in the ninth month after bade [H.] to be among the num-
ber of [his] friends' (*S.* 1.6.61–2).

C. Cilnius Maecenas was an equestrian originally from Arretium
in Etruria.[8] It is not known when or why he came to Rome, but he
was already a trusted adviser to Octavian by the time of the war
against the 'liberators' (Intro. 2), and he would continue in that
capacity until the late twenties BC.[9] His talents seem to have been
more political than military, and he had a reputation for decadence
and effeminacy (1.10, 9.13–14, 14.1nn.),[10] but he was with Octavian at
Philippi (*Eleg. Maec.* 43–4) and, accompanied by H., in parts of the
war against Sextus Pompeius (Intro. 2) and at Actium (9.3n.).

Maecenas was extremely wealthy, had pretensions as a writer,[11]
and was a friend to a number of famous poets. From later antiquity
on his relationship with these men has been seen as more or less that
of a 'patron' to his 'clients'.[12] But in the case of H., at least, this seems
to be a distortion. As he presents it, H.'s friendship with Maecenas
is based above all on a mutual regard and affection that is inde-
pendent of the 'positions' of the two (1.2, 23–4nn.; cf. *S.* 1.6, 9.45–
60, 2.6.29–58). Maecenas gave him gifts, as friends do (1.31n., *C.*
2.18.11–13, 3.16.38, *Ep.* 1.7), but there is no evidence that H., himself
an *eques* and *scriba* (above), was dependent on these for a livelihood.[13]

---

[7] The date of publication of *Satires* 1 is not certain, but it may have been as
late as 32 BC (Mankin (1988a) 68).

[8] For Maecenas, cf. N–H on *C.* 1.1.1, *RE* XIV 207–29, Armstrong (1989)
20–4.

[9] It is not clear why Maecenas 'faded from the scene'; cf. *RE* XIV 212–13,
Syme (1939) 409.

[10] Cf. Sen. *Ep.* 19.9, 92.35, 101.10–15, 114.4–6, 120.19, *RE* XIV 214.

[11] Poetic fragments in *FPL* pp. 132–4, Courtney (1993) 276–81; cf. 17.67n.,
N–H on *C.* 2.12.10.

[12] E.g. Porph. on *C.* 4.12.15, Schol. on *C.* 1.1.2, 3.16.38, *S.* 2.6.31, also Suet.
Vit. Horat., Juv. 7.94. There are countless modern versions of this; for a cri-
tique, cf. Armstrong (1986).

[13] It is often stated that H. owed his 'Sabine farm' (1.31–2n.) to Maecenas,
but neither he nor Suetonius says this. It seems to be an inference from *C.*
2.18.12–14 (cf. Porph., Schol. *ad loc.*), which is usually taken to mean 'now

Little is known about the externals of H.'s life after the period that is the focus of the *Epodes*.[14] At some point Octavian (by then 'Augustus') invited him to become his personal secretary or at least a member of his household, but H. declined (Suet.). Octavian also seems to have invited him to compose certain poems, including *Ep.* 2.1 (the 'epistle to Augustus'), the odes concerning Tiberius and Drusus (*C.* 4.4, 14), and the *Carmen saeculare*, which was performed at the Secular games of 17 BC (Suet.).[15] Following that there is silence until the notice of H.'s death, which occurred on 27 November 8 BC, shortly after the death of Maecenas (cf. *C.* 2.17).

2. HISTORICAL BACKGROUND

H.'s early works, *Satires* I and the *Epodes* (Intro. 4), belong to a time of great tension (42–32 BC), then great conflict (32–30 BC) among the Romans. For over a century Rome and Italy had been ravaged by strife both external and internal.[16] The Gracchi and their supporters had been murdered in the city (133, 121 BC), there was a huge invasion of German tribes (105–101) followed by more civil disorder (100), then a war with the Italian allies (91–88), and a full-scale civil war, the first in Rome's history (88–81). A relatively peaceful interval (80–50) was nevertheless punctuated by rebellions, conspiracies, and slave revolts (79–71 (Sertorius), 78 (Lepidus), 72–71 (Spartacus), 63 (Catiline)), and, increasingly, civil disorder in the city (58–52). This culminated in yet another civil war, which left Julius Caesar the sole ruler of the state (50–44).

When Caesar was killed by Brutus and the other 'liberators' (44), it appeared at first that the Republic might be restored. But it was not long before factions began to vie for control, one consisting of

that he has given me a Sabine estate, I need ask nothing from my powerful friend' (=Maecenas; cf. 13.6n.). But the passage makes more sense in its context if H. is saying 'Since I have an estate that belongs to me [i.e. makes me independent], I do not have to ask anything from a powerful friend.'

[14] Cf. Putnam (1986) 15–30, Armstrong (1989) 135–6.

[15] The Suetonian *uita* cites evidence (a letter of Augustus) only in regard to *Ep.* 2.1, and some scholars have been justly sceptical about Augustus' involvement with *Odes* 4 (Fraenkel (1957) 364–5, Putnam (1986) 20–3).

[16] For the history of Rome in this period, cf. Syme (1939), Scullard (1982), Brunt (1988).

the 'liberators', another of M. Antonius (Antony) and his followers, and a third of Caesar's heir Octavian and his followers.[17] When Octavian and Antony made common cause as members of the 'second triumvirate'[18] they turned on the others, proscribing and murdering prominent citizens, including Cicero, at Rome, and defeating the armies of the 'liberators' at Mutina (43) and finally at Philippi (42).

After Philippi Octavian and Antony consolidated their power and set about, as they put it, 'restoring the state'. Their only rivals were a few die-hard senators and Sextus Pompeius, the son of Pompey the Great, whose fleet of Romans, ex-slaves, and foreigners was a serious threat to Italian food supplies and shipping. In 41–40 Octavian fought a brutal war against Romans holed up in Perusia and led by Antony's brother. This came close to erupting into another full-scale civil war, but the triumvirs managed to salvage and cement their coalition by in effect dividing the Roman world between them, with Octavian attending to the western, Antony to the eastern empire ('treaty of Brundisium' 40). A personal bond was created by the marriage of Antony to Octavian's sister Octavia.

An accord was also reached with Sextus Pompeius, who received, among other things, control of Sicily ('treaty of Misenum' 39). But when Antony went east to prepare for war against Parthia, Octavian and Sextus soon fell out. Their war began with Octavian capturing Sardinia (38), but he then suffered a series of naval defeats and disasters, including one off Cape Palinurus, at which Maecenas and probably H. were present.[19] It was not until he put M. Vipsanius Agrippa, Maecenas' 'man-of-action' counterpart,[20] in charge and received some assistance from Antony, that he was able to defeat Sextus, first at Mylae (July or August 36), then decisively at Naulochus (3 September 36).[21]

---

[17] For the name 'Octavian', cf. 1.3n.

[18] The 'triumvirate' also included M. Aemilius Lepidus, but 'this flimsy character' (Syme (1939) 166) was essentially irrelevant even before Octavian forced him to 'retire' shortly after Naulochus.

[19] Cf. C. 3.4.28 with the discussion of Wistrand (1958) 16–17.

[20] Agrippa (C. 1.6, S. 2.3.185, Ep. 1.12) is 'conspicuous by his absence' from the Epodes; cf. 9.7–8n.

[21] Cf. 9.7–10 with notes.

Antony had come to Italy after Octavian's first setbacks, and they renewed the triumvirate with another treaty (Tarentum, spring of 37).[22] But when Antony returned east it was to Cleopatra, who had become his ally and probably more as early as 42, but with whom he now lived openly, apparently preferring her and their children to Octavia and his legitimate Roman offspring. In 34, after a successful campaign in Armenia, he celebrated some sort of triumph and seems to have promised various territories which might have interested Rome to Cleopatra and her children.

It is not certain whether Antony meant to throw in his lot with Cleopatra and become a kind of eastern 'king' or whether Octavian, wishing to be rid of his last rival, convinced Romans that this was Antony's plan.[23] In any case, relations between west and east deteriorated until 32, when it became clear that war was inevitable (7 intro.). Both sides began their preparations, Antony divorced Octavia, and Octavian declared war on Cleopatra (9.27n.) as if it were a foreign, not a civil conflict. At Actium (9 intro.) Antony and Cleopatra were defeated; they fled back to Alexandria, where they committed suicide, he while Octavian's army advanced on the city (1 August 30), she after it had been captured (8 August).

The 'Alexandrian war' would be the last Roman civil war for nearly a century, but at the time nobody could have known this. People would eventually come to think, or at least hope, that the replacement of the Republic with a 'principate' was one way of guarding against a recurrence of civil strife. This suggests, and the works of some authors make this plain, that many Romans attributed the civil wars above all to the *contentio dignitatis*, the 'competition' among the foremost men of the city to achieve the highest honours in war and peace.[24] For many centuries this competition had remained only that because it was checked partly by fear of external enemies but also, in a more positive way, by the participation of these men in institutions that educated them to subordinate rivalry

[22] H. may have accompanied Maecenas to this 'summit conference' (*S.* 1.5), but cf. E. Gowers, *P.C.P.S.* 39 (1993) 48–66.

[23] Cf. Pelling on Plut. *Ant.* 53–5, 60.1, Huzar (1978) 185–208.

[24] This represents what seems to be H.'s own view of these matters (7.5, 18, 16.1, 2, 3–10nn., N–H on *C.* 2.1, 3.4.65–8) and it is not entirely different from the views of Sallust and Livy in their prefaces. Cf. Jal (1963).

to a sense of what made them fellow citizens and, in Roman terms, *amici*.

With the destruction of Carthage (146 BC) and the increasing 'corruption' of Roman society by wealth there was a decline in both the external and internal restraints on the Romans. Not only were different groups at odds, but within each group rivalries began to verge towards enmity. The Gracchi were killed by fellow senators, their deaths applauded even by some relatives. In the Social War, Romans got used to the idea of killing their former comrades-in-arms. Sulla had been an assistant to Marius, Caesar the father-in-law of Pompey, Octavian the brother-in-law of Antony. Whatever the cause of each civil war, it always came down to men connected by these and by even more intimate bonds of *amicitia* killing each other and thus repeating again and again the 'crime of Romulus' (7.17–20).

3. THE *EPODES* AND EARLY GREEK *IAMBUS*

Five of the seventeen *Epodes* (1, 4, 7, 9, 16) are explicitly concerned with the last stages of the story just recounted (Intro. 2), and it is possible to relate most, if not all, of the others to this theme.[25] It is clear, then, that, as a whole, the Epode book was meant as a 'response' to the crisis of the end of the Republic. But in addition to its 'political' content, there is much that seems to be more purely 'literary', and it has not been clear to most commentators how this aspect of the collection is also relevant to its historical context.[26]

H. draws on a wide range of earlier literature both Greek and Latin,[27] but he leaves no question as to his chief model, the early Greek *iambi* of Hipponax and especially Archilochus (6 intro.).[28] At a

[25] Cf. the introductions to the individual Epodes.

[26] The following discussion is based on the editor's doctoral thesis, 'The *Epodes* of Horace and Archilochean iambus' (University of Virginia 1985).

[27] See Index 2 s.v. 'Alcaeus', 'Anacreon', etc.

[28] It has become fashionable to state (not argue) that the *Epodes* were also influenced by the *Iamboi* and perhaps the *Ibis* of Callimachus. But there is no evidence that H. even knew these poems, let alone made them his 'secret' models. Cf. 15.7–9n. and nn. 44 and 61 below.

later time (around 20 BC) he would summarize his achievement (*Ep.* 1.19.23–5):

> Parios ego primus iambos
> ostendi Latio, numeros animosque secutus
> Archilochi, non res et agentia uerba Lycamben.

Most of this is borne out by even a cursory look at H.'s *Iambi*.[29] His metres are Archilochean down to minute details (Intro. 6), while his subject matter (*res*) and the targets of his *uerba* are not the same as those of Archilochus. But it is not entirely clear what he means by *animi*, 'spirit', and many have doubted whether in this respect H. in fact owes as much to the early Greek poet as he claims.[30]

One reason for these doubts is that most Latinists have laboured under what appears to be a mistaken interpretation of the nature of early Greek *iambus*. Until fairly recently, it was assumed that Archilochus and the others 'wrote' primarily from personal experience, and that the main function of their *iambi* was to 'settle scores' with real people who had in some way offended them. H.'s *Epodes*, with their 'stock figures' (below), seem far removed from this. But some new discoveries (cf. 11 intro.) and, especially, a reassessment of the evidence have completely changed the way in which Hellenists, at least, interpret *iambus* and produced a picture of that genre which makes it more evident why H., in the late Republic, would choose to imitate its 'spirit'.[31]

The genre *iambus* 'had its heyday in the seventh and sixth centuries [BC]' (West (1974) 33), and although it probably had many practitioners, those best known to later antiquity were Archilochus of Paros and Thasos (*fl.* mid seventh century), Hipponax of Ephesus (*c.* 540), and Semonides of Amorgos (mid seventh century).[32] It

---

[29] This was H.'s own title for the *Epodes* (Intro. 4). For his claim of 'primacy', see Intro. 6.

[30] E.g. Leo (1900), Fraenkel (1957) 36–41, Fedeli (1978) 124–8.

[31] The account of early Greek *iambus* given here is based on the following: K. J. Dover, 'The poetry of Archilochus', in *Archiloque*, ed. B. Snell (Entr. Hardt 10, Geneva 1964) 181–212, West (1974) 22–39, Nagy (1979) 222–52, M. R. Lefkowitz, *The lives of the Greek poets* (Baltimore 1980), A. P. Burnett, *Three archaic poets* (Cambridge Mass. 1983), Gentili (1988) 107–14, 179–96.

[32] H. does not mention Semonides, but may owe a few touches to him; see Index 2 s.v.

may have originated as a 'cult song' associated with Demeter and
Dionysus whose characteristic form was what would later be called
'iambic' metre. But *iambi* could also be composed in other meas-
ures, including 'elegy' and the related 'mixed' forms of epodes
and *asynarteta* (Intro. 4). The common element, what made *iambus*
a distinct genre, was that it was essentially 'blame poetry' which in
one way or another and with varying degrees of hostility (below)
found fault with behaviour that was seen as somehow inappropriate
or dangerous.[33]

The sense of what was inappropriate or dangerous was provided
not so much by the individual iambist's sensibilities as by the norms
of his society. *Iambus* was composed primarily for an audience drawn
from that society, whether the citizens in the assembly, or smaller
groups in the predominant social context of archaic Greece, the
symposium. In either circumstance, the *iambus* was meant to remind
the audience of what might be a threat to the very shared customs,
morals, and so on which brought them together and united them
as an audience. Whether as fellow citizens or as drinking compan-
ions, the members of the audience would consider themselves *philoi*
('friends') and what they shared as *philotēs* ('friendship'), a term which
has the same complex range of meaning in Greek as *amicitia* has in
Latin (Intro. 2).

The 'affirmation of *philotēs*'[34] through blame could be accom-
plished in various ways. The poet, speaking more or less in his own
person as a member of the group, could attack someone directly,
either another member or an 'outsider' (below). Or he could adopt
an 'identity' not his own and reveal 'himself' to be guilty of some
misconduct by in effect 'saying the worst things about himself'.[35]
Or he could tell a story, a 'blame narrative' (5 intro.) combining
such 'self-indictments' with accounts of reprehensible acts. There

---

[33] There are, of course, other types of blame poetry, including 'Old
Comedy' (perhaps derived from *iambus*; cf. West (1974) 35–7) and Roman
satire and its antecedents (cf. Mankin, *A.J.Ph.* 108 (1987) 405–8).

[34] Nagy (1979) 251.

[35] The phrase comes from an 'attack' on Archilochus by the fifth-century
BC sophist Critias (88 B D–K = Aelian, *V.H.* 101.3 = Arch. fr. 295 West); cf.
Gentili (1988) 181–2.

were also different 'levels' of blame, ranging from admonition and humorous chiding directed at members of the group to more virulent attacks, usually reserved for 'outsiders'.

It appears that these 'outsiders' tended to be figures who had originally been members of the group but had 'alienated' themselves through the worst forms of misconduct. It also appears that most such figures were not real people, but 'stock characters' with significant names embodying or symbolizing what the iambist and his society found most inimical.[36] A scenario, either known to or repeated for the audience, would explain how such an exemplary (in a bad sense) figure had become an 'outsider' and serve as a warning against such behaviour.

The parallels between all this and H.'s *iambi* are not hard to discover. His audience, where he indicates it, is either his fellow citizens (7, 16) or his friends in the context of a symposium (3, 9, 11, 12, 13). These friends are real people, but his 'enemies', like those in early *iambus*, are mostly 'stock figures' (1.33–4, 2.67, 4.1, 5.15, 25, 29, 41–4, 73, 6.1, 10.2, 11.6, 24, 12.18, 14.16, 15.11nn., App. 2). He speaks in his own person but also poses as an 'Alfius' (2; cf. 4 intro.) and frequently says 'the worst things about himself' (4, 6, 8, 11, 12, 14, 15, 17). Most of the poems pretend to be 'direct speech', but there is a 'blame narrative' (5) and a 'dialogue' that suggests that this may also have been a technique of early *iambus* (17 intro.). Within other poems there is considerable use of narration and 'talking characters' (4, 7, 11, 12, 13, 15).

It may also be possible to discover, or at least suggest, why H. chose to re-create early Greek *iambus* at Rome in the late thirties BC. In the midst of a crisis which could be seen as a result of the decline and failure of traditional Roman *amicitia* (Intro. 2), H. turned to a type of poetry whose function had been the affirmation of 'friendship' in its community. It is doubtful whether he believed that his or anyone else's poetry could avert disaster (cf. 16 intro.). But he may have hoped that his *iambi* would somehow 'blame' his friends and fellow citizens into at least asking themselves *quo ruitis?* (7.1).

---

[36] Cf. West (1974) 26–7, Nagy (1979) 243–9. For arguments that Lycambes, at least, may have been a real person, see Gentili (1988) 294–5.

4. THE EPODE BOOK

The idea of the *Epodes* as a response to the historical events of the late thirties BC depends, of course, on the hypothesis that H. composed them or at least wanted his audience to think that he composed them during this period. This is only a hypothesis, but it seems to make more sense than any of the other suggestions that have been made concerning the chronology of the *Epodes*.[37]

There is one certain date in the collection, that of the battle of Actium (2 September 31 BC), the setting for Epode 9. It has been argued that this is only a *terminus ante quem* for the 'political poems', and that other poems could have been written as early as 42 BC, when H. (by his own account), began 'making verses' (*Ep.* 2.2.49–54; cf. Intro. 1). The usual criteria for deciding on an 'early' or a 'late' date for each Epode are its supposed level of 'maturity' and, in the case of the political poems, its attitude (if this can be determined) towards Octavian. Thus Epode 10 (a 'mature' H. would not imitate his model so closely), Epodes 8 and 12 (or use so much obscenity), and Epode 16 (or express such pessimism with Octavian triumphant) are considered 'early', while Epode 13 (it resembles certain Odes) and Epode 1 (it seems to express a 'commitment' to Octavian (but cf. 1.2, 5, 23–4nn.)) are considered 'late'.[38]

Even if the criteria for distinguishing 'early' and late Epodes were more objective, there would be a basic difficulty with this approach. Unless their sensibilities were the same as those of H.'s modern 'chronographers', the members of H.'s original audience hearing or reading the Epode book for the first time would have nothing to go on except the order in which the poems are arranged. When they encountered Epodes 1, 4, and 7, for instance, they would see these poems as anticipating a war which, when they finally read Epode 9,

---

[37] For surveys of the dating of the *Epodes*, see Carrubba (1969) 15–17, Setaioli (1981).

[38] This approach, which informs most recent scholarship on the *Epodes* (for exceptions, see n. 39 below), can be traced to C. Franke, *Fasti Horatiani* (Berlin 1839). The views of earlier commentators, where they can be recovered, are closer to that presented here (e.g. Bentley (1728) xix–xx).

they might naturally assume to be the Actian war. It would also be natural to take Epodes 13 and 16, coming 'later' in the collection, as referring to a time 'later' than that of Epode 9.[39]

There are other indications that the Epode book invites such a 'linear' or 'sequential' reading.[40] Perhaps the most objective is the metrical sequence (Intro. 6): ten poems in a combination of iambic lines are followed by a poem (11) in which a dactylic element 'intrudes', an entirely dactylic poem (12), a mostly dactylic poem with an iambic element (13), poems containing a balance of dactyls and iambics (14, 15, 16), and finally a poem which returns to pure iambics (17).[41] The first word of the book is *ibis* (1.1), the last is *exitus* (17.81n.). Epode 14 seems to alert the reader to the fact that the book is coming to an end (14 intro.). There are numerous 'cross-references' from poems 'back' to those 'preceding' them (e.g. 2.1–8, 3.4, 5.15, 6.16, 8.11, 10.1, 11.5, 12.23, 13.6, 14.6, 15.7, 16.1–14, 17.1–18nn.).

This is not to say that the movement of the book is entirely 'linear': there is also a kind of 'architecture'[42] by which poems separated from each other in the space (or time?) of the volume nevertheless seem to be paired. They do not form a pattern as neat as those detected in Virgil's Eclogue book and in Propertius' '*monobiblos*' (book 1), and there does not seem to be any 'numerology' such as can be found in those works.[43] But besides Epodes 1 and 17 (above), there are correspondences between 1 and 9, 2 and 16, 3 and 14, 4 and 6, 5 and 17, 7 and 16, 8 and 12. None of these, however, violates the

[39] For this interpretation, cf. Schmidt (1977), Kraggerud (1984) 9–20, Porter (1987) 254–9.

[40] For these terms and other 'principles of arrangement' in Latin poetry books, see J. Van Sickle, *The design of Virgil's Bucolics* (Rome 1978), Santirocco (1986), Porter (1987).

[41] Cf. H. Belling, *Studien über die Liederbücher des Horatius* (Berlin 1903) 137, Carrubba (1969) 18–21. It is possible that H. imitated an arrangement of metres in a collection of Archilochus, although there is no way of proving this (Carrubba (1969) 87–103). It is worth noting that H.'s arrangement is quite different from that of Callimachus in his *Iamboi* (above, n. 28).

[42] For this term, see the studies cited in n. 40 above, and, for its application to the Epode book, see Carrubba (1969) 22–86, Schmidt (1977), and H. Dettmer, *Horace: a study in structure* (Hildesheim 1983) 77–109.

[43] Cf. Van Sickle (above, n. 40), B. Otis, *H.S.C.Ph.* 70 (1965) 22–86.

apparent 'chronological sequence', i.e. there is no instance where a reader might think that the events in a poem 'later' in the book are supposed to have occurred 'earlier' than those in the poem with which it seems to be paired.

Although it is clear that H. himself called this collection his *Iambi* (14.7, *C.* 1.16.24, *Ep.* 1.19.23, 2.2.59, cf. *Ars* 79), it has become conventional to call it the 'Epodes', and that practice is continued here. But it should be noted that the title *Epodi* or *Epodon Liber* is not attested before Porphyrio (Intro. 7) and even later *grammatici* (*ThLL* v 2.695–6), and that it is in any case inappropriate, since the last poem of the collection is not, technically, an *epodus* (Intro. 6).[44]

5. LANGUAGE AND STYLE

The language of Archilochus and the other early iambists has been characterized as a 'stylized Ionic', somewhere between and drawing on both the spoken form of that Greek dialect and the elevated 'Kunstsprache' of epic.[45] The *Epodes* can likewise be seen as occupying a kind of 'mid-stage', not only between the colloquial and the poetic, but in terms of H.'s own works, 'between [his] informal hexameter poetry and his lyric poetry'.[46]

H. achieves this 'mid-stage' by combining, in various proportions in various contexts, 'poetic' with 'unpoetic' language.[47] The 'poetic' consists of words, forms, phrases, and constructions which evidence

[44] Cf. N. Horsfall, *B.I.C.S.* 28 (1981) 109. For this reason it seems unlikely that there is a connection with *epodai*, (Greek) 'magical spells' (cf. Gowers (1993) 282). Since some ancient books were referred to by their opening words (e.g. *arma uirumque* = the *Aeneid*; cf. Jocelyn on Enn. *trag.* 350, Kenney, *C.R.* 20 (1970) 290), it has been suggested that H. may have intended *ibis* (1.1) as a kind of title and as an 'allusion to Callimachus' invective poem *Ibis*' (Heyworth (1993) 86). But there is no evidence that any of H.'s books were known by an '*incipit*', or that his *Iambi* owe anything to Callimachus (above, n. 28).

[45] A. Scherer, 'Die Sprache des Archilochos', in *Archiloque* (above, n. 31) 89–107, West (1974) 77–111.

[46] Armstrong (1989) 55. For H.'s own placement of the *Epodes* 'between' his other works, cf. *Ep.* 2.2.59–60. The chief studies of the language of the *Epodes* are Blok (1961), Grassman (1966), and Hierche (1974) 93–125.

[47] For these terms, cf. Axelson (1945) and P. Watson (1985).

suggests would have been perceived by the original audience either
as appropriate to 'elevated' types of poetry (epic, tragedy) or as 'old-
fashioned' ('archaism') or foreign ('Graecism').[48] The 'unpoetic', on
the other hand, would be more familiar to that audience either from
standard (i.e. Ciceronian, Caesarian) prose ('prosaic') or from the
spoken language ('colloquial', 'vulgar').[49]

As if anticipating the advice he would later give the Pisones (*Ars*
47–59), H. also creates his own poetic language with neologisms
(Index 2 s.v.) often 'formed on the analogy of Greek' (Brink on *Ars* 53
(*uerba*) *Graeco fonte ... parce detorta*). These include what seem to be
new words (1.19, 20, 2.11, 3.18, 5.34, 95, 7.8, 8.20, 11.15, 28, 13.18,
14.14, 16.38, 41, 43, 51, 57, 58, 60), previously attested words used in
new senses (1.15, 2.5, 4.12, 17, 5.50, 89, 7.12, 10.7, 9, 11.10, 11, 19, 28,
12.8, 14, 13.5, 14.4, 16.7, 8, 48, 17.33), and Greek-style constructions
(1.23–4, 2.19, 20, 64, 3.7, 5.68, 8.16, 9.20, 10.16, 15.1).[50] It would be
interesting to know how many of these could be traced to analogies
in early Greek *iambus*, and whether the neologisms in the *Odes* in turn
reflect Greek lyric models.[51]

Like other Greek and Latin poetry, including early *iambus*, the
Epodes contain their share of poetic 'figures' such as 'hendiadys'
(5.16n.), 'metonymy' (2.29n.), and 'personification' (2.17–18n.).[52] Their

[48] The fragmentary state of 'elevated' poetry before H. often makes it ne-
cessary to risk anachronism by bringing in texts which might have been influ-
enced by H. or which themselves combine various styles. Another problem
specific to the study of iambic and lyric verse is the loss of most early Latin
tragedy, an 'elevated' genre which, unlike hexameter epic, was composed in
metres that accommodate words containing a 'cretic' sequence $(- \cup -)$. There
are a number of such words in the *Epodes* (73 occurrences – 61 words), but it is
seldom possible to determine their stylistic level (cf. 2.40, 3.6, 13, 18, 5.43,
50, 70, 99, 11.13, 26, 13.4, 14.8, 16.14, 18, 62, 17.14, 49, 75nn.). See Appen-
dix 3.
[49] The evidence for the spoken language is provided by 'lower' genres of
verse (comedy, satire, epigram) and prose (letters, novels, inscriptions). The
term 'vulgar' is used here of language that would probably not be acceptable
to 'polite company' in H.'s day (cf. Adams (1982) 1–2, Richlin (1992) 1–31).
[50] For Greek borrowings that are attested earlier than the *Epodes*, see Index
2 s.v. 'Graecism'.
[51] For the *Odes*, cf. Bo III, Index s.v. *uocabula noua*, and A. Waltz, *Des varia-
tions de la langue et de la métrique d'Horace* (Paris 1881).
[52] For such 'figures', cf. LHS II 772–838 and Fantham (1992) 35–41.

stylistic level is also 'raised' by similes, metaphor, and more subtle uses of imagery, and they are 'ornamented' (although rarely, if ever, 'for ornament's sake') with mythological and geographical names and epithets. Finally, H. anticipates the intricacy of the *Odes* with various techniques involving word order, including 'transferred epithet', '*apo koinou* construction', 'zeugma', 'postposition', and 'hyperbaton' (Index 2 s.vv.).

It might be expected that the language and style of the *Epodes* would have been influenced by that of Catullus and the other 'new poets' who were active during H.'s youth.[53] There are suggestions of such an influence (Index 2 s.v. 'Catullus'), but there are also many differences, and even where H. seems to adopt elements that modern scholars consider 'hallmarks' of Neoteric style, he does not 'ape' them (cf. *S.* 1.10.19).[54] In this respect he distinguishes himself not only from those putative 'models' but also from his contemporaries Virgil (of the *Eclogues*) and, it would seem, Gallus (Index 2 s.v.). On the other hand, the *Epodes* do seem to owe a considerable debt, if not in 'philosophy', at least in word choice and some aspects of style, to Lucretius (Index 2), which is not surprising in view of that poet's influence on H.'s other works.[55]

6. METRE

All but one (17) of H.'s *Iambi* are composed in 'epodic' couplets, in which a verse of one metrical structure and length is followed by a

[53] This is the view of, among others, Newman (1967) 270–82 and E. McDermott, 'Greek and Roman elements in Horace's lyric program', *ANRW* II 31.3 (1981) 1644–9. For the 'new poets' or 'Neoterics', cf. Courtney (1993) 198–253.

[54] These 'hallmarks' (cf. Ross (1969) 17–112) include postponed particles (1.12n.), adjectives in *-osus* (3.16n.), diminutives (8.15–16n.), compound adjectives (17.12n.), elided *atque* (2.40n.), and 'the vocabulary of urbane Rome: *delicatus, dicax, elegans, facetiae, ineptiae, lepos, sal, urbanus,* and *uenustus* with their other forms and opposites' (Ross (1969) 105–6), none of which occur in the *Epodes*. Although Catullus' 'polymetrics' and the Neoteric fragments allow some 93 'cretic-containing words' (above, n. 48), they contain only nine that also occur in the *Epodes* (*aestuosus, antea, curiosus, immerens, impudicus, laboriosus, obliuio, otiosus, umbilicus*), and of these only one is not attested in still earlier Latin poetry (*obliuio* (5.70, 14.2, Bib. *Poet.* 3 *FPL*, but cf. Acc. (?) fr. 697 Ribbeck)).

[55] Cf. W. Rehmann, *Lukrez und Horaz* (Freiburg 1969).

verse of a different length and, in some cases, metrical structure. The ancient grammarians called this second verse the *epōdos*, something 'added' (*epi*) to the song (*ōdē*), but with a looseness typical of Greek and Latin literary terminology this word was also used of the two verses together as a couplet and of whole poems consisting of such couplets.[56]

Archilochus was sometimes reckoned the 'inventor' of epodes,[57] and fragments and citations indicate that he used at least nine different combinations.[58] It appears that at some point his poems in these metres were arranged in a separate collection evidently called both *Epōdoi* and *Iamboi*.[59] Since the content of these and other early Greek epodes seems to have been neither more nor less 'iambic' than that of poems composed in stichic metre or (for Archilochus) elegiac couplets, it appears likely that they differed from other forms of *iambus* not in 'genre' but in how they were performed. The *testimonia* concerning Archilochus as a musician and as an 'inventor' of *parakatalogē* ('recitative') suggest that epodes represent a mode of performance somewhere between speech unaccompanied by music and full-scale song.[60]

Although H. draws on all of Archilochus' poetry (Intro. 3), it is possible that his choice of metres and, perhaps, their sequence in his book owe something to the separate collection of Archilochian epodes.[61] All but two of his combinations are attested for Archilochus, and it seems likely that even the 'missing' ones (Systems iv,

---

[56] LSJ s.v. *epōdos*, ThLL v 2.695–6.

[57] Cf. Tarditi (1968) 212–16 ('testimonia de metris Archilochi').

[58] Frr. 168–204 West; cf. Rossi (1976) 223–9.

[59] Cf. the *testimonia* to Arch. frr. 182, 187, 188–92, 200, 201 West, and West (1974) 22. The collection is sometimes thought to be Hellenistic, but there is no sure evidence for this, and it is clear that there were texts of Archilochus in circulation in the Classical period, if not earlier (cf. Tarditi (1968) 'Index auctorum', Pfeiffer (1968) Index s.v. 'Archilochus').

[60] Rossi (1976) 215–16. This is not to say that Archilochus' elegiacs (a kind of epodic combination) were not also accompanied by music; cf. West (1974) 9–10, 13–15, Gentili (1988) 35. For Archilochus and the lyre, see 13.9n.

[61] Carrubba (1969) 87–103, Setaioli (1981) 1688–9. It may be worth noting (cf. above, n. 28) that H. uses none of the combinations attested for the *Iamboi* of Callimachus, that the only verse types they share are the common iambic trimeter (*a*) and dimeter (*b*), and that H. avoids altogether the choliamb (a trimeter with a long at pos. 11), although it is the 'signature' measure of Hipponax as well as Callimachus and was popular with the Neoterics.

vii) would 'turn up' if further evidence were available.[62] His usage, especially in the *asynarteta* (Verse Type *e*), but also in the more common iambic trimeter (Verse Type *a*) seems in some respects distinctly 'Parian'. It appears, moreover, that he recognized the status of epodic verse as somewhere between speech and song or, in terms of his own works, between his hexameter *sermo* and his lyric *carmen*.[63]

At *Ep.* 1.19.23–4 (Intro. 3) H. claims that he 'first displayed Parian *iambi* to Latium'. Since 'iambic' verse had a long earlier history at Rome, this claim has been taken as an exaggeration or even a conscious 'slighting' of such poets as Catullus and Varro.[64] But H. is not talking about metre alone (Intro. 3), and even if he were, his 'iambics' (i.e. trimeters) differ from those of his Latin predecessors (Verse Type *a*), and he does seem to have been the 'first' to 'display' epodic combinations.[65]

This is not to say that H.'s metrical usage is entirely 'Greek'. His prosody (treatment of syllables as 'short' or 'long') is in general the same as that of his Latin precursors and contemporaries,[66] and his

---

[62] Until the discovery of the 'Cologne epode' (Arch. fr. 196a West; cf. Intro. 3) it was thought that H. might have 'invented' the metre of Epode 11 (System 11).

[63] H. pretends, at least, that some epodes would be accompanied by the lyre (13.9, 14.12n.; cf. 17.39n.), and he would later describe Archilochus' *numeri* as *modos et carminis artem* (*Ep.* 1.19.24–7), a phrase that might suggest a musical element (cf. *C.* 1.23.5, 2.1.40 etc., *OLD* s.v. *modus* 8). For his placement of *iambi* 'between' *carmen* and *sermo*, cf. *Ep.* 2.2.59–60 (above, n. 46).

This is not the place to discuss if and how H.'s works were performed, but the prevailing view that they were essentially 'book poetry' runs against the many references in H. to 'singing', his attention in the *Ars* and elsewhere to the needs of an 'aural' audience, the evidence for the public performance of the lyric *Carmen saeculare* (above, n. 1), and Ovid's claim (if his words can be taken at face value) that he heard H. himself playing the lyre (*Tr.* 4.10.49–50).

[64] Cf. Newman (1967) 273.

[65] It seems likely that [Virg.] *Cat.* 13, composed in 'System 1', is later than the *Epodes* (R. Westendorp Boerma, *P. Vergili Maronis Catalepton* 11 (Assen 1963) 77–92). Epodic combinations have been postulated for Laevius (2, 21 *FPL* cf. Courtney (1993) 121, 135) and Varro (*Men.* 78, 141; cf. Astbury's app. crit.), but the arguments are not very convincing.

[66] See Index 2 s.v. 'prosody'. The *Epodes* also seem to be more 'Latin' than 'Greek' in avoiding unelided monosyllables at verse end (11.21, 17.63 (trim.), 12.23, 15.7, 16.15 (hex.), 12.6, 14, 16, 24 (dact. tetr. cat.), 11.16 (hemiepes) = 2% of the verses), although these are not common in Greek iambic

dactylic hexameter (Verse Type *c*) follows the Ennian, rather than the Homeric (or Archilochian), model. In regard to the 'rules' governing elision and hiatus he also follows Latin practice, although the incidence of elision in the *Epodes* is distinctly lower than in any previous Latin verse, including his own hexameters.[67] He has been criticized for apparently paying little attention to the 'natural gait of Latin talk', i.e. for failing to accommodate the Latin word accent to his metrical structures.[68] But this may be in keeping with the nature of those structures as neither speech nor song (above).

What follows is an account of the different measures (Verse Types) and combinations (Systems) employed by H. in the *Epodes*. In the schemes, the subscript numbers indicate verse position,[69] while the superscript numbers show the ratio of long to short syllables at positions in the iambs where either can occur ('anceps'). The principal break ('caesura') in each verse type is indicated by a single bar, verse end or its image (in the *asynarteta*; cf. Verse Type *e*) by a double bar.[70]

poetry either (Van Raalte (1986) 223). In this respect, as in others (Intro. 5), the *Epodes* fall between the *Odes*, where the incidence is even lower (0.3% in *Odes* 1–3, 1.5% in *Odes* 4 and *Saec.*), and the hexameter poetry, in which it tends to be considerably higher (12% in *Sat.* 1, 8% in *Sat.* 2, 9% in *Ep.* 1, 6% in *Ep.* 2.2 and *Ars*, but 2% in *Ep.* 2.1). Cf. Soubiran (1988) 368–70 (other Latin iambic verse), and J. Hellegouarc'h, *Le monosyllable dans l'hexamètre latin* (Paris 1964) 50–68.

[67] Cf. Soubiran (1966) s.v. 'Horace'. An indication of this is provided by comparing H.'s trimeters, in which there are 55 elisions in 311 verses (=1.8 per 10 verses) to the trimeters and choliambs of Catullus and Varro, in which there are 131 in 228 verses (=5.7 per 10).

[68] Gratwick (1993) 41, 58–9. H. himself provides some of the evidence for the existence of an *ictus* ('verse accent') in iambic metre (Brink on *Ars* 253, 274), something recent scholars find difficult to accept (Soubiran (1988), Gratwick (1993) 40–1, 59–60). In the *Epodes* there seems to be no correlation between word accent and any positions in the verse where this *ictus* might be located.

[69] The 'positions' are numbered according to the schemes in Van Raalte (1986).

[70] 'Verse end' or, in some metres, 'period end' (cf. West (1982) 4–6, N–H on *Odes* 1, Intro. 3) can be recognized as a position where usage permits either a short syllable where a long would be expected (*brevis in longo*), as in pos. 12 of the iambic trimeter (Verse Type *a*), or hiatus (lack of elision) between a final vowel, diphthong, or (in Latin) *-m* in one verse and an initial vowel or diphthong in the next. For the 'signs' of verse end in *asynarteta*, cf. Verse Type *e*.

Verse Types

a. Iambic trimeter

$$\overset{1:1}{\underline{\cup}_1}\ \overline{\underline{\cup}}_2\ \cup_3\ \overline{\underline{\cup}}_4\ \overset{2:1}{\overline{\cup}_5}\ |\ \overline{\underline{\cup}}_6\ \cup_7\ |\ \overline{\underline{\cup}}_8\ \overset{1:1}{\overline{\cup}_9}\ -_{10}\ \cup_{11}\ \overline{\cup}_{12}\ \|$$

H.'s trimeter resembles both that of the Greeks of all periods and of Latin poets who composed 'Greek-style' iambics[71] in regard to the location of the caesura at either pos. 5 or pos. 7 (cf. 1.19, 6.11nn.). But it may be particularly 'Archilochian' in its frequency of verses having word end (w/e) simultaneously at both caesura positions (5 + 7).[72] Its ratio of long to short syllables in anceps (total 1.3 : 1) is closer to that of early Greek poetry (1.4 : 1 in tragedy), including Archilochus (1.1 : 1), than to those of earlier Latin, in which longs predominate, and of Hellenistic epigram, which is more balanced.[73] Like early Greek, but unlike most Hellenistic and 'Greek-style' Latin, it allows 'resolution' of the long into two shorts at the non-anceps pos. 2 (2.33, 67, 5.15, 85, 91, 10.19, 11.27, 17.6, 12, 78), 4 (1.27, 2.35, 57, 61, 3.17, 5.15, 10.7, 17.42, 63, 74), 6 (2.23, 39, 5.25, 49, 7.1, 17.12, 65), and 8 (17.12, 74).[74] On the other hand, H. shows little regard for 'Porson's Law', the tendency in most Greek trimeters outside of comedy to avoid w/e after long anceps at pos. 9 (1.27, 29, 2.13, 33, 47, 3.9, 13, 4.13, 5.17, 19, 93, 7.1, 13, 8.1, 15, 9.27, 10.7, 21, 11.3, 5, 27, 17.13). It is possible that H. was not aware of this 'law', or

[71] These include Catullus (iambic trimeters and choliambs) and fragments of Varro's *Menippea* (cf. System VII). The 'trimeter', if it is that (cf. *Ars* 250–62), of Republican drama and of Lucilius is almost a different 'species', especially in allowing anceps and resolution at all positions save 11 (Gratwick (1993) 40–62).

[72] In both H. and Arch. 35% of the trimeters have w/e at both pos. 5 and 7. This is a higher frequency than in any other Greek poetry (Van Raalte (1986) 171, 183) and than in Catullus' trimeters (15%) and choliambs (22%) and Varro's trimeters (4%).

[73] In Varro the ratio is 2.3 : 1, in Hellenistic epigram it is 1 : 1. For other Greek poetry, see Van Raalte (1986) 105–11. Greek and Latin choliambs, which in other respects resemble iambic trimeters, provide no basis for comparison, since they have only two anceps positions (1 and 5).

[74] Leo (1900) 17. H. seems to agree with Arch. and other early *iambus* in avoiding 'split resolution' (distribution of the shorts between two words), but cf. 2.33n. and 17.74 (elision). For what appear to be resolutions at anceps positions, cf. 2.35n.

that Archilochus did not observe it as 'strictly' as his fragments suggest, or that whatever its significance for the rhythms of Greek it is not relevant to Latin.[75]

In the trimeters of Epode 16 (System VI) there are no long syllables at anceps positions (but cf. app. crit. at 16.4, 14, 36). Such 'pure trimeters' occur intermittently both in the *Epodes* (1.3, 13, 15, 17, 23, 31, 2.1, 7, 41, 4.3, 5, 9, 17, 5.3, 7, 9, 43, 71, 7.15, 9.21, 10.1, 3, 11, 17.22, 23, 28, 38, 40, 41, 64, 75) and in other iambic verse (e.g. Arch. frr. 48.5, 177.3, 196a.50 West). But H. may owe something to Cat. 4 and 29, the only surviving poems earlier than the *Epodes* composed entirely, or almost entirely (cf. Fordyce on 29.3, 20, 23) in this measure.

b. Iambic dimeter

$$\overset{2:1}{\cup}_1 \ \overline{\cup\cup}_2 \ \cup_3 \ \overline{\cup\cup}_4 \ \overset{7:1}{\cup}_5 \ -_6 \ \cup_7 \ \overline{\cup}_8 \ \|$$

This measure is less common than the trimeter, and the surviving examples in Archilochus (frr. 172–8, 180–1, 193–4, 196, 196a = 27 complete verses) differ from those of H. in having a more regular break at pos. 6 (w/e in 74% of the verses, 47% in H.).[76] They also have more short syllables at pos. 5 than at pos. 1 (the inverse of H.), but their total ratio of long to short (2.8:1) resembles that of H. (3.5:1) in being considerably higher than in both poets' trimeters (Verse Type *a*). There are no resolutions in Arch. and few in H.

[75] For 'Porson's Law', cf. West (1982) 42, Van Raalte (1986) 248–56. It appears that the first Latin poet to 'observe' it is Seneca, who still has 'violations' (F. X. Bill, *Beiträge zur lex porsoniana* (Westphalia 1932) 60–84, Soubiran (1988) 368–70). H. and other Latin poets also ignore 'Knox's Law', avoidance of a trochee-shaped ($-\cup$) word filling pos. 8 and 9 (West (1982) 42), and they tend to have a higher overall incidence of w/e at pos. 9 (30% of H.'s trimeters, 47% of Cat., 30% of Var.) than in non-comic Greek verse (10–20%; cf. Van Raalte (1986) 251). This might be because such w/e usually results in coincidence of word accent with the presumed *ictus* (above, n. 68) at pos. 8 and 10, although if this were the intent, one might expect an even higher incidence. For the corresponding pos. 5 in the dimeter, see Verse Type *b* and n. 77 below.

[76] For other iambic dimeters, cf. Hipp. fr. 118 West (System 1), Call. *Iamb.* 5 (combined with choliambs), Laev. *poet.* 1, 4, 6, 15, 18, 21 (?), 23, 27 *FPL*, and A. M. Dale, *The lyric metres of Greek drama* (Cambridge 1968) 75–7 (occasional 'runs' and cola in tragedy and comedy).

(2.62, 3.8, 5.48, 15.24), and both poets violate the dimeter's version of 'Porson's Law' (cf. Verse Type *a*) by allowing w/e after long anceps at pos. 5 (Arch. frr. 180, 196a.17 (?) West, 88 examples in H.), although the overall incidence of w/e at this pos. is lower in Arch. (19% of verses) than in H. (48%).[77]

c. Dactylic hexameter

$$-_1 \;\; \overset{\smile}{_{2a}}\overset{\smile}{_{2b}} \;\; -_3 \;\; \overline{\overset{\smile}{_{4a}}\overset{\smile}{_{4b}}} \;\; -_5 \;|\; \overline{\overset{\smile}{_{6a}}\overset{\smile}{_{6b}}} \;\; -_7 \;\; \overline{\overset{\smile}{_{8a}}\overset{\smile}{_{8b}}} \;\; -_9 \;\; \overset{\smile}{_{10a}}\overset{\smile}{_{10b}} \;\; -_{11} \;\; \overline{\overset{\smile}{}}_{12} \;\; \|$$

There seems to be nothing distinctive about the hexameters of Archilochus (frr. 1–17 (elegy), 193.2 West = 21 verses), and in any case H. seems to follow the Latin model established by Ennius in his preference for caesura at pos. 5 rather than (the Greek custom) at pos. 6a. But he may be somewhat 'Greek' in avoiding w/e at pos. 8a ('Herman's Bridge'),[78] and in his frequency of 'dactylic feet' (double short for single long where permitted), which is higher than in most Republican Latin, including his own *Satires* and *Epistles*.[79]

d. Dactylic tetrameter catalectic

$$-_1 \;\; \overset{\smile}{_{2a}}\overset{\smile}{_{2b}} \;\; -_3 \;\; \overline{\overset{\smile}{_{4a}}\overset{\smile}{_{4b}}} \;\; -_5 \;\; \overset{\smile}{_{6a}}\overset{\smile}{_{6b}} \;\; -_7 \;\; \overline{\overset{\smile}{}}_8 \;\; \|$$

This was used by Archilochus (System III), but only one example survives (fr. 195 West), and others in Greek and Latin come from lyric rather than *iambus* (e.g. *C.* 1.7, 28, Alcman, fr. 3, Ibycus, fr. 282 *PMG*, Laev. *poet.* 20 *FPL*). Both this measure and the hemiepes (*e*) are more 'dactylic' than the hexameter, with spondees occurring only at pos. 4 (12.8, 14, 22), although in the *Odes* H. allows them at pos. 2 as well. It is possible, if not demonstrable, that the frequency of mono-

---

[77] H. also 'violates' the dimeter's version of 'Knox's Law' (above, n. 75); cf. 2.42, 46, 48, 3.14, 14.4.

[78] For 'Hermann's Bridge' in Latin, cf. Skutsch on Enn. *Ann.*, Intro. 47. It is 'observed' more or less by Lucr., Cat. (in poem 64), Virg., and H. himself in his *sermo* but not, curiously enough, in the 'lyric hexameters' of his *Odes* (*C.* 1.7.3, 28.1, 23, 25, 4.7.5 = 10% of 48 verses).

[79] The ratios of spondee to dactyl at positions 2, 4, 6, and 8 are 1 : 3, 1 : 1, 2 : 1, and 2 : 1 respectively, with an overall ratio of 1 : 1, the same as in the hexameters of the *Odes*. This is far less dactylic than in most Greek (e.g. 1 : 2 in Homer) but still more 'balanced' than in any other Latin before Virgil's *Eclogues* (also 1 : 1). For spondees at pos. 10, see 13.9n.

syllables at verse end (cf. n. 66) in the *Epodes* (12.6, 14, 16, 24) as opposed to the *Odes* (none in 34 verses) has something to do with the difference in genre.

e. Hemiepes

$$-_1 \quad \smile_{2a}\smile_{2b} \quad -_3 \quad \smile_{4a}\smile_{4b} \quad \overline{\smile}_5 \quad \|$$

The hemiepes ('half dactylic hexameter') is used as an independent verse (e.g. *C.* 4.7, Arch. frr. 182–7, 198 West), as a unit ('colon') in longer measures (the elegiac 'pentameter' = 2 hemiepe, the 'D' element in dactylo-epitrite lyric), and in the combinations known as *asynarteta* ('unjoined measures'). In these the hemiepes is associated with another measure, often an iambic dimeter (Verse Type *b*), but the unit that comes first, whether the hemiepes ('elegiambus') or the dimeter ('iambelegus'), is supposed to act as if it were a separate measure, i.e. to exhibit in its final element the signs of period end (hiatus, *brevis in longo*).[80] Of the extant *asynarteta* only those of Archilochus and of H. actually behave in this way (Systems II, IV), an almost certain indication of direct 'Parian' influence on H.'s metre.[81]

Systems

I. 'Iambic'[82]: iambic trimeter (*a*)|| iambic dimeter (*b*)|| (Epodes 1–10, Arch. frr. 172–81, Hipp. fr. 118 West, [Virg.] *Cat.* 13). In H. grammatical periods ('complete sentences') fill couplets (10% of the verses), quatrains (24%), and units of six lines (30%) or longer (35%); grammatical cola ('clauses') often 'spill over' within couplets (enjambment), but only rarely from one couplet to the next (3.4–5, 20–1, 5.30–1, 32–3, 48–9, 9.2–3, 24–5).

II. 'Third Archilochian': iambic trimeter (*a*)|| hemiepes (*e*)|| iambic dimeter (*b*)|| (Epode 11, Arch. frr. 196, 196a West). In H. there is enjambment within couplets, but not from one to the next, although

---

[80] See n. 70 above and Rossi (1976).

[81] Rossi (1976).

[82] For the titles of the different systems (all from late Greek and Latin grammarians), see Carrubba (1969) 19, 87–103.

this does occur in Archilochus (fr. 196a.5–6, 11–12, 14–15, 23–4, 32–3, 44–5 West).

III. 'First Archilochian': dactylic hexameter (c)|| dactylic tetrameter catalectic (d)|| (Epode 12, C. 1.7, 28, Arch. fr. 195 West). H. has enjambment both within and between couplets.

IV. 'Second Archilochian': dactylic hexameter (c)|| iambic dimeter (b)|| hemiepes (e)|| (Epode 13; cf. Arch. fr. 199 West (testimonia for the 'iambelegus')). H. has enjambment both within and between couplets.

V. 'First Pythiambic': dactylic hexameter (c)|| iambic dimeter (b)|| (Epodes 14, 15, Arch. frr. 193–4 West). In H. enjambment between couplets is rare (14.6–7, 14–15).

VI. 'Second Pythiambic': dactylic hexameter (c)|| 'pure' iambic trimeter (a)|| (Epode 16, [Homer], *Margites* fr. 1 West, Arcesilaus, *EG* 957–60 (=Diog. Laert. 4.30), Nicanaetus, *EG* 3002–7 (=*AP* 13.29)). In H. enjambment between couplets is rare (16.18–19, 30–1).

VII. Stichic iambic trimeter (a)|| (Epode 17, Arch. frr. 18–87, Sem. frr. 1–38 West, Call. *Iamb.* 8, 10, Cat. 4, 29, 52, Var. *Men.* 37, 77, 95–6, 111, 269–73, 306, 349–55, 385, 485–6, 578).

7. THE TEXT

It appears that after their publication in the late first century BC H.'s works went in and out of fashion but never ceased to be read in parts, if not the whole, of the Roman world.[83] Nevertheless, the earliest manuscripts (MSS) containing them date only to the ninth century AD, when there may have been a kind of 'Horatian revival' at the court of Charlemagne.[84] These MSS seem to be the ancestors

---

[83] For the history of H.'s text, see Perret (1964) 168–84, Brink (1971) II 1–43, and Tarrant (1983) 182–5.

[84] Perret (1964) 180, M.-B. Quint, *Untersuchungen zur mittelalterlichen Horaz-Rezeption* (Frankfurt am Main 1988).

of the countless others from later centuries, and are the only ones that modern scholars draw on for composition of the text.[85]

For most of H.'s text, the MSS offer a single reading, but there are a significant number of places where some of them offer at least one variant. Since it is not always the same ones that offer the variant, it is not possible to classify the MSS on these grounds.[86] But the consistent presence of the variants suggests that the extant MSS testify to the earlier existence of two distinct textual traditions derived, ultimately, from two ancient copies or editions.[87]

In addition to these traditions, there seems to have been a third which somehow survived in only a single MS, the 'most ancient' of several discovered in a Belgian monastery by J. Cruquius (ed. 1565). This MS, the *Blandinianus Vetustissimus* (**V**), was lost when the monastery was destroyed in 1566, but Cruquius' excerpts survive, and it may have been copied at least once.[88] It seems to have agreed in general with the other MSS, but in a few cases (e.g. *S.* 1.6.126) it offered readings that are unique. Most of these are in the hexameter poems, but it is not without significance for the *Epodes* (see app. crit. at 2.20, 9.17).

The ancient commentators (Scholia) on H. are also significant for the text. There are two of these, one an abbreviated version of a full commentary by Pomponius Porphyrio (Porph., **P**), a scholar of the third or fourth century AD, the other 'a miscellaneous body of ancient material put together perhaps in the fifth century' and surviving along with much later material among the marginal notes in some of H.'s MSS (Schol., **S**, Pseudacro).[89] The MSS of Porphyrio are as early as those of H., and at times their *lemmata* seem to display

---

[85] For accounts of the MSS, see Brink (1971) 1–11, Tarrant (1983) 183–4, and the editions of Keller and Holder (1899) and of Klingner (1959).

[86] Brink (1971) 12–20, Tarrant (1983) 184–5.

[87] Brink (1971) 27–38.

[88] Brink (1971) 8–9. Cruquius' extracts for the *Epodes* are reprinted at the end of Vol. 1 of Keller and Holder (1899).

[89] The citation is from Tarrant (1983) 186. For the scholia, see the editions of Porphyrio by Holder (Innsbruck 1894) and of 'Pseudacro' by Keller (Stuttgart 1902), N–H on *Odes* 1, Intro. 4, Brink (1971) 38–43, Tarrant (1983) 186. The marginal scholia are called 'Pseudacronian' because in some MSS they are attributed (impossibly) to the ancient scholar Helenius Acro (*fl.* AD 200).

independence (app. crit. at 7.13, 9.17, 13.9). But both sets of scholia
are most valuable for the text when they comment explicitly on a
variant, indicating that it was in H.'s text in late antiquity, if not
earlier (e.g. 4.8, 5.1, 102, 6.3–4, 9.17, 15.15, 16.41, 17.77).[90]

In the apparatus criticus of this edition the aim is to provide read-
ers with information about the ancient, rather than the mediaeval,
traditions for the text of the *Epodes*. The individual readings are
identified, not by the surviving MSS which contain them,[91] but
according to whether they occur in all or most of these (**C**), in one or
two (**c**), or in some but not in others, in which case they are dis-
tinguished as the variant printed in the text (**A**) and that not printed
in the text (**B**).[92] The readings of the possible 'third tradition' are
identified separately (**V**), as are those commented on by Porphyrio
(**P**) and the other scholia (**S**). At two places (9.1, 17.17; cf. nn.) the
reader is alerted to the fact that variants are supported by the testi-
mony of ancient grammarians (**T**).[93]

As for the text of this edition, it relies mostly on the ancient evi-
dence, but some conjectures have been adopted (1.15, 4.8, 5.58, 7.12,
15.15, 17.22) and others, both from later MSS (**D** = *Deteriores*) and
from more recent scholars, have been mentioned in the app. crit.
and the commentary.[94]

---

[90] Cf. Mankin (1988b) 272–3. It is not possible to reconstruct a 'Por-
phyrian' or 'Pseudacronian' edition because in their surviving forms both
commentaries are selective and do not always comment where the MSS or **V**
offer variants.

[91] This information can be found in the editions of Keller and Holder,
Vollmer, Klingner, Bo, and Borzsák. It has not been possible to examine any
MSS for the present edition, but this seems to be unnecessary (Brink (1971) 2).
Certain Horatian MSS seem to preserve traces of ancient orthography
(Brink (1971) 7), but in this respect the present edition generally follows the
'standard' of *OLD*.

[92] For this and other methods of presentation, see Brink (1971) 21.

[93] There are full collections of *testimonia* in the editions of Keller and
Holder, Klingner, and Borzsák.

[94] Still other conjectures can be found in the editions of Bentley, Peerl-
kamp, Campbell, and Shackleton Bailey.

Q. HORATI FLACCI
IAMBORVM LIBER

SIGLA

For details, see Intro. 7.

A = one ancient tradition of variants
B = the other ancient tradition of variants
C = all or nearly all of the chief MSS
c = one or two of the chief MSS
V = the *Blandinianus Vetustissimus*
P = Porphyrio (commentary, not lemma)
S = 'Pseudacronian' scholia (commentary, not lemma)
T = testimony of ancient grammarians
D = readings in derivative MSS

Q. HORATI FLACCI
IAMBORVM LIBER

EPODE 1

Ibis Liburnis inter alta nauium,
  amice, propugnacula,
paratus omne Caesaris periculum
  subire, Maecenas, tuo:
quid nos, quibus te uita si superstite,   5
  iucunda, si contra, grauis?
utrumne iussi persequemur otium
  non dulce, ni tecum simul,
an hunc laborem, mente laturi decet
  qua ferre non mollis uiros?   10
feremus et te uel per Alpium iuga
  inhospitalem et Caucasum
uel Occidentis usque ad ultimum sinum
  forti sequemur pectore.
roges tuum labore quid iuuem meo   15
  imbellis ac firmus parum:
comes minore sum futurus in metu,
  qui maior absentis habet,
ut assidens implumibus pullis auis
  serpentium allapsus timet   20
magis relictis, non, ut adsit, auxili
  latura plus praesentibus.
libenter hoc et omne militabitur
  bellum in tuae spem gratiae,
non ut iuuencis illigata pluribus   25
  aratra nitantur meis

1.3 caesaris **CP**: caesari **c**   5 si *om.* **c**   10 qua **A**: quem **B**   15 labore
Glareanus: laborem **C**   21 adsit **A**: ut sit **BP**(?): uti sit **D**   26 meis **C**: mea **c**

pecusue Calabris(ante sidus feruidum)
    Lucana mutet pascuis
neque ut superne uilla candens Tusculi
    Circaea tangat moenia.   30
satis superque me benignitas tua
    ditauit; haud parauero
quod aut auarus ut Chremes terra premam,
    discinctus aut perdam nepos.

EPODE 2

Beatvs ille qui procul negotiis,
    ut prisca gens mortalium,
paterna rura bubus exercet suis
    solutus omni fenore
neque excitatur classico miles truci   5
    neque horret iratum mare
forumque uitat et superba ciuium
    potentiorum limina.
ergo aut adulta uitium propagine
    altas maritat populos   10
aut in reducta ualle mugientium
    prospectat errantis greges
inutilisque falce ramos amputans
    feliciores inserit
aut pressa puris mella condit amphoris   15
    aut tondet infirmas oues.
uel cum decorum mitibus pomis caput
    Autumnus agris extulit,
ut gaudet insitiua decerpens pira
    certantem et uuam purpurae,   20

---

28 pascuis **A**: pascua **B**   29 superne **c**: superni **CS**   candens **A**: tangens **B**
34 perdam **A**: perdam ut **B**   2.18 agris **CV**: aruis **c**   20 purpurae **C**:
purpura **cV**

quá muneretur te, Priape, et te, pater
   Siluane, tutor finium.
libet iacere modo sub antiqua ilice
   modo in tenaci gramine:
labuntur altis interim ripis aquae,   25
   queruntur in siluis aues
fontesque lymphis obstrepunt manantibus,
   somnos quod inuitet leuis.
at cum tonantis annus hibernus Iouis
   imbris niuisque comparat,   30
aut trudit acris hinc et hinc multā canē
   apros in obstantis plagas
aut amite leui rara tendit retia:
  (turdis edacibus) dolos
pauidumque leporem et aduenam laqueo gruem,   35
   iucunda captat praemia.
quis non malarum quas amor curas habet
   haec inter obliuiscitur?
quodsi pudica mulier in partem iuuet
   domum atque dulcis liberos,   40
Sabina qualis aut perusta solibus
   pernicis uxor Apuli,
sacrum uetustis exstruat lignis focum
   lassi sub aduentum uiri
claudensque textis cratibus laetum pecus   45
   distenta siccet ubera
et horna dulci uina promens dolio
   dapes inemptas apparet:
non me Lucrina iuuerint conchylia
   magisue rhombus aut scari,   50
si quos Eois intonata fluctibus
   hiems ad hoc uertat mare,

23 *continuant epodon* **APS**: *nouum incipiunt* **BS**   25 ripis **A**: riuis **BV**   29 at
C: aut **c**

non Afra auis descendat in uentrem meum,
   non attagen Ionicus
iucundior quam lecta de pinguissimis   55
   oliua ramis arborum
aut herba lapathi prata amantis et graui
   maluae salubres corpori
uel agna festis caesa Terminalibus
   uel haedus ereptus lupo.   60
has inter epulas _ut_ iuuat pastas oues
   uidere properantis domum,
uidere fessos uomerem inuersum boues
   collo trahentis languido
postosque uernas, ditis examen domus,   65
   circum renidentis Lares.
haec ubi locutus fenerator Alfius,
   iam iam futurus rusticus,
omnem redegit Idibus pecuniam
   quaerit Kalendis ponere.   70

EPODE 3

PARENTIS olim si quis impia manu
   senile guttur fregerit,
edit cicutis alium nocentius.
   o dura messorum ilia!
quid hoc ueneni saeuit in praecordiis?   5
   num uiperinus his cruor
incoctus herbis me fefellit? an malas
   Canidia tractauit dapes?
ut Argonautas praeter omnis candidum
   Medea mirata est ducem,   10
ignota tauris illigaturum iuga
   perunxit hoc Iasonem,

65 postosque **c**: positosque **C**   3.3 edit **CVPS**: edat **c**

hoc delibutis ulta donis paelicem
   serpente fugit alite.
nec tantus umquam siderum insedit uapor   15
   siticulosae Apuliae
nec munus umeris efficacis Herculis
   inarsit aestuosius.
at si quid umquam tale concupiueris,
   iocose Maecenas, precor,   20
manum puella suauio opponat tuo
   extrema et in sponda cubet.

EPODE 4

LVPIS et agnis quanta sortito obtigit,
   tecum mihi discordia est,
Hibericis peruste funibus latus
   et crura dura compede.
[licet superbus ambules pecunia,]   5
   fortuna non mutat genus.
uidesne, Sacram metiente te Viam
   cum bis trium ulnarum toga,
ut ora uertat huc et huc euntium
   liberrima indignatio?   10
'sectus flagellis hic triumuiralibus
   (praeconis ad fastidium
arat Falerni mille fundi iugera
   et Appiam mannis terit
sedilibusque magnus in primis eques   15
   Othone contempto sedet.
quid attinet tot ora nauium graui
   rostrata duci pondere
contra latrones atque seruilem manum
   [hoc, hoc tribuno militum?']   20

4.8 trium *Barth* (*cf.* **PS**): ter **C**   16 contempto **CS**: contento *ed. Veneta 1478*

EPODE 5

'AT o deorum quidquid in caelo regit
    terras et humanum genus,
quid iste fert tumultus? aut quid omnium
    uoltus (in unum me) truces?   5

hostile

per liberos te, si uocata partubus
    Lucina ueris affuit,
per hoc inane purpurae decus precor,
    per improbaturum haec Iouem,
quid, ut nouerca, me intueris aut uti   *as*
    petita ferro belua?'   10

lament

ut haec trementi questus ore constitit
    insignibus raptis puer,
impube corpus, quale posset impia
    mollire Thracum pectora,
Canidia breuibus illigata uiperis   *little*   15
    (crinis et incomptum caput | *ref.*
iubet sepulcris caprificos erutas,
    iubet cupressos funebris
et uncta turpis oua ranae sanguine
    plumamque nocturnae strigis   20
herbasque [quas Iolcos atque Hiberia
    mittit uenenorum ferax]
et ossa ab ore rapta ieiunae canis
    flammis aduri Colchicis.
at expedita Sagana per totam domum   25
    spargens Auernalis aquas
horret capillis ut marinus asperis
    echinus aut currens aper.
abacta nulla Veia conscientia
    ligonibus duris humum   30

5.1 regit **AVPS**: regis **B**   3 aut **A**: et **B**   15 illigata **AP**: implicata **BS**
21 iolcos **AVP**: colchos **BS**   atque **A**: aut **B**   28 currens **CS**: Laurens
N. Heinsius

exhauriebat ingemens laboribus,
quo posset infossus puer
longo die bis terque mutatae dapis
   inemori spectaculo,
cum promineret ore, quantum exstant aqua   35
   suspensa mento corpora,
exsecta uti medulla et aridum iecur
   amoris esset poculum,
interminato cum semel fixae cibo
   intabuissent pupulae.   40
non defuisse masculae libidinis
   Ariminensem Foliam
et otiosa credidit Neapolis
   et omne uicinum oppidum,
quae sidera excantata uoce Thessala   45
   lunamque caelo deripit.
hic irresectum saeua dente liuido
   Canidia rodens pollicem
quid dixit aut quid tacuit? 'o rebus meis
   non infideles arbitrae,   50
Nox et Diana, quae silentium regis,
   arcana cum fiunt sacra,
nunc, nunc adeste, nunc in hostilis domos
   iram atque numen uertite.
formidulosis dum latent siluis ferae   55
   dulci sopore languidae,
senem, quod omnes rideant, adulterum
   latrant Suberanae canes,
nardo perunctum, quale non perfectius
   meae laborarint manus.   60
quid accidit? cur dira barbarae minus
   uenena Medeae ualent,

---

37 exsecta **CV**: exsucta **c**   55 formidulosae **AB**: formidulosis **cS**   58 latrant *Housman, Zielinski*: latrent **CS**   60 laborarint **AV**: laborarunt **B**

quibus superbam fugit ulta paelicem,
    magni Creontis filiam,
cum palla, tabo munus imbutum, nouam 65
    incendio nuptam abstulit?
atqui nec herba nec latens in asperis
    radix fefellit me locis:
indormit unctis omnium cubilibus
    obliuione paelicum. 70
a, a, solutus ambulat ueneficae
    scientioris carmine!
non usitatis, Vare, potionibus,
    o multa fleturum caput,
ad me recurres nec uocata mens tua 75
    Marsis redibit uocibus:
maius parabo, maius infundam tibi
    fastidienti poculum,
priusque caelum sidet inferius mari
    [tellure porrecta super,] 80
quam non amore sic meo flagres uti
    bitumen atris ignibus.'
sub haec puer iam non, ut ante, mollibus
    lenire uerbis impias,
sed dubius unde rumperet silentium 85
    misit Thyesteas preces:
'uenena magnum fas nefasque, non ualent
    conuertere humanam uicem.
diris agam uos: dira detestatio
    nulla expiatur uictima. 90
quin, ubi perire iussus exspirauero,
    nocturnus occurram furor

---

63 superbam **AV**: superba **BS**   65 imbutum **A**: infectum **B**   69 indormit
CP: an dormit *Sh. Bailey*: num dormit *Mankin*   71 a a **AS**: *om.* **B**   87 mag-
num **CP**: miscent *Garnsey*: *alii alia*

petamque uoltus umbra curuis unguibus,
   quae uis deorum est Manium,   95
et inquietis assidens praecordiis
   pauore somnos auferam.
uos turba uicatim hinc et hinc saxis petens
   contundet obscenas anus.
post insepulta membra different lupi
   et Esquilinae alites   100
neque hoc parentes, heu mihi superstites,
   effugerit spectaculum.'

EPODE 6

QVID immerentis hospites uexas canis
   ignauus aduersum lupos?
quin huc inanis, si potes, uertis minas
   et me remorsurum petis?
nam qualis aut Molossus aut fuluus Lacon,   5
   amica uis pastoribus,
agam per altas aure sublata niuis
   quaecumque praecedet fera;
tu, cum timenda uoce complesti nemus,
   proiectum odoraris cibum.   10
caue caue, namque in malos asperrimus
   parata tollo cornua,
qualis Lycambae spretus infido gener
   aut acer hostis Bupalo.
an si quis atro dente me petiuerit,   15
   inultus ut flebo puer?

---

98 contundet **A**: contundat **B**   102 effugerit **AP**: effugerint **B**   6.3–4
uertis ... petis **AS**: uerte ... pete **BV**   14 bupalo **CP**: Bupali *Kenney*
15 petiuerit **A**: oppetiuerit **B**

EPODE 7

Qvo quo scelesti ruitis? aut cur dexteris
    aptantur enses conditi?
parumne campis atque Neptuno super
    fusum est Latini sanguinis,
non ut superbas inuidae Carthaginis   5
    Romanus arces ureret
intactus aut Britannus ut descenderet
    Sacra catenatus Via,
sed ut secundum uota Parthorum sua
    Vrbs haec periret dextera?   10
neque hic lupis mos nec fuit leonibus,
    numquam nisi in dispar feris.
furorne caecus an rapit uis acrior
    an culpa? responsum date.
tacent et albus ora pallor inficit   15
    mentesque perculsae stupent.
sic est: acerba fata Romanos agunt
    scelusque fraternae necis,
ut immerentis fluxit in terram Remi
    sacer nepotibus cruor.   20

EPODE 8

Rogare longo putidam te saeculo
    uiris quid eneruet meas,
cum sit tibi dens ater et rugis uetus
    frontem senectus exaret
hietque turpis inter aridas natis   5
    podex uelut crudae bouis!

7.12 numquam *ed. Veneta 1490*: umquam **CS**   13 caecus **C**: caecos **cP**
(*lemma*)   15 albus ora pallor **A**: ora pallor albus **B**

sed incitat me pectus et mammae putres,
   equina quales ubera,
uenterque mollis et femur tumentibus
   exile suris additum.   10
esto beata, funus atque imagines
   ducant triumphales tuum,
nec sit marita quae rotundioribus
   onusta bacis ambulet:
quid, quod libelli Stoici inter Sericos   15
   iacere puluillos amant,
illiterati num minus nerui rigent
   minusue languet fascinum?
quod ut superbo prouoces ab inguine,
   ore allaborandum est tibi.   20

EPODE 9

QVANDO repostum Caecubum ad festas dapes
   uictore laetus Caesare
tecum sub alta (sic Ioui gratum) domo,
   beate Maecenas, bibam,
sonante mixtum tibiis carmen lyra,   5
   hac Dorium, illis barbarum?
ut nuper, actus cum freto Neptunius
   dux fugit ustis nauibus,
minatus Vrbi uincla quae detraxerat
   seruis amicus perfidis.   10
Romanus eheu (posteri negabitis!)
   emancipatus feminae
fert uallum et arma miles et spadonibus
   seruire rugosis potest
interque signa turpe militaria   15
   Sol aspicit conopium.

8.8 quales **A**: qualis **B**: qualia *Madvig*   17 minus **CPS**: magis *N. Heinsius*
9.1 repostum **AT**: repositum **BP**   9 uincla **A**: uincula **B**

at huc frementis uerterunt bis mille equos
    Galli canentes Caesarem
hostiliumque nauium portu latent
    puppes sinistrorsum citae.   20
io Triumphe, tu moraris aureos
    currus et intactas boues?
io Triumphe, nec Iugurthino parem
    bello reportasti ducem
neque Africanum, cui super Carthaginem   25
    uirtus sepulcrum condidit.
terra marique uictus hostis punico
    lugubre mutauit sagum:
aut ille centum nobilem Cretam urbibus,
    uentis iturus non suis,   30
exercitatas aut petit Syrtes Noto
    aut fertur incerto mari.
capaciores affer huc, puer, scyphos
    et Chia uina aut Lesbia
uel, quod fluentem nauseam coerceat,   35
    metire nobis Caecubum.
curam metumque Caesaris rerum iuuat
    dulci Lyaeo soluere.

EPODE 10

MALA soluta nauis exit alite
    ferens olentem Meuium.
ut horridis utrumque uerberes latus,
    Auster, memento fluctibus,
niger rudentis Eurus inuerso mari   5
    fractosque remos differat;

---

17 at huc **V**(*v.l.*)**P**(*?*): at hoc **P**(*?*): ad hunc **AV**(*?*)**P**(*lemma*)**S**: adhuc **B**   frementis *edd.*: frementes **C**   25 africanum **AS**: africano **B**   27 *epodon continuant* **CPS**: *nouum incipiunt* **cS**   10.2 meuium **AS**: maeuium **BPS**

insurgat Aquilo, quantus altis montibus
  frangit trementis ilices;
nec sidus atrā nocte amicum appareat
  quā tristis Orion cadit,   10
quietiore nec feratur aequore
  quam Graia uictorum manus,
cum Pallas usto uertit iram ab Ilio
  in impiam Aiacis ratem.
o quantus instat nauitis sudor tuis   15
  tibique pallor luteus
et illa non uirilis eiulatio
  preces et auersum ad Iouem,
Ionius udo cum remugiens sinus
  Noto carinam ruperit!   20
opima quodsi praeda curuo litore
  porrecta mergos iuuerit,
libidinosus immolabitur caper
  et agna Tempestatibus.

EPODE 11

PETTI, nihil me, sicut antea, iuuat
  scribere uersiculos amore percussum graui,
amore, qui me praeter omnis expetit
  mollibus in pueris aut in puellis urere.
hic tertius December, ex quo destiti   5
  Inachiā furere, siluis honorem decutit.
heu me, per Vrbem (nam pudet tanti mali)
  fabula quanta fui, conuiuiorum et paenitet,
in quis amantem languor et silentium
  arguit et latere petitus imo spiritus.   10

---

8 frangit **C**: plangit *Wakefield*   19–20 sinus noto **AP**: sinu notus **BV**:
sinus notus **c**   22 iuuerit **CPS**: iuueris **D**   11.2 percussum **A**: per-
culsum **B**   8 et **C**: ut *Bentley*

'contrane lucrum nil ualere candidum
   pauperis ingenium?' querebar applorans tibi,
simul calentis inuerecundus deus
   feruidiore mero arcana promorat loco.
'quodsi meis inaestuet praecordiis   15
   libera bilis, ut haec ingrata uentis diuidat
fomenta uolnus nil malum leuantia,
   desinet imparibus certare summotus pudor.'
ubi haec seuerus te palam laudaueram,
   iussus abire domum ferebar incerto pede   20
ad non amicos heu mihi postes et heu
   limina dura, quibus lumbos et infregi latus.
nunc gloriantis quamlibet mulierculam
   uincere mollitie amor Lycisci me tenet;
unde expedire non amicorum queant   25
   libera consilia nec contumeliae graues,
sed alius ardor aut puellae candidae
   aut teretis pueri longam renodantis comam.

EPODE 12

QVID tibi uis, mulier nigris dignissima barris?
   munera quid mihi quidue tabellas
mittis nec firmo iuueni neque naris obesae?
   namque sagacius unus odoror
polypus an grauis hirsutis cubet hircus in alis   5
   quam canis acer ubi lateat sus.
qui sudor uietis et quam malus undique membris
   crescit odor, cum pene soluto
indomitam properat rabiem sedare, neque illi
   iam manet umida creta colorque   10

---

11 contrane **CV**: contraque **c**   18 summotus **C**: commotus *Sh. Bailey*
pudor **C**: furor *Mankin*   12.3 mittis **AS**: mittes **B**   firmo iuueni **A**:
iuueni firmo **B**   7 qui **A**: quis **B**   8 crescit **A**: crescat **B**

stercore fucatus crocodili, iamque subando
  tenta cubilia tectaque rumpit!
uel mea cum saeuis agitat fastidia uerbis:
  'Inachia langues minus ac me;
Inachiam ter nocte potes, mihi semper ad unum   15
  mollis opus. pereat male, quae te
Lesbia quaerenti taurum monstrauit inertem,
  cum mihi Cous adesset Amyntas,
cuius in indomito constantior inguine neruus
  quam noua collibus arbor inhaeret.   20
muricibus Tyriis iteratae uellera lanae
  cui properabantur? tibi nempe,
ne foret aequalis inter conuiua, magis quem
  diligeret mulier sua quam te.
o ego non felix, quam tu fugis ut pauet acris   25
  agna lupos capreaeque leones!'

EPODE 13

HORRIDA tempestas caelum contraxit et imbres
  niuesque deducunt Iouem; nunc mare, nunc siluae
Threicio Aquilone sonant. rapiamus, amici,
  occasionem de die, dumque uirent genua
et decet, obducta soluatur fronte senectus.   5
  tu uina Torquato moue consule pressa meo.
cetera mitte loqui: deus haec fortasse benigna
  reducet in sedem uice. nunc et Achaemenio
perfundi nardo iuuat et fide Cyllenaea
  leuare diris pectora sollicitudinibus,   10
nobilis ut grandi cecinit Centaurus alumno:
  'inuicte, mortalis dea nate puer Thetide,

---

22 properabantur **A**: properabuntur **B**   13.3 amici **CPS**: amice *Bentley*
9 cyllenaea **P** (*lemma*): cyllenea *uel* cyllenia **CS**   11 grandi cecinit **A**: ceci-
nit grandi **B**

te manet Assaraci tellus, quam frigida parui
   findunt Scamandri flumina lubricus et Simois,
unde tibi reditum certo subtemine Parcae   15
   rupere, nec mater domum caerula te reuehet.
illic omne malum uino cantuque leuato,
   deformis aegrimoniae dulcibus alloquiis.'

EPODE 14

Mollis inertia cur tantam diffuderit imis
   obliuionem sensibus,
pocula Lethaeos ut si ducentia somnos
   arente fauce traxerim,
candide Maecenas, occidis saepe rogando.   5
   deus, deus nam me uetat
inceptos olim, promissum carmen, iambos
   ad umbilicum adducere.
non aliter Samio dicunt arsisse Bathyllo
   Anacreonta Teium,   10
qui persaepe caua testudine fleuit amorem
   non elaboratum ad pedem.
ureris ipse miser. quodsi non pulchrior ignis
   accendit obsessam Ilion,
gaude sorte tua: me libertina nec uno   15
   contenta Phryne macerat.

EPODE 15

Nox erat et caelo fulgebat luna sereno
   inter minora sidera,
cum tu, magnorum numen laesura deorum,
   in uerba iurabas mea,
artius atque hedera procera astringitur ilex   5
   lentis adhaerens bracchiis,

13 parui **CS**: praui **S**: flaui *N. Heinsius*

dum pecori lupus et nautis infestus Orion
　　turbaret hibernum mare
intonsosque agitaret Apollinis aura capillos,
　//fore hunc amorem mutuum,   10
o dolitura meá multum uirtute Neaera!
　　nam si quid in Flacco uiri est,
non feret/assiduas potiori té dare noctes
　　et quaeret iratus parem,
nec semel offensi cedet constantia formae,   15
　　si certus intrarit dolor.
et tu, quicumque es felicior atque meo nunc
　　superbus incedis malo,
sis pecore et multá diues tellure licebit
　　tibique Pactolus fluat   20
nec te Pythagorae fallant arcana renati
　　formaque uincas Nireá,
heu heu, translatos alio maerebis amores,
　　ast ego uicissim risero.

EPODE 16

ALTERA iam teritur bellis ciuilibus aetas
　　suis et ipsa Roma uiribus ruit.
quam neque finitimi ualuerunt perdere Marsi
　　minacis aut Etrusca Porsenae manus
aemula nec uirtus Capuae nec Spartacus acer   5
　　nouisque rebus infidelis Allobrox,
nec fera caeruleá domuit Germania pube
　　parentibusque abominatus Hannibal,
impia perdemus deuoti sanguinis aetas
　　ferisque rursus occupabitur solum,   10
barbarus heu cineres insistet uictor et Vrbem
　　eques sonante uerberabit ungulá,

(quaeque carent uentis et solibus) ossa Quirini
 (nefas uidere!) dissipabit insolens.
forte quid expediat: communiter aut melior pars   15
 malis carere quaeritis laboribus?
nulla sit hāc potior sententia: Phocaeorum
 uelut profugit exsecrata ciuitas
agros atque Lares patrios habitandaque fana
 apris reliquit et rapacibus lupis,   20
ire pedes quocumque ferent, quocumque per undas
 Notus uocabit aut proteruus Africus.
sic placet? an melius quis habet suadere? secunda
 ratem occupare quid moramur alite?
sed iuremus in haec: simul imis saxa renarint   25
 uadis leuata, ne redire sit nefas,
neu (conuersa domum) pigeat dare lintea quando
 Padus Matina lauerit cacumina,
in mare seu celsus procurrerit Appenninus
 nouaque monstra iunxerit libidine   30
mirus amor, iuuet ut tigres subsidere ceruis,
 adulteretur et columba miluo,
credula nec rauos timeant armenta leones
 ametque salsa leuis hircus aequora.
haec et quae poterunt reditūs abscindere dulcis 35
 eamus omnis exsecrata ciuitas,
aut pars indocili melior grege; mollis et exspes
 inominata perpremat cubilia!
uos quibus est uirtus, muliebrem tollite luctum,
 Etrusca praeter et uolate litora.   40
nos manet Oceanus circumuagus: arua beata
 petamus, arua diuites et insulas,

---

14 uidere **A**: uideri **BVS** 15 quid **CS**: quod **D** 16 carere **CPS**: leuetque
uel sim. Kenney 33 rauos **AVS**: flauos **B**: fuluos **c**: saeuos **c** 36 omnis
APS: omnes **B** 37 exspes **APS**: exper **BP(?)S** 41 circumuagus **AS**:
circum uagus **BP**

reddit ubi Cererem tellus inarata quotannis
   et imputata floret usque uinea,
germinat et numquam fallentis termes oliuae   45
   suamque pulla ficus ornat arborem,
mella caua manant ex ilice, montibus altis
   leuis crepante lympha desilit pede.
illic iniussae ueniunt ad mulctra capellae
   refertque tenta grex amicus ubera,   50
nec uespertinus circumgemit ursus ouile,
   nec intumescit alta uiperis humus.
pluraque felices mirabimur, ut neque largis
   aquosus Eurus arua radat imbribus
pinguia nec siccis urantur semina glaebis,   55
   [utrumque rege temperante caelitum.]
non huc Argoo contendit remige pinus,
   neque impudica Colchis intulit pedem;
non huc Sidonii torserunt cornua nautae,
   laboriosa nec cohors Vlixei.   60
nulla nocent pecori contagia, nullius astri
   gregem aestuosa torret impotentia.
Iuppiter illa piae secreuit litora genti,
   ut inquinauit aere tempus aureum,
aere, dehinc ferro durauit saecula, quorum   65
   piis secunda [uate me] datur fuga.

EPODE 17

IAM iam efficaci do manus scientiae
supplex et oro regna per Proserpinae,
per et Dianae non mouenda numina,
per atque libros carminum ualentium
refixa caelo deuocare sidera,   5

48 lympha **AP**: nympha **B**   51 ouile **A**: ouili **BV**
CS: *post* 52 *transposuit Heynemann, post* 56 *Bentley*
65 aere **A**: aerea **B**   17.5 refixa **AS**: defixa **B**

61–2 *in hoc loco habent*
61 astri **A**: austri **B**

Canidia, parce uocibus tandem sacris
citumque retro solue, solue turbinem.
mouit nepotem Telephus Nereium
in quem superbus ordinarat agmina
Mysorum et in quem tela acuta torserat.   10
luxere matres Iliae additum feris
alitibus atque canibus homicidam Hectorem,
postquam relictis moenibus rex procidit
heu peruicacis ad pedes Achillei.
saetosa duris exuere pellibus   15
laboriosi remiges Vlixei
uolente Circa membra; tunc mens et sonus
relapsus atque notus in uoltus honor.
dedi satis superque poenarum tibi,
amata nautis multum et institoribus: 20
fugit iuuentas et uerecundus color,
relinquor ossa pelle amicta lurida,
tuis capillus albus est odoribus;
nullum a labore me reclinat otium,
urget diem nox et dies noctem neque est   25
leuare tenta spiritu praecordia.
ergo negatum uincor ut credam miser
Sabella pectus increpare carmina
caputque Marsa dissilire nenia.
quid amplius uis? o mare et terra, ardeo   30
quantum neque atro delibutus Hercules
Nessi cruore nec Sicana feruida
uirens in Aetna flamma: tu, donec cinis
iniuriosis aridus uentis ferar,
cales uenenis officina Colchicis?   35
quae finis aut quod me manet stipendium?

---

11 luxere **A**: unxere **BV**   17 circa **AT**: circe **B**   18 relapsus **A**: relatus **B**
22 relinquor *Peerlkamp*: reliquit **C**   amicta **A**: amictus **B**   33 uirens **CV**:
urens, furens **D**

effare: iussas cum fide poenas luam,
paratus expiare, seu poposceris
centum iuuencos, siue mendaci lyra
uoles sonari: 'tu pudica, tu proba   40
perambulabis astra sidus aureum.'
infamis Helenae Castor offensus uice
fraterque magni Castoris uicti prece
adempta uati reddidere lumina:
et tu (potes nam) solue me dementia,   45
o nec paternis obsoleta sordibus
neque (in sepulcris pauperum) prudens anus
nouendialis dissipare puluered;
tibi hospitale pectus et purae manus
tuusque uenter Pactumeius et tuo   50
cruore rubros obstetrix pannos lauit,
utcumque fortis exsilis puerperā.
'quid obseratis auribus fundis preces?
non saxa nudis surdiora nauitis
Neptunus alto tundit hibernus salo.   55
inultus ut tu riseris Cotytia
uolgata, sacrum liberi Cupidinis,
et Esquilini pontifex uenefici
impune ut Vrbem nomine impleris meo?
quid proderit ditasse Paelignas anūs   60
uelociusue miscuisse toxicum?
sed tardiora fata te uotis manent:
ingrata misero uita ducenda est in hoc,
nouis ut usque suppetas laboribus.
optat quietem Pelopis infidi pater   65
egens benignae Tantalus semper dapis,

---

40 sonari **A**: sonare **B**   42 uice **AS**: uicem **BS**(?)   50 pactumeius **CPS**:
partumeius **c**   53 *carmen continuant* **APS**: *nouum incipiunt* **BS**   57 sacrum
APS: sacra **BS**   62 sed **A**: si **BP**   64 laboribus **A**: doloribus **B**

optat Prometheus obligatus aliti,
optat supremo collocare Sisyphus
in monte saxum: sed uetant leges Iouis.
uoles modo altis desilire turribus,   70
modo ense pectus Norico recludere,
frustraque uincla gutturi nectes tuo
fastidiosa tristis aegrimonia.
uectabor umeris tunc ego inimicis eques
meaeque terra cedet insolentiae.   75
an quae mouere cereas imagines,
ut ipse nosti curiosus, et polo
deripere lunam uocibus possim meis,
possim crematos excitare mortuos
desiderique temperare pocula,   80
plorem artis in te nil agentis exitus?'

67 aliti **AV**: alite **B**   72 nectes **A**: innectes **B**   77 polo **CS**: choro **P**
80 pocula **A**: poculum **BPS**   81 agentis **A**: habentis **B**   exitus **A**: exitum **B**

COMMENTARY

EPODE 1

Introduction

Maecenas will share Octavian's danger: should H. and M.'s other friends also share it, or stay behind? They will follow M. wherever he goes. If M. wonders how H. can help him, he cannot, but his fear for his friend will be less if he is with him. In this and every war H. will serve in hope only of M.'s good will and not, as some might, for the sake of enriching himself.

The setting is probably Rome sometime before the Actium campaign (Intro. 2), perhaps in the spring of 31 BC, when Octavian assembled his forces at Brindisi, the embarkation point for Greece (Dio 50.11.5; cf. 9.3n.). With its announcement of a journey, the poem resembles a *propempticon* ('bon-voyage poem': 10.1–10n.), except that H., unlike the well-wishers in other examples of the genre (e.g. Tib. 1.1.), will also be a traveller, and he is less concerned with the destination and outcome of the voyage than with the opportunity it offers for him to define and affirm his friendship with Maecenas.

Some have wondered why a poem on friendship should introduce a collection of *iambi* (Intro. 4). Besides dedicating the book to Maecenas (cf. *C.* 1.1, *S.* 1.1, *Ep.* 1.1), it could be intended to recall the importance of friends (*philoi*) as the audience and context for early Greek *iambus* (Intro. 3). There, too, friendship is defined through contrast with unfriendly or inimical behaviour (25–34n.) and tested by moments of crisis (e.g. Arch. fr. 15 West (App. 1) 'Glaucus, an ally is only a friend until there is a battle', frr. 88–114 (military expeditions)). H.'s depiction of his friendship with Maecenas may thus serve as a kind of 'touchstone' for assessing the conduct of the characters, both friends and enemies, in the epodes that follow.

1–4 Maecenas will go among the enemy ships, ready to endure the danger threatening Octavian.

1 Ibis: the second sing., picked up throughout (*amice, tuo* etc.), seems to emphasize that H.'s concern is for the individual Maecenas, not necessarily for Octavian or his cause (2n.). For the theory that *ibis* was a kind of title for the Epode book, cf. Intro. 4, n. 44.

Liburnis 'with (Octavian's) Liburnians'. *Liburnae*, so called because the Romans borrowed their design from the Illyrian *Liburni*, were light, fast galleys able to outmanoeuvre, but at a disadvantage in a set battle against, larger ships (S. Panciera, *Epigraphica* 18 (1956) 130–56).

1–2 inter ... propugnacula: since these seem to be the cause of Maecenas' danger, H. probably means the *propugnacula* of the enemy fleet, although at Actium both sides would have vessels equipped with 'turrets' that allowed marines to fight 'as if from walls' (Plin. *Nat.* 32.3; cf. Virg. *A.* 8.691–3, Pelling on Plut. *Ant.* 61.1, 66.3). The word order, with *amice* literally 'amid' the words for the ships, seems to emphasize the threat. H. is fond of such effects with *inter* (e.g. 8.5, 9.15–16, *C.* 1.12.47, 3.3.37, 6.26, 10.6, 15.5, 18.13, 27.51, 4.3.14).

2 amice: a key word, indicating that H.'s fear and willingness to share danger stems from his *amicitia*, not from attachment to a cause (5, 11–14, 23–4nn.) or desire for gain (25–34). The hyperbaton *amice ... Maecenas* may suggest that H. places his feeling for his friend prior to his regard for the man's 'name' and connection with Octavian (cf. *C.* 3.8.5–13, 29.1–3, *Ep.* 1.1.1–3).

3 omne: probably 'every', as at 27, indicating Maecenas' general readiness to support Octavian. But as a specific danger is at hand (*hunc* 9, *hoc* 27), it could mean 'the whole danger', i.e. from start to finish (13.17n.).

Caesaris: Octavian early dropped the last element in his adopted name C. Iulius Caesar Octavianus, but modern scholars use it to distinguish him from his great-uncle and his post-civil-war incarnation as Augustus (Kienast (1982) 7–9, 79–80). H. knows him only as 'Caesar' in the *Epodes*, *Satires*, and *Odes* 1, although the Caesar of *S.* 1.9.18 and *C.* 1.2.44 is the dictator. The Iulius of *S.* 1.8.49 cannot be identified, and the Octavius of *S.* 1.10.82 seems to be a historian and noted drunk (K–H *ad loc.*). In his other works H. still prefers name to title (N–H on *C.* 2.9.19, Brink on *Ep.* 2.1.5, 2.2.48).

3–4 Caesaris periculum | subire ... tuo 'endure Caesar's peril at your own'. The abl. *tuo* (sc. *periculo*) could be instrumental, as at 15 below, or related to the idiom *meo periculo*, 'at my own risk'

(*OLD* s.v. *periculum* 4b, Sh. Bailey (1956) 43–4). This would suggest that Maecenas will share the danger unordered or even contrary to Caesar's wishes, exactly what H. claims he himself will do (7–10). The idiom is not common in verse outside of comedy (Ov. *Met.* 10.545), but not out of place for the stylistic level of the *Epodes*.

Some prefer the variant *Caesari*, which, with *tuo*, would equal *pro Caesare tuo*, 'on behalf of your Caesar' (Brink (1982) 34), but Porph. comments on the gen. and it seems more likely that *-is* would be corrupted to *-i* than vice versa (Keller).

4 subire 'endure'; cf. *S.* 1.3.120, *Ep.* 1.17.41, Cic. *Fam.* 15.4.12 *mitto quod inuidiam, quod pericula, quod omnis meas tempestates et subieris et, multo etiam magis si per me licuisset, subire paratissimus fueris.* The idea of endurance could imply that Maecenas may share the danger, but be no more able to help Caesar than H. Maecenas (15–16, 19–22). His passivity is in keeping with the initial image of the Liburnians 'amid' but not attacking the enemy.

5–10 The happiness of Maecenas' friends depends on his survival. In the crisis, should they follow orders and remain behind, or face the danger like men?

The first pers. pl. (5–14) may include not only H., but the others who make up the group of *amici* of which Maecenas is the central figure (Babcock (1974) 12). Such a group, what the Greeks called a *hetaireia*, is the main context and audience for *iambus* (Intro. 3).

5 quid nos: sc. *faciamus*. The ellipse of the verb in a question seems to be colloquial (5.3n., *S.* 1.2.10, 4.136, 2.3.31, 99, *Ep.* 1.1.91, 2.10, 3.9, Hofmann (1951) 47–8).

5–6 quibus ... grauis 'for whom life, if (lived) with you surviving, is sweet, if (lived) otherwise, tiresome'. Some consider the second *si* (= *sin*; cf. *C.* 3.29.53, *S.* 1.3.6, *Ep.* 1.5.6) 'superfluous' (Porph.), and its omission by some MSS has paved the way for such conjectures as *sit* (Aldus).

5 superstite: this is usually taken to mean 'present' or 'safe', but elsewhere in H. and in most other Classical Latin *superstites dicimus qui supersint mortuis* (Non. p. 630M; cf. 5.101, *C.* 2.2.8, 17.7, 3.9.12, 16, *Saec.* 42). If that is its meaning here, then H. would seem to imply that life would be happy even if those with Maecenas – including Caesar – were to perish, so long as Maecenas 'survived' them. H.'s focus on a single friend and his indifference to the fate of the rest is

almost 'Achillean'; cf. Hom. *Il.* 16.98–100 (Achilles to Patroclus)
'May none of the Trojans escape, | nor any of the Argives, but may
you and I avoid doom, | so that we alone may sack Troy.'

Not surprisingly, commentators find it hard to believe that this is
what H. means. Some take *superstitem pro praesenti* (Schol.), others as a
synomym for *incolumis* or *saluus*. But it is harder to believe that H.'s
audience would recognize meanings of *superstes* that are attested only
in a few passages of early Latin (cf. Non. (above), Fest. p. 395M,
Don. on Ter. *An.* 487, Pl. *As.* 17 (but cf. 21), *Cas.* 818, *Tru.* 387, fr. 6,
Acc. *trag.* fr. 21 *ROL*, Cic. *Mur.* 26 (legal mumbo-jumbo)).

6 iucunda: cf. Cic. *Am.* 55 *uita inculta et deserta ab amicis non possit
esse iucunda, Fin.* 1.6 *nullo modo sine amicitia firmam et perpetuam iucundita-
tem uitae tenere possumus. iucundus* does not occur in the *Odes* (9× in the
hexameters), and its distribution in other Latin suggests that it is less
elevated than *gratus* and *dulcis*, but less colloquial than *suauis* (Watson
(1985) 439).

si contra: euphemistic for *te mortuo*; cf. N–H on *C.* 2.10.14 *alteram
[=malam] sortem.*

7 utrumne: the superflous *-ne* seems to be colloquial, and even
without it *utrum ... an* occurs only rarely in poetry (Axelson (1945)
90).

iussi 'at your insistence', suggesting that Maecenas has already
urged his friends to this course, and that H. would not 'pursue lei-
sure' unless 'ordered' to do so. The part. also identifies the speaker
and his companions (5–10n.) as male, and may thus prepare for the
phrase *non mollis uiros* (10).

iubeo often means 'insist', 'ask', or even 'invite' (11.20, *S.* 1.1.63,
104), yet the phrasing here has a military ring and, with the other
indications of war, might create the initial impression that H.'s rela-
tion to M. is that of subordinate to commander. But this impression,
already weakened by *amice* (2), is further undermined by what follows
(15–22n.).

persequemur otium: this may be an oxymoron. *sequor* with
otium or the like is an accepted usage (*OLD* s.v. *sequor* 20), but the
intensive *persequor*, when not used lit. of 'chasing' living things (*C.*
1.23.10, 3.2.14, *S.* 1.9.16, *OLD* s.v. *persequor* 1–2), normally has as its
object something to be attained, explored, or attacked (s.v. 3–9) or
an activity to be 'pursued' (s.v. 10). *laborem* (9) would be an appro-

priate object, *otium* a paradoxical one. 'H. sees *otium*, without Maecenas, as a toil more taxing than a relentless journey that must be pursued' (Miles). Cf. Cic. *Off.* 3.1 *nam et a re publica forensibusque negotiis armis impiis usque prohibiti, otium persequimur.*

otium is 'a word capable of many implications, both good and bad' (N–H on *C.* 2.16; cf. J. André, *L'otium dans la vie morale et intellectuale romaine* (Paris 1966) 455–99 (on H.)). Here it seems to have both a positive sense, of ease and pleasure, and negative, of shirking toil.

8 ni: only here and at *C.* 4.6.21 in H.'s lyric, but 14× in the hexameters, and its usage elsewhere also suggests that it may be colloquial (Hierche (1974) 118).

9–10 'Or shall we (pursue) this labour, set on enduring with (that) mind, with which it befits strong men to endure?' With the punctuation adopted here (Nauck), *persequemur*, supplied from 7, is the main verb, with *laturi* in apposition but still part of the question, which is answered in reverse order, *laturi* by *feremus* (11), *persequemur* by *sequemur* (14). Others punctuate to make either *laturi* (sc. *sunt*, but cf. 17n.) or, with the question extended through 14, *feremus* (11) the main verb (Housman (1971) 5, Sh. Bailey).

9 laborem: sc. *persequemur* (7n.). There is a similar *apo koinou* at *Ep.* 1.3.9 *quid* [sc. *struit* (6)] *Titius, Romana breui uenturus in ora.*

mente: with *qua* (10) = *ea mente qua*. The placement of the rel. pronoun after its verb is unusual for H. (cf. *S.* 1.4.39, 81, 9.25, 2.3.298 *dixerit insanum qui me, Ep.* 2.1.201 *sonum referunt quem nostra theatra*) and may put special emphasis on *decet*.

laturi: fut. part. expressing purpose (2.68, 3.11, 15.3, *C.* 1.22.6, 4.13.24, *S.* 1.5.87, 10.73, 2.8.85, *Ars* 476).

10 non mollis uiros: for *mollis* cf. 11.4, 24, 12.16, 14.1, 16.37, *C.* 1.15.31 (Paris on the battlefield) *sublimi fugies mollis anhelitu.* Maecenas himself had a reputation for *mollities* (Intro. 1), and there may be 'a note of defiance in *non mollis*, with H. daring his readers to smile, sc. "I know what people say about M., but he is not *mollis* when danger to Octavian is imminent" ' (Kenney).

11–14 They will endure and follow Maecenas, whether through the Alps and Caucasus mountains, or all the way to the furthest gulf of the west.

From *hoc bellum* (23–4) there can be no doubt that they are committing themselves to the war against Antony. Yet it is striking that

H. does not mention a possible destination in the eastern Mediterranean, the area of operations for that war. Expeditions to the NW, NE, and W would involve travel by land, not sea (but cf. 13n.), and battles, not against fellow Romans, but against Gauls, Germans, Parthians, and Spanish tribes (12, 13nn.). The eruption of civil war had left unfinished business with these peoples which Octavian was to resume as soon as things were settled (Scullard (1982) 246–59, Kienast (1982) 274–310). H. may imply what he elsewhere makes explicit, that the swords of the Romans were better directed against such enemies than each other (7 intro.).

The theme of friend journeying with friend is a familiar one (Kroll on Cat. 11, N–H on *C.* 1.22.5, 2.6, 2.17), and H. may be working a variation on a topos or 'genre' (Cairns (1972) 141–2). But his focus on 'trouble spots' of military concern distinguishes this context from many of the supposed parallels, in which the destinations include impossibly remote or even fabulous places.

11 et te uel per: an unusual word grouping. In his trimeters H. avoids monosyllables at pos. 4, 5, and 7, and nowhere else has a cluster of more than three (2.31).

Alpium iuga: into Gaul, which was still far from pacified, especially in view of the German threat (Scullard, Kienast (11–14n.)).

12 inhospitalem = Greek *axenos*, an epithet given to the Black Sea region from Pindar (*P.* 4.203) on. Mention of the Caucasus could suggest a campaign against Parthia, as operations in that area were apparently a prelude to the most recent Parthian expedition, that of Antony in 35 BC (Pelling on Plut. *Ant.* 34.10).

et: postponed, as at 2.20, 3.22, 10.18, 13.14, 16.2, 32, 40, 42, 45, 17.2, 3. For other postponed particles, cf. 34, 9.31 (*aut*), 8.11, 17.4 (*atque*), 10.11 (*nec*), 14.6, 17.45 (*nam*), 16.29 (*seu*), 43 (*ubi*). Postposition of particles is supposed to be a Neoteric innovation based on Hellenistic Greek practice (Norden (1926) 402–4, Marouzeau (1949) 70–91, 105–8, Ross (1969) 67–9). But postponed *et*, which first occurs at *CE* 55.6 (late Republic?), and in Virgil (*Ecl.* 1.34 etc.) and H., does not appear to be Neoteric. Of the 80-odd postponed particles in H., nearly half are *et* and nearly all (90%) are *metri causa*. In the Neoteric Catullus, by contrast, only 9 of 16 (60%) postpositions are metrically expedient. This suggests that for H. technique was more a convenience than the stylistic marker it had been for his predecessors.

13 Occidentis ... ultimum sinum: the epithet suggests an unfamiliar place (cf. *C.* 1.35.29, Cat. 11.11, 29.4, 12 (of Britain), *C.* 2.18.4 (Africa), 2.20.28 (Scythia), Virg. *G.* 1.30, *A.* 4.481, 8.687, 12.334 (Thule, Ethiopia, Bactria, Thrace)), perhaps the *Sinus Aquitanicus* (Bay of Biscay), a region as yet relatively unknown to the Romans. Its southern coast, the territory of the Cantabri, would be the focus of Octavian's Spanish war of 26-25 BC (*C.* 3.14.3-4, Scullard, Kienast (11-14n.)). Most commentators take H. to mean Gades (Cadiz), but by the triumviral period this was a Roman colony, although in anachronistic (*C.* 3.3.45 (set in 714 BC)) and 'mock-heroic' contexts (*C.* 2.2.10, N-H on 2.6.1) it could still be evoked as the western boundary of the world.

usque ad: in a local sense only here in H.'s lyric (cf. *S.* 1.2.26, 6.105, *Ep.* 2.2.170).

sinum: cf. Virg. *G.* 2.123 (the Indian Ocean) *extremi sinus orbis.*

15-22 Maecenas may ask how H. could possibly help him. H.'s fear will be less if he is with his friend, just as a mother bird is more afraid for her chicks when she is away, although even when present she can hardly protect them.

At this point, close to the centre of the poem, Maecenas' imagined question, H.'s response, and especially the complex simile (19-22n.) shift the focus from the general situation to the particulars of the relation between the two friends. With the shift come surprises. H. no longer speaks as part of a group (*iuuem meo* 15) and is revealed to be, both in M.'s estimation and his own, not quite the 'man' he seemed (15-16). But the simile in turn reveals that the hint at the beginning (4n.) of M.'s passivity was justified (19-22n.). Both men are caught up in a dangerous situation, in which it becomes essential for H. to rehearse, and so reaffirm, his personal reasons for fighting at his friend's side (23-34n.).

15 roges = *si roges,* a colloquial parataxis (8.1-2, *C.* 1.27.9-14, 4.4.65-8, Hofmann (1951) 109-10).

labore: a necessary correction (Glareanus ed. 1585) for the unmetrical but more obvious *laborem* of the MSS.

quid: acc. of reference in a double acc. construction (23-4n., 11.1,

17, *Ep.* 2.2.212 *quid te exempta iuuat spinis de pluribus una?*, LHS II 40, 43).

iuuem: this seems to be the first instance of *iuuo* where 'usu deflexo iuuantur res malae' rather than the people afflicted by them (*ThLL* VII 2.747). But the usage is obvious enough (cf. *OLD* s.v. *adiuuo* 7, *subleuo* 3, *opitulor*, *subuenio*, *succurro*) and is probably colloquial rather than a Horatian coinage.

16 imbellis ac firmus parum: cf. the Homeric reproach (*Il.* 2.201, 9.35, 41) *aptolemos kai analkis* ('unwarlike and defenceless'). *ac* occurs only here and at 12.14 in the *Epodes*, and is rare in other verse, apparently because it is practically identical in sense and prosody to *et* (Axelson (1945) 82–3, LHS II 477–8).

firmus parum: this is probably a polite way of saying *mollis* (Ion.; for *parum*, cf. *C.* 1.12.59, 30.7, 2.18.22, 4.1.35, *S.* 2.6.45, *Ars* 448) rather than, as some take it, a suggestion that H. is ill.

17 sum futurus: in H. the so-called 'future periphrastic' (fut. act. part. as a main verb) always includes a form of *sum* (cf. 9–10n.) and indicates, not simple futurity, but likelihood or tendency (*C.* 1.9.13, *S.* 1.2.112, 5.27, 2.3.261, 6.7, 56, 8.66).

18 maior: adj. for adv., as often in Latin (2.55–6, 3.18, 16.51, *S.* 1.8.4, 2.4.16, LHS II 171–3).

habet: this and Virg. *Ecl.* 7.40 seem to be the first examples of *habeo* in the sense of emotions 'gripping' people (*ThLL* VI 2431). The usage may be a Graecism (cf. LSJ s.v *echō* A 8).

19–22 'just as a hen tending to her unfledged chicks fears the attacks of snakes (even) more for them (the chicks) left behind (by her), not that, even if she should be at hand, she would bring more help to them being present'. The simile illustrates H.'s anxiety and weakness: he is like a terrified and helpless mother bird. But if the mother corresponds to H., then the chicks, the object of concern, must correspond to Maecenas. The comparison, which implies that M., too, may be *imbellis ac firmus parum*, is hardly flattering. Yet it serves to heighten the sense of danger symbolized by the ominous snakes (20n.).

The image of the bird and her young is not uncommon (Hom. *Il.* 9.323–7, Aesch. *Sept.* 291–3, Moschus 4.21–7, Stat. *Ach.* 1.212–16), but H. may refer specifically to Hom. *Il.* 2.308–20, where Odysseus describes the portent of Troy's destruction. If so, the simile becomes even more ominous, since Troy, her 'mother city', is often a symbol for Rome (10.11–14n.).

19 assidens: cf. 5.95, *S.* 1.1.81–2 (if you are sick) *habes qui | assideat, fomenta paret, medicum roget.*

implumibus: first here and at Virg. *G.* 4.512–113 (a nightingale) *amissos queritur fetus, quos durus arator | obseruans nido implumis detraxit,* which may imitate Hom. *Il.* 9.323 *aptēsi neossoisi* ('unfledged young') or *Od.* 16.218 *paros peteēna genesthai* ('before the wings (of the chicks) are full grown').

The caesura in this verse consists of a 'cut' (*tmesis*) between *im* and *plumibus* (11.15, 16.8). This type of caesura is not attested in the fragments of early *iambus,* but it does occur in Greek tragedy and comedy (Van Raalte (1986) 204–5) and in Roman comedy (Soubiran (1988) 150–1).

20 serpentium allapsus: the Romans considered snakes ominous; cf. Pease on Cic. *Div.* 1.36, 2.62–5, where Cicero translates the *Iliad* passage cited above (19–22n.). *allapsus* first occurs here and may be a Horatian coinage (Blok (1961) 27).

20–1 timet | magis relictis 'fears more for (them) left behind'. For the construction, *timeo* x (acc.) on behalf of y (dat.), cf. Virg. *Ecl.* 6.50 *collo timuisse aratrum, A.* 2.130 *quae sibi quisque timebat, OLD* s.v. 2b. Some take *relictis* as an abl. absolute, 'she fears more greatly when they are left behind' (Lambinus, Brink (1982) 34–5).

21 ut adsit: concessive, 'even if she should be at hand' (*S.* 1.4.69, *Ep.* 1.12.8, *OLD* s.v. *ut* 35). The variant *ut sit* may have arisen from an attempt to make a 'future periphrastic' (17n.) with *latura* (22).

22 latura: fut. part. indicating likelihood (5.74, 6.4, 9.30, 15.11, *C.* 1.28.30, 4.2.3, 7.10, *S.* 1.8.29, 33, 10.89, 2.1.12, 8.44, *Ep.* 1.3.9, 2.2.38, 48, 86, 161, *Ars* 155).

praesentibus: this is usually taken as dat. ('for them being present'), but unless H. intends a kind of *figura etymologica* (4.15n.; cf. Pl. *Ps.* 1142 *praesens praesentem uides*), it seems redundant after *adsit.* Another possibility is that it is abl. of (compendious) comparison (LHS II 826), 'not that she would bring more help *than* those present', i.e. she could no more help the chicks than they themselves. For the construction, cf. *Ep.* 1.17.43–4 *de paupertate tacentes | plus poscente ferent.*

23–34 This and every war will be fought in hope of Maecenas' good will. H. does not expect riches in exchange: Maecenas has already given him enough and more. His reward will be immaterial, something he can neither hoard nor squander.

As the poem ends H. identifies the 'danger' and 'labour' as a war, and an imminent one (*hoc*), and extends his commitment beyond, to 'every war' (23). To his other motives he adds the hope of M.'s *gratia*. This word has several meanings, but H. is careful to indicate that he seeks, not the 'gratitude' of a patron, but the 'good will' of a friend (24n.). Finally, he blames, both indirectly (25–30n.) and directly (33–4), those who, unlike himself, would profit from the crisis.

23 libenter: only here in H.'s lyric (in the hexameters at *S.* 1.1.63, 3.63, 141, 5.34, 2.6.20, *Ep.* 1.11.24, 2.1.262). Its rarity in other verse aside from comedy suggests that it is unpoetic (Axelson (1945) 63, 149).

militabitur: this verb is surprisingly uncommon, perhaps because it preserves its association with *miles*; *duces*, not *milites*, are the focus of most Roman accounts of warfare (Blok (1961) 28–9). Here H., apparently for the first time (*ThLL* VIII 967), extends its meaning from 'serve as a soldier' to 'fight a war', but the connection with *miles* may still be important, suggesting that in every war, H. will fight as a 'common soldier' – in US Army slang, as a 'grunt' – with all the hardships traditional to that status (2.5n). The passive may suggest the anonymity of 'soldiery' and also provide a sense of 'greater resolution; the identity of the participant fades away as wholly unimportant, so that what matters is only the task and its completion' (Heinze).

23–4 hoc et omne ... bellum: internal or 'cognate' accusatives made the subjects of a passive verb (*C.* 2.8.1, 3.19.4, *S.* 2.5.27, *Ep.* 1.16.25). The passive construction is rare in Latin, even in comedy, where the internal acc. is common (cf. Pl. *Per.* 232 *militia* [sc. *amoris*] *militatur*, LHS II 29). It is more frequent in Greek (K–G I 126–7) and H. may be imitating something in Archilochus.

omne ... | bellum: the idea that they may survive this war to fight others, perhaps against foreign enemies (11–14n.), is the first dubious note of optimism in the poem. Some see in this anticipation of future wars a commitment by H. to the 'cause' of Octavian (Babcock (1974) 28) or even a reference to the 'loyalty oath' which

Octavian imposed on Italy in 32 BC (Kraggerud (1984) 29–32; cf. Reinhold on Dio 50.6.6). But H.'s focus is on Maecenas, not Octavian, and the only 'cause' he mentions is his friend's *gratia*.

24 in: expressing purpose (17.63, *S*. 2.5.47 etc.).

gratiae: since H. cannot really help Maecenas (11–22), and since he rejects the idea of material reward (25–34), *gratia* here would seem to mean 'good will' (*OLD* s.v. 1) or 'amity' (s.v. 2) and not, as some take it (e.g. Kraggerud (1984) 32), the 'gratitude' owed by a patron to a client (s.v. 3). On *gratia* in general and in the political vocabulary of the late Republic, cf. Hellegouarc'h (1972) 202–8, Brunt (1988) 389–90.

25–30 In denying that he is motivated by greed, H. perhaps indirectly 'denounces the mentality and debauchery of those among [his] contemporaries for whom war and, in particular, civil war, presented a useful opportunity for plunder' (Martina (1989) 51). Such 'indirect blame' is an important feature of Horatian, as it was of Archilochean, *iambus* (Intro. 3). For greed and profiteering during civil war, cf. Cic. *Phil.* 5.32, Sall. *Cat.* 10.13, Vell. 2.3.3, Jal (1963) 384–91.

25 iuuencis: technically 'bullocks' in the 'second stage of life', older than *uituli*, younger than *tauri* (Var. *R.* 2.5.6). But the word occurs only rarely in prose and may be poetic, somewhat like 'kine' in English (Blok (1961) 29–30).

illigata: cf. 3.11, 5.15, *C.* 1.27.23. *illigo* is rare in verse, probably because most of its forms are not suited to dactyls; cf. the tmesis at Virg. *A.* 10.794 *inque ligatus.*

pluribus: the comparative probably suggests that H. already has some *iuuenci* (31–2n; cf. 9.33n.).

26 nitantur: the ploughs, rather than the bullocks, 'toil', and the flocks 'change pastures' without shepherds or dogs (27–8), implying, perhaps, a kind of golden age 'automation' (cf. 2.61–4, 16.43–50).

meis: the hyperbaton seems to give the adj. special emphasis: 'the oxen are mine, not the property of the landlord or the result of borrowing' (Naylor; cf. 2.3, *C.* 3.24.3–4, Brink on *Ep.* 2.2.21). Since *meis* gives *iuuencis* two epithets and leaves *aratra* without one, some prefer the reading *mea*. But H. seems to 'exempt' possessive adjectives from the 'two-epithet rule' (*C.* 1.1.2, 3.6.10–11, 13.15–16, 4.9.32, *S.* 2.3.18,

Ep. 2.2.21–2, LHS II 160–1), and *mea*, like *laborem* (15n.) and the variants *quem* (10), *pascua* (28), and *superni* (29n.), probably arose from assimilation to the case of the nearest noun.

27–8 'Transhumance' of flocks from summer to winter pasture was a regular practice in southern Italy until fairly recently (Var. *R.* 2.1.16, 2.2.9, White (1970) 306). It would be a mark of great wealth to own an estate big enough to include both types of pasture (2.11–12n., *Ep.* 2.2.177–9 *quidue* [sc. *prosunt*] *Calabris | saltibus adiecti Lucani, si metit Orcus | grandia cum paruis non exorabilis auro?*).

27 Calabris: Calabria was famous for its sheep (N–H on *C.* 1.31.5, Plin. *Nat.* 8.190).

ante sidus feruidum: before the 'dog days' signalled by the heliacal rising of Sirius in late July (3.15–16, 16.61–2, N–H on *C.* 1.17.17, 3.13.9–10, *S.* 2.5.39, Arch. fr. 107 West, Virg. *G.* 2.353).

28 mutet 'substitutes Lucanian for Calabrian pastures'. For the construction, cf. 9.28, *C.* 1.17.2, 2.12.23, 16.19, 3.1.47, *S.* 2.7.10, *Ep.* 1.1.100, 7.36. H. also 'gives x [acc.] in exchange for y [abl.]' (*C.* 1.16.26, 29.15, 34.13).

29–30 Tusculum stood on a hill above what is now Frascati only 15 miles from Rome. Its view of the surrounding country and proximity to the city made it a popular place for villas (*RE* VIIA 1482–90).

29 superne: probably with *candens*, 'shining from above' (*S.* 1.5.26 *impositum saxis late candentibus Anxur*). The phrase 'expresses the arrogance of the profiteer and also his pretension in possessing a villa which stands on high, visible from far away, the object of admiration and envy' (Martina (1989) 51). Many editors prefer the better attested *superni*, but the adj., especially in the sense 'lofty', is much rarer than the adv. (cf. Ov. *Met.* 15.128, Sen. *Phaed.* 926, Leo, *A.L.L.* 10 (1896–8) 435–7), and the altitude of the town seems less relevant than the attractions of the villa (Bentley, Brink (1982) 36).

30 Circaea: Circe (17.15–18n.) and Ulysses were the parents of Telegonus, the legendary founder of Tusculum (*C.* 3.29.8, West on Hes. *Th.* 1014). The epithet is first attested at Cic. *Caec.* 57 *Circaeo poculo*, which may echo something in Roman tragedy. Here it may suggest the lofty pretensions of a profiteer and also, since the Mamilii, a leading family of Tusculum, claimed descent from Telegonus (Dion. Hal. 4.45, Fest. p. 116M), such a creature's wish 'to acquire, along with property, escutcheon and lineage' (Martina (1989) 52; cf. 4.6, 8.11–12).

tangat moenia: since Tusculum was on top of the hill (29–30n.) a villa right near the town would be most conspicuous (29n.) and also offer the best scenic outlook.

31-2 Thanks to Maecenas' generosity H. has no need to profit from the war.

Commentators from Porph. on detect a reference to the Sabine farm which M. is supposed to have given H. sometime between 33 and 30 BC (Intro. 1). Although H. seems to own bullocks (25n.) and, presumably, land for them to plough, he does not say he owes these things to his friend. In fact, he is quite vague as to how M. has 'enriched' him. It is striking that the Sabine farm, however important in the 'poetic landscape' of *Satires* 2, the *Odes*, and *Epistles* 1, does not figure at all in the *Epodes*. Except in two poems (9, 13 intro.), H. seems to situate himself in the city and, in Epode 2, even rejects the kind of *laudes ruris* that are so much a part of his other works.

31 satis superque: a colloquial phrase (17.19, *S.* 1.2.65–6, Fordyce on Cat. 7.2).

benignitas: the fact that H. owes something to M.'s 'generosity' does not necessarily make him a 'client' in the technical sense (24n.). Along with its near synonyms *beneficentia* and *liberalitas*, *benignitas* is used of actions, not only by superiors towards inferiors, but among friends of equal status (Cic. *Off.* 1.20, 42–57, 2.52–64, Hellegouarc'h (1972) 217–19).

ditauit: a word rare in both verse and prose, and possibly an archaism (17.60, *Ep.* 1.6.6, Brink on *Ars* 57, *Rhet. Her.* 4.66, Lucr. 2.627, *ThLL* v 1555).

32 haud: only here in H.'s lyric, 17× in his hexameters. *haud* is common in Plautus, but later restricted mostly to formulae (*haud scio an* etc.)) and litotes (LHS II 778), and is much rarer in lyric and elegy than in epic and satire (Axelson (1945) 91–2).

parauero: the fut. perf. is either *metri causa* (5.102, 15.24, Kenney on Apul. *Met.* 5.24.5, LHS II 323) or perhaps 'the poet situates himself mentally at the moment when he would have already enriched himself' (Plessis).

33-4 H.'s ridicule of Chremes and the prodigal provides a kind of 'comic relief' from the seriousness of the rest of the poem and may also be 'programmatic' for the role of 'stock figures' in his other *iambi* (Intro. 3)

quod ... premam | ... perdam: rel. clause of purpose (2.21, 5.32, 9.35n.).

33 auarus: like *discinctus* (34) this probably goes with 'I' (the subj. of the verbs), but 'both epithets are felt again with *Chremes* and *nepos* respectively' (Naylor).

Chremes: a stock name in comedy (cf. Greek *chrēmata*, 'money'), usually for a *senex*. H. probably refers to a lost play, since none of the extant Chremetes (Ter. *An.*, *Eu.*, *Hau.*, *Ph.*; cf. *S.* 1.10.40, Brink on *Ars* 94, Lucil. fr. 815 *ROL*) hide money in the ground.

34 discinctus: lit. 'unfastened' (*S.* 1.2.132), hence 'relaxed' (*S.* 2.1.73) and, in a bad sense, 'dissolute' (Pers. 3.31 *ad morem discincti uiuere Nattae*). But *discingo* can also mean 'disarm' (*OLD* s.v.), and H. may suggest that the *nepos*, unlike Maecenas and himself, is a 'slacker'. Cf. Serv. on Virg. *A.* 8.724 [*discinctos Afros*] *uel discinctos dixit militiae inhabiles. omnes enim qui militant cincti sunt, alioqui inefficaces, ut contra praecinctos strenuos dicimus. Horatius* [*S.* 1.5.5–6]: *iter ... praecinctis unum.*

aut: postponed (12n.).

perdam: with *ut* supplied from 33. The variant *perdam ut* is *lectio facilior*.

nepos 'prodigal' (*S.* 1.4.49, 8.11, 2.1.22, 53, 3.225, *Ep.* 1.15.36, 2.2.193, *OLD* s.v. 4).

EPODE 2

Introduction

'Happiness is to be found, not in urban commerce, politics, or soldiering, but in the old fashioned country life of the rustic. For him each season offers its pleasures, and a frugal wife and well-ordered home make him self-sufficient.' So spoke the usurer Alfius, intending to become a rustic, but he instead returned to his trade.

The epode draws on many types of poetry (1–3, 5–8, 17–18, 23–4, 39–48, 49–60nn.), but its quasi-dramatic form, with a character revealing unpleasant things about himself, is almost certainly modelled on the 'indirect blame' so important in early Greek *iambus* (Intro. 3). Two notable examples (cf. Arist. *Rhet.* 3.17) are Arch. fr. 19 West (App. 1), in which a certain 'Charon the carpenter' displays his narrow parochialism by deriding Gyges, the king of Lydia, and fr. 122, where a 'father' (perhaps Lycambes) expresses amazement at the conduct of his daughter (Neobule?).

It is not certain whether these poems also revealed the identities of their speakers only at the end, or if their audience was supposed to be 'duped' into accepting them in a straightforward way until that 'revelation'. Some have argued that this is the case here, and that the bulk of Epode 2 is meant as 'genuine' praise of country life, with the final lines serving to 'iambicize' the poem and also allowing H. 'to mix the strong expression of what he really cared for with a dose of ... self-mockery' (Fraenkel (1957) 60). But, as the commentary attempts to show, the speech of 'Alfius' is riddled throughout with distortions and downright errors such as are absent from other poems in which H. praises the country in his own person (*C.* 1.17, 20, 31, 2.3, 6, 11, 15, 16, 18, 3.1, 6, 8, 13, 16, 18, 29, 4.12, *S.* 2.6, *Ep.* 1.7, 10, 11, 14, 16). It seems likely that while some of H.'s original audience might be fooled for a time or even until the final lines forced a second reading, the more alert would pick up on the 'clues' and realize almost from the beginning (1–8n.) that the speaker is a ridiculous impostor.

Alfius' 'self-indictment' is comic, but may also have more serious implications. Unlike H. himself (Epode 1, but cf. Epode 16), he hopes to escape the coming war (5–6), yet, as a usurer, he is probably among those who will profit from it (1.25–30n.), perhaps even obtaining his estate from the proscribed or dispossessed. There is no place for any nobler sentiments in his 'dream country', not even for friends with whom he might share his country feasts (cf., by contrast, *S.* 2.6.60–76). Some readers might be amused, others infuriated to find such a creature evoking Roman and Italian traditions (9–38, 21–2, 39–48nn.) and appropriating Lucretius' Epicureanism (23–4n.).

It has been suggested that H.'s blame of Alfius is also a critique of Virgil's *Georgics*, to which there seem to be a number of references (1, 7–8, 14, 17–18, 21, 28, 35, 40, 48, 57nn.), unless Virgil is the imitator. But this interpretation assumes that Virgil's poem is unadulterated praise of country life, which is far from being the case (cf. Thomas (1988) Intro. 7). In fact, it might be argued that both poets, in different genres and styles, express similar misgivings about the possibility and morality of escapism.

Epode 2 is among the most popular of H.'s works, often imitated (e.g. Mart. 1.49, 10.47), translated, and set to music, sometimes, however, without the epilogue or any other hint that it is not what it seems (Wilkinson (1951) 165–6). But one imitation, even if indirect, that preserved the original spirit, was an American TV show of the 1960s called *Green Acres*. This featured a typical Manhattan lawyer (67n.) who was inspired by delusions similar to those of Alfius to move away from the city and take up farming, with endlessly catastrophic and amusing results.

1–8 Happy the man who works his own property far from the troubles that disturb the soldier and the city-dweller.

Even in these opening lines there are hints, more evident on a second reading, that prepare for the ending. The speaker seems to envisage agriculture as free from toil (1n.), while his interest in just that (4n.) and in property suggests that he defines happiness in terms of wealth (1n.). And someone who rejects military and political concerns (5–8) can hardly be the H. of the first Epode.

1–3 Beatus ille qui ... exercet: the phrasing is that of a *makarismos*, a declaration that someone is for some reason (usually, as here, described in a rel. clause) exceptionally 'happy' (*makar, olbios, eutuchēs, beatus, felix, fortunatus*). There are other examples in H. (1n.; cf. 8.11–14, 15.17, N–H on *C.* 1.13.17) and throughout ancient literature from Homer and Hesiod on (G. Dirichlet, *De ueterum makarismis* (Giessen 1914)). Some fragments of Archilochus (70.8, 112.12 West) and Hipponax (43, 117.6, 177) contain *makarismoi*, but these do not appear to be H.'s models. For the possible influence of book 2 of Virgil's *Georgics*, cf. 2 intro.

1 beatus ille: sc. *est*. The ellipse seems to be characteristic of *makarismoi* (e.g. 12.25, *C.* 1.13.17, 4.13.21, *S.* 1.6.52, 9.12, 2.7.31, Hom. *Od.* 5.306, 6.154, Hes. *Op.* 172, Virg. *G.* 2.490 *felix qui potuit rerum cognoscere causas*, 493 *fortunatus et ille deos qui nouit agrestis*). The term *beatus* has an ambiguity appropriate to this context (Miles). At first sight, it seems to mean 'happy' in a general sense (*OLD* s.v. 1), but it will turn

out that the speaker means 'wealthy' (s.v. 3). The difference between
these two senses of *beatus*, the one philosophical, the other, it seems,
popular, is a theme of great interest to H. (*C.* 1.4.14, N–H on 2.2.18,
3.7, 16.28, 18.14, 3.9.4, 16.32, 29.11, 4.9.46, *S.* 1.1.19, 117, 3.142,
2.6.74, 96, *Ep.* 1.6.47, 10.14, 16.18, 18.32, Brink on 2.1.139). Cf. Sen.
Ep. 45.9 *si utique uis uerborum ambiguitates diducere, hoc nos doce, beatum
non eum esse quem uulgus appellat, ad quem pecunia magna confluxit, sed illum
cui bonum omne in animo est.*

procul: cf. *S.* 1.6.52 *ambitione procul*, Virg. *G.* 2.459 *procul discordibus
armis*. The use of *procul* as a preposition (*S.* 1.4.101, 6.52) rather than
as an adverb (4× in H.) or with *ex* (2×) seems to be poetic, occurring
first at Enn. *Sc.* 260 Vahlen *patria procul* but not in prose before Livy
and then only rarely (LHS II 271).

negotiis: like *beatus*, this could be ambiguous. The speaker could
mean general 'tasks', 'difficulties', 'troubles' (*OLD* s.v. 2, 3, 4) or, in
keeping with what turns out to be his trade, 'commercial activities'
(s.v. 8). His idea of rural life as somehow 'remote' from any of these
things may also suggest how little he really knows about it: *negotium*
can be used of agricultural labours (Cato, *Agr.* 145.1, 156.4, Col. 1 pr.
20, 1.1.2, 8 etc.).

negotium seems to be a prosaic word avoided by other late Repub-
lican and Augustan poets (Brink on *Ep.* 2.1.1, Axelson (1945) 107). In
H. it usually has negative connotations (*C.* 3.29.49, *S.* 2.1.80, 3.19,
Ep. 2.1.1), especially in relation to city life (*C.* 3.5.53, *S.* 2.6.33, *Ep.*
1.7.59, 14.17).

2 prisca gens mortalium: the phrase combines two familiar
ideas about the past: that it was 'happier' than the present, and that
early man lived a rural, agricultural life. The ideas are also com-
bined in Aratus' golden age (*Phaen.* 108–14), in Varro (*R.* 3.1.1–4),
and Virgil (*G.* 2.532–40 – but cf. Thomas *ad loc.* and on 1.118–46),
and in H.'s own vision of ancient Italy (*C.* 2.15, 3.6, *S.* 2.2.89–93
(parody), *Ep.* 2.1.139–44). But more often the ideal past is considered
happy precisely because there is no need for work, including agri-
culture (1.26, 16.43–50, Hes. *Op.* 90–2, 109–26, 172–3, Smith on Tib.
1.3.41, Gatz (1967) index s.v. *felix priscorum temporum status*). Despite
the many activities in his dream country, the speaker imagines for
himself something like the toil-free version of the golden age (3, 11–
12, 19–20, 23–7, 44, 61–4). Cf. 59–60n.

prisca: 'not only "old", but also "of the old type"' (Brink on *Ep.* 2.1.139 *agricolae prisci, fortes, paruoque beati*; cf. *C.* 3.21.11, 4.2.40, *Saec.* 58, *Ep.* 2.2.117, *Ars* 214). While not an exclusively poetic word, *priscus* 'often carries a nuance of respect or veneration' (E–M s.v.).

gens = *genus* (16.63, *C.* 1.3.26, 12.49).

mortalium = *hominum*, an elevated expression avoided in ordinary prose but favoured by Sallust and other archaizers and by poets in solemn or mock-solemn contexts (*C.* 1.3.37, 3.29.31, *S.* 1.6.37, 9.60, 2.6.58, Skutsch on Enn. *Ann.* 366).

3 The mention of ploughing begins what is essentially a calendar of rural activities (9–38n.) which continues, even with the shift in focus to the farmer's wife (39–48) and to the speaker himself (49–60), until the Terminalia (59) and the ploughing oxen (63–4) bring the reader full circle back to early spring. Ploughing, especially in rich soil – for an Alfius, only the best – normally took place with the coming of spring in the middle of February and thus signalled the beginning of the agricultural year (N–H on *C.* 1.4.3, Thomas on Virg. *G.* 1.43, Var. *R.* 1.30, Col. 2.4.3, 9, White (1970) 180).

paterna: cf. *C.* 2.16.13–14, *S.* 2.3.184, *Ep.* 1.18.60. In some versions of the golden age myth there is no private property (*C.* 3.24.11–13, Lucr. 5.1110–16, Virg. *G.* 1.126–7, Tib. 1.3.43–4, Gatz (1967) index s.v. *absentia rerum privatarum*). But that might be going too far for the speaker, who soon imagines himself sacrificing to Terminus, the protector of such property (59n.).

exercet: the word implies that toil is part of the happy life, but the speaker's fantasies run more to watching than working (2n., 11–12, 63–4). *exerceo* seems to be 'a normal word for working one's land' (Mynors on Virg. *G.* 1.99; cf. 1.220, 268, 2.356, 415, *A.* 1.431 etc.), but its proximity here to *fenore* may hint at a legal idiom for Alfius' profession, *fenus exercere* (Miles; cf. *OLD* s.v. *exerceo* 6).

4 solutus: cf. 5.71, 9.38, 10.1, 12.8, 13.5, 17.7, 45, *S.* 1.6.129 *solutorum misera ambitione*, 2.6.68–9 *solutus | legibus insanis*.

fenore: another ambiguous term. The context suggests 'debt carrying interest' (*OLD* s.v. 2; cf. *Ep.* 1.1.80, *Ars* 421 (= *S.* 1.2.13)), but the *fenerator* really means the payments of 'interest' (s.v. 1) which he will be busy calling in on the Ides (69–70).

Tacitus seems to say (the text is difficult) that those 'noble savages', the Germans of his time, were innocent of usury (*Ger.* 26.1). But there appears to be no parallel for *fenus* as an evil absent from the ideal past, and the speaker's mention of it may betray an obsession.

5-8 The speaker's preference for farm living over soldiering and city life continues the idea of the happy past, from which warfare and cities were absent (2n.). But it also contrasts with the stand taken by H. himself in the previous poem (1.23, 25-30).

The comparison between diverse modes of life (*bioi*) is a familiar topos from early Greek poetry on (Solon 13.43-62 West, N-H on *C.* 1.1, 2.13.13-20, 16.1-12, *S.* 1.1.4-12, Virg. *G.* 2.503-12, Smith on Tib. 1.1.1-5, Cairns (1978) 80-1).

5-6 The *miles* is probably the subject of both clauses (Turolla): not only is he rudely awakened for battles on land, but he must face the danger of the sea in naval warfare. Since catalogues of *bioi* (5-8n.) often include that of the merchant, some supply *mercator* or *nauta* as the subject of *horret* (6). But the soldier of the period of Naulochus and Actium would expect to serve *terra marique* (1.1, 11-14, 4.17-20, 7.3-4, 9.27).

5 excitatur: sc. *somno*; cf. Bacchylides, *Paean.* 4.75-6 Maehler, Tib. 1.1.4 *Martia cui somnos classica pulsa fugent*, Virg. *G.* 2.539 (in Saturn's golden age) *necdum etiam audierant inflari classica.*

classico: the *classicum* was a horn with which the commander of any army signalled, among other things, his departure into battle (Vegetius, *Epitoma rei militaris* 2.22, Caes. *Civ.* 3.82.1, Virg. *A.* 7.637, Liv. 2.59.6). Its mention here may indicate that the soldier is 'roused', not for ordinary reveille, but for some important event.

miles 'as a soldier'. For the predicate noun, cf. 4.15, 5.13, 92-3, 6.1, 9.13n., 10.21, 12.17, 16.15, 36, 17.33-4, 41, 47, 52, 58, 74.

truci: this seems to be the first time where *trux*, normally used of living things, is applied to an 'instrument of cruelty or savagery' (*OLD* s.v. 1e). Either the horn is announcing some particularly awful battle or the speaker considers anything that would disturb sleep 'cruel and savage'.

6 iratum mare: cf. *C.* 1.3.40 *iracunda fulmina*, 3.9.22-3 *improbo | iracundior Hadria*, 4.5.19 *pacatum ... per mare*, Andr. fr. 18.2 *FPL mare saeuom*, Lucr. 5.1002-3 *mare ... saeuibat*.

7 forumque: the site of financial and political activity (*Ep.* 1.19.8-9, Virg. *G.* 2.501-2 (the man who knows the rural gods) *nec ferrea iura | insanumque forum et populi tabularia uidit*).

7-8 superba ... limina: where the *cliens* or other cultivator of
the powerful would have to waste time. Cf. Virg. *G.* 2.461-2 (for-
tunate the farmer) *si non ingentem foribus domus alta superbis | mane salu-
tantum totis uomit aedibus undam.*

superba: transferred epithet, as at 7.5, 8.19; cf. N-H on *C.*
1.37.31, 2.14.27, Lucr. 4.1178, Virg. *G.* 2.461-2 (above). *superbus* and
superbia nearly always have a negative connotation both in H. (e.g.
4.5) and, especially when used of the powerful (8n.), in other late
Republican authors (Hellegouarc'h (1972) 439-41).

8 potentiorum: when used of political 'power' *potens* and *poten-
tia*, like *superbus* (7-8n.), often have a pejorative sense (*C.* 1.35.23-4,
2.18.12, *Ep.* 1.18.44, 86 (but cf. *C.* 3.30.12), Hellegouarc'h (1972) 238-
42, 442-3).

9-38 Not only does the happy rustic plough (3-4), but he tends
vines, herds, trees, hives, and flocks in spring and summer (9-16),
enjoys fruit, thanks the gods, and relaxes in autumn (17-28), and
hunts in winter (29-36). These activities, pleasant in themselves, also
bring forgetfulness of desire (38-9).

At first sight this calendar (9-36n.) includes pursuits both honest
and honourable by Roman standards and seems legitimate enough.
But on closer inspection it suggests the ignorance and naïvety of an
'armchair' rustic. At least one item may be out of temporal sequence
(11-12n.), undue space is given to relaxation (23-8n.) and hunting
(29-36n.), and the rustic would have to be Superman to do everything
alone (9-36, 10nn.), yet it is only later in the poem, when Alfius is
talking about himself (49), that there is any mention of slaves (65-5).
Finally, the *rus*, apparently suitable for agriculture, viticulture, ani-
mal husbandry, arboriculture, apiculture, and hunting, has the fab-
ulous quality of H.'s 'happy islands' (Epode 16) or of Varro's (*R.*
1.2.3-6) and Virgil's (*G.* 2.136-76) *laudes Italiae*. For in reality there
was no place, even in the *magna parens frugum* (*G.* 2.173) where the
same land could be used for so many purposes (cf. Thomas, Mynors
on *G.* 2.109 *nec uero terrae ferre omnes omnia possunt*, White (1970) 56-85).

9-36 The implicit movement from early spring to summer (9-16)
is followed by explicit announcements of changes in season (17-18,
29-30). The temporal framework indicates that the disjunctive par-
ticles (*aut ... aut* etc.) should be interpreted to mean, not that the

rustic does one task to the exclusion of the others, but that he sooner or later does all of them, with his choice of activity depending on the time of year.

9–10 Like ploughing (3n.) the training-in of vines to support trees (*uitis insitiua* or *arbustiua*) usually took place in early spring (Mynors on Virg. *G.* 2.323, Col. 4.29.4, 11.2.23, 26). The speaker uses the proper language for this system of viticulture, but he describes only its final stages and ignores the arduous preparations necessary. Among other things, it took three years for the 'layer' (9n.) to be ready for training, and six years for the poplar (10n.) to be ready to receive it (White (1970) 236).

9 ergo: since he has no other concerns (37–8n.). *ergo* seems overly forceful in this context, and may suggest a usurer's 'balance sheet mentality'. H. generally avoids inferential (illative) conjunctions: *ergo*, although at home in all types of poetry (*ThLL* v 2.760–1), occurs only three other times in H.'s lyric (17.27, *C.* 1.24.5, 2.7.17), *igitur, itaque*, and the like not at all. In the hexameter poetry such conjunctions are restricted mostly to formal arguments and mock-philosophical language (Brink on *Ep.* 2.2.145, Axelson (1945) 80).

adulta ... propagine: he joins the poplars 'with the mature layer of vines'. The plain abl. (one might expect *cum* or the dat., as with *iungo* and *coniungo*) may be idiomatic; cf. Col. 11.2.79 *ulmi quoque uitibus recte maritantur*, Ov. *Ep.* 4.134 *et fas omne facit fratre marita soror*, and perhaps *C.* 3.5.5–6 *milesne ... coniuge barbara | turpis maritus uixit*.

propagine: a 'layer' is formed by 'bending over the top (so as to form an *arcus*) or some part of the parent tree [or vine], and burying it until it forms its own root system' (Thomas on Virg. *G.* 2.26–7). A vine 'propagated in this way quickly grows strong, and in the third year will be separated from its mother [vine]' (Col. *Arb.* 7.3), at which point it will be mature enough (*adulta*) to be trained on to its support (10n.).

prŏpago seems to be the normal scansion and, given H.'s preference for short anceps at pos. 9 (Intro. 6), probably what he intended here. But Virgil has the first syllable long at *G.* 2.26 and 63.

10 altas: the poplars needed to be 'nurtured' (*altas* participial) for six years before receiving their vines (Col. *Arb.* 16.3), but a

beholder might admire them as impressively 'lofty' (*altas* adjectival).
For a similar word play, cf. *C.* 3.4.37–42 *Caesarem altum* ... [sc.
Camenae] *almae*.

maritat: a technical term (Cato, *Agr.* 32.2, Fordyce on Cat.
62.49; cf. N–H on *C.* 2.15.4–5, 4.5.30).

populos: the black poplar and the elm were considered the best
trees for *uitis insitiua* (Mynors on Virg. *G.* 2.221, Col. 5.6.4, *Arb.* 16.1,
Plin. *Nat.* 17.200). But the poplar would be an odd choice for some-
one who also expected to feed livestock: *populus, quia raram neque ido-
neam frondem pecori praebet, a plerisque repudiata est* (Col. 5.6.5).

11–12 These lines do not fit well in the calendar. According to
Varro (*R.* 2.5.11) and Columella (6.22.2) cattle move to mountain
pastures in the summer (*aestus, aestas*). The phrase *in reducta ualle*
could refer to such pasturage (11n.), but the summer setting jars with
the spring activities on either side (9–10, 13–14n.). Since both Varro
and Columella contrast summer only with winter (*hiems, hiberna*) and
do not mention the other seasons, they may mean it in the loose
sense of 'warm weather' that would include spring (*OLD* s.v. *aestus* 1,
2a). It is also possible that the speaker is confused about the
sequence of tasks, or that the couplet should be transposed to follow
14 (Fabricius) or 16 (L. Mueller). A scribe's desire to join *aut* (9) with
aut (11) might have caused the dislocation.

11 in reducta ualle: *depressa siue secreta aut certe flexuosa, dum sequi-
tur montes* (Schol.). The phrase also occurs at *C.* 1.17.17, Virg. *A.*
8.609, both mountain or hill settings, and *A.* 6.703, where the topo-
graphy (in the underworld) is less certain.

mugientium: the substantive is first attested here, but seems to
be modelled on such poeticisms as *balantum* (Enn. *Ann.* 169 Skutsch,
Lucr. 2.369, Virg. *G.* 1.272, *A.* 7.538), *natantum* (*G.* 3.541), *uolantum*
(Lucr. 2.1083), and *hinnientium* (Laev. *poet.* 27.6 *FPL*).

12 prospectat: the verb may suggest that the rustic watches
from on high, perhaps on a hill or mountain (cf. *C.* 3.2.6–8, 25.10,
Ep. 1.10.23, Virg. *A.* 1.180–5 *Aeneas scopulum* ... *conscendit* ... *tris litore
ceruos* | *prospicit errantes*), and that 'nihil hic diutini operis est, sed
breuis tantum intermissio et uoluptas' (Bentley). If the rustic were
tending, rather than admiring the herd, he would probably be down
in the valley with them and also have assistants (Var. *R.* 2.10).

errantis: cf. Virg. *Ecl.* 1.9, 2.21 *mille meae Siculis errant in montibus agnae*, *G.* 3.139, *A.* 1.185 (above).

13–14 Grafting of fruit trees (below) was yet another spring task (Cato, *Agr.* 40.1, 41.1, Col. 5.11.1, 11.2.11, 26), although the exact time varied according to tree type and regional climate (Var. *R.* 1.41.1, Col. 11.2.96, Plin. *Nat.* 17.113–14). There seems to have been no fixed time for pruning (cf. Col. 11.2.6, 16, 19, 32, 41, 79).

According to the speaker, the rustic first prunes, then replaces the 'useless boughs' with 'more productive' ones. The language is correct, but Alfius again betrays his ignorance, this time by conflating two separate activities. In the agricultural writers pruning and grafting are unrelated procedures, and even in Pomona's magic garden they are quite distinct (Ov. *Met.* 14. 627–31). When a shoot from one standing tree was attached to another tree near it, the insertion was sometimes made at the site of a severed bough (Var. *R.* 1.40.6, Col. 5.11.14). But this is not what is described here, and grafts were normally attached, not where other boughs had been removed, but into the trunk of the host tree (Cato, *Agr.* 40.2, Virg. *G.* 2.78–82, Col. 5.11.3, Plin. *Nat.* 17.101–2). Some take these lines to describe the grafting of vines, but in autumn the rustic harvests pears, presumably from the *rami* (cf. *inserit* (14), *insitiua* (19)), and the language here seems more appropriate to arboriculture. In particular, the agricultural writers use *ramus* of trees and shrubs (56), but not of vines.

13 inutilisque: cf. *C.* 3.17.10 *alga ... inutili*, *S.* 1.8.1 *inutile lignum*, Virg. *G.* 1.88, Col. 5.6.37 *arbustum ... inutile et inuenustum*. The *-que* (*-ue* Bentley) seems to interrupt the sequence of disjunctive particles, but cf. 9–36n., 35, 16.30, and the use of *et* for *aut* (LHS II 484) at *C.* 1.3.9, 3.11.49, Virg. *G.* 2.25.

amputans: Cato, Varro, and Virgil have only *puto*, but Cicero's figurative use of *amputo* (*Sen.* 52, *Tusc.* 3.13) and its frequency in Columella indicate that it was a standard term (*ThLL* I 2020).

14 feliciores: the root meaning of *felix* is 'fruitful' (16.53, Paul. *Fest.* 92M *felices arbores Cato dixit quae fructum ferunt*, Thomas on Virg. *G.* 2.80–1 *ingens | exiit ad caelum ramis felicibus arbos*).

inserit: another technical term (Cato, *Agr.* 40.1 etc., Thomas on Virg. *G.* 2.302).

15–16 Honey was gathered in the autumn and late spring (Thomas on Virg. *G.* 4.231) but also in early summer (Col. 9.14.5, 15.1). The last date both accords with the temporal sequence (9–38n.) and coincides with the time for shearing, *inter aequinoctium uernum et solstitium* (Var. *R.* 2.11.6; cf. Col. 11.2.44).

Once again the speaker focuses only on the final stages and says nothing about the yearly toil involved in bee- and sheep-rearing. He also seems to be unaware that bees and sheep make poor neighbours: (*apibus*) *inimicae et oues difficile se e lanis earum explicantibus* (Plin. *Nat.* 11.62; cf. Mynors on Virg. *G.* 4.10).

15 The style seems to wax poetic (17–28n.): 15 is 'almost a golden line' (Miles). It has a pair of epithets followed by a pair of nouns, but the verb is not between. Cf. 47, 5.19, 16.48, and, for another variant of the pattern, 2.43, 10.1, 14.7, 16.2, 9, 34, 46. There are true golden lines at 12.5, 13, 13.11 (cf. n.), 16.7, 33, 55.

pressa: cf. 13.6, Virg. *G* 4.140–1 (the Corycian gardener) *primus ... spumantia cogere pressis | mella fauis.*

mella: poetic plural. H., Lucr., Virg., and, it seems, Varro of Atax (18.3 *FPL*) avoid *mel* in the nom., acc., and voc., but prefer the sing. in the oblique cases. Columella (9.4.4 etc.) seems to be the first to use pl. for sing. in prose (*ThLL* VIII 605, LHS II 16–17).

amphoris: the speaker may have his jars mixed up, as none of the agricultural writers mention storing honey in *amphorae*, which were normally used for water or wine (*ThLL* I 1987).

16 infirmas: *quae aestu uelleribus premantur* (Schol.). The epithet may also refer to the proverbial stupidity of sheep (Plin. *Nat.* 8.199 *infirmissimum pecori caput*, Otto (1890) 261) or even to Alfius' 'peculations', since in Latin as in English people can be 'fleeced' of their money (Pl. *Bac.* 241–2, 1095, 1121–5, *Capt.* 266–8, *Epid.* 311, *Merc.* 526, Enk on Prop. 2.16.8, Otto (1890) 45).

17–28 The thought of autumn, with its fruits (17–22) and relaxation (23–8) is especially attractive to the speaker. He devotes more space to it (12 lines) than to spring and summer combined (8 lines), and his language becomes less technical and more poetic (17–18, 20, 21–2, 26, 27nn.).

17–18 *poetica fantasia finxit Autumnum quasi corporalem deum pomis coronatum* (Porph.). Autumn is personified at Ar. *Pax* 523, 706–11, in Greek art (Roscher III 931, *LIMC* s.v. *opōra*), and in Latin poetry from

Lucretius on (1.175, 5.743; cf. N–H on *C.* 2.5.11, 4.7.11, Bömer on Ov. *Met.* 2.29, *F.* 4.897).

caput | Autumnus agris extulit: the phrase is similar to Virg. *G.* 2.340–1 *uirumque | terrea progenies duris caput extulit,* but it is hard to decide which poet is the imitator and what to make of the imitation.

18 agris: the variant *aruis* may come from Virg. *G.* 2.340 (17–18n.). Despite the pronouncements of *grammatici,* there seems to be little difference in meaning between the two words (*ThLL* I 1282, II 731).

19 ut gaudet 'how he rejoices'. The subject is still the *beatus.* For exclamatory *ut,* cf. 61, 16.31, 53, 17.56, 59, *C.* 1.11.3, *S.* 2.5.18, 6.53, 8.62, *Ep.* 1.18.16–17, 19.19.

gaudet ... decerpens: *gaudeo* with the participle seems to be a Graecism, modelled on the typical construction with *hedomai, chairo* etc. (LHS II 364; cf. 3.7n., *C.* 3.4.73, *Ep.* 2.2.107).

20 certantem ... purpurae 'the grape competing [in hue] with purple'. *certo* with dat. seems to be poetic (11.8, *C.* 2.6.15, *S.* 2.5.19, Coleman on Virg. *Ecl.* 5.8, 8.55, *G.* 2.99, *ThLL* III 894) and may imitate Greek use of that case with *machomai* ('fight'). Cf. the dat. with *altercor* (*S.* 2.7.57), *decerto* (*C.* 1.3.13), *luctor* (*C.* 1.1.15, *Ep.* 2.2.74), *pugno* (*S.* 1.2.73). For postponed *et,* cf. 1.12n.

purpurae: either cloth dyed with an extract from the *purpura,* a type of mollusc (*OLD* s.v. 3), or the dye itself (s.v. 2). *purpura* was an expensive commodity (N–H on *C.* 2.16.7–8, 2.18.8, 3.1.42, 4.13.13), and might be an unlikely term of comparison for a genuine rustic, although quite appropriate for an Alfius.

21–2 In his enthusiasm the speaker addresses the gods directly, as if he, not the rustic, were making the offering. For similar apostrophes 'expressing subjective participation' (Norden on Virg. *A.* 6.14), cf. 9.11, 21–6, 10.15–16, Virg. *G.* 2.20, 2.388, 529, Janko on Hom. *Il.* 13.602–3, 15.365–6.

The piety displayed here is commendable, but it is possible that the usurer's mentality intrudes. Grapes were a normal offering to Priapus, a protector of gardens and vineyards (*S.* 1.8, Thomas on Virg. *G.* 4.110–11, *Priap.* 85.5, 86.14, *RE* XXII 1914–42), but there is no evidence that they were offered to Silvanus, a god of flocks and boundaries (22n.), or that this old Italian spirit was associated in cult with the Asiatic and Greek Priapus (*RE* above 1938; at Tib. 1.1.13–

18 the god mentioned with Priapus is probably Pan). This may be a case of honouring two gods 'for the price of one'.

21 qua muneretur: rel. clause of purpose dependent on *decerpens* (1.32n.). *munero* and especially its deponent form may be colloquial (Ter. *Hau.* 300, Cic. *Att.* 7.2.3, *ThLL* VIII 1641).

pater: this does not appear to be a regular title for Silvanus, but cf. Virg. *G.* 2.494 *Siluanumque senem*, Lucil. frr. 24–7 *ROL nemo sit nostrum* [*sc. deorum*] *quin ... pater siet ac dicatur ad unum.*

22 Siluane: cf. *C.* 3.29.23, *Ep.* 2.1.143 [*agricolae prisci*] *Siluanum lacte piabant,* Virg. *Ecl.* 10.24, *G.* 1.20, 2.494 (21n.), *A.* 8.600–1 *Siluano ... aruorum pecorisque deo, RE* IIIA 117–25.

tutor finium: cf. 59n., *Gromat.* I 302.13 Lachmann *omnis possessio quare Siluanum colet? quia primus in terram lapidem finalem posuit.* It is probably an accident that this is the first instance of *tutor* used of a god, since gods often *tuentur, tutantur,* and keep things *in tutela.* On the other hand, *tutor* is so common as a legal term that the speaker's use of it may be a lapse into his *sermo forensis.*

23–8 After so much hard work (!) the rustic deserves a siesta. His resting-place is the *locus amoenus* familiar from poetry and art (N–H on *C.* 2.3) and probably by H.'s day a hackneyed theme (Kirn (1935) 41). A number of MSS and one of the scholia begin a new poem with 23, which may indicate that this part of the epode was excerpted as a 'purple passage'.

23–4 The theme of the happy past (2n.) returns with what seems to be a reference to Lucr. 5.1392–4 (primitive men) *saepe itaque inter se prostrati in gramine molli | propter aquae riuum sub ramis arboris altae | non magnis opibus iucunde corpora habebant.* Lucretius himself echoes an earlier part of his poem (2.29–33), evidently to suggest that the life of early man came close to the Epicurean ideal (Costa on 5.1392–6). Perhaps the speaker fancies himself an Epicurean; that would explain why H. puts so many echoes of Lucretius into his mouth (25, 39, 39–40, 41, 43–4, 45, 46, 62–3, 65, 66, 70nn.).

23 sub antiqua ilice: cf. 10.8, 15.5, 16.47, *C.* 3.13.14, 23.10, 4.4.57, *Ep.* 1.16.9–10 *quercus et ilex | multa fruge pecus, multa dominum iuuet umbra,* Virg. *Ecl.* 7.1, *G.* 3.333–4. The ilex (holm oak) is an evergreen and would provide shade even in late autumn. For *antiqua,* 'long standing', cf. Virg. *G.* 3.332, *A.* 2.626, 714, 6.179, 7.178.

24 tenaci: the grass is so comfortable that it seems to 'restrain' somebody lying in it (K–H). This interpretation is preferable to that of the Scholia, 'because [the grass] grips the earth with roots and sod', but *tenax*, while appropriate to ivy (Cat. 61.34), laurel (Virg. *G.* 2.134), and moss (Sen. *Phaed.* 1044) is still an odd epithet for grass. Kenney suggests *feraci*.

Even excluding those unsuited to dactyls (*efficax, pertinax, peruicax*) adjectives in -*ax* occur with greater frequency in H.'s lyric (20 adjectives, 56 occurrences = 1.5 per 100 verses) than in his hexameters (16 adjectives, 35 occurrences = 0.9 per 100 verses), which suggests that he considered them poetic. For others in the *Epodes*, cf. 34, 3.17, 5.22, 9.33, 12.4, 16.4, 20, 17.1, 14, 39.

25 labuntur: cf. N–H on *C.* 1.2.19, 2.14.2, *Ep.* 1.2.43, Lucr. 2.362 *flumina . . . summis labentia ripis.*

altis ... ripis: since *altus* can mean either 'high' (1.1, 2.10, 9.3, 10.7, 17.70) or 'deep' (6.7, 16.52n., 17.55), it could go well with either *ripis* or the variant *riuis*. But the former seems more likely, 'quippe auctumno, cum arescunt flumina, non alti sunt riui, sed altae ripae' (Bentley). Cf. Lucr. 2.362 (above).

26 queruntur ... aues: a poetic touch (Ov. *Am.* 3.1.4 *latere ex omni dulce queruntur aues*) which may, however, sound a 'discordant' note. Elsewhere in H. *queror* and its cognates are used of genuine 'lamentation', and in other contexts where creatures 'complain' they usually have a reason (e.g. Cic. *Div.* 1.14, Lucr. 4.545–6, Virg. *G.* 1.378, 3.328, 4.511–12, *A.* 8.215–16). Perhaps these birds do not like the company they must keep.

27 fontesque: cf. Lucr. 5.945 *at sedare sitim fluuii fontesque uocabant.* Some prefer the conjecture *frondesque* (Markland; cf. Prop. 4.4.4 *multaque natiuis obstrepit arbor aquis*), but if *fontes* is 'superfluous' with *lymphis* that may be the point: the speaker is 'pouring it on'; cf. 17.55n.

lymphis ... manantibus: instrumental abl.; cf. Ov. *F.* 6.10 [*nemus*] *obstreperetur aquis. lympha* is a poetic word (16.48, N–H on *C.* 2.3.12, 11.20, 3.11.26, 13.16, *S.* 1.5.24, *Ep.* 2.2.146, *ThLL* VII 1942).

obstrepunt: this verb usually indicates loud, crashing noises (e.g. *C.* 2.18.20, 3.30.10, 4.14.48), hardly the sort to 'invite sleep'. But an Alfius, used to much worse (5), might find even the 'obstreperous' sounds of the country relaxing.

28 somnos ... leuis: cf. *C.* 2.16.15–16, Virg. *G.* 2.470–1 (for happy rustics) *mollesque sub arbore somni | non absunt*, and, for other country siestas, N–H on *C.* 1.1.22, 2.3.6, 11.13–14, 3.1.21, *Ep.* 1.14.35, 17.6, 2.2.78, Gow on Theocr. *Id.* 1.15, Virg. *Ecl.* 1.55, *Cul.* 42–97.

quod inuitet: consecutive rel. clause (5.57), 'that which tends to invite carefree naps'.

29–36 Farmers hunt, especially in winter (N–H on *C.* 1.1.25, Mynors on Virg. *G.* 1.307), and the speaker seems to know the proper methods (but cf. 33, 35nn.). Yet his rustic's hunting 'is aimed not at protecting his herds but from first to last at filling his belly' (Cairns (1978) 88). The bag consists of 'Roman gastronomic delicacies' (Miles), which later allow the speaker to scorn imported ones (49–60n.). Furthermore, since there were many other tasks to do in winter (Hes. *Op.* 536–63, Cato, *Agr.* 37.3, 39, Var. *R.* 1.36, Virg. *G.* 1.300–10, Col. 11.2.6–14, 95–6), the focus on hunting only may be surprising and unrealistic (Miles).

29 at: the contrast is with the inactivity of autumn.

Iouis = *caeli*, an example of 'metonymy' (Latin *denominatio* (*Rhet. Her.* 4.43)) 'by which the names of gods are used for the objects with which they are concerned or associated' (Fordyce on Virg. *A.* 7.113; cf. Cic. *De orat.* 3.167, *Nat.* 3.41, Lucr. 2.655–60, LHS II 779). The figure occurs in Greek poetry as early as Homer (e.g. *Il.* 2. 426 (Hephaestus = fire); cf. Arch. fr. 9.11 West) and in Latin from Andronicus (9.38n.) and Naevius on (*inc.* 30a–c *ROL cocus edit Neptunum Cererem | et Venerem expertam Vulcanum Liberumque absorbuit | pariter*). Cf. 7.3, 9.38, 13.2, 16.19, 17.55.

annus hibernus 'winter [season of the] year'. Cf. *C.* 3.23.8, 4.7.7, Virg. *Ecl.* 3.57 *nunc formosissimus annus*, *A.* 3.139, 6.311 *frigidus annus*.

30 imbris niuisque: cf. 13.1–2, Lucr. 6.107 (clouds can) *cohibere niues gelidas et grandinis imbres*.

31 acris: cf. 12.6, 25, *Ep.* 2.2.29, Virg. *Ecl.* 10.56 *acris uenabor apros*. Here *acris* may be 'proleptic with *trudit* i.e. "drives into wilderness"' (Naylor). For other proleptic epithets, cf. 3.7, 16, 5.95, 6.3, 11.16.

hinc et hinc: poetic for *hinc et illinc* (5.97, *C.* 3.4.58–9, *S.* 1.1.17–18; cf. 4.9, *S.* 1.1.112, 2.4–8, 3.49–50, 4.27, 2.2.64, 3.59, 141, *Ep.* 1.17.39–41, 2.2.67–9, 75, *Ars* 45, 363–5, 439).

multa cane: instrumental abl. (1on., *S.* 2.6.114–15 *domus alta Molossis | personuit canibus*, *Ep.* 1.1.94, 19.13, 2.2.72). *multus* with the sing.

('many a') seems to be poetic (*C.* 1.5.1, 15.6, 4.5.33, *Ep.* 1.13.18, *Ars* 293, Virg. *Ecl.* 1.33, Ov. *F.* 4.772 *in stabulo multa sit agna meo*, LHS II 161). The mention of dogs could be a mistake, since they were seldom used in winter hunting, especially if there was snow (Miles; cf. 6.5–10n. Xen. *Cyn.* 8.2, J. K. Anderson, *Hunting in the ancient world* (Berkeley 1985) 48, 134).

32 apros: the Romans were great connoisseurs of wild boar meat (*C.* 3.12.13, *S.* 2.2.42, 89, 3.234, 4.40–2, 8.6, Juv. 1.141 [*aper*] *animal propter conuiuia natum*, André (1961) 118–19).

plagas: short nets hung between bushes to trap the boar after it had been flushed by the dogs (N–H on *C.* 1.1.28). Like herding (12n.), this kind of hunting must have required assistants, but the speaker does not mention them.

33 amite 'fowler's pole'. *ames*, a rare technical term (*ThLL* I 1989), does not appear elsewhere in verse. Its first syllable could be long, and some scan *amite leuī*, but H. avoids split resolution in his iambs (Intro. 6).

leui: *ideo leui quia asperitas lignorum tollitur quando ad usum uocantur* (Schol.). With *leui* (above), the pole would be 'light in weight'.

rara: this may be another mistake. Thrushes are not very big and would be able to escape from a 'loosely woven' net. The *retia rara* at Virg. *A.* 4.131 are for wild goats, boars, and lions (153–9), while Mart. 11.21.5 *quae rara uagos expectant retia turdos* seems to imitate this passage.

34 turdis: another delicacy (*S.* 1.5.72, 2.2.74, 5.10–11, *Ep.* 1.15.40–1, André (1961) 125). As *turdi*, like *grues* (35n.), are migratory birds (Var. *R.* 3.5.7), the speaker's scorn for imported fowl (53) will ring hollow.

edacibus: cf. the imitation at Mart. 3.58.26 *tendis auidis rete subdolum turdis*. But in fact thrushes are fastidious (Col. 8.10.4 (for feeding *turdi*) *multi uarietatem ciborum, ne unum fastidiant, praebendum putant*), and the epithet here may apply more to the speaker (cf. *S.* 2.2.92, *Ep.* 2.1.173 *edacibus in parasitis*) than to the birds.

dolos: in apposition to *retia*, as *praemia* (36) is to *leporem* and *gruem* (35).

35 pauidumque: this is the only example of resolution at a non-anceps position (Intro. 6) in H.'s iambs that has not been explained as synizesis (cf. on *laqueo*), contraction (*postosque* (65n.)), or consonantal *i* (5.79, 11.23; cf. 12.7, 13.2). But it, too, could be contracted; cf. Kroll on Cat. 40.1 *Rauide* (= *Raude*), and the word plays on *audi* and *auidi* (Pl. *Bac.* 276) and on *cauneas* and *caue ne eas* (Cic. *Div.* 2.84). *pauidus* is rare in prose before Livy with the telling exception of Sallust (3×), and may be poetic (*C.* 1.1.14, 2.11, 23.2, 3.16.6, *S.* 2.6.113).

leporem et ... gruem: the two delicacies are also paired at Virg. *G.* 1.307-8. For hares, cf. *S.* 2.2.9, 4.44, *Ep.* 1.15.22, André (1961) 121-2; for cranes, *S.* 2.8.87, Mynors on Virg. *G.* 1.120, Ov. *F.* 6.176, Plin. *Nat.* 10.60.

aduenam: another error. Wild cranes winter in east Africa and come to Italy in the summer (Plin. *Nat.* 10.61 *illas* [storks] *hiemis, has* [cranes] *aestatis aduenas*). *aduena* seems to be a technical term (Var. *R.* 3.5.7, *ThLL* I 89).

laqueo 'noose', usually in H. for strangling people (*C.* 3.24.8, *S.* 2.2.99, *Ep.* 1.16.37), but cf. *Ep.* 1.16.51-2, Virg. *G.* 1.139-40 *tum laqueis captare feras et fallere uisco* | *inuentum*. For the synizesis *laqueo*, cf. *C.* 3.7.4 (*fidei*), *S.* 1.8.43 (*cerea*), 2.2.21 (*ostrea*).

37-8 Hunting is a traditional cure for love (N-H on *C.* 1.1.27) but since *amor* was not included among the evils of city life (1-8) the introduction of this topos here comes as a surprise. Some see a transition to the next topic, the farmer's wife, but she is hardly a love-object (39-60n.). Perhaps H. means the reader to be left wondering what this *amor* is until the end of the poem, where Alfius' greed identifies it as *amor habendi* (cf. *Ep.* 1.7.85). The conjecture *Roma quas curas habet* (Scrinerius, *Mnem.* 15 (1887) 325, Sh. Bailey) is attractive, but the corruption would be hard to explain. On the other hand, the idea of *Roma* may be suggested, through the familiar anagram, in *amor* (cf. Ahl (1985) 265).

quis ... obliuiscitur 'who does not forget among these things the distressing cares which love possesses?'

37 malarum ... habet = *malarum curarum quas amor habet.* For the attraction of the noun into the rel. clause, cf. 6.8, *C.* 4.13.18, *S.* 1.1.1, 4.2, 10.16, 2.2.59. The construction seems to be Lucretian (cf. Bailey on Lucr. 1.15), but the 'anticipatory position of the adjective [*malarum*] here is without parallel' (Giarratano).

38 haec inter: postponement of *inter* is not unusual (12.23, *C.* 3.3.11, 10× in the hexameters), even in prose. For other prepositions, cf. 7.3n.

39–66 The calendar sequence continues: at first it is still winter (43, 45–6, 52nn.), then the sorrel and mallow (57–8, but cf. 55–8n.), the Terminalia (59), and the ploughing oxen (63–4) indicate a return to spring. But the speaker's focus shifts from the rustic to his wife (39–48), diet (49–60), and household (61–6).

39–48 The farmer's wife, with her *pudor* and devotion to the home, resembles the matrons praised on Roman epitaphs (Miles; cf. Lattimore (1962) 295–9), the chaste women in some versions of the golden age (Prop. 2.32.51–2, Juv. 6.1–24, Gatz (1967) 131–2), and Tibullus' Delia as he wishes her to be (1.2.71–4, 5.21–34, 10.39–42). Yet in other respects she is more farm-hand than wife. Some of her tasks are traditional for women (43–4, 47–8nn.), but others are usually performed by men (41, 45–6nn.), and *in partem* (39) may be ironic: she does the man's 'share' as well as her own (Miles).

39 quodsi: in the protasis of a condition *quodsi* often anticipates a climax (10.21, 11.15, 14.13n., N–H on *C.* 1.1.35, 3.1.41, *Ep.* 1.1.70 etc., Brink on *Ep.* 2.1.90). The reader might expect something like 'but if the rustic should have an excellent wife, then his happiness would be complete', but gets instead the ludicrous apodosis, 'then there would be no need to buy fancy imported delicacies' (49–60).

mulier: like Lucretius and Catullus, H. has no qualms about using this word (11.23, 12.1, 24, 16.39 etc.), but other late Republican and Augustan authors seem to regard it as unpoetic and prefer *femina* (Axelson (1945) 57–8). Cf. 42n.

in partem 'for [i.e. so as to fulfil] her part' (Page). *pro parte* is the usual phrase and *in partem*, which occurs only rarely, may be colloquial or modelled on Greek *en merei* or *kata meros* (*ThLL* x 463).

40 domum ... liberos: there may be an echo of Lucr. 3.894–5 (once dead) *non domus accipiet te laeta neque uxor | optima, nec dulces occurrent ... nati*, Virg. *G.* 2.523–4 *interea dulces pendent circum oscula nati, | casta pudicitiam seruat domus*. The fact that *liberi* is almost always plural (*OLD* s.v.) makes it unsuited to hexameters, but it does not seem to be unpoetic (5.5, 17.57, Enn. *Sc.* 120 etc., Cic. fr. 42.2 *FPL*).

atque dulcis: in most Classical Latin verse, *atque* is used chiefly before vowels, but in H., for reasons that are not clear (Axelson (1945) 83–5, N–H on *C.* 2.19.11), it occurs either as often (*Satires*) or much more often (lyric, *Epistles*) before consonants (cf. (cons.) 4.19, 5.54, 7.3, 15.17, 16.19, 17.4, 12, 18, (vowel) 5.21, 8.11, 15.5).

41 Sabina: sc. *mulier* or *uxor*. The Sabines were paragons of old-time virtue and industry (*C.* 3.6.37–44, Virg. *G.* 2.167, 532 *hanc olim ueteres uitam coluere Sabini*, Liv. 1.18.4, Col. 1. pr. 19, 12. pr. 10).

perusta solibus: the phrase suggests work in the fields; cf. Tib. 2.3.9 (if the poet were ploughing) *nec quererer quod sol graciles exureret artus*. But Italian farm women, even the bailiff's mate (*uilica*), a slave, seem to have been restricted to household tasks (Cato, *Agr.* 143, Virg. *G.* 1.293–6, Col. 12.1–3), and sunburns were considered unattractive (12.2n., Gow on Theocr. *Id.* 10.27, Ov. *Ars* 3.303, *Med.* 13, Juv. 6.425).

If Alfius echoes Lucr. 5.251–2 *pars terrai nonnulla perusta | solibus assiduis* he may be trying to sound learned and only inadvertently equating the woman with dirt.

solibus: the pl. signifies 'the sun day after day' (Mynors on Virg. *G.* 2.332; cf. 16.13, *C.* 4.5.8, *Ep.* 1.20.4).

42 pernicis 'agile' seems inappropriate of a farmer, but is used of hunters (Cat. 2.12, Virg. *A.* 11.718, Grat. 120 (a hunting spear) *pernix Lucania*, Col. 7.12.8), and in proximity with 31–6 may suggest that this Apulian is a *uenator tenerae coniugis immemor* (*C.* 1.1.26).

uxor: only here in the Epodes, but 7× in the *Odes* and 11× in the hexameters. As with *mulier* (39n.), H. uses *uxor* in defiance of contemporary preference, in this case for *coniunx* (Brink on *Ep.* 2.1.142, Axelson (1945) 57–8).

Apuli: for the scansion, see 3.16n.

43–4 The absence of a particle connecting this couplet with 39–42 makes for a sequence (as Ross (1979) 42 diagrams it) A (39–42) asyndeton B (43–4) C (45–6) *que et* D (47–8). This sequence is not paralleled in H., but there are examples in Lucretius (4.1197–8, 6.529–30, LHS II 515–16) and it may be in keeping with other Lucretian touches here (23–4n.). Attempts to eliminate the asyndeton include *iuuans* (Turnebus), *sacrum et* (dett.), and *sacrumue tostis* (Ross; cf. 43n.).

43 sacrum ... focum: the hearth was sacred to Vesta and the Lares (66n.), and tending it was actually a task for women (Cato, *Agr.* 143.2, Wissowa (1912) 157–8).

uetustis 'aged', so as to burn better. Since *uetustus* is rare in prose before Livy and in verse often occurs in elevated contexts, it has been argued that it is too 'loftily poetic' here (Ross (1979) 243, proposing *sacrumue tostis*). But its use in Columella of, among other things, 'aged' seawater, dung, and cheese (2.14.9, 3.11.4, 6.7.2; cf. 8.5.4, 9.11.2, 12.20.6, 22.2, 23.1) suggests that it may be a technical term, and even if it was poetic in the late Republic, one poet who uses it is Alfius' 'model' (23–4n.) Lucretius (2.1174, 3.774, 5.160, 827, 1084).

exstruat 'pile high', not stinting of the firewood, an indication that it is still winter. For the construction *exstruo* x (acc.) with y (abl.), cf. Cic. *Tusc.* 5.62 *mensae ... epulis exstruebantur.*

44 lassi: possibly from his hunting (42n.). *lassus* seems to have been colloquial in origin, and formal prose continued to prefer *fessus,* but it was made poetic by usage in Ennius, Lucretius, H. (*C.* 2.6.7, *S.* 1.5.37, 10.10, 2.2.10, 7.94, 8.8, *Ep.* 2.2.27), and Virgil (Axelson (1945) 29–10).

45–6 Penning and milking flocks do not figure among the ordinary tasks for women (41n.). A *uilica* was expected to be present (*interesse*) 'when the [male] shepherds are milking the ewes at sheepfolds or putting the lambs or the young of other animals to nurse' (Col. 12.3.9), but this is not the same as her doing these things herself.

The Romans used sheep milk more than other types, and it was most abundant when the ewes had lambed, another winter occurrence (Plin. *Nat.* 8.187, White (1970) 277–8, 303, 310–11).

45 cratibus 'hurdles' plaited from various twigs and used for temporary fencing (Var. *R.* 2.2.9, Virg. *G.* 1.166, Col. 12.15.1).

laetum: it appears that *laetas segetes etiam rustici dicunt* (Cic. *De orat.* 3.155; cf. *Orat.* 81), but the epithet occurs in this sense of 'sleek' in other poetic contexts (*C.* 4.4.13, Lucr. 1.14, 2.343, Thomas on Virg. *G.* 1.1, 2.144, 3.320).

46 distenta ... ubera: cf. *S.* 1.1.110, Virg. *Ecl.* 4.21–2, 9.31, all based, it seems, on Lucr. 1.258–9 *candens lacteus umor | uberibus manat distentis.*

47 horna ... uina 'this year's wines' (poetic pl.; cf. 9.34, 13.6, N–H on *C.* 1.18.5), what the French call 'vin naturel', home-made and less expensive. *hornus* seems to be a rustic word (*C.* 3.23.3, *S.* 2.6.88, *ThLL* vi 2.2972, E–M s.v.).

dulci: transferred epithet; cf. Cat. 27.2 *calices amariores,* Mart. 11.104.19–20 *dulcia ... pocula.*

48 dapes inemptas: cf. Virg. *G.* 4.133 (the Corycian gardener) *dapibus mensas onerabat inemptis.* It is possible that H. has borrowed the phrase 'with satirical intent' (Kenney (1984) liv). *daps* is an archaism found chiefly in verse (*ThLL* vi 36–7). In H. it usually = *cibus* or *cena* (3.8, 17.66, *C.* 3.1.18, 4.4.12, *S.* 2.6.67, 89, 108, *Ep.* 1.17.51, *Ars* 198), but in some cases it seems to have its original sense of 'religious feast' (5.33n., 9.1, *C.* 1.32.13, 37.4, 2.7.17).

apparet: the wife may 'exit' on an unpoetic note, since *apparo* of food seems to be as humdrum as American 'fixes dinner'. Outside of comedy it occurs in this sense only here and at Mart. 1.99.12, and even in other senses is rare in verse (*ThLL* ii 269–70).

49–60 Like H.'s Ofellus (*S.* 2.2), the speaker is suspiciously well informed about the exotic imports he rejects. His claim of moderation is undercut by the hunting passage (29–36): he 'has no need of urban delicacies because he has his own rural ones, some of which are foreign – *aduenam gruem* – and all of which are *inemptas*' (Miles).

Food was an important topic in various types of ancient poetry, including *iambus*, lyric, comedy, bucolic, and satire (N–H on *C.* 1.31.15, Rudd (1966) 202–6, West (1974) 31, Gowers (1993) 1–49).

49 me: the speaker (Alfius), who manages to place himself in the scene just in time for dinner.

iuuerint: since it is parallel to the pres. subj. *descendat* (53), the perf. subj. is probably a metrical convenience (cf. 1.32n., *S.* 2.4.90–1 *quamuis . . . referas cuncta, | non tamen interpres tantundem iuueris*).

Lucrina . . . conchylia: shellfish from the Lago Lucrino near Baiae and Puteoli ranked among the best in the world (N–H on *C.* 2.15.3, *S.* 2.4.32, Plin. *Nat.* 9.168, André (1961) 107–8).

50 rhombus aut scari: the 'turbot' comes from the Adriatic (*S.* 1.2.116, 2.2.42, 8.30, Plin. *Nat.* 9.169, André (1961) 103–4), the 'parrot wrasse' from further east (52n.) in the Mediterranean (Enn. *var.* 40–1 Vahlen, Plin. *Nat.* 9.62–3, Col. 8.16.9).

51 Eois . . . fluctibus: an inflated way of referring to the familiar Aegean and Carpathian seas. The epithet *Eous* is normally used of points much further east (*C.* 1.35.31, *OLD* s.v.). The phrase goes with *intonata* either as a locative, 'thundered in', or as a dat., 'thundered at' (cf. Ov. *Am.* 1.7.45–6). For the scansion *Ēŏus*, cf. Cinna, *poet.* 6.1 *FPL*, Virg. *G.* 1.288, *A.* 2.417, 3.588, 6.831, 11.4. H. also has *Ēous* (*C.* 1.35.31; cf. Virg. *G.* 1.221, 2.115, *A.* 1.489, West on Hes. *Op.* 548).

intonata: *intono*, a poetic word (Norden on Virg. *A.* 6.607, *ThLL* VII 26), occurs only here in H. and only here in Classical Latin as a deponent (Prisc. *GLK* II 473.14, 520.25). Cf. 5.39, 16.8nn., and *inuictus* (13.12), *cenatus* (*S.* 1.10.61), *potus* (*C.* 4.13.5 etc.), *pransus* (*S.* 1.5.25, 6.127, *Ars* 340), LHS II 290–1.

52 hiems 'winter storm', a sense of *hiems* found chiefly in poetry (*ThLL* VI 3.2774). Cf. Greek *cheimon* (e.g. Arch. fr. 105.3 West (App. 1)).

ad hoc ... mare: the speaker must mean the southern *mare Tyrrhenum* or even the *mare Ionium* (Adriatic), since the *scarus*, 'which runs in great numbers from the shores of all Asia and Greece as far as Sicily, has never swum as far as the Ligurian sea or through Gaul to the Iberian' (Col. 8.16.9). An attempt was made to stock the Tiber mouth with *scari*, but that was in the time of Tiberius (Plin. *Nat.* 9.62–3).

53 Afra auis: probably the *gallina Africana* or *Numidica* ('guinea fowl'), an especially prized and expensive bird (Var. *R.* 3.9.18–19, André (1961) 13–14). The *grus* (35n.) is also from Africa, but *inempta*.

descendat: this seems to be the first instance of *descendo* in the sense 'is swallowed', but it may be a colloquialism or a medical usage (Sen. *Ep.* 108.15 *oblectamenta* ('appetizers') ... *facile descensura, facile reditura, ThLL* V 1.647–8).

54 attagen Ionicus 'francolin', another gourmet fowl (Plin. *Nat.* 10.133, Mart. 13.61, André (1961) 126).

55–8 Olives, sorrel (*lapathus*), and mallow (*malua*) are often mentioned as homely, healthy food (N–H on *C.* 1.31.15, *S.* 2.2.46, 4.29, West on Hes. *Op.* 41, Kenney on *Mor.* 72). Yet this salad seems to belong to the golden age (2n.) or the 'happy islands' (16.45). Sorrel and mallow are spring perennials (Plin. *Nat.* 19.170), appropriate fare for the Terminalia (59n.). But at this time of year olives, which are harvested in the autumn (White (1970) 225), would have to be 'plucked' (55n.), not from the bough, but from the jar.

55 iucundior: the adj. is parallel to the adv. *magis* (50; cf. 1.18n.).

55–6 lecta ... oliua: the point seems to be that the fruit is *inempta* (48), unless the speaker naively imagines that olives can be eaten right off the tree without any curing (cf. Cato, *Agr.* 117–19, Col. 12.49). *pinguissimis* is another transferred epithet (47n.); cf. Virg. *G.* 2.425 *pinguem et ... placitam Paci nutritor oliuam* (16.45n.).

57 herba lapathi: cf. *S.* 2.4.29 *lapathi breuis herba* and, for the gen., *C.* 2.3.14, 3.15.15, 29.3, 4.10.4 (*flos/flores rosae*), *S.* 2.4.69 *baca* ... *oliuae*, Virg. *Ecl.* 5.26 *graminis* ... *herbam. lapathus* is a Greek word for *rumex* ('sorrel'), a favourite in salads and other simple dishes (*S.* 2.4.29, Pl. *Ps.* 815, Lucil. fr. 200 *ROL*, André (1961) 31–2).

prata amantis: cf. 16.34, Thomas on Virg. *G.* 2.113, 3.315 *amantis ardua dumos*, 4.124 *amantis litora myrtos. amo* in this sense seems to belong to the language of agriculture (*ThLL* I 1956).

58 maluae salubres: for the 'salubrious' qualities of mallow, cf. N–H on *C.* 1.31.15, Cels. 2.29, Plin. *Nat.* 20.222–3, Mart. 10.48.7–8. The speaker will need plenty if he eats everything mentioned in the poem.

59–60 'His vegetable diet is varied with meat on rare occasions' (Wickham). This was true for most ancient Italians, especially peasants (André (1961) 137–9), who rarely had access to the supplies of game that Alfius imagines for his rustic (29–36).

59 The Terminalia in early spring (23 February) honoured Terminus, the protector of *termini*, 'boundary markers' (Bömer on Ov. *F.* 2.639–84, Scullard (1981) 79–80). *termini* were unknown in the golden age (3n.), but since they marked a major type of loan security, they would be important to a usurer. The slaughtered lamb may also be at odds with the idealized past, as blood sacrifice was absent not only from the golden age (Mynors on Virg. *G.* 2.537, Gatz (1967) 165–71), but from the Terminalia as celebrated in early Rome (Plut. *Quaest. Rom.* 15, *Numa* 16.1).

agna: Roman custom prescribed male victims for male gods (Scullard (1981) 23; cf. 9.22n.), but in poetry, if not in cult, Terminus and Faunus seem to be exceptions (Ov. *F.* 2.655–6 (*agnus* and *porca* for Terminus), N–H on *C.* 1.4.12 (*agna* or *haedus* for Faunus), Ov. *F.* 2.361 (*capella* for Faunus), Bömer on 4.653 (ewe for Faunus)).

60 haedus ereptus lupo: *iucunde expressit rusticorum frugalitatem* (Porph.): the kid would not be eaten unless it were dead or dying anyway. But cf. the proverb 'animals eaten by wolves have sweeter meat' (Plut. *Symp.* 2.9), which apparently means that the wolf, a 'bon connoisseur' (Plessis), is likely to single out the tastiest animal. H.'s phrase seems to be echoed at Mart. 10.48.14 *haedus inhumani raptus ab ore lupi*.

61–2 As he dines the speaker contemplates with pleasure the return of his flocks and oxen and the gathering of his slaves around the household gods.

For all his talk about country labours, he now imagines himself watching (62–3), not working, and despite his earlier silence on the matter (12, 32n.), his dream house turns out to be full of slaves (65). Nor is that house the simple cottage tended by the *pudica mulier* (39–40), but a *ditis ... domus* (65) in which even the Lares bask in prosperity (66).

61 epulas: a more prosaic term than *dapes* (48n.; cf. *ThLL* v 1.36).

iuuat: sc. *me* (49). With the indicative verb, fantasy seems to have become reality (cf. 68n.).

62–3 uidere ... | uidere: the repetition has a Lucretian ring (e.g. 2.955–6); cf. 11.2–3, 16.41–2, 64–5.

63–4 Back to ploughing time (3n.). For the image of returning oxen, cf. *C.* 3.6.42–3, 13.10–12, Virg. *Ecl.* 2.66 *aspice, aratra iugo referunt suspensa iuuenci*, Bömer on Ov. *F.* 5.497 (63n.).

63 uomerem inuersum: object of *trahentes* (64). The word order *fessos uomerem* may be meant to suggest *fessos uomere* (Naylor). The plough is 'turned upside down' so that its blades will not cut into the ground as it is dragged back (Virg. *Ecl.* 2.66, Ov. *F.* 5.497 *uersa iugo referuntur aratra*).

64 collo: cf. *C.* 3.3.14–15 *uexere tigres indocili iugum* | *collo trahentes*. These seem to be the only examples of *collum* as a 'distributive sing.' (several creatures 'sharing' a single part or attribute), a usage that is either colloquial or based on Greek practice (Löfstedt (1956) 12–26).

65 postosque uernas: the slaves are 'in position' either to wait on their master or to dine themselves. *uernae*, 'house-born slaves', were thought to be more efficient than imported ones (Brink on *Ep.* 2.2.6), but the point here is probably that even the slaves on this estate are *inempti*.

The contracted form *postos* (cf. 9.1n., Lucr. 1.1059 etc., Cat. 68.39, Virg. *G.* 3.527, Norden on *A.* 6.24) occurs in only one MS but is probably required by the metre (35n.).

ditis ... domus: 'the slaves born in the house advertised by their number the wealth of the owner' (Giarratano; cf. Tib. 2.1.23 *turba uernarum, saturi bona signa coloni*, Petr. 53.2, White (1970) 370). *ditis* is metrically expedient (cf. *C.* 1.7.9, *S.* 1.1.40, 5.91, 7.19, 9.51,

2.7.52). Otherwise H., like most Latin authors, prefers *diues* (*ThLL* v 1.1588).

examen: lit. 'swarm', as of bees, suggesting a large number. The metaphor is a 'live' one; cf. N–H on *C.* 1.35.31, *Ep.* 1.19.23, Cic. *Har.* 25, Var. *R.* 3.16.30, Mynors on Virg. *G.* 4.21.

66 renidentis: there may be a play on two senses of *renido*: the Lares are 'smiling' (*C.* 3.6.12, *OLD* s.v. 2), as often in art, but also 'sleek' or 'glowing' with wealth (N–H on *C.* 2.18. 2, Lucr. 2.27, Virg. *G.* 2.282, *OLD* s.v. 1).

Lares: the household gods who resided at the hearth (43n.) and were thought to participate in meals. Cf. 5.50n., *S.* 2.5.14, 6.66–7 *ante Larem proprium uescor uernasque procaces | pasco libatis dapibus,* Wissowa (1912) 149.

67–70 Alfius, the usurer and someday rustic, finishes his speech and goes back to business.

The surprise ending – if it is that – shows that Alfius will never realize his dream. The money that he might have used to buy an estate he quickly loans out again.

67 haec ubi locutus: most commentators supply *est*, which makes this a subordinate clause ('when he said these things') and *redegit* (69) the main verb. The asyndeton between *redegit* and *quaerit* (70), also a main verb, may serve to emphasize the suddenness of Alfius' final action. Some take *locutus* as a participle and *ubi* with *redegit* ('having said these things, when he collected . . .'), which would eliminate the asyndeton but involve accepting an unnatural word order. Still others ('nonnulli' cited by Lambinus), in what is clearly an attempt to salvage the poem as 'sincere praise' of country life, supply *sum* with *locutus*, as if H. were all along the speaker and Alfius his unconverted audience ('after I said these things, Alfius (all the same) returned to usury').

ubi: the postposition of *ubi* (16.43, 19 of 55 occurrences in H.) and of most other rel. particles and pronouns does not appear to be an affectation (1.12n.), as it is frequent in prose as well as verse and may even have been the 'rule' in early Latin (Marouzeau (1949) 122–35).

fenerator: for the loathing inspired by usurers, cf. *S.* 1.2.14–15, 3.85–9, 2.3.69–70 (one named Cicuta, 'hemlock'), Cato, *Agr.* 1.1, Var. *Men.* 37 *auarus fenerator,* Sall. *Cat.* 33.1, Cic. *Off.* 1.150 *primum* *improbantur ii quaestus qui in odia hominum incurrunt, ut portitorum* [customs collectors], *ut feneratorum.*

Alfius: cf. Col. 1.7.2 '*uel optima nomina non appellando fieri mala*' ['even the best loans go bad if they are not called in'] *fenerator Alfius dixisse uerissime fertur.* This is the only other reference to Alfius, but his presence in H. and the association with the proverb may indicate that he was a famous usurer, the 'Cato' of his profession (cf. *disticha Catonis*), or that, like Chremes (1.33n.), he was a stock figure in drama. The name might even be connected with Greek *alphē*, 'gain' (Orelli).

In American slang, usurers ('loan sharks') are known as 'Shylocks' even to people who have never heard of Shakespeare. The lawyer on *Green Acres* (2 intro.) was named 'Oliver Wendell Douglas'.

68 iam iam: 'the implication often conveyed by *iam iam* or *iam iamque* [is] of an action so imminent that it seems to have happened already' (Fordyce on Cat. 63.73; cf. 17.1, N–H on *C.* 2.20.9). Here it seems to pick up on the shift to indicative at 61.

futurus rusticus 'meaning to become a rustic'; the fut. part. expresses purpose (1.9n.). Elsewhere in H. *rusticus*, whether substantive ('yokel') or adjective ('clownish') is usually pejorative (*C.* 3.23.2, *S.* 1.3.31, 2.2.3, 6.80, 115, 7.28, *Ep.* 1.2.41–2, 7.83, 13.12–13, 2.1.146, 2.39, *Ars* 213; the exception is *C.* 3.6.37–8).

69–70 *exigit, inquit, a debitoribus pecuniam comparaturus praedia, cogitans scilicet iucunditatem uitae illius quam in rusticis laudet. sed rursus stimulatus cupiditate usurarum quaerit eam faenori dare* (Porph.). Interest was reckoned by the month, from one Kalends, Nones, or Ides to the next (*S.* 1.3.87, Cic. *Ver.* 2.170, *Catil.* 1.14, *Att.* 10.5.3, 14.20.2, Ov. *Rem.* 561, Crook (1967) 209–13). Alfius calls in his debts on the Ides, the last settlement day of the month, intending to put the money to better use, but is up to his old tricks by the Kalends, the first lending day of the month following.

69 redegit 'collected', a technical term (Cic. *Caec.* 56, *Rab. Post.* 37, *OLD* s.v. 5).

70 quaerit ... ponere: for *pono* in the technical sense 'lend out', cf. *Ars* 421 (= *S.* 1.2.13) *diues agris, diues positis in fenore* [4n.] *nummis, OLD* s.v. 14b. The inf. with *quaero* seems to be poetic (16.16n., *C.* 1.16.26, 37.22, 3.4.39, 24.27–8, 27.55–6, 4.1.12, *S.* 1.9.8, 2.1.77, 7.114, *Ep.* 1.1.2–3, Lucr. 1.103).

EPODE 3

Introduction

Garlic, rather than hemlock, should be used to execute parricides.
Something is burning inside of H.; is it poison? It must be what
Medea used to protect Jason and to destroy her rival. The heat is
worse than that in Apulia, and not even Hercules' poisoned robe
burned as much. If Maecenas ever again plays such a joke, may he
suffer the consequences of garlic breath.

The setting is clearly a banquet, one of the main contexts for
early Greek *iambus*, and Maecenas' joke and H.'s response seem akin
to the many *iambi* in which mockery or even verbal abuse among
friends serves to reaffirm their *philotēs* (Intro. 3; cf. Arch. frr. 96, 117,
124, 125, 168 West, Nagy (1979) 244–6). There is also a similarity
with certain poems of Catullus (6, 10, 12, 14, 22, 35, 44, 50, 103),
which do not, however, contain anything like H.'s mythic *exempla*.

These *exempla*, like others in the *Epodes* (5.61–6, 6.13–14, 9.7–10,
10.11–4, 13.11–18, 14.9–14, 15.5–10, 17.7–8, 30–5, 42–4, 65–9) and,
perhaps, in Archilochus (9–14n.), are not simply 'ornaments' or
comic hyperbole, but are vital to understanding the poem (9–18n.).
Maecenas' joke, however lightly meant, seems to come dangerously
close to disrupting his friendship with H., and thus parallels the poi-
sons of Canidia (17–18) and other malignant forces (e.g. 4.1–10n., 6
Intro., 7.15–20) that are setting Romans against each other.

1–4 In comparing garlic to hemlock, H. suggests a parallel between
himself and the parricide, as if he, too, were justly condemned to
die. But in the sequel he presents himself as an unsuspecting (5–8)
and undeserving (9–18) victim, and finally directs the blame where it
belongs, at Maecenas (19–22).

H.'s physical pain may be compounded by anxiety that he is about
to be tested on his pledge (Epode 1) to follow Maecenas to war
(Gowers (1993) 295), as garlic was a regular battle ration for Greek
soldiers (Ar. *Ach.* 164, *Equ.* 493–4, 946, *Lys.* 690, E. Capso, *Phoen.* 47
(1993) 115–20), and, it seems, Roman soldiers (Pl. *Poen.* 1313–14; cf.
Cic. *Att.* 13.42.3, Suet. *Vesp.* 8.3, and imperial Latin *scordaliae*
('brawl'), *scordalus* ('brawler'), derived from *skordon*, the Greek word
for 'garlic').

1–3 Parentis ... edit: H. parodies Roman legal formula (e.g. *Dig.* 48.9.1 *lege Pompeia de parricidiis* [55 or 52 BC] *cauetur ut, si quis patrem ... occiderit* [2n.] *... ut poena ea teneatur, quae est legis Corneliae de sicariis, Cod. Justin.* 9.17 *si quis parentis* [1n.] *... fata properauerit ... insutus culleo* [a sack] *et inter eius ferales angustias comprehensus serpentium contuberniis misceatur et ... uel in uicinum mare uel in amnem proiciatur*). Such parody is common in Greek and Roman comedy and satire, including H. (e.g. *S.* 1.2.47–8, 2.1.7–9, 2.51). The language here and in 19–22 may also suggest a curse (Kirn (1935) 42); cf. 5.89, 10.1–10, 16.18nn., N–H on *C.* 2.13.1–10, Naev. *com.* 18–19 *ROL ut illum di perdant, qui primum holitor protulit | caepam* [onion].

1 Parentis = *patris* or *matris*, an archaism or legal usage (*C.* 1.7.25, 10.6, 12.13, 2.13.5, 37, 19.21, 3.10.12, 11.34, *S.* 1.2.7, 6.7, 2.3.134, *Ars* 313, Blok (1961) 38); cf. *Cod. Justin.* 9.17 (1–3n.), Fest. p. 260M *si parentem puer uerberit ast ille plorassit parens, puer diuis parentum sacer esto.*

olim: with the fut. (2n.) *olim = aliquando, posthac, umquam* (*C.* 2.10.17, *S.* 1.4.137, 6.85, 2.5.27, *Ep.* 1.3.18, 10.42, Brink on *Ars* 386–7 *si quid tamen olim | scripseris, in Maeci descendat iudicis auris*).

impia: cf. 5.13, 84, 7.1, 10.14, 16.9, 66, *S.* 2.1.53–6 *Scaeuae uiuacem crede nepoti | matrem: nil faciet sceleris pia dextera ... | sed mala tollet anum uitiato melle cicuta* (3n.).

2 senile: *ad augmentum sceleris dixit senile, qui etiam si occisus non esset mori potuerit* (Schol.). The epithet is probably transferred (5.13, 10.14, *C.* 1.27.6, 3.1.17, 4.4.46), although the focus on the 'aged' appearance of the parent's throat may increase the horror.

guttur fregerit: cf. *C.* 2.13.5–6 (the man who planted a tree that almost crushed H.) *illum et parentis crediderim sui | fregisse ceruicem.* Since *guttur* can often indicate the palate or oesophagus (*ThLL* VI 2375), the parricide's 'punishment that afflicts the throat (*edit alium*)' seems to fit the crime (Miles).

fregerit: fut. perf. (cf. 19), as in the legal texts (1–3n.) and elsewhere with *olim* (1n.).

3 edit: an old form of the subj. (=*edat*) appropriate to the archaic language of legal formula (1–3n.). Cf. *S.* 2.8.89–90 (also legalese?) *leporum auolsos, ut multo suauius, armos, | quam si cum lumbis quis edit.*

cicutis: poetic pl. (2.15, 47nn.). At Rome hemlock was used for poisoning and as a topical remedy for various ailments (*S.* 2.1.53–6 (ɪn.), Brink on *Ep.* 2.2.53; cf. 2.67n., Pers. 5.143–5, Plin. *Nat.* 25.151–4), but at Athens *kōneion* served to execute parricides and other capital felons, such as Socrates (Plin. *Nat.* 25.151, Sen. *Ep.* 13.14, Juv. 13.185–7). Hemlock's effect of fatal cold and numbness is the opposite of garlic's (Ov. *Am.* 3.7.13–14, Plin. *Nat.* 25.151, Juv. 7.205–6 *Athenae | nil praeter gelidas ausae conferre cicutas*).

alium: by the late Republic garlic was considered fare for rustics (4n.) and other low or unsophisticated types, but it was also recalled nostalgically as a staple of those hardy *maiores* who had brought Rome to greatness (Var. *Men.* 63). In rejecting it, H. seems to display *urbanitas* (1.31–2n.) and at the same time the *mollities* (1.10, 16nn.) of one who 'is not a man with guts, an old Roman or a peasant' (Gowers (1993) 293).

For the properties, effects, and 'lore' of garlic, cf. Plin. *Nat.* 20.50–7 *alio magna uis ... serpentes abigit et scorpiones odore atque, ut aliqui tradidere, bestias omnes* [11–12n.] *... facit et somnos atque in totum rubicundiora corpora – uenerem quoque stimulare cum coriandro uiridi tritum potumque e mero* [17–18n.]. *uitia eius sunt, quod oculos hebetat, inflationes facit, stomachum laedit copiosius sumptum, sitim gignit* [15–16n.], Gowers (1993) 290–7.

4 A howl of agony: the garlic is now burning in H.'s innards. For garlic in rural food, cf. Virg. *Ecl.* 2.10–11 (below), Kenney on *Mor.* 87, 116, Col. 10.112, 314, 11.3.16, 20, 22, André (1961) 10. Its absence from the meals imagined by the speaker of Epode 2 may be yet another hint (2 intro.) of his identity as a 'city-slicker', but it is possible that H. actually disliked the stuff, since he does not mention it in any of his other scenes of country eating.

messorum 'reapers' who have worked up an appetite. Cf. Virg. *Ecl.* 2.10–11 *Thestyllis et rapido fessis messoribus aestu | alia serpyllumque* [thyme] *herbas contundit olentis. messor*, a rare word, occurs chiefly in poetry (*ThLL* vɪɪɪ 861), but cf. Cic *De or.* 3.46 (an orator's voice) *non mihi oratores antiquos, sed messores uidetur imitari*, where it seems to be a term of abuse.

ilia: their 'innards' (*S.* 2.8.30, Virg. *A.* 7.499, Ov. *Ib.* 167, *Met.* 3.67). The use of *ilia*, lit. 'arteries' (Plin. *Nat.* 11.208), as a euphemism for *intestina* or *inguen* (e.g. *Ep.* 1.1.9, Cat. 11.20) seems to be poetic (Blok (1961) 43, Adams (1982) 50–1).

5–8 Since H. has already mentioned garlic, it is odd that he now asks what has 'poisoned' him. Perhaps the increase in his pain (4n.)

causes him to think – or at least pretend to think – that 'something worse than garlic must be afflicting him; it is surely some kind of poison, but he cannot make out its precise nature' (Miles).

5 quid hoc ueneni 'what (is) this (in the sphere) of poison?' The gen. is of the sort 'sometimes called the genitive of the rubric, that is the class to which an individual belongs' (Kenney on Lucr. 3.832; cf. 5.1, 15.12). For *uenenum*, cf. 5.22n., 62, 87, 17.35.

saeuit: cf. *C.* 1.25.13–15, Petr. 17.8 *maior enim in praecordiis dolor saeuit*, Tac. *Ann.* 13.15 (in a *uenenum*) *temperamentum inerat ne statim saeuiret*.

praecordiis: lit. 'parts of the body under the heart', here the site of physical pain ('heartburn'); cf. 17.26, *S.* 2.4.26, *OLD* s.v. 1. Elsewhere in H. the *praecordia* are a seat of emotion (5.95, 11.15, *S.* 1.4.89, *OLD* s.v. 2); cf. 5.37n. and Greek use of *thumos*, *phrēn*, and the like (e.g. Arch. fr. 120.2, 124b.4, 128.1, 131.1, 172.2, 191.3 West).

6 num: even in direct questions *num* does not necessarily expect a negative answer (8.17) but can indicate the emotional state of the speaker, in this case amazement and indignation (cf. *S.* 2.5.58 (7n.), LHS II 463).

uiperinus ... cruor: for the epithet, cf. *C.* 1.8.9, 2.19.19, Acc. *trag.* 552–3 *ROL ex uiperino morsu uenae ... | ueneno imbutae.* 'The ancients not unnaturally regarded snake's blood as poisonous' (N–H on *C.* 1.8.9; cf. Ov. *Pont.* 4.7.36 *quae uipereo tela cruore madent*, Plin. *Nat.* 11.279). Vipers often figure in magic (5.15, Tupet (1976) 64–5).

H.'s slight preference in the *Epodes* for *cruor* (7.20, 17.32, 51) over *sanguis* (7.4, 5.19, 16.9) may be due to its convenience in iambic verse. In the hexameter poetry the proportion is reversed, while in other Latin, including the *Odes*, *sanguis* occurs from 4 to 16× more often than *cruor* (Blok (1961) 44, *ThLL* IV 1242).

7 incoctus herbis 'added by cooking to these herbs'. The verb suggests that H. ate some kind of soup or porridge (André (1961) 28–9) rather than a *moretum*, which was not cooked (Kenney on *Mor.* 116). Hipponax mentions two garlicky concoctions (frr. 26.2, 39.4 West), and given the interest of the genre in both food (2.49–6on.) and 'low' activity (3n., Intro. 3), it would not be surprising if garlic figured in other *iambi* as well (Gowers (1993) 293).

fefellit: with *incoctus* (5.67–8, *C.* 3.16.32, *Ep.* 1.17.10). The construction, which is not attested before H., seems to be based on

Greek *lanthanō* ('escape notice') and the participle (2.19n.). *fefellit* sug-
gests that the effect of the 'poison' was all the worse because un-
expected (11–12n.). There may be a play on *fefellit* and *fel*, 'gall',
'bitterness', 'venom' (Gowers (1993) 299).

an: the second question does not present an alternative, but 'cor-
rects and completes the first' (Giarratano). If there was poison in the
food, then Canidia and no one else put it there. For this use of *an*, cf.
7.13–14, *S.* 2.3.262–3, 278–80, 5.58 *num furis? an prudens ludis me obscura
canendo?*, *Ep.* 1.3.31–4, 11.5–6, *Ars* 265–7, LHS 11 465–7.

7–8 malas ... dapes: the epithet is proleptic: the food became
'noxious' (*OLD* s.v. *malus* 4) as a result of Canidia's 'handling'. Cf. *S.*
2.8.94–5 (dinner guests rejected their dishes) *uelut illis | Canidia afflas-
set, peior serpentibus Afris.* For *tracto*, cf. N–H on *C.* 2.13.9–10 (the tree
planter (2n.)) *et quidquid usquam concipitur nefas | tractauit*, for *daps*,
2.48n., and for Canidia, App. 2.

9–18 H.'s attempt to explain his mishap in terms of myth and
nature is obviously meant to be comic and bathetic, an effect
enhanced by the combination of elevated with unpoetic language
(Blok (1961) 58–9). Yet the passage is also essential to the logic and
meaning of the poem. As he rants, H. seems gradually to 'cool off',
both literally, from the heat of the garlic, and figuratively, from his
shock and anger. When he refers to Medea, he implies that he has
been viciously attacked, and by a friend (9–14n.). But he reconsiders:
perhaps the garlic itself, a natural force like the Dog Star, rather
than any human agency, is responsible for his pain (15–16). Finally,
by comparing it to Deianira's 'gift', he seems to concede that the
garlic, although dire in its result, may have been well-intended (17–
18n.). With this he regains his composure, and the poem ends with
joking banter rather than a serious rupture of friendship (3 Intro.).

9–14 Whatever the reader knows about Canidia (App. 2), she is
clearly a witch, and the reference to Medea, the archetypical sor-
ceress, follows naturally (5.61–6n.). In his version of the story, H.
emphasizes Medea's power not only to harm her enemies (13–14) but
to help her friends (9–12). This raises the question of why Maecenas
has harmed a friend (9–18n.). At 5.61–6, by contrast, Canidia speaks
only of Medea's destructive arts.

The *exemplum* takes the form of a miniature narrative, a common
device in Greek poetry and one almost certainly employed by Archi-

lochus (17–18n.). It is not known if Archilochus mentioned Medea and could therefore be H.'s source, but elements of the myth appear in other lyric (e.g. Pind. *P.* 4), not to mention early epic and tragedy (13, 14nn.), and there is no reason to think that his model here was Hellenistic (Fedeli (1978) 112). For early versions of the Medea story, cf. Page (1971) xxi–xxx, *RE* xv 29–65, and, for H.'s use of it, 5.24, 61–6, 16.57–8, 17.35, *C.* 2.13.8, 4.4.63, Brink on *Ars* 123, 185.

9 ut 'when' (5.11, 16.64, *C.* 4.4.42, *S.* 1.6.27 etc.; cf. 7.19n.).

Argonautas ... omnis: the phrase seems to go both with *candidum*, 'handsome beyond all the (other) Argonauts', and *mirata est* (10). Cf. Ap. Rhod. 3.443–4 'amazingly among all (the Argonauts) the son of Aeson excelled | in beauty and grace'. Since this is not likely to be H.'s model (11n.), the two poets may have drawn on a common source.

Most Latin poets avoid *praeter* (Axelson (1945) 81), but H. uses it in all of his works (11.3, 16.40, 6× in Odes, 13× in hexameters). Here it seems to be equivalent to Greek *exocha*, 'beyond', 'surpassingly'.

candidum: Jason was famous for his good looks (Pind. *P.* 4.78–92, Ap. Rhod. 3.443–4, Ov. *Ep.* 12.11–12). In the sense 'fair-skinned, fair (usu. implying beauty)' (*OLD* s.v. 5) *candidus* is used chiefly in poetry and either of gods (N–H on *C.* 1.18.11) or of girls and young boys, not of mature heroes (cf. 11.27, *C.* 1.13.9, 3.9.2, 4.1.27, *S.* 1.2.123, *Ep.* 2.2.4, *ThLL* iii 241). If H. is suggesting that Jason, his 'stand-in' in the *exemplum*, is delicate or effeminate, then he may be alluding to the relation between himself and Maecenas (here = Medea) in Epode 1 (1.15–22n.). There may also be an ironic play on *candidus* in the sense 'honest' (11.11, 14.5), the opposite of what Jason turns out to be (13n.).

9–12 candidum | ... ducem | ... illigaturum ... Iasonem: the sequence reads like a riddle. H. may be creating an 'aura of mystery and romance' (Miles) or, perhaps, describing Jason from Medea's point of view (cf. 13n.): the hero's looks, status, and mission impress her before she finds out his name.

11–12 Jason's yoking of the bulls is mentioned in most versions of the myth, but H. seems to be alone in having Medea protect her lover with the same substance as she will later use to destroy her rival. In its dual nature her potion is like most *uenena* (5.22n.), but it also resembles garlic (Gowers (1993) 303), which causes sickness yet

can be a potent medicine and is able to ward off dangerous creatures
with its smell (3n.). Medea's two methods of administering the potion
recall, too, Canidia's poison, more dangerous because 'hidden' in
the soup (7n.). To help Jason, Medea anointed him, presumably with
his knowledge and consent, but to harm the *paelex*, she concealed the
stuff in 'gifts'.

11 ignota ... iuga: poetic pl., object of *illigaturum*. The yoke was
'unfamiliar' because the bulls had not yet been broken. H. differs
here from Apollonius Rhodius, who has Aeetes boast that he himself
often yoked and drove the bulls (3.409–15).

tauris: H. does not mention that these were fire-breathing, but
yoking bulls, rather than bullocks (1.25) or oxen (2.3, 63–4), would be
a dire task in itself. Cf. 6.11–12, 12.17, Mynors on Virg. *G.* 1.45–6.
The dat. probably goes both with *ignota* ('unknown to') and *illigaturum*
('put the yoke on').

illigaturum: fut. part expressing purpose (1.9n.). For the verb,
cf. 1.25n.

12–13 perunxit hoc ... | hoc ... fugit: both the position and
the repetition of *hoc* make it emphatic: 'it was with *this* that she (must
have) anointed him, | by means of gifts dipped in *this* that having
avenged herself she fled'.

12 perunxit: cf. 5.59, *Ars* 277, both 'ludicrous scenes' (Blok (1961)
49), which, along with its rarity in other verse, suggests that *perungo*
may be unpoetic.

13 delibutis: cf. 17.31, Pac. *trag.* 209–10 *ROL* (a passage known
to H. (*S.* 2.3.60–2)) *reliquias ... sanie delibutas.*

donis: at Eur. *Med.* 1156–1221 there are two gifts, a crown and a
robe, but other versions mention only the crown (Page (1971) xxvi).

paelicem 'concubine' (5.63, 70, *C.* 3.10.15, 27.66), a term of abuse
expressing Medea's view of the situation (9–12n.); Jason, of course,
thought he was taking a *noua nupta* (5.65–6). The *magni Creontis filia*
(5.64) is not named by Euripides either, but elsewhere she is called
Glauce or Creusa (Page (1971) xxv). *paelex* is rare in Republican prose
and verse but, perhaps as a result of H.'s example, becomes a
favourite of Ovid (44×) and Senecan tragedy (26×; cf. Blok (1961)
49–50).

14 H.'s source is probably Eur. *Med.* 1321–2, although the evi-
dence of vase-paintings suggests that the story of the serpent chariot

was older than Euripides (Page (1971) xxvii, *RE* xv 45). Cf. Pac. *trag.* 242 *ROL angues ingentes alites iuncti iugo*, Var. *Men.* 284 *dixe* [?] *regi Medeam aduectam per aera in reda anguibus.*

serpente ... alite: this may be a comic oxymoron, 'flying creeper' (or 'creeping flier'). The sing. is poetic, as is *ales* (*ThLL* I 1524), whether an adj. (*C.* 1.2.42, 3.12.4, 4.1.10, 4.1, 11.26) or a substantive (5.100, 10.1, 16.24, 17.12, 67, *C.* 1.6.2, 2.20.10, 16, 3.3.61, 4.78, 4.6.24).

15–16 For the heat of Apulia, cf. 2.41–2, *C.* 3.30.11, Var. *R.* 1.6.3, Sen. *Ep.* 87.7, White (1970) 73–4. H.'s almost gratuitous slur on the climate of his homeland (*C.* 3.4.9, 30.10–11, *S.* 1.5.77, 2.1.34–8) may be an iambic touch, recalling Archilochus' blame of his own Paros and Thasos (frr. 20, 21, 22, 228 West), although this kind of thing does occur in other types of poetry (e.g. Hes. *Op.* 639–40, Hom. *Od.* 9.21–7, 13.242–7).

15 siderum: poetic pl. for the *sidus feruidum*, the Dog Star (1.27n.).

insedit 'oppressed', perf. of *insideo* (*OLD* s.v. 5) or *insido* (s.v. 1c), and only here in H., although the two words occur elsewhere in both prose and verse.

uapor 'heat', a Lucretian term (1.491 etc.) occurring only here in H. (cf. *Ep.* 1.16.7 *uaporet*). The word may also suggest the effects of garlic, which induces thirst (3n.) and produces its own 'exhalation' (*OLD* s.v. *uapor* 1; cf. Miles, Gowers (1993) 300).

16 siticulosae: first attested here and, with its cretic shape, rare in other verse (cf. *Priap.* 61.12, 63.3), but its use in imperial prose (*OLD* s.v.) suggests that it was a technical term.

siticulosus, aestuosus (18), and *iocosus* (20) are three of 13 forms in *-osus* occurring 15× in the *Epodes* (5.43, 55, 9.14, 10.23, 16.54, 60, 62, 17.15, 16, 34, 73, 77). The cluster here may recall Catullus (3 intro.), in whom such forms are relatively frequent, but in general H.'s usage is different from his predecessor's. In Latin poetry *-osus* forms appear to have at least three functions (Ernout (1949) 13–85): (1) some provide an epic colour in imitation of Greek forms in *-oeis* and *poly-*, (2) others are colloquial, and (3) still others are 'normal' words, occurring in prose and verse without any obvious resonance. In Catullus most of the *-osus* forms belong to the first two categories (Ross (1969) 53–60). Those in the *Epodes*, by contrast, with only two

or three exceptions (5.55, 9.14, 17.15nn.), are of the third type, as
are the majority in H.'s other works as well.

H. elides -*ae* only here and at 17.11, *C.* 3.4.78, *S.* 1.1.20, 2.100, 6.38,
2.1.72, 3.276, 4.7, 6.84, and possibly *C.* 3.8.27, *S.* 1.2.82, 5.100, and
Ep. 1.6.26 (cf. the app. crit. in Klingner and Sh. Bailey).

Apuliae: the district is *Āpŭlia* (*S.* 1.5.77, Pl. *Cas.* 72, Lucil. fr. 950
ROL etc.), but an inhabitant is an *Āpŭlus* (2.42, *C.* 1.33.7, 3.4.9, 5.9,
16.26, 4.14.26, *S.* 2.1.34, 38, Pl. *Cas.* 77, *Mil.* 648). The evidence is
unambiguous (but cf. the variants *limen Apuliae* (for *limina Pulliae*) at
C. 3.4.10 and *mare Apulicum* (for *mare publicum*) at 3.24.4), but the cause
of the variation in quantity is uncertain.

17–18 Unlike Medea's *dona*, Deianira's *munus* was not meant to
hurt anyone, but to win back Hercules' love for her. In this respect it
resembles garlic, which was thought to be an aphrodisiac (3n., Gow-
ers (1993) 296).

At least part of Deianira's story – Hercules' battle for her with the
river Achelous, the centaur Nessus' attempt to abduct her – was told
by Archilochus (frr. 34 (?), 259 (cf. 17n.), 286–9 West). The form and
content of his account is unknown, but it is probably, as here, an
exemplum rather than a self-contained narrative (Gentili (1988) 184).
Other important versions of the myth include Hes. fr. 25.18–25 M–
W, Bacch. *Dith.* 16 Maehler, and the *Trachiniae* of Sophocles (cf.
Easterling (1982) 15–19). H. again refers to the poisoned robe at
17.31–2. For Hercules in his other works, cf. Brink on *Ep.* 2.1.5–17,
10–12, Oksala (1973) 166.

17 munus = *donum*. There seems to be no difference in meaning
in H., who with only one exception (*Ep.* 1.18.75) uses forms of *munus*
where those of *donum* are metrically impossible (5.65, 12.2 etc.).

The poisoned robe is called a 'gift' (*dōron, dōrēma*) a number of
times in the *Trachiniae*; cf. especially 758 (Hyllus to Deianira) *son ...
dōrēma, thanasimon peplon* ('your gift, the deadly robe').

umeris: dat. with *inarsit* (11.15). In Sophocles the robe sticks to
and burns Hercules' sides, lungs, bones, and blood as well as his
shoulders (*Trach.* 765–70, 1050–6).

efficacis: the epithet is probably ironic, since for all his might
Hercules could not overcome this threat. Cf. Soph. *Trach.* 1058–1102
(= Cic. *Tusc.* 2.20–2). Archilochus (fr. 259 West) is cited for a version
of the proverb *oude Hēraklēs pros duo* ('not even Hercules (could win)

against two (enemies)'). It is possible that he used it in a context similar to this, with the two enemies Deianira and the dead centaur Nessus.

efficax, with its cretic, is rare in verse (17.1, *C.* 4.12.20, Sen. *Her. F.* 1273), but it occurs, although later than H., in elevated prose (*ThLL* v 2.159–63), and both here and at 17.1 may be 'quasi-grandiloquent' (Blok (1961) 52). For other forms in -*ax*, cf. 2.24n.

18 inarsit: a poetic word (Virg. *A.* 8.623, Ov. *Met.* 7.83, [Sen.] *Her. O.* 251, Stat. *Theb.* 3.539) first attested here and possibly a Horatian coinage (Blok (1961) 52; cf. 11.15n.).

aestuosius: probably an adj. agreeing with *munus* (1.18n.) rather than the comparative of the adverb, which is not attested even in the positive. *aestuosus* is similar to *siticulosus* (16) in its distribution, except that it occurs more often in verse (16.62, *C.* 1.22.5, 31.5, 2.7.16, Cat. 7.5), including Latin tragedy (Pac. *trag.* 80 *ROL*).

19–22 The end recalls the beginning (19n.) with H. again decreeing a punishment, this time for Maecenas, who is at last identified as the culprit. But by now H. is quite 'cool' (9–18n.): this is evident from his language, which is quite colloquial, suggesting a normal tone of voice (Blok (1961) 59), from the fact that he gives Maecenas a second chance, and from the penalty itself which, although it still 'fits the crime' (2n.), is a far cry from an execution. The key word is *iocose*: H. recognizes that he is the victim, not of judicial poisoning, magic, revenge, natural disaster, or tragic reversal, but of a friendly joke to be repaid, if at all, in kind.

19 at: not adversative (2.29, 5.25, 9.17), but introducing with 'expletive force' (*OLD* s.v. 11) a threat (cf. *S.* 2.1.44 and, for similar uses, 5.1n., N–H on *C.* 1.28.23, 3.7.22, *S.* 1.4.19, 8.37, 2.2.40, 6.54, *Ep.* 1.7.16). This type of *at* is especially common in comedy, and is probably colloquial in origin (*ThLL* II 955).

si quid ... concupiueris 'if you ever (again) desire such a thing', i.e. to perpetrate another practical joke. H. could mean 'desire (to eat) something similar (to garlic)' (Lambinus), but on the present occasion it was H., not Maecenas, who ate the garlic, and Maecenas' punishment would be more comic if he should suffer – perhaps through divine agency (*precor*) – the effects of garlic without having eaten it. The fut. perf. is parallel to that in line 2, as *si quid* is to *si quis* (1), *umquam* to *olim*, and *opponat ... cubet* (11–12) to *edit* (3).

concupisco (only here in H.) is rare in verse, and even in prose seems to belong to a low stylistic level (Blok (1961) 53).

20 iocose: the epithet both fits the present context and is proleptic for the future. For other 'proleptic vocatives', cf. 9.4, 13.12, *C.* 1.2.37, 4.14, N–H on *C.* 2.2.2, 3.4.42, 5.39–40. *iocosus* belongs to the third category of *-osus* forms (16n.) and is H.'s favourite, occurring 10× (*C.* 1.10.7, 12.3, 20.6, 3.3.69, 21.15, 4.15.26, *S.* 1.4.104, 10.11, *Ep.* 1.18.89), more than in any other Classical Latin poet.

precor: sc. *deos*, whichever ones would make Maecenas reek of garlic (19n.). The punctuation accepted here (Bentley, most edd.) makes *precor* parenthetical (*OLD* s.v. 5) with *opponat* and *cubat*, like *edit* (3), optative subjunctives. But the verb could govern *manum . . . cubet* as an object clause (s.v. 1b). There is a similar uncertainty at *C.* 1.3.7–8.

21–2 Cf. Simulus' reaction to his own garlicky *moretum* (Mor. 105–8): *saepe uiri nares acer iaculatur apertas | spiritus et simo damnat sua prandia uultu, | saepe manu summa lacrimantia lumina terget | immeritoque furens dicit conuicia fumo.*

21 puella: probably an attractive guest at the banquet, or perhaps the Licymnia of *C.* 2.12.23–8, but hardly Maecenas' wife Terentia (Schol.). For such 'girls', cf. 11.4, 6, 23, 27, 12.14–17, 14.15–16, 15.11, Griffin (1986) 15–29.

suauio: cf. Prop. 2.29.39 (Cynthia) *opposita propellens suauia dextra.* *suauium* (only here in H.) and *basium* (not in H.) are colloquial, the 'correct' term being *osculum* (*C.* 1.13.15, 36.6, 2.12.25, 3.5.41; cf. Axelson (1945) 35). There is probably a play on the etymology (Gowers (1993) 306): Maecenas' *suauium* will be anything but *suaue*. Cf. the 'god' Suauisauiatio (Pl. *Bac.* 116, 120). H. avoids elision of long vowels (*suaui(o) opponat*) in his lyric and *Epistles* (cf. 22n., 2.9, 4.1, 5.9, 8.15, 15.12, 17.24).

22 extrema et: it seems natural to take *extrema* as abl. agreeing with *sponda*, 'on the outermost (part of the) bed frame' (cf. *Ep.* 1.1.6, Prop. 3.21.8 (Cynthia) *extremo dormit amicta toro*), rather than as nom. with *puella* (L. Mueller), 'the girl as far (from M.) as possible'. The objection to the abl. is that this is the only case in the *Epodes* of a long vowel elided at a verse position that requires a short. But H. allows such elisions in his other works (*C.* 3.4.17, 5.21, 25× in the *Satires*, *Ep.* 1.2.29, 7.24, 14.37, 18.112, 2.2.69; cf. Soubiran (1966) 207–18, 310–15). For the postponed *et*, cf. 1.12n.

sponda: lit. 'frame' or 'edge' of the bed. The girl will be even further away than Propertius' reluctant Cynthia *extremo ... toro* (above). *sponda* is a rare word of uncertain origin, and H. could be making a kind of metrical joke: *sponda* forms a 'spondee' (cf. *Ars* 256) in the last (*extrema*) place in the last dimeter in the poem where such a foot can occur.

EPODE 4

Introduction

The speaker is the 'natural enemy' of a man who seems to have been a criminal but now parades his wealth. The loiterers on the Sacra Via also declare their anger at this ex-slave taking a choice seat in the theatre and serving as tribune of the soldiers at the very time when a war against slaves is imminent.

The date of the epode is uncertain, and could be before either Naulochus or Actium, with its position in the book suggesting the latter (17–20, 19nn.). Its unnamed target has been identified (Porph., Schol., MS titles) as Pompeius Menas, an ex-slave of Pompey who became an *eques* (Dio 48.45.7) and was a naval commander for Sex. Pompeius before defecting to Octavian in time to be on the winning side at Naulochus (9.10n., Pelling on Plut. *Ant.* 32.1, 35, Reinhold on Dio 49.1.4.). But there is no evidence that this man, who died well before Actium (Dio 49.37.6), was ever a *tribunus militum* (20), and it seems more likely that the attack here is on a stock figure (Jacoby (1914) 459).

In this respect the poem resembles other Epodes (1.33–4n.) and also a number of early Greek *iambi* involving 'exemplary characters' (Intro. 3), but is less like a poem of Anacreon (fr. 388 *PMG*, a lyric attack on an upstart) and various Latin invectives to which it has been compared, where the targets are named or readily identifiable as real people (e.g. Cat. 28, 29, 33, 39, 40, 42, 54, 57, 93, 94, 97, 98, 108, 113, 114, 115, Calvus, frr. 17, 18 *FPL*, *Cat.* 10, 13).

Another 'iambic' or at least 'Archilochean' aspect of the poem is that both the speaker and the 'crowd' (9–10) seem even more reprehensible than the upstart they attack (1–10, 2, 3–4, 11–20nn.; cf. 2

intro.). It is possible that the speaker is not H. at all: the opinion of ex-slaves expressed here is quite different from H.'s own (6n.), and the resentment against the man's military tribunate resembles that experienced by H. himself (20n.). Since there is no indication of the speaker's sex it could even be a woman (cf. 1.7, 12.9nn., *C*. 3.12 (a girl's monody)). Perhaps he or she is supposed to 'represent' narrow-minded snobs whose loathing for fellow Romans would be particularly disturbing and dangerous in a time of civil strife.

1–10 The enemy is initially presented as an alien who belongs, as it were, to a different species or, with less hyperbole, is possibly of foreign (3n.) or slave (3–4n.) origin. Yet it turns out that this creature wears, with ludicrous ostentation, but evidently as his right, a toga, the mark of a Roman citizen (8n.). The speaker's hatred is thus directed against a *fellow Roman*, and for no better reasons than the man's supposed *genus*, good fortune, and manner of walking down the street.

For the possibility that the speaker is not H., cf. 4 intro.

1 Lupis et agnis: dat. with *obtigit* (below). The word order seems to indicate that the speaker (*mihi*) corresponds to the sheep, the enemy (*tecum*) to the wolves, which suggests that he is a figure like Lycambes, Archilochus' 'wolf-dancer' adversary (6.13n.). For wolves and the enmity of wolves and sheep, cf. 2.60, 6.2, 7.11–2, 12.25–6, 15.7, *C*. 3.18.13, Ov. *Ib*. 43–4 *pax erit haec nobis, donec mihi uita manebit,* | *cum pecore infirmo quae solet esse lupis*, and (H.'s model?) Hom. *Il*. 22.262–5 (Achilles to Hector) 'as there are no pacts between lions and men, | nor do wolves and sheep have agreement, | but they always hate each other, | so it is not for me and you to be friends'.

sortito obtigit 'was assigned by lot', a 'lot' (*sors*) of fate or nature not subject to *fortuna* (6). Cf. Pl. *Merc*. 136 (of a disaster) *tibi sortito id obtigit*, and H.'s use of *sors* and *sortior* at 14.15, *C*. 2.3.27, 3.1.15, *S*. 2.6.93–4 *terrestria quando* | *mortalis animas uiuunt sortita, Ars* 219, 403.

Both *sortito* (only here) and *obtingo* (Cat. 107.1, Sen. *Tro*. 980) are rare in verse outside of comedy. In prose they are used of legal and public assignments and allotments (*OLD* s.vv.), and rather than being unpoetic here (Axelson (1945) 69, Blok (1961) 60), they may have a quasi-official air in keeping with other political language in the poem (2, 5, 10, 11, 19). For the elided long vowel, cf. 3.21n.

2 tecum mihi: in H., as in most Latin, the normal order is *ego et tu* and not, as in English, 'you and I'. When H. inverts the order elsewhere, it seems to be significant, showing real or mock deference (*C.* 2.6.21, *S.* 2.5.33, *Ep.* 1.7.15, 16.16, 2.2.79, *Ars* 103) or indicating that one person is of lower status than the other (*S.* 2.7.40, 75, 80–1 (Davus to H.)). Here the inversion serves the metre, but it also aligns *tecum* with *lupis*, *mihi* with *agnis* (1n.), and may suggest that the speaker considers the addressee somewhat formidable.

discordia: at first sight, this would seem to indicate a private feud (cf. *S.* 1.7.15, Pl. *Truc.* 420, Ter. *Hec.* 693, Cic. *Q.fr.* 2.6.2). But as it becomes clear that this enmity is 'natural' (1n.) and not personal, and that – at least according to the speaker – it is felt by many other people, H.'s audience might think of the main sense of *discordia* in the late Republic: 'it designates above all oppositions of a general type that occur within the state, and thus is found in such phrases as *discordia ciuium, ciuitatis, ciuilis*' (Hellegouarc'h (1972) 134). Cf. Virg. *Ecl.* 1.71–2 *en quo discordia ciuis | produxit miseros*, Thomas on *G.* 2.496 *infidos agitans discordia fratres*.

3–4 The speaker says that the adversary was scarred by ropes and fetters; the crowd, on the other hand, cites the whips of the *triumuiri* (11–12). The contradiction may be meant to suggest that both are ignorant of the true cause, and that their accounts are malicious inventions. Since the man makes no effort to hide his scars, and seems even to flaunt them (3n.), it is possible that, despite his enemies' claims, he acquired them honourably.

3 Hibericis ... funibus: ropes woven from *spartum*, a plant common in the Iberian region (Plin. *Nat.* 19.26) and still called 'Spanish broom'. Since such ropes were used especially on ships (Plin. *Nat.* 19.30), the speaker may be hinting that the upstart got his scars at sea, perhaps as a galley slave (Orelli). Cf. Petr. 105.4, where *nautae* on a ship beat Encolpius and Giton with *funes*. Rope was sometimes used in floggings at Rome (Pl. *Pers.* 282 (to a slave) *caedere hodie tu restibus*, [Hor.] *S.* 1.10.5*–6* (school punishment?)), but the normal instruments were whips (11n.), clubs (*S.* 1.3.101, 134, 5.23, 2.3.112, Brink on *Ep.* 2.1.154), and rods (*S.* 2.7.58, *OLD* s.v. *uirga* 2, P. Garnsey, *Social status and legal privilege in the Roman Empire* (Oxford 1970) 136–41).

Hibericis: lit. of the *funes*, but the epithet may also suggest that the man himself is a Spaniard (Naylor, Buechner (1970) 57). Cf. Cic. *Phil.* 11.12 (attack on a new senator) *accedit Saxa nescio quis, quem nobis Caesar ex ultima Celtiberia tribunum plebis dedit, castrorum antea metator, nunc, ut sperat, urbis: a qua cum sit alienus, suo capiti saluis nobis ominetur,* Opelt (1965) 149–51.

Hibericus is well-suited to iambs, yet since it occurs only here, at Var. *Men.* 403 (prose?), and in some later prose, its stylistic level cannot be determined (Blok (1961) 61). More usual are *Hibernus,* especially in verse (*C.* 1.29.15, *S.* 2.8.46, Lucil. 426 *ROL* etc.), and *Hispanus,* especially in prose (but cf. *C.* 3.6.31, 8.21, 14.3, Skutsch on Enn. *Ann.* 471). Silius seems to have coined *Hiberiacus* (13.510) for his hexameter.

peruste: both 'seared by beating' (*S.* 2.7.58 *uri uirgis, Ep.* 1.16.47 *loris non ureris,* Cat. 25.11 (11n.)), and 'chafed by manacles' (*Ep.* 1.10.42–3 *calceus ... uret,* 13.6 *uret sarcina*). For another use of *peruro,* cf. 2.41n.; for the tmesis at pos. 5 (*per|uste*), 1.19n.

latus | et crura: accusatives of respect ('Greek acc.') with *peruste.* The construction is poetic; cf. 5.16, LHS II 36–8.

The man's *crura* are probably exposed as he walks (8n.), but for his *latus* with its scars to be visible he must not be wearing the usual tunic under his toga (D–S V 347–52). Omitting or removing the tunic was an ancient practice (Plin. *Nat.* 34.23) affected by later Romans either to show their old-fashioned virtue (Brink, Rudd on *Ars* 50) or to elicit sympathy in trials by allowing the crowd to see their battle scars (Cic. *de Or.* 2.124, 195, Ogilvie on Liv. 2.23.4, Quint. *Inst.* 2.15.7).

4 dura compede: cf. Tib. 1.7.42 (echoing H.?) *crura licet dura compede pulsa sonent.* The sing. *compede* is poetic (N–H on *C.* 1.33.14, 4.11.24, *Ep.* 1.3.3, *ThLL* III 2059); H. has the pl. only at *Ep.* 1.16.77 (cf. Ov. *Am.* 2.2.47, *Ep.* 20.85).

5 licet 'although'; cf. 15.19n.

superbus: a term of opprobrium, especially in political contexts (2.7n.).

ambules 'strut' (*OLD* s.v. 4), a manner of walking that H. found particularly hateful (5.71, 8.14 (cf. 17.41), *S.* 1.2.25, 4.51, 66). There may be a reference here to Cat. 29.6–7 (of Mamurra) *et ille nunc superbus et superfluens | perambulabit omnium cubilia;* cf. 5.69n. *ambulo* is unpoetic and possibly colloquial (Blok (1961) 65, *ThLL* I 1870).

pecunia: cf. *Ep.* 1.6.36–7 *scilicet uxorem cum dote fidemque et amicos | et genus et formam regina Pecunia donat.*

6 fortuna 'good luck' (*C.* 1.31.10, 37.11, 3.27.75, 4.4.71, *S.* 1.9.45, *Ep.* 1.5.12, 8.17, 2.1.32), but still only luck (*C.* 1.34, 3.29.49–56). Cf. 13.7n.

genus '(low) birth'; cf. *C.* 2.4.15, 4.7.23, *S.* 2.5.8, *Ep.* 1.6.37 (5n.), 20.22. The speaker's view of the importance of ancestry is very different from that expressed by H. in *S.* 1.6 (4 intro.).

7 Sacram ... Viam: the main street of ancient Rome, running from the Velia through the Forum to the Capitoline (Richardson (1992) 338–40). It was the scene of processions (7.8), but also 'a fashionable place for loungers' (Page). Cf. *S.* 1.9.1.

metiente: even when used of walking *metior* never loses its primary sense of 'measure' (*ThLL* VIII 883, 887; cf. Cic. *Phil.* 11.12 (3n.)). Perhaps the man uses the remarkable 'measurements' of his toga (8n.) as a gauge for his strides.

8 bis trium ulnarum: gen. of quality (5.41, 12.3, 16.9). *ulna* as a measure occurs chiefly in verse (Blok (1961) 66) as an equivalent to either a cubit (*c.* 1.5 feet) or a fathom (6 feet; cf. *RE* IXA 559–63). Unless the speaker wildly exaggerates, the meaning here must be six cubits (9 feet). Most commentators rightly take this of the width of the toga, evident because it billows as the man walks, thus exposing his *crura* (3n.). For sizes of togas, cf. *S.* 1.3.14, 31 (below), 2.3.77, *Ep.* 1.1.96, 14.32, 18.30, 19.13, Smith on Tib. 1.6.40, D–S v 348. Some argue that the problem is not with the toga's width, but with its length, as at *S.* 1.3.31 (*amico*) *rusticius tonso toga defluit* (*diffluit* Sh. Bailey). But a man with a toga dragging on the ground could hardly *ambulare* or *metiri*.

trium: the MSS offer the adverb *ter*, but 'twice thrice' would not be normal Latin, and it seems necessary to amend to the adj. (Barth), which is perhaps implied by the comments (but not the *lemmata*) in the scholia (*cum bis ter ulnarum toga, hoc est cum sex ulnarum toga* (Porph.), *ter ulnarum toga: sex enim ulnis habebat diffusam togam* (Schol.)). The corruption may have arisen from a misunderstood abbreviation.

toga: the first indication that the man not only lives in Rome, but is a Roman citizen. Cf. *C.* 3.5.10, *Ep.* 2.1.57, Enn. *Ann.* 514 Skutsch *dum quidem unus homo Romanus toga superescit,* Virg. *A.* 1.282 *Romanos, rerum dominos gentemque togatam, OLD* s.vv. *toga* 5, *togatus* 3.

9–10 Appeal to the anonymous *uox populi* is a device as old as Homer (e.g. *Il.* 2.271–7) and Archilochus (fr. 172.3–4 West (App. 1)). The effect here may be to 'objectify' the speaker's disgust by suggesting that, since it is shared by others, it is justified (Jacoby (1914) 460).

9 ora uertat: their anger causes the passers-by to stare at the man. Cf. Brink on *Ep.* 2.1.196 *elephans albus uulgi conuerteret ora*, Var. *R.* 2.1.22 *cum conuertissent in eum ora omnes*, *OLD* s.v. *conuerto* 5d. The interpretations of Porph., *significant autem populum ex indignatione ... detorquere ab illo aspectum* (i.e. they look away in anger) and Peerlkamp (so also K–H), 'indignatio mutat colorem, qui est in ore et uultu' are less natural; cf. Horsfall (1973) 136–7. *uerto* for *conuerto* seem to be a case of '*uerbum simplex pro composito*', a colloquial but also poetic usage (Ruckdeschel (1910) 1 25–31, Bo III 387–9). Cf. 5.54 (*uerto* for *auerto*), 58 (*latro* for *adlatro*), 13.7 (*mitto* for *omitto*), 14.3 (*duco* for *adduco*), 17.56 (*rideo* for *derideo*).

huc et huc euntium: the other 'loungers' (7n.) on the Sacra Via. *huc et huc* is poetic for *huc et illuc* (2.31n.).

10 liberrima 'most free' in expressing itself, as is proved by the speech that follows. Cf. 11.16, 26, *S.* 1.3.52, 4.5, 90, 103, 132, 2.7.4, 8.37, *Ep.* 1.18.1, Brink on *Ep.* 2.1.147, *Ars* 282. There may also be a play on *liber* in the sense 'free-born', since the crowd thinks (3–4n.) that the target of their *indignatio* is a *libertinus* (Miles).

indignatio: cf. Cic. *Inv.* 1.100 *indignatio est oratio per quam conficitur ut in aliquem hominem magnum odium aut in rem grauis offensio concitetur*. For *indignatio* and related terms (the word itself occurs in verse only here and at Juv. 1.79, 5.120) in Roman rhetoric and satire, cf. W. S. Anderson, *Essays on Roman satire* (Princeton 1982) 423–7.

11–20 The marks of a renegade slave are on the man, yet he owns a great estate and wears out the road visiting it. In the theatre he sits in the orchestra – and by right, for he is an *eques*. Why war against brigands and slaves when this man is a tribune of the soldiers?

The crowd's hatred of the man seems to be based, not on anything he has done, but on their interpretation – possibly erroneous (3–4n.) – of his scars, on the signs of his prosperity, and on his high status at Rome and in the army. It is as irrational as that of the speaker (1–10n.) and even more sinister, since it leads them to confuse this fellow citizen, *eques*, and commander of troops with the real enemy (4 intro.).

11 flagellis: the whip (*flagrum, flagellum, lorum*) was the instrument of choice for punishing slaves or, because of that association, for adding insult to injury of citizens. Cf. *C.* 3.5.35, *S.* 1.2.41, 3.119, *Ep.* 1.16.47, [Hor.] *S.* 1.10.5*, Kroll on Cat. 25.11 *inusta turpiter tibi flagella conscribillent*, Garnsey (3n.) 137.

triumuiralibus: the *tres* (*trium*, III) *uiri capitales* or *nocturni* were minor magistrates responsible for 'keeping the peace' by imprisoning or inflicting corporal punishment on criminals and renegade slaves. Cf. Pl. *Am.* 153–6 (the slave Sosia) *qui me alter est audacior homo ... qui hoc noctis solus ambulem? | quid faciam nunc si tresuiri me in carcerem compegerint? | ind' cras quasi e promptaria cella depromar ad flagrum*, Crook (1967) 69.

triumuiralibus is one of only three 'sesquipedalian' or longer words in the *Epodes* (8.13, 13.10, cf. *Ars* 97). It may be intended to add solemnity here, as if the crowd were pronouncing sentence on the man. Cf. E. Staedler, *Glotta* 27 (1939) 199–206, Blok (1961) 68–9.

12 praeconis: it is not clear which of the various types of *praeco* is indicated here. Among the possibilities are (1) an auctioneer (*S.* 1.6.86, 2.2.47, *Ep.* 1.7.56, Brink on *Ars* 419, *RE* XXIII 1198–9) 'disgusted' (*S.* 2.2.14, 4.78, 6.86, *OLD* s.v. *fastidium* 3) because the man's scars will lower his sale value (Miles); (2) a bailiff in the service of the *tresuiri* (11n.) 'weary' (s.v. 2) of proclaiming this habitual offender's crimes and punishments (Orelli, K–H). There is no other evidence for such a functionary, but *praecones* were part of the praetor's retinue at trials (*RE* XXIII 1194, 1197); (3) a herald (*RE* 1196) who, while summoning the people to the theatre (15–16), displays his 'contempt' (12.13, *Ep.* 1.10.25, 2.1.215, *OLD* s.v. 4) for this creature about to take one of the best seats (Miles); (4) an announcer of elections (*RE* 1196) 'revolted' at finding the man's name among the candidates for *tribunus militum* (20n.).

ad fastidium: with *sectus*, 'cut to the point of (arousing) disgust'. This seems to be the first instance of *ad* with *fastidium* (*ThLL* VI 318), but cf. *S.* 1.2.41–2 *flagellis | ad mortem caesus*, *OLD* s.v. *ad* 12.

13 arat 'has under cultivation' (*S.* 1.1.51 (below), *OLD* s.v. 1b).

Falerni ... fundi: an especially lucrative property; the *ager*

Falernus in Campania was famous for its wine (N–H on *C.* 1.20.10, 27.10, 2.3.8, 6.19, 11.19, 3.1.43, *S.* 1.10.24, 2.2.15, 3.115, 4.19, 24, 55, 8.16, *Ep.* 1.14.34, 18.91 (if genuine; cf. Klingner's app. crit.), Mynors on Virg. *G.* 2.96, White (1970) 72–3). An absentee owner would travel there by the Via Appia (14).

mille ... iugera: *c.* 750 acres (*OLD* s.v. *iugerum*), a sizeable estate. Cf. *S.* 1.1.49–51 *dic quid referat intra | naturae finis uiuenti, iugera centum an | mille aret?* For *mille* as a large round number, cf. *C.* 3.7.12, *S.* 2.1.4, 3.70, 116, 226, 325, *Ep.* 1.6.19.

14 mannis: 'Gaulish ponies much prized for their speed' (Kenney on Lucr. 3.1063 (the restless man) *currit agens mannos ad uillam praecipitanter*). Cf. *C.* 3.27.7, *Ep.* 1.7.77.

terit: cf. 16.1n. *tero* in the sense 'wear out (a road)' seems to be poetic (Cic. *Arat.* 236, Lucr. 1.927, Virg. *G.* 1.380, Ov. *Ars* 1.491).

15–16 The tribune L. Roscius Otho's *lex Roscia theatralis* (67 BC) reserved orchestra seats (15n.) for members of the equestrian order, defined, for this purpose, if not in general, as citizens (15n.) with at least (16n.) 400,000 HS (*Ep.* 1.1.62, Cic. *Mur.* 40, *Phil.* 2.44 etc., Asc. 78 Clark, Vell. 2.32.3, Liv. *Per.* 99, Juv. 3.153–8, 14.323–4; cf. H. Hill, *The Roman middle class in the Republican period* (Oxford 1952) 111, 160).

15 sedilibusque ... in primis: an exaggeration; in fact the seats were the fourteen rows behind those reserved for the senators. According to Porph., *ex quattuordecim autem ordinibus, quos lege Roscia Otho tribunus plebis in theatro equestri ordini dedit, duo primi ordines tribuniciis* [i.e. *tribunis militum*] *uacabant*, but there is no other evidence for this, and it may be an inference based on 19–20.

The *figura etymologica* (LHS II 790–3) *sedilibus ... sedet* is one of four in the *Epodes* (5.75–6, 89, 9.10–14, cf. 10.8n.); H. uses the device more often in the *Odes* (G. Huber, *Wortwiederholung in den Oden des Horaz* (Zurich 1970)). *sedile* is a 'poetic and silver word' (Brink on *Ars* 205; cf. Virg. *G.* 4.350, *A.* 1.167, 5.837, 8.176, Blok (1961) 72).

eques: not being full citizens, *libertini* technically were not eligible for equestrian status, although their sons, including H. himself, were (S. Treggiari, *Roman freedmen during the late Republic* (Oxford 1969) 64–5, Armstrong (1986) 256–63). This man may have evaded the legal restrictions, as seems to have been the case with Pompeius Menas (4 intro.) and others during the chaos of the Triumviral period (Treggiari 65). But it is also possible that his slave origin is an invention of his enemies (3–4n.) and that he is an *eques* and *tribunus militum* (19–20) by right.

16 Othone contempto: an indication of how wealthy the man is. The law stipulated a minumum *census* of 400,000 HS (15–16n.): 'quisquis igitur [as this man] supra illum censum longe euectus fuit, contemnere potuit Othonem, et legi eius impune oppedere' (Bentley). Some (Jacoby (1914) 454–62, Miles) prefer the conjecture (ed. Veneta 1478) *contento*, 'with Otho satisfied', i.e. in accordance with the law. But this would make the verse an 'unmotivated attack', not on the upstart, but on the *lex Roscia* itself (K–H).

contempto: cf. *C.* 3.16.25, *S.* 1.1.65, 4.68, 10.77, 2.3.14, 5.36, 7.85, *Ep.* 1.1.29, 50. *contemno* (2× in the lyrics, 8× in the hexameters) seems to be more prosaic than *sperno* (6.13), which is preferred by H. in the *Odes* and by a number of other Latin poets (Blok (1961) 72–3).

17–20 The arrangement of the Epode book suggests that these lines refer to the war against Antony and not, as most commentators suppose, that against Sex. Pompeius. Cf. 19n., Intro. 4.

17 quid attinet 'what does it achieve'; cf. *C.* 1.19.12, 3.23.13, *S.* 2.2.27. *attineo* may be an unpoetic word (Axelson (1945) 101, Blok (1961) 73), but cf. Ov. *Ep.* 1.2 (*attamen* MSS: *attinet* Aphthonius, Goold).

ora nauium: lit. 'faces of ships', a novel expression in Latin (*ThLL* IX 1092), but cf. Virg. *A.* 5.157–8 [*naues*] *ambae iunctisque feruntur | frontibus*, Prop. 3.22.14 (of *Argo*) *in faciem prorae pinus adacta nouae*. Greek and sometimes Roman ships were described and pictured as having 'cheeks', 'eyes' and 'noses' (Hom. *Il.* 2.367, *Od.* 9.125, 11.124, Aesch. *Suppl.* 716, 743–4, *Pers.* 559–60, O. Crusius, *Rh.M.* 44 (1889) 451).

The repetition of *ora* (9) seems unmotivated, unless the ships are supposed to mimic the angry stares of the crowd.

17–18 graui | . . . pondere: the phrase suggests larger warships rather than Liburni (1.1n.). Commentators cite Dio 49.1.1–2 on the preparations for the war against Sex. Pompeius, but Octavian also had such ships in his fleet at Actium (Pelling on Plut. *Ant.* 6.14, Reinhold on Dio 50.18.6, 31.1–35.6).

18 rostrata: having *rostra*, 'beaks', for ramming other ships (*OLD* s.v. *rostrum* 2b). *rostratus* is rare in verse (Enn. (?) *Ann. spuria* 9 Skutsch, Virg. *A.* 8.684) but in prose occurs mostly in elevated contexts and may be an archaism (Blok (1961) 74).

19 This seems to be appropriate of the rag-tag host of Sex. Pompeius (9.9–10n.), but Antony was also accused of enlisting brigands and slaves (Pelling on Plut. *Ant.* 61.1, 62.1).

latrones: lit. 'brigands' (*S.* 1.3.106 (cf. 122), 4.67, 69, 2.1.42, *Ep.* 1.2.32), but *latro* was also a term of abuse often applied to dangerous citizens such as Catiline, Clodius, and Antony (*OLD* s.v. 2b, Opelt (1965) 132–2). After Ennius (Skutsch on *Ann.* 57) *latro* seems to be an unpoetic word (Blok (1961) 74).

atque: for unelided *atque*, cf. 2.40n.

seruilem manum: for Antony's slaves and slavery, cf. 9.12n. *seruilis* (*S.* 1.8.32, 2.7.111) appears to be another unpoetic word (Blok (1961) 74).

20 hoc, hoc: the *anadiplosis* (*geminatio*, 'doubling') indicates strong emotion; cf. 5.5n., 53, 71, 6.11, 7.1, 11.2–3, 21, 14.6, 15.23, 16.41–2, 64–5, 17.2–4, N–H on *C.* 2.14.1, Bo III 397–8.

tribuno militum: since military tribunes normally served on land (*RE* VIA 2439–45), it appears that the coming war will be fought *terra marique*. This suits Actium (9.27n.) better than Naulochus (9.7–10n).

The man's attainment of the military tribunate arouses indignation because (1) as senior officers in the legions military tribunes, whatever their ancestry (15n.), commanded Roman citizens, and (2) although less important than in earlier times, the office was still a stepping stone for *noui homines* towards senatorial status (T. P. Wiseman, *New men in the Roman senate* (Oxford 1971) 143–7). Twenty-four of the military tribunes were elected by the people; it is thus possible that the crowd is also angry because their own votes are at least partly to blame for their enemy's ascent. For the *inuidia* directed at H. because of his own military tribunate (Intro. 1), cf. *S.* 1.6.46–8.

EPODE 5

Introduction

A kidnapped boy asks his captors, a group of witches, why they threaten him. They ignore him and go about preparing to torture him to death and turn parts of him into a love potion. Their leader Canidia prays to her gods and announces that a previous love charm directed against a certain Varus has failed, but that the man will not escape her new magic. The boy speaks again, this time to curse the witches, predict that his ghost will haunt them, and prophesy that a mob will stone them and leave their bodies for scavengers.

The circumstances of the boy's kidnapping are not given, and he is not identified except as a citizen (7n.) whose parents are living (101). His abductors are witches with appropriate names (15, 25, 29, 41–4nn.), but Canidia, at least, has the look of a Roman matron (5–10, 9, 57, 73nn.), and the setting is probably her house near the Subura and Esquiline (11, 29, 53, 58, 69–70, 100nn.). The purpose of her magic, if not all of its details, is clear, to bring back her lover or husband (73n.) from his 'mistresses'. But its results are quite different: it is not said whether Varus returns, but the innocent boy is transformed into a supernatural force of vengeance.

The poem's form, third person narrative 'enclosing' direct speech by characters 'saying the worst things about themselves' (2 intro.), was once thought to be 'un-iambic', but it is now evident that this kind of thing, although later associated with mime, bucolic, and the 'novel' (Fedeli (1978) 101), also figured in early Greek *iambus* (59–60n., Intro. 3; cf. Arch. frr. 23, 30–49, 176–7, 187, 196a, Hipp. frr. 25, 92 West, West (1974) 32). *Iambus* was likewise interested in magic (Hipp. frr. 78, 92, 104 West, West (1974) 142–5), as was other early Greek poetry (22n. 17.17n. (Circe), Ingallina (1974) 24–32, Tupet (1976) 107–50).

H. may have drawn on these, perhaps on Hellenistic poetry (Theocr. *Id.* 2 (cf. 58n., Fedeli (1978) 67–97)), and on more immediate sources, including 'curse tablets' (17.2n.), papyri (5.15, 17–18, 19, 20, 23, 37–8, 39, 45–6, 48, 51, 59, 17.4nn.), and, possibly, his own experience (5.37n.; cf. 17.58). Magic was common in Rome at all periods, including the late Republic (Ingallina (1974) 16–24, Liebeschuetz (1979) 126–39, 226–7). In 29 BC Maecenas is supposed to have advised Octavian to 'hate and punish those alienating Roman religion ... (and) not permit anyone to be an atheist or sorcerer ... and not permit there to be any magicians' (Dio 52.36.1–3).

Although usually operating in private and secret, magic can threaten society when it seems to attack or 'travesty' more approved forms of ritual ('religion'). It is possible that Canidia's chief sorcery here is such a travesty, in this case of the Matronalia celebrated on

the Kalends of March in honour of Juno Lucina (6n.) in her temple
on the Esquiline (11–28, 15, 52nn.; cf. *RE* x 1115–16, Scullard (1981)
85–7, Richardson (1992) 214–15). This feast was restricted to women
(but cf. Macr. 6.4.13 (men in disguise)), and seems to have been
aimed at promoting fertility and family continuity, something a rov-
ing husband (73n.) might disrupt. It may be significant that Archi-
lochus seems to have described some sort of profanation of a sanc-
tuary of Hera (= Juno), perhaps at Thasos (Diosc. *AP* 7.351.7–8
(= Arch. frr. 30–87 West); cf. Gentili (1988) 188–90).

With all this, Epode 5 still remains one of the most mysterious
poems in Latin. It has been interpreted as an 'exposé' of actual sor-
cerous activity, as an entertaining 'ghost story' (cf. the imitation
'Lost hearts' in M. R. James' *Ghost stories of an antiquary* (London
1904)), and as some kind of 'symbolic' narrative. Much depends on
the identification of Canidia (App. 2). If she represents Rome itself
or some other force whose 'charms' both allure and destroy, then the
most significant image may be that of the boy, whose murder seems
in a sense to repeat and perpetuate the curse arising from the mur-
der of Remus (7.19–20).

1–10 The speaker is a young boy, alone and frightened by the noise
and hostile faces of four women. He 'sees dimly that the hags have
some dreadful intent; though he knows not what' (Wickham). In the
sequel that intent is revealed (32–40), but not the identity of the boy,
how he was abducted, or why he was singled out as a victim. The
boy's anonymity magnifies the horror: it suggests that any Roman
child (or Roman?) could be transformed from an innocent suppliant
into a vengeful fiend.

1–2 At ... genus: an exclamation, like 'good lord!' or 'oh my
god!', rather than a true prayer. Both *at* (3.19n.) and *o* (49, 74, 3.4,
10.15, 12.25, 15.11, 17.30, 46, N–H on *C.* 1.9.8) suggest strong emotion.

1 deorum quidquid: cf. *C.* 2.1.25 *deorum quisquis*, where 'the
comprehensive *quisquis* reflects the conventional blanket-clause of
cult' (N–H; cf. their note on *C.* 1.32.15, Appel (1909) 78–9). But the
use of the neuter *quidquid* with the partitive gen. seems to be prosaic
(Cic. *Ver.* 2.135, Liv. 2.5.7, 23.9.3 etc.) and colloquial (*S.* 1.6.1–2, For-
dyce on Cat. 3.2, 9.10, 31.14 *quidquid est domi cachinnorum*, LHS II 52,
56).

caelo: the seat of the gods in the traditional Roman (and Greek) order of things and thus the object of assault by forces such as magic which challenge that order (45–6, 78–9, 13.1–2n., 17.78).

regit: a term from the language of prayer; cf. 51, *C.* 1.3.3, 12.57, 35.1, 3.4.48, *OLD* s.v. 7c.

2 The verse has the sound of a prayer formula; cf. N–H on *C.* 1.12.14, *Ep.* 2.1.7 (heroes) *dum terras hominumque colunt genus*, Pl. *Rud.* 1 (Jupiter) *qui gentes omnes mariaque et terras mouet*, and Arch. fr. 177 West (App. 1), may be H.'s model (Fraenkel (1957) 64).

3 quid ... tumultus: *quid sibi uult hic tumultus* (Porph.). For *fero* in the sense 'convey' a message or meaning, cf. Pl. *Merc.* 161 *quid fers? dic mihi*, Tib. 1.8.1–2 *non ego celari possum, quid nutus amantis | quidue ferant miti lenia uerba sono*, *OLD* s.v. 26a, d. The interpretation 'what (evil) does it bring' (*ThLL* VI 549), although supported by parallels in H. (*S.* 1.4.130, 2.2.76, 96, *Ars* 175), seems less appropriate to the context.

iste 'this (your)', addressed to Canidia (5–6n.). *iste* is colloquial and, for most authors, unpoetic (Axelson (1945) 71, LHS II 184). H. uses it 24× in his hexameter verse, but only here in his lyrics.

aut: cf. 7.1, *Ep.* 2.1.91, *OLD* s.v. 4. *aut* introducing a question seems to be colloquial (LHS II 465, 498–9). It is more frequently so used than *et* (II 480) which some editors prefer here as less likely to occur to a scribe (*lectio difficilior*). The ellipse of *sunt* after *quid* is also colloquial (1.5n., cf. *S.* 2.3.128, 275, 7.75, 8.2).

3–4 omnium ... in unum me: the four witches 'gang up' on the lone boy. Cf. *C.* 1.36.17–18 *omnes in Damalin putris | deponent oculos*.

4 uoltus ... truces: cf. 93, *C.* 1.2.39–40 *acer et Mauri peditis cruentum | uoltus in hostem*. For *trux*, cf. 2.5n.

5–8 per ... | per ... | per: the repetition of words (*anadiplosis*; cf. 4.20n.) is a regular feature of prayer language. Cf. 53, 71, 17.2–4, 7, 9–10, 25, 38–9, 42–3, N–H on *C.* 2.19.7, Norden on Virg. *A.* 6.46.

5–6 The boy singles out Canidia (*te*), evidently because she looks like a *matrona* (9, 73n.) who would be susceptible to appeals *per liberos*. There is no indication in this poem whether she actually has children, but cf. 17.50–2.

5 per liberos: cf. 2.40n., Ter. *An.* 538–40 *per te deos oro et nostram amicitiam ... | perque unicam gnatam tuam et gnatum meum*.

te: emphatic at the caesura and because dislocated from what seems to be the idiomatic word order, which in such phrases puts the pronoun between *per* and its object (N–H on *C.* 1.8.2 *per omnis | te deos oro*, Ter. *An.* 538 (above)).

5–6 uocata ... adfuit: more prayer-language. For *uoco = inuoco*, cf. *C.* 1.2.25, 43, 14.10, 30.2, 32.16, 2.18.40, 3.22.3, 4.5.13, *S.* 1.8.33; for *adsum = tueor, iuuo*, 53, *C.* 3.21.21, 27.66, *S.* 2.6.15, *ThLL* II 923, Appel (1909) 115–16.

6 Lucina: protector of women in childbirth, identified with Greek Ilithyia (*Saec.* 13), Diana (Cat. 34.13–14, Virg. *Ecl.* 4.10), and especially Juno (*RE* x 1115–17, XIII 1648–51). The temple of Juno Lucina on the Esquiline was the site of the Matronalia on the first of March (Scullard (1981) 85; cf. 5 intro.).

ueris: i.e. if she has any children that are her own and not, like the speaker, kidnapped (Plessis). Cf. Prop 2.9.17–18 (if the text is sound) *tunc* [during the Trojan war] *ueris gaudebat Graecia natis, | tunc etiam felix inter et arma pudor*. The slur on Canidia, for which H. 'apologizes' in his palinode (17.50–2), strikes some critics as inappropriate among the *mollia uerba* (83–4) of a young boy. But it is no worse than the ensuing comparisons with a stepmother and a wild beast, and there seems to be no reason to suppose that 'the biting mockery is only possible in the mouth of the poet [in his own person]' (K–H), or that there is some kind of double meaning (Orelli), or that *ueris* should be emended to *uentris* (Peerlkamp).

7 inane: both 'empty' (*C.* 2.20.21, 3.11.26, *S.* 1.6.127, 2.2.14, 7.9) because stripped off the boy (12) and, as he fears, 'useless' (6.3, *S.* 1.2.113, 2.3.212, *Ep.* 1.17.41, 2.2.206, *Ars* 230, 443) to protect him.

purpurae = *uestis purpurea* (2.20n., N–H on *C.* 2.18.8, 3.1.42, 4.13.13, *OLD* s.v. 3), in this case the *toga praetexta* with its purple stripe worn by Roman magistrates and by citizen boys until they 'assumed' the *toga uirilis* of maturity. The *praetexta*, like the *bulla* (12n.), was thought to have protective power: cf. Plin. *Nat.* 9.127 (*purpura*) *pro maiestate pueritiae est*, Pers. 5.30 (12n.), Quint. *Decl.* 340 *sacrum praetextarum ... quo infirmitatem pueritiae sacram facimus ac uenerabilem*, Bömer on Ov. *F.* 3.771.

decus: the use of *decus* with a defining gen. seems to be elevated, if not poetic (*C.* 1.1.2, 32.13, N–H on 2.17.4, 3.16.20, 25.5, 4.6.27, *ThLL* v 237).

8 improbaturum: litotes or *extenuatio* ('understatement'; cf. Cic.

De or. 3.202, Quint. *Inst.* 9.2.3) for *uindicaturum* or the like. *improbo* occurs only here in H. and appears to be unpoetic (*ThLL* VII 686). For the future part., cf. 1.22n.

Iouem: the boy's death while still *praetextatus* (7n.) would anger Jupiter who, along with Iuuentas and Liber Pater, governed the transition to the *toga uirilis* (Wissowa (1912) 135–6).

9 nouerca: stepmothers are assumed to be hostile to their acquired children. Cf. *C.* 3.24.17–18, West on Hes. *Op.* 825, Eur. *Alc.* 309–10, Pl. *Ps.* 313–14, Cat. 64.402, Virg. *Ecl.* 3.33, *G.* 2.126–8, 3.283–4 (*nouercae* as poisoners), Sen. *Con.* 4.6 *quid alterum [fratrem] nouercalibus oculis intueris?*, Opelt (1965) 202, A. Gray-Fow, *Lat.* 47 (1988) 741–57, and the American expression 'love (someone) like a stepmother'.

m(e) intueris: the elided long vowel (3.21n.) on a monosyllable is unparalleled in the *Epodes*. *intueor* occurs only here in H., and is rare in verse outside of comedy before the empire.

uti: cf. 37, 81; H.'s use of this older form of *ut* (3× in *Odes*, 11× in *Sat.*, 3× in *Ep.* 1) may be due to the influence of Lucretius, the last poet in whom it occurs with any frequency (83×). Cf. Axelson (1945) 129.

10 For the image, cf. *C.* 1.23.9–10, Hom. *Il.* 11.546 (Ajax) 'retreated, glaring at the throng like a wild beast', Call. *Hymn* 6.50–2.

petita 'attacked' (93, 97, 6.4, 15, *C.* 1.3.38, *S.* 1.2.66, 2.1.39, 52, 55). *belua* is a common term of abuse (*Ep.* 1.1.76, Opelt (1965) 143–4).

11–28 Canidia ignores the boy's plea and begins preparing her sorcery. Her initial acts and those of Sagana, while not without magical significance (19, 20, 23, 24), seem in essence to be travesties of the purifications (*piamina, februa, lustra*) which preceded Roman sacrifices (Tupet (1976) 18–29, 309–10; cf. Bömer on Ov. *F.* 2.19, 25, 35, Wissowa (1912) 390–2).

11 haec: internal acc. (1.23n.) with *questus*; cf. 74n., *OLD* s.v. *queror* 1d.

trementi ... ore: cf. *C.* 4.2.7–8 *profundo ... ore, Ars* 94, 323, Ov. *Tr.* 3.11.54 *ore tremente* (v.l. *gemente*), *ThLL* IX 1080–1. The form *trementi* is unusual for H.: the few cases where he has the *i* ending of the abl. sing. of the pres. part. are either *metri causa* (*C.* 2.3.3, 19.5) or, as seems to be the case here, to avoid too many *e* sounds (*C.* 1.25.17, 2.16.1, *S.* 1.2.30). Otherwise he prefers an *e* ending regardless of whether the form is participial or adjectival in sense (Bo III 97–8, LHS I 438).

consistit: probably 'became quiet' (*OLD* s.v. *consisto* 4), although it could mean 'came to a halt' (s.v. 1, 2), i.e. 'in the courtyard of the house (of Canidia) where he had been dragged' (Kiessling).

12 insignibus: a boy's *insignia* consisted of the *toga praetexta* (7n.) and a *bulla*, a kind of amulet which served both as a sign of free birth and as a charm against evil. Cf. Pers. 5.30–1 *cum primum pauido custos mihi purpura cessit | bullaque succinctis Laribus donata pependit*, *RE* III 1048–51.

13 impube corpus 'a childish shape' (Page), in apposition to *puer*. The phrase seems to be poetic; cf. Austin on Virg. *A.* 6.582–3 *hic et Aloidas geminos immania uidi | corpora*, Skutsch on Enn. *Ann.* 88, and Greek periphrases with *demas* and *sōma* (e.g. Aesch. *Eum.* 84, Eur. *Herc.* 1036, *Tro.* 201). For *impubes*, cf. *C.* 2.9.15, Virg. *A.* 7.382 *impubesque manus*.

13–14 impia | ... pectora: for the transferred epithet, cf. 3.1n. The savagery of the Thracians was proverbial (N–H on *C.* 1.27.2, Arch. fr. 42.1, Hipp. fr. 115 West (App. 1), *RE* VIA 402).

15 Canidia: for the name, cf. App. 2. Its metrical form allows it to begin the verse wherever it occurs in H. (3.8, 5.48, 17.6, *S.* 1.8.24, 2.1.48, 8.95).

breuibus ... uiperis: at *S.* 1.8.54 Priapus calls Canidia and Sagana 'Furies', and here Canidia is depicted with the snaky hair that from Aeschylus on (*Cho.* 1048–9; cf. Paus. 1.28.6) was a feature of those creatures. Cf. N–H on *C.* 2.13.35, Enn. *Sc.* 30 Vahlen, Cat. 64.193, Thomas on Virg. *G.* 4.482–3 *caeruleosque implexae crinibus anguis | Eumenides*, *A.* 7.346, 450, 12.848, Ov. *Ep.* 2.119 *Allecto breuibus torquata colubris*, *PGM* IV 2864 (Selene with snake hair). The resolution at pos. 4 (Intro. 6) may be meant to express the quick movement of the tiny snakes (Giarratano). For vipers in magic, cf. 3.6n.

illigata: this seems preferable to the variant *implicata* because it was known to Porph., is a rarer word (1.25n.), and is more suited to a possible travesty of the rites of Juno Lucina (5 intro.), where women had to *unbind* their hair and any knots on their persons (Bömer on Ov. *F.* 3.257 *siqua tamen grauida est, resoluto crine precetur* (to Lucina), Serv. on Virg. *A.* 4.518 *Iunonis Lucinae sacra non licet accedere nisi solutis nodis*). It is true that at times witches, including Canidia (*S.* 1.8.23–4), mimic rather than mock such unbinding (cf. Virg. *A.* 4.509–21), but in general knots seem to be as essential to magic as their absence is to the traditional cults to which it is opposed (cf. 71, 17.45, 67, 72, *C.* 1.27.23, *S.* 1.8.30–1, 50, Theocr. *Id.* 2.3 (= *HA* 576), Virg. *Ecl.* 8. 77–8, Smith on Tib. 1.8.5, Bömer on Ov. *F.* 2.575, Tupet (1976) 45–8).

16 crinis … caput = *crinis incomptos capitis*, an example of 'hendiadys' (*unum [sensum] in duo diuisit* (Porph. on *C.* 2.15.18–20), cf. 16.42, Kenney on Lucr. 3.346, Apul. *Met.* 4.33.2.8, LHS II 782–3). For the 'Greek' accusatives, cf. 4.3, *C.* 2.7.7–8, 11.15, N–H on *C.* 2.11.23, 4.8.33, 11.5, Brink on *Ep.* 2.1.110 *fronde comas uincti. crinis*, like *coma* (II. 28), is poetic, although H., in contrast with the writers of epic and tragedy, is not averse to the prosaic *capillus* (27, 15.9, 17.23). In this he resembles, or perhaps is followed by, the elegists and Ovid (Axelson (1945) 51).

incomptum: not at odds with *illigata*, as a woman's hair can be 'tied up' yet still 'dishevelled'. Cf. N–H on *C.* 2.11.23.

17–18 For the *arbores purae* of true purifications (Bömer on Ov. *F.* 2.25, Fugier (1963) 81–2, Tupet (1976) 309–10). Canidia substitutes wood from trees associated with death and burial, the wild fig (Prop. 4.5.76, Mart. 10.2.9, Pers. 1.25, Juv. 10.145, *PGM* LXI 59) and the cypress (N–H on *C.* 2.14.23, Skutsch on Enn. *Ann.* 223–4, Plin. *Nat.* 16.139 (*cypressus*) *Diti sacra et ideo funebri signo ad domos posita, PGM* LVII 15).

17 iubet: with *aduri* (24). The hyperbaton is mitigated by the fact that the intervening accusatives could be taken as direct objects of *iubet*. Since they are surrounded by past tenses (11, 31, 49, 86), *iubet* and *horret* (27) must be historical presents.

caprificos: in addition to its funereal associations (17–18n.), the 'goat fig' was thought of as a destructive growth (Pers. 1.25, Juv. 10.145, Isid. *Orig.* 17.7.18 *appellata eo, quod parietes quibus innascitur carpit*), and here may be meant to help 'break down' Varus' defences (Ingallina).

19–24 Cf. Prop. 3.6.25–30 (imitating this passage), where the poet's *puella* complains of another woman's spells: *non me moribus illa, sed herbis improba uicit:* | *staminea rhombi ducitur ille* [Prop.] *rota;* | *illum turgentis ranae portenta rubetae* | *et lecta exsectis* [*exsuctis* Burman (37n.)] *anguibus ossa trahunt* | *et strigis inuentae per busta iacentia plumae* | *cinctaque funesto lanea uitta toro.*

19 uncta ... sanguine 'the eggs of a foul toad smeared with (its own) blood'. Some take *oua* with *strigis* (cf. Ov. *Am.* 1.12.20), but the word order adj. A, adj. B, noun A, noun B forming a self-contained unit has numerous parallels in H. (Naylor; cf. 2.15, 47, 51–2, 55–6, 3.6–7, 4.13, 5.29, 39–40, 61–2, 67–8, 9.23–4, 12.19, 14.1–2, 16.4, 48, 17.66).

turpis ... ranae: probably the *rubeta* (Greek *phrynē*), a type of tree toad (Plin. *Nat.* 8.110). It was used for poisons and their antidotes (Plin. *Nat.* 11.280, 18.303, 25.123, 32.49–52, Juv. 1.70, 6.659, Tupet (1976) 361–3), but also for aphrodisiacs (Prop. 3.6.27 (19–24n.), Plin. *Nat.* 32.52 (73n.)) and possibly other magic (*PGM* III 508). Eggs were also used in magic (Pers. 5.185, Plin. *Nat.* 10.154, 28.19, 30.131, *PGM* XXXVI 283 (crow's eggs)), although there seems to be no parallel for what H. describes here (Tupet (1976) 310). They seem to have figured in purifications (Juv. 6.518, Apul. *Met.* 11.16), and this may be another travesty.

20 plumamque ... strigis: Propertius (19–24n.) interprets this as a love charm (cf. Petr. 134.1, where *striges* are blamed for Encolpius' impotence), but it may be directed against the boy, since *striges* were thought to attack small children (Bömer on Ov. *F.* 6.131, Titin. *inc. fab.* xxii Ribbeck *si forte premet strix atra puellos,* | *uirosa immulgens exertis ubera labris,* Plin. *Nat.* 11.232). The *strix*, an undetermined type of screech owl (Plin. *Nat.* 11.232), is mentioned in many contexts of magic and ill omen (Fest. p. 414M, Bömer (above), Smith on Tib. 1.5.52, Ov. *Am.* 1.12.20, *Met.* 7.269, Sen. *Med.* 733–4, Luc. 6.689, *PGM* XXXVI 265 etc.). Witches were thought to assume its shape and roam as vampires (Pl. *Ps.* 820–1, Prop. 4.5.17, Ov. *Am.* 1.18.13–14, *F.* 6.141–2, Apul. *Met.* 3.21). In Romania the vampire is still called a *strigoï* (Barber (1988) 31).

21 herbasque: these imported (*mittit*) herbs seem to be different from the *herba* and *radix* which Canidia herself gathered for her previous spell (67–8). For magic plants, cf. Tupet (1976) 59–64.

Iolcos atque Hiberia: places associated with Medea (24, 61–6, 3.9–14n.), Iolcos as the setting of her rejuvenation of Aeson and murder of Pelias in a magic cauldron (Eur. *Med.* 9–10, Prop. 2.1.54, Bömer on Ov. *F.* 2.41, *Met.* 7.1–356), and Hiberia (modern Georgia) where Thessalians who pursued her after the disaster at Corinth were said to have settled (Tac. *Ann.* 6.34). The place-names also serve as a kind of synecdoche for regions notorious for magic and witches, Thessaly (45, N–H on *C.* 1.27.21, Brink on *Ep.* 2.2.209) and the eastern Black Sea (24n., Virg. *Ecl.* 8.95–6). *Colchos*, the unmetrical reading of some MSS and scholia, is 'prope sollemnis error' for *Iolcos* (Housman on Man. 5.34; cf. the app. crit. at Prop. 2.1.54, Ov. *Met.* 7.158, Sen. *Med.* 457). For *atque* preceding a vowel, cf. 2.40n.

22 uenenorum: not necessarily 'poisons', but 'enchantments', good or bad. This is the etymological sense of *uenenum* (E–M), which is related to *u(V)enus*. Cf. 71, 87, 3.9–12n., *C.* 1.27.22 (71n.), *S.* 1.8.19, Afran. *com.* 380–1 Ribbeck *aetas et corpus tenerum et morigeratio:* | *haec sunt uenena formosarum mulierum*, Coleman on Virg. *Ecl.* 8.95, Gowers (1993) 300–1. The Greek terms *pharmakon* and *philtron* (from *phileō*, 'love') have a similar ambiguity; cf. Hom. *Od.* 4.228–30 'such cunning *pharmaka* did the daughter of Zeus [Helen] possess, | good ones, which Polydamna gave her, the wife of Theon, | from Egypt, where the life-giving land produces the greatest number | of *pharmaka*, many good ones, when mixed, and many bad ones', Arch. fr. 13.7 West (App. 1).

ferax: for the gen. construction, cf. *C.* 4.4.58, *Saec.* 19–20, Var. *R.* 1.9.7, LHS II 77–8, and H.'s use of *benignus* (*C.* 1.17.15, *S.* 2.3.3), *fecundus* (*C.* 3.6.17), *felix* (*S.* 1.9.11–12), *fertilis* (*Saec.* 29, *S.* 2.4.31), *prosper* (*C.* 4.6.39), and *uber* (*C.* 2.19.10).

23 ossa: probably the bones of a corpse, as at *S.* 1.8.22 (Priapus cannot stop the witches) *quin ossa legant herbasque nocentis*; cf. 17.47n., Smith on Tib. 1.2.47–8 *haec* [*saga*] *cantu finditque solum manesque sepulcris* | *elicit et tepido deuocat ossa rogo*, Ov. *Ep.* 6.89–90 (Medea), Luc. 6.550–3, Apul. *Met.* 3.17 *extorta dentibus ferarum trunca caluaria* (skulls), *PGM* IV 1886.

ieiunae canis: 'sympathetic magic'; the dog's desire for food, like the boy's (33–4), symbolizes the amorous desire that Canidia wants to arouse in Varus (Tupet (1976) 312). According to *PGM* CXXVII 9, a stone bitten by a dog can 'cause a fight at the banquet'.

24 aduri: the objects are burned as in *piamina* (11–28n.), but the act may also be intended to 'light a fire' in Varus (81–2).

Colchicis: like those Medea used to heat her cauldron (21n.). Colchis, her homeland (16.58), was another hotbed of sorcery (17.35, N–H on *C.* 2.13.8, *C.* 4.4.63; cf. the drug *Colchicum* (Plin. *Nat.* 28.129) and modern 'colchicine'). The form *Colchicus* seems to be more prosaic than the nouns turned adj. *Colchus* and *Colchis* (Brink on *Ars* 32, *ThLL* Onom. II 529).

25 at 'meanwhile' (*OLD* s.v. 2). H. avoids the unpoetic *autem* (*Ars* 53, Brink on *Ep.* 2.1.199, 260, Axelson (1945) 85–6).

expedita 'ready for action', like a soldier (*OLD* s.v. 1); cf. *S.* 1.8.23–4 *uidi egomet nigra succinctam uadere palla | Canidiam.*

Sagana: Canidia's sole companion in *S.* 1.8. As with Canidia, the scholiasts identify her as a real person (*memini me legere apud Helenum Acronem* [Intro. 7] *Saganam nomine fuisse Pompei sagam senatoris, qui a trium-uirilibus proscriptus est* (Porph. on *S.* 1.8.25)), but she, too, is probably a stock figure. Her name comes from *sāga*, 'witch' (Prisc. *GLK* II 120 *sagana enim et saga idem significant*), which is in turn related to (*prae*)*sagus*, *sagio*, and *sagax* (Brink on *Ep.* 2.2.208, Pease on Cic. *Div.* 1.65, E–M s.v. *sagus*). For the initial short *a*, cf. *sagax* and such pairs as *lăbi, lăbāre, sĕdes, sĕdere*. The second short *a* is harder to explain, since in the Latin the termination is always *-ānus*, but it may be meant to suggest a foreign origin (cf. Greek *aganos, ganos, origanos* etc.).

26 Auernalis aquas: an inversion of the pure water required for lustration (11–28n.). Cf. Pease on Virg. *A.* 4.513 (Dido or a priestess) *sparserat et latices simulatos fontis Auerni.* The *lacus Auernus* near Cumae was thought to have its source in the underworld (Cic. *Tusc.* 1.37, Lucr. 6.739–847, Austin and Hardie (appendix) on Virg. *A.* 6.236–63). The form *Auernalis* is much rarer in verse (Prop. 4.1.49, Ov. *Met.* 5.540, Stat. *Silv.* 2.6.101, 5.3.172) than the quasi-adjectival (24n.) *Auernus* (*ThLL* II 1315).

27–8 horret … | echinus: Sagana may have her hair in a 'bristle cut'; at *S.* 1.8.48 she wears a *caliendrum*, evidently a kind of wig (Porph.: cf. Var. *Men.* 570). The comparison with the *echinus* (sea urchin) may also refer to this creature's strange way of moving (Plin. *Nat.* 9.100 *ingredi est his* [*echinis*] *in orbem uolui, itaque detritis saepe aculeis* [spines] *inueniuntur*) and to its witch-like affinity with the moon (Lucil. fr. 1222 *ROL luna alit ostrea et implet echinos*). H. may be thinking of Archilochus' *echinus* which 'knows one big thing' (fr. 201 West (App. 1)) but this seems to be a hedgehog. For *capillus*, cf. 16n.

28 currens aper: cf. [Ov.] *Hal.* 60–1 *actus aper saetis iram denun-tiat hirtis | et ruit oppositi nitens in uulnera ferri*, Sil. 1.421–4, Stat. *Theb.* 11.530–1, all of which seem to indicate that boars 'bristle' even when they are attacking. On the other hand, this is usually said to occur when they are brought to bay (Hom. *Il.* 13.471–3, *Od.* 19.439–47, Virg. *A.* 10.707–18), and Bentley makes a strong case for Heinsius' conjecture *Laurens* (cf. *S.* 2.4.42, Virg. *A.* 10.709, Mart. 9.48.5).

29–46 Veia prepares the torture and murder of the boy, while Folia causes the descent of the moon. The latter is a traditional practice of witches (45–6n.), but the former, 'the essential operation' of the poem, seems to be without any exact parallel (Tupet (1976) 313).

29 abacta nulla … conscientia: either 'excluded from no complicity' (i.e. party to every kind of abomination), or 'deterred by no remorse' (*OLD* s.v. *conscientia* 3d). The first sense of *conscientia* is the more common (*OLD* s.v. 1). For the abl. of separation with *abigo*, cf. *C.* 3.24.39–40, *S.* 2.2.44–5.

Veia: 'the robust servant, perhaps a slave, assigned the dirty jobs' (Tupet (1976) 297). The name occurs in inscriptions (*CIL* v 1356 etc.), but it may be significant. According to Paul. Fest. (p. 368M), *ueia* was the Oscan word for *plaustrum*; a nickname 'wagon' would suit her role in the 'coven'. Other possibilities are a connection with Veiouis (Vediouis, Vedius), a god of the dead (Düntzer (1892) 606), or that she is supposed to be from Veii (cf. Prop. 4.10.31 *dux Veius*) and steeped in the lore of that Etruscan city (Ingallina (1974) 204).

30 ligonibus 'mattocks' (*C.* 3.6.38, *Ep.* 1.14.27). The plural is either poetic (2.47n.) or suggests that the ground is shattering the tools. *duris* is probably felt as well with *humum* (*enallage*; cf. 11.22, *C.* 4.4.57, *S.* 1.1.28, Mynors on Virg. *G.* 2.355 *duros iactare bidentis*, *A.* 6.148) and may even, like Sisyphus' 'pitiless rock' (Hom. *Od.* 11.598), suggest the 'cruelty' of the entire operation (cf. *C.* 3.11.31, Thomas on Virg. *G.* 3.515–16 *duro fumans sub uomere taurus | concidit*).

humum: possibly the soil in the *impluuium*, the area under the open part of a Roman roof. For *humus* of the 'ground' inside a building, cf. *Mor.* 93–4 *contemptaque passim | spargit humi atque abicit* ('scattering all over the floor and discarding what he rejected' (Kenney)), *ThLL* vi 3122, and *Ep.* 1.14.26 (in a *taberna*) *salias terrae grauis*.

31 exhauriebat: the verb is normally used of liquids, but cf. Col. 1.6.15 *puteorum in modum … exhausta humus*.

laboribus: probably dat.; cf. Lucr. 5.207–9 *uis humana … | uitai causa ualido consueta bidenti | ingemere*, Virg. *G.* 1.45–6 *incipiat … taurus* *aratro* | *ingemere*, and H.'s use of that case with *in* compounds at 34, 69, 1.25, 2.51 (cf. n.), 3.6, 11, 16, 17, 10.15, 11.15.

32 quo = (*idcirco*) *ut*, a rare and archaic usage when introducing a final clause without a comparative (*OLD* s.v. *quo* 3a, LHS II 679).

infossus: cf. Nep. *Paus.* 5.5, Virg. *A.* 11.205 (both of corpses), Luc. 6.529-30 (Erictho the witch) *uiuentis animas et adhuc sua membra regentis* | *infodit busto. infodio* is an agricultural term (Cato, *Agr.* 37.3, Virg. *G.* 2.262, 348, 3.535); cf. American 'plant a stiff'.

33 longo die: the adj. seems to be predicative, 'in the length of a day' (Kenney on Apul. *Met.* 6.11.4), although it could reflect the viewpoint of the boy (cf. *Ep.* 1.1.20-1 *ut nox longa quibus mentitur amica diesque* | *longa uidetur opus debentibus*, Cat. 80.3-4 *cum te octaua quiete* | *e molli longo suscitat hora die*).

bis terque = *saepe* (Brink on *Ars* 358, 440). *daps* here probably means simply 'food', although the witches may have prepared some kind of ritual meal (2.48n.). Cf. the special food given to Greek *pharmakoi* (10.1, 21-4n.) before their torment (Burkert (1985) 82-3) and the 'sacred pancakes' fed to Celtic 'bog men' before they were sacrificed (A. Ross, D. Robins, *The life and death of a Druid prince* (New York 1991) 36-40).

34 inemori: this seems to be a Horatian coinage combining the senses of *immorior* ('die amid' (something); cf. *Ep.* 1.7.85 *immoritur studiis*) and *emorior* ('die slowly' (*OLD* s.v. 1)).

spectaculo: anticipating 102, where the boy predicts that his tormentors will furnish another kind of *spectaculum*.

35-6 The exact method of the boy's murder seems to be unparalleled in ancient texts (Tupet (1976) 327). Perhaps the most important detail is the comparison with bodies floating in water, which may be intended to evoke the fate of Tantalus (17.66, cf. *S.* 1.1.68-9), an apt symbol for the unquenchable desire which the resulting potion is meant to induce. Cf. Hom. *Od.* 11.582-92, especially 582-3 'and I saw Tantalus with his harsh sufferings | stuck in a swamp. And it [the swamp] washed against his chin', Cic. *Tusc.* 1.10 (quoting a verse from an unidentified tragedy (= 67 *ROL*) *mento summam aquam attingens enectus siti Tantalus.*

35 ore: probably abl. of measure, 'by (the length of) his face'. Cf. N-H on *C.* 2.8.3.

36 suspensa mento: cf. Cic. *Tusc.* 1.10 (35-6n.), Ov. *Pont.* 2.3.39-

40 *mitius est lasso digitum supponere mento* | *mergere quam liquidis ora natantis aquis*, Petr. 43.4 *illius mentum sustulit* (i.e. 'saved from (figurative) drowning').

37–8 More sympathetic magic, with the boy's desire for food, like the dog's (23n.), symbolizing amatory desire. As physical structures (below, on *aridum*) marrow and especially liver figure in Roman folk medicine (Plin. *Nat.* 28.4 *alii* [seeking cures] *medullas crurum quaerunt et cerebrum infantium*, 197 (cures for hepatitis) *lupi iecur aridum ... asini iecur aridum*), divination (Wissowa (1912) 419), and magic (Ov. *Am.* 3.7.30, *Ep.* 6.91–2, *Met.* 7.273 (Medea)). But they may also be significant here as seats of emotion, including love (*medulla*: *Ep.* 1.10.28, Cic. *Tusc.* 4.24, Lucr. 3.250, Cat. 45.16 [*amoris*] *ignis mollibus ardet in medullis*, 66.23 *maestas exedit cura medullas*, Prop. 2.12.17 *quid tibi* [*Amor*] *iucundum est siccis habitare medullis?*, *PGM* CIX I (cf. Betz's note); *iecur*: N–H on *C.* 1.13.4, 25.15 (cf. 3.4.77 with Lucr. 3.984–94), 4.1.12, *S.* 1.9.66, *Ep.* 1.18.72, Arch. fr. 234 West (App. I), 'for you do not have anger in your liver').

37 exsecta 'cut out' (*S.* 1.5.59, *OLD* s.v. 1). The variant *exsucta* may have arisen because 'sucking out' is the normal way of eating marrow (Luc. 7.843 *totas auidae* [*ferae*] *sorbere medullas*, Juv. 8.90 *ossa ... uacuis exsucta medullis*). There is a similar textual confusion at Prop. 3.6.28 (19–24n.; cf. Sh. Bailey, *C.Q.* 40 (1949) 27).

aridum: the fact that only the liver is specified as 'dry' suggests autopsy on H.'s part. As a seat of emotion, *medulla* can 'burn', 'be eaten', and 'dry up' in a metaphorical sense (37–8n.). But 'real bone marrow from a victim of starvation (let alone passion) would appear no "drier" to the naked eye than that from any other corpse. The starved liver, however, suffers an obvious increase in (hard) fat content and decrease in blood supply' (K. Mankin, MD), which might make it look drier than normal. It is possible that *aridum* means here 'preserved by drying' after removal (cf. Plin. *Nat.* 28.197 (37–8n.)) and that it is to be taken *apo koinou* with *medulla* (K–H). Some critics insist on a parallel epithet for *medulla*, either *exsucta* as an adj. (a rare usage; cf. Sen. *Ep.* 30.1 *infirmi corporis et exsucti*), *exsicca* (D, Cunningham, Brink (1982) 37–8, Sh. Bailey) or *exesa* (Heinsius, Bentley). But in an era before freeze-drying it would take weeks for the organs to be ready for Canidia to use in her potion (Tupet (1976) 314).

38 amoris ... poculum 'love potion' (*philtron*). Cf. 78, 17.80,

Pl. *Truc.* 43–4 *si semel amoris poculum accepit meri | eaque intra pectus se penetrauit potio.*

39 interminato ... cibo: probably dat. with *fixae*; cf. 17.5, *C.* 3.15.2, 24.5–6, Virg. *A.* 1.482 *diua solo fixos oculos auersa tenebat*, 6.469, Sil. 13.822 *oculos terrae fixos.* The passive use of the normally deponent *interminatus* may be colloquial (Ruckdeschel (1911) II 36), but H. uses other deponents as passives even in elevated contexts (16.8, 38, *C.* 1.1.25, 32.5, 2.15.15, 3.3.22, 5.24, 6.10, 24.12, *S.* 2.2.114, 124, *Ars* 263). Cf. 2.51n.

semel 'once and for all' (N–H on *C.* 1.24.16, 28.16, 3.5.29, 29.48, 4.3.1, 7.21, 13.14, *Saec.* 26, *Ep.* 1.18.71, *Ars* 331).

40 intabuissent: lit. 'had become putrescent' (*OLD* s.v. 1; cf. Virg. *G.* 3.523 *oculos* [of a dying ox] *stupor urget inertis*), but given the manner and purpose of the boy's death there may be a hint of (*in*)*tabesco* in the sense 'waste away with desire or other emotion' (*S.* 1.1.111, Kroll on Cat. 68.55–6 *maesta neque assiduo tabescere lumina fletu | cessarent*, Prop. 3.6.23, Ov. *Met.* 2.780; cf. N–H on *C.* 1.36.17 *putres ... oculos*, Norden on Virg. *A.* 6.442, and Greek (*kata*)*tēkō* (e.g. Theocr. *Id.* 1.91; also in magical papyri; cf. *PGM* IV 115–19, VII 981–3 etc.)).

41–4 With her possibly Roman name, unusual sexuality, specific home town, and association with Naples, Folia seems more real than the others, and is the peg on which hang most theories for identifying the coven as real people (App. 2). But the details may be merely circumstantial, 'intended to give an air of truthfulness to the story' (Wickham). The scholia, so full of 'information' on Canidia, say nothing about Folia, her name could be that of a stock figure (42n.), and it is striking that this supposedly historical figure is credited with the one truly supernatural act described in the poem (45–6n.).

41 masculae libidinis: gen. of quality (4.8n.) with *Foliam.* For the expression, cf. *Ep.* 1.19.28 *mascula Sappho*, unless H. there refers to Sappho's poetic vigour rather than her sexual interests (Fraenkel (1957) 346). The Romans seem to have regarded female as more peculiar than male homosexuality (e.g. Pl. *Per.* 227, *Truc.* 262–3, Ov. *Tr.* 2.365, *Ep.* 15.15–20, Sen. *Contr.* 1.2.23, Sen. *Ep.* 95.21, Juv. 2.47–8, 6.311, 320–6, Lilja (1982) 28, 72). Both *masculus* (*C.* 3.6.37) and *libido* (16.30, *C.* 1.18.10, 25.13, 4.12.8, 7× in hexameters) are rare in elevated verse and may be unpoetic (*ThLL* VII 1300–7, VIII 426).

Ariminensem: from Ariminum (Rimini) on the Adriatic (Cic.

Ver. 1.36). A magic herb called *reseda* grew in its vicinity (Plin. *Nat.* 27.131) and a rooster spoke Latin there in 78 BC (*Nat.* 10.50), but otherwise the town had no special reputation for the supernatural. Perhaps its pairing with Naples on the Tyrrhenian is meant to imply that Folia was notorious from 'coast to coast' of Italy. The epithet might also suggest a connection with Ariminius, a Persian god of evil and death (Arist. *G.A.* 27, *RE* II 825) or, despite the difference in quantity, with the mysterious *Arima* or *Arimoi*, the 'bed of the monster Typho' (Hom. *Il.* 2.783, cf. West on Hes. *Th.* 304), sometimes identified as Aenaria (Ischia) off the bay of Naples (Virg. *A.* 9.716, Ov. *Met.* 14.89, Strab. 13.626, 16.784, Plin. *Nat.* 3.82). Adjectives of place in *-ensis* are rare in Latin verse (H. has only two others (*Ep.* 1.4.3, 6.63)), and the effect here may be similar to Catullus' *Bononiensis Rufa Rufulum fellat* (59.1).

Foliam: commentators cite the name Folius (*RE* VI 2828), but Folia could suggest *follis* ('scum-bag' (Juv. 6.373b; cf. Adams (1982) 75)) or, by its similarity to *folia*, the Greek love-names Phyllis and Petale (Düntzer (1892) 607).

43 otiosa ... Neapolis: Naples and the surrounding *oppida* in Campania (Puteoli, Baiae, Capua, Cumae, Surrentum, Tarentum) were famous for Greek leisure and luxury (Virg. *G.* 4.563–4, Ov. *Met.* 15.711–12 *in otia natam* | *Parthenopen* (the poetic name for Naples), Griffin (1986) 8–9, N–H on *C.* 2.6). This line seems to be the only basis for the story (Porph. on 3.7–8, 5.43, *S.* 1.8.23–4) that Canidia was from Naples. *otiosus* is one of the most common *-osus* adjs. (3.16n.; cf. *C.* 3.18.11, Ernout (1949) 46), occurring both in prose and non-dactylic verse (Enn. *Sc.* 238 Vahlen, Cat. 50.1).

45–6 quae ... deripit: the indicative verb (a historical present; cf. 17–18, 27) shows that H. is resuming the narrative. Some take the relative clause to be part of the characterization of Folia ('she can force down the stars and the moon' (Luck (1985) 74), but this, besides probably requiring the subjunctive, would leave her without any specific task. The drawing down (*kathairesis*) of the moon, stars, or both, possibly to allow rituals to proceed in secret (*S.* 1.8.35–6), is a well-attested practice of witches (13.2n., 17.4–5, 48, Plato, *Gorg.* 513a, Ar. *Nub.* 749, Virg. *Ecl.* 8.69 *carmina uel caelo possunt deducere lunam, A.* 4.489, Prop. 1.1.23–4, Tib. 1.2.45, *PGM* I 124 etc., Tupet (1976) 92–103, Roscher II 3165).

45 excantata: a technical term (Plin. *Nat.* 28.17–18 *non et legum ipsarum in duodecim tabulis uerba sunt: 'qui fruges excantassit', et alibi, 'qui malum carmen incantassit'*). Cf. 72n. For *uox* in the sense 'incantation', cf. 76, 17.6, 78, *S.* 1.8.45, *Ep.* 1.1.34, 2.23.

47–82 Canidia appeals to Night and Diana to punish her enemies, the women whose houses in the Subura Varus frequents. She had tried, with the magic once used by Medea, to keep him beside her, but some more powerful sorceress released him. Next time, with her new spell, nothing will help him: he will return to her, burning with desire.

This interpretation depends on taking 55–60 as Canidia's account of what Varus is doing while she speaks (D. Drew, *C.R.* 37 (1923) 24–5, Zielinski (1935) 439–51, Miles, D. Bain, *Lat.* 45 (1986) 125–31). Another view is that the lines are her prayer for the first spell to work (Porph., Schol., most commentators). There are problems with the first interpretation (58, 69–70nn.), but even greater ones with the second. Among other things, it requires the reader to believe that what would seem to be the 'essential operation' (29–46n.) of the poem, the sacrifice of the boy, is nothing more than a 'contingency plan' set in motion before Canidia and the coven are even sure that it will be necessary.

47 hic 'at this point' (*OLD* s.v. 6), a usage common in H.'s *sermo* (*S.* 1.5.7, 30, 82, 9.7, 2.8.16, cf. Cat. 10.24), but not alien to more elevated verse (Enn. *Ann.* 446 Skutsch, Virg. *A.* 1.728, 2.533 etc.).

irresectum: the better to claw people (93) and animals (Prop. 4.5.16 [*Acanthis*] *cornicum immeritas eruit ungue genas*) or dig in graveyards (*S.* 1.8.26–7 (the witches began) *scalpere terram | unguibus*). Canidia, of all people, would also be aware of the magic and superstitions associated with fingernail parings (Tupet (1976) 49, 84; cf. Plin. *Nat.* 28.28, West on Hes. *Op.* 742–3, *PGM* 1 4–10).

dente liuido: probably her one remaining natural tooth; she loses her false ones at *S.* 1.8.48. Cf. the description of the hag in many Irish folk tales: 'she had one tooth, and that long enough to use as a crutch'. This disgusting feature (8.3, N–H on *C.* 2.8.3, *C.* 4.13.10–11, *Ep.* 1.18.7) may also symbolize Canidia's malignant nature (6.15).

48 rodens pollicem: nervous or jealous frenzy (*S.* 1.10.71, Prop. 2.4.3 *saepe immeritas corrumpas dentibus ungues*, 3.25.4, Petr. fr. 3 (cited by Schol. here) *pollice usque ad periculum roso*, Mart. 4.27.5 *nigros conrodit liuidus* [with *inuidia*] *ungues*) or, perhaps (there seem to be parallels in other cultures (e.g. *PGM* III 420–1), if not in Rome), an apotropaic gesture of some sort (W. Friedrich, *Hermes* 77 (1942) 223–4, I. Opie, M. Tatem, *A dictionary of superstitions* (Oxford 1992) s.v. 'thumbs').

49 quid ... tacuit: i.e. she left nothing, even the unspeakable, unspoken (*Ep.* 1.7.72 *dicenda tacenda locutus*, Cat. 64.405 *omnia fanda nefanda ... permixta* (87–8n.); for such 'polar expressions' in Greek, cf. West on Hes. *Op.* 3–4, Soph. *O.C.* 1001, LSJ s.v. *arrhētos*). Another possibility (K–H, Ingallina (1974) 145) is that she spoke partly aloud, partly 'silently' or under her breath (cf. *Ep.* 1.16.57–62, Smith on Tib. 2.1.84, [Tib.] 3.12.16, Ov. *Met.* 7.248–51 (Medea) *terrenaque numina ... | rapta cum coniuge regem ... | placauit precibusque et murmure longo*, Bömer on *F.* 2.572, Luck (1985) 24). The shift here to interrogative may suggest epic style; cf. Hom. *Il.* 5.703–4 'whom first and last did Hector and Ares kill?', 8.273, 11.299–300, 16.692–3 (cf. Virg. *A.* 11.664–5), 22.202–4, *Od.* 9.14, and the contexts where the poet questions the Muse or another god (*Il.* 1.8 etc., West on Hes. *Th.* 114–15, Virg. *A.* 9.77, 10.316, 12.500).

49–60 Canidia's prayer is a kind of *apopompē* ('sending away'), an averting (*auerto, auerrunco*) of a divinity's wrath (*iram* 54) from the speaker to another target (Miles; cf. N–H on *C.* 1.21.13, Fraenkel (1957) 410–14 (on *C.* 4.1), Brink on *Ep.* 2.1.136, Kroll on Cat. 63.92, Appel (1909) 125–7), often an enemy (10.13–14, Arch. fr. 13.7–9 West (App. 1)). In such prayers it is important that the new target be an attractive one: Night, and especially Diana 'who rules the silence', would find the disturbance caused by Varus' escapades particularly obnoxious. A number of details in this passage are imitated by Ovid at *Met.* 7.192–219 (Medea about to rejuvenate Aeson (21n.)).

50 non infideles: this may be an overly familiar way of addressing gods, as if Canidia, in common with many sorcerers, considers herself their equal (17.53–81). Although *fides* is a concern of the gods (*ThLL* VI 665), the terms *fidelis, fidus*, and their opposites seem normally to be used only of humans, animals, and their attributes (VI 656–9, 703–7; Ov. *Met.* 7.192 *Nox ... arcanis fidissima* seems to be imitating H. (49–60n.)). The chief exceptions are the homely Lares and Penates (Virg. *A.* 7.121, Ov. *F.* 6.529, *ThLL* VI 704); Ovid even compares the former to 'faithful dogs' (*F.* 5.137–42). *arbitra* is first attested here, but may be more conventional (*C.* 1.3.15, Ov. *F.* 3.73 (Mars) *arbiter armorum*, 5.665–6, Liv. 9.1.7 *diis arbitris foederis*, 21.10.3, *Prec. Ter.* 4 (*PLM* I 138) *caeli et maris diua arbitra rerumque omnium*, *ThLL* II 406–7).

51 Nox et Diana: there seems to have been no formal or state cult of Night (Bömer on Ov. *F.* 1.455, *RE* XVII 1670; cf. Cic. *Nat.* 3.44), but she figures in chthonic rites (Virg. *A.* 6.249–50), mystery doctrine (*RE* XVII 1666–9), and magic (Ov. *Met.* 7.192 (50n.), 14.403–5, *PGM* IV 2858, Tupet (1976) 13). Diana, in her identification with Greek Artemis Trioditis ('of the crossways'), Selene, and especially Hecate (*S.* 1.8.33), is also a divinity of the underworld, darkness, and magic (Virg. *A.* 4.511, Bömer on Ov. *F.* 1.414, *Ep.* 12.67–70, Sen. *Med.* 6–7 *tacitisque praebens conscium iubar | Hecate triformis*, Tupet (1976) 14–15). But she may be invoked here in her more traditional aspects of mistress of wild beasts (55–6; cf. *C.* 1.21.5–8, 3.22.1, 4.6.33–4, *Saec.* 1) and of 'averter' of evil (49–60n., N–H on *C.* 1.21.13–16). The scansion *Dīana* (17.3, *C.* 3.4.71, *Saec.* 1, 75, *Ars* 16, 454) seems to be poetic (Skutsch on Enn. *Ann.* 240); H. also has the original *Dĭāna* (*C.* 1.21.1, 2.12.20, 4.7.25, *Saec.* 70).

silentium: sc. *noctis*, the usual time for magic and other unorthodox rituals (15.1–2n., *S.* 1.8.21–2, Cic. *Leg.* 2.21, 37, *PGM* VII 321–5, Tupet (1976) 13).

52 arcana ... sacra: cf. Ov. *Ep.* 12.79 *per triplicis uultus arcanaque sacra Dianae. arcanus*, which occurs chiefly in verse (11.14, 15.21, *ThLL* II 434), seems to be a technical religious term (E–M; cf. *arceo* (e.g. *C.* 3.1.1)). *sacer*, too, seems normally to be applied to religion (cf. 7.20n, 16.18, 36), and its use in connection with magic (17.6, 57) could be either travesty or a kind of 'survival of primitive thought' (Fugier (1963) 89–106).

53 nunc, nunc ... nunc: more ritual (or ritual-sounding) *anadiplosis* (5.8n.). Cf. Sen. *Med.* 13 *nunc nunc adeste sceleris ultrices deae.*

hostilis domos: the houses of Varus' *paelices* in the Subura (47–82n.). The plural makes it unlikely that Canidia could mean Varus' house (Porph.), even if he does not live with her (69–70n.).

54 uertite: for *auertite*, a technical term in *apopompē* (49–60n.; cf. 10.13, Lucil. 858 *ROL deum rex auertat uerba obscena*, Virg. *A.* 3.265, 620 *di talem terris auertite pestem*, 9.78). *numen* is 'stronger and more comprehensive than *ira*' (Ingallina (1974) 213); cf. 15.3, 17.3, Virg. *A.* 4.611 (Dido) *meritumque malis aduertite numen*, *RE* XVII 1273–8).

55–6 Scenes contrasting night-time sleep and quiet with the rest-lessness of a god or human are as old as Homer (*Il.* 2.1–2, 10.1–2, 24.677–9; cf. 15.1, Alcman, fr. 89 *PMG*, Sapph. fr. 168B Voigt, Ap. Rhod. 3.744–53 (imitated by Var. At. fr. 8 *FPL desierant latrare canes urbesque silebant:* | *omnia noctis erant placida composta quiete*), Pease on Virg. *A.* 4.522, Bömer on Ov. *F.* 5.429–44). The emphasis here on the sleep of wild beasts seems appropriate in a prayer to Diana (49–60n.).

55 formidulosis 'frightening' (*C.* 2.17.18, *OLD* s.v. 1), although this prosaic word (*ThLL* VI 1100) can also mean 'frightened' (s.v. 2; cf. Gell. 9.12.1). Cf. Sal. *Cat.* 52.13 *loca taetra inculta foeda atque for-midulosa*, Virg. *G.* 4.468 *caligantem nigra formidine lucum*. The variant *formidulosae* would violate the 'two-epithet rule' (1.26n.) and, as Bent-ley notes, neither meaning of the adj. 'conuenit feris, dum sopore languidae sunt'.

57–60 Canidia's description of Varus is an 'enclosed invective' (Intro. 3) like the attack on Neobule in Arch.'s Cologne epode (fr. 196a.23–34 West).

57 senem ... adulterum: cf. *S.* 1.4.51, Pl. *Cas.* 239–40 *eho tu nihili, cana culex ...* | *senectane aetate unguentatus per uias, ignaue, incedis?*, McKeown on Ov. *Am.* 1.9.4 *turpe senilis amor.* The term *adulter* can be used of any kind of 'illicit or clandestine lover' (*OLD* s.v. 1), but it may imply here that Varus is Canidia's husband (73n.).

quod omnes rideant: consecutive rel. clause (2.28n.) following on the idea of Varus' decrepitude ('old (and therefore) a thing which all ridicule'). With the traditional view of this passage (47–82n.) the phrase is sometimes taken as a wish.

58 latrant: the emendation of Housman (*apud* J. Gow, *Horace Odes and Epodes* (Cambridge 1896)) and, it seems independently, of Zielinski (1935). Dogs are a well-known hazard for clandestine lovers (*C.* 3.16.2, *S.* 1.2.128, Pl. *As.* 184–5 (the speaker is a *lena*) *et quoque catulo meo* | *subblanditur nouus amator, se ut quom uideat gaudeat,* Smith on Tib. 1.6.31–2, 2.4.32, Prop. 3.16.17, 4.5.73–4, Ov. *Am.* 2.19.39–40; cf. Liv. 5.47.3 [*canis*] *sollicitum animal ad nocturnos strepitus*).

The subj. *latrent* could have arisen from confusion with *latent* (55) or by attraction to *rideant* (57) and *laborarint* (60). It might suit the interpretation accepted here if 55–60 are taken as a rhetorical ques-tion (Drew, *C.R.* 37 (1923) 25). Questions unmarked by interrogative pronouns or particles are not uncommon in H. (9.21–2n., 17.33–5, 56–9, *C.* 1.15.22, 25.8, 27.10, 29.5, 3.28.8, 4.1.2, *S.* 1.1.83, 87, 2.19,

3.94, 4.93, 6.42, 9.75, 2.3.65, 123, 132, 186, 201, 213, 7.42, 103, *Ep.*
1.1.82, 2.33, 16.37, 18.18, 2.1.54, 2.19, 66, 80, 154, *Ars* 5, LHS II 456,
460–1, 467). With the other interpretation, *latrent* is thought to be
optative ('may the dogs bark'), the climax of Canidia's prayer. This
is based on supposed parallels where the barking of dogs alerts
witches that their spells have succeeded (Virg. *Ecl.* 8.107) or that
their patron goddess Hecate (51n.) is present (Theocr. *Id.* 2.11–13
(= *HA* 584–6), Ap. Rhod. 3.1216–17, Virg. *A.* 6.257–8, Ov. *Met.*
14.403–11). The transitive use of *latro* (*S.* 2.1.85, *Ep.* 1.2.66) seems to
be colloquial (Ruckdeschel (1910) 28).

Suburanae: the Subura, the valley between the Viminal and
the Esquiline, 'was notorious for its bustle, noise, dirt, and shady
morality' (I. A. Richmond in *OCD* s.v.). Cf. Prop. 4.7.15 *uigilacis furta
Suburae,* [Tib.] *Priap.* 40.1 *nota Suburanas inter Telesina puellas,* Pers.
5.32, Mart. 2.17, 6.66, 11.61.3–4, 78.11–12.

59 nardo: Canidia's first potion, modelled on that of Medea (61–
6) and likewise meant to harm *paelices* (63, 70) although not with fire,
but with Varus' forgetfulness of them (69–70). Doctored unguents
were a stock-in-trade of witches (17.23, Prop. 4.5.25–6, *PGM* IV
1496–1595, XXXVI 333–60). The mention of nard here is clearly the
source for the story that Canidia was a 'perfumer' by profession (*hinc*
[i.e. from line 59] *scias illam, ut diximus* [on 3.7–8], *unguentariam fuisse*
(Porph. on 59)). For other uses of nard, cf. 13.8–9n.

quale: the appositive acc. instead of the usual abl. of comparison
(*C.* 4.2.37–8) seems to be colloquial. Cf. *S.* 1.5.41–2 *animae, qualis* [for
qualibus] *neque candidiores* | *terra tulit,* Virg. *Ecl.* 3.105 *tris pateat caeli spa-
tium non amplius ulnas* [for *ulnis*], LHS II 110.

60 laborarint: the potential subj. ('my hands could not have
made better') is preferable to the indic. ('my hands have not (to this
point) made better') because it suggests why Canidia now resorts to
something completely different from nard. Transitive *laboro* (= *ela-
boro*) seems to be colloquial and, later, poetic (*ThLL* VII 808).

61 quid accidit? 'Why is it happening?', i.e. why is Varus at
large (55–60) and not asleep in bed (69–70)? The question is ad-
dressed to Night and Diana (51), but Canidia answers it herself
(71–2). For *quid* alternating with *cur* ('why ... why'), cf. *C.* 1.8.3–13,
2.11.11–13, 17.1–6, *Ep.* 2.2.177–83, Brink on *Ars* 53, LHS II 458.
With *latrent* as an optative (47–82, 58nn.), *quid accidit* is supposed to

mean 'What is happening?' and to indicate that Canidia finally realizes, evidently from the silence of the dogs, that her first spell has failed.

61–6 The account of Medea's vengeance seems intended to show the power of her spells and make it all the more puzzling that on this occasion they have failed. Cf. 17.76–81. For the Medea myth and H.'s possible sources, cf. 3.9–14n. At *Id.* 2.15-16, Theocritus' Simaitha ('a suburban Medeia' (Dover *ad loc.*)) claims to have used the *pharmaka* of Medea, Circe, and a certain Perimede (cf. Hopkinson *ad loc.* (*HA* 588–9)).

61 barbarae: almost a perpetual epithet of Medea, with reference both to her foreign origin (24n.) and to her cruelty (Eur. *Med.* 256, Ov. *Ep.* 6.19 (71n.), 81 *barbara paelex*, 12.105, *Met.* 7.144, 276, *Tr.* 2.526).

minus = *non*, a colloquial euphemism (8.17–18, *C.* 1.2.27, 4.3.16, *S.* 1.3.29, 93, 2.2.48, *Ep.* 1.10.18, 2.2.90, 156, Hofmann (1951) 146).

62 ualent 'are potent' (87, 11.11, 16.3, 17.4); cf. Prop. 2.4.7–8 *non hic herba ualet, non hic nocturna Cytaeis,* | *non Perimedaea gramina cocta manu,* Plin. *Nat.* 23.145 *minus ualent in remediis dulces* [almonds].

63 superbam ... paelicem: expressing Medea's view, as *nouam ... nuptam* expresses Jason's (3.13n.). For *superbus,* cf. 2.7n.

64 Creontis: the king of Corinth who received Jason and Medea after the murder of Pelias (21n.). At Eur. *Med.* 1204–21 he, too, is killed by the poisoned robe when he tries to save his daughter.

65 tabo: lit. 'putrescent matter', but here 'a substance causing putrescence' (cf. *tabes*). For the image, cf. 40n. *tabum* is 'a word almost peculiar to epic poetry' (Kenney on Lucr. 3.661).

munus imbutum: for *munus = donum,* cf. 3.17n. The variant *infectum* probably arose as a gloss on the more unusual *imbutum.*

67 atqui 'and yet' (*S.* 2.1.68, *Ep.* 1.2.33). Despite its frequency in H. (3× in odes, 8× in hexameters), *atqui* seems to be an unpoetic word (Axelson (1945) 103–4).

67–8 The most powerful herbs usually grow in inaccessible places (Ov. *Met.* 7.418 [*aconita*] *nascuntur dura uiuacia caute,* Tupet (1976) 61).

68 radix: Greek witches were sometimes called *rhizotomoi* ('root-cutters'; cf. LSJ s.v.), and this was the title of a play by Sophocles about Medea (Macr. 5.19.8). Cf. Laev. fr. 27.4 *FPL* (ingredients for *philtra*) *radiculae, herbae, surculi.*

fefellit: for the Greek construction, cf. 3.7n. The essential part of the magical *moly* was its root, but this was 'difficult for mortal men to uncover' (Hom. *Od.* 10.302–6; cf. Ov. *Met.* 14.292). Cf. Virg. *Ecl.* 4.24 *fallax herba ueneni* and (in a different sense) *G.* 2.152 (in Italy) *nec miseros fallunt aconita legentis.*

69–70 The couplet seems to contradict both 55–60 (cf. 47–82n.) and *ambulat* (71). It is possible that *indormit* here means, not that Varus is sleeping while Canidia speaks, but that 'the bed he sleeps in (normally, when he is at home) has been smeared with a drug to make him forget all other mistresses' (Wickham; so also Campbell (edition), Bain (47–82n.) 130–1). On the other hand, Canidia could be indulging in sarcasm ('he sleeps – sure he does'; cf. 8.7–10) or asking an indignant rhetorical question (Vollmer). Sh. Bailey's *an* [or should it be *num* or *quin* (6.3–4n.)?] *dormit* would make this clearer, but cf. 58n.

69 unctis: i.e. with the nard (59), here designated by its intended effect (*obliuione*). For 'forgetfulness' as a liquid to be poured or drunk, cf. 14.1–4. Despite an apparent echo of Cat. 29.7 (Mamurra) *perambulabit omnium cubilia*, the *cubilibus* here (poetic plural, as at 12.12, 16.38) have to be Varus' (69–70n.) and not those of the *paelices* (Peerlkamp, Miles, Luck (1985) 624). That Canidia was able to anoint them may be another indication that Varus is her husband (73n.)

obliuione: cf. 14.2, *C.* 4.9.34. *obliuio* is not suited to dactyls, where the preferred term is *obliuia* (*S.* 2.6.62, Norden on Virg. *A.* 6.715). But it is rare even in other verse (*ThLL* XI 2.107–9) and may be unpoetic.

71 a, a: '*a* is very rare in H. and shows an affectation of strong emotion' (N–H on *C.* 1.27.18; cf. their note on *C.* 2.17.5). For the hiatus in or after an interjection, cf. 12.25, 15.23, *C.* 1.15.9, *S.* 2.3.265, *Ep.* 1.19.19, *Ars* 301.

solutus: cf. 15n., 17.7, *C.* 1.27.21–2 *quae saga, quis te soluere Thessalis | magus uenenis, quis poterit deus?*, Virg. *A.* 4.479–87 (a sacerdos) *quae mihi [Dido] reddat eum uel eo me soluat amantem | ... | haec se carminibus promittit soluere mentes*, Tib. 1.2.61–2 *nempe haec eadem [saga] se dixit amores | cantibus aut herbis soluere posse meos.* For the colloquial *ambulo* ('strut'), cf. 4.5n.

ueneficae: in comedy and oratory this is often a term of abuse,

used of slaves and other low characters (Hofmann (1951) 87, Opelt
(1965) index s.v.). Cf. Ov. *Ep.* 6.19 (Hypsipyle of her rival Medea)
barbara narratur uenisse uenefica tecum. Canidia, while grudgingly admit-
ting her enemy's superior knowledge, may be disparaging her as a
kind of 'dime-store witch'. The fact that *ueneficus* means primarily
'enchanter' rather than 'poisoner' (E–M s.v., *OLD*) is further evi-
dence that *uenenum* is a neutral term (22n.).

72 carmine 'incantation', an ancient meaning of *carmen* often
evoked by Latin poets (17.4, 28, *S.* 1.8.19, 2.1.82, *Ep.* 2.1.138, *Ars* 401,
Virg. *Ecl.* 8.67–71, Pease on *A.* 4.487, *ThLL* iii 464–5, Tupet (1976)
166–78). Cf. 17.29n. (on *nenia*) and Intro. 4 (on the title 'Epodes').

73 non usitatis: the litotes recurs in a different context at *C.*
2.20.1. For *potio* (a prosaic word (*ThLL* x 2.322)), cf. Pl. *Truc.* 44
(38n.)., Cic. *Clu.* 40, 173, Plin. *Nat.* 32.52 *amorem concitari et iurgia* [when
a bone from the *rubeta* (19n.) is added] *in potionem,* Suet. *Cal.* 50.2
creditur [Caligula] *potionatus a Caesonia uxore amatorio quidem medicamento,
sed quod in furorem uerterit.* The word 'poison' is derived from *potio,* and
in English a 'potion' is usually a special or magical drink (cf. the
popular song 'Love Potion Number Nine').

Vare: a number of details (5–6, 69–70, 75 (*recurres*)) suggest that
this is Canidia's husband (Zielinski (1935) 448). Varus is a Roman
cognomen, but identifying its individual bearers is notoriously dif-
ficult (N–H on *C.* 1.8; cf. Cat. 10.1, Virg. *Ecl.* 6.7). As with the
witches, the name's literal meaning may be important: 'bandy-legs'
(cf. *S.* 1.3.47) might be an apt term of abuse for an aged reprobate
(Düntzer (1892) 605, E. R. Garnsey, *Epilegomena on Horace* (London
1907) 28). Cf. Pl. *Mer.* 639 (of a *senex amator*) *canum, uarum, uen-
triosum, bucculentum, breuiculum,* Juv. 2.22 (a homosexual named Varil-
lus, 'little straddler'), Quint. *Inst.* 11.3.125 *uaricare supra modum et in
stando deforme est et, accedente motu, prope obscenum.* The other male
associated with Canidia, Albucius (*S.* 2.1.48 *Canidia Albuci, quibus est
inimica,* [*minitatur*] *uenenum*), may be a Lucilian character (cf. *S.*
2.2.66–8, Lucil. frr. 87–93 *ROL*), but his name could be from *albucus*
('asphodel'); cf. Plin. *Nat.* 21.108 *tradunt et ante foras uillarum* [*albucum*]
satum remedio esse contra ueneficiorum noxiam.

74 multa: internal acc.; cf. Virg. *G.* 3.226 *multa gemens,* 4.320
multa querens. The sing. *multum* is more usual (15.11, 17.20).

caput = *homo,* a usage that is both colloquial (*S.* 2.1.27, 5.74, *Ep.*

2.2.189, Pl. *Per.* 184 *uerbereum caput*, Cic. *Phil.* 11.1, *ThLL* III 404–5)
and poetic (N–H on *C.* 1.24.2, 28.20, Calv. fr. 3 *FPL*, Cat. 68.119–20
etc.). Cf. Hom. *Il.* 8.281 'Teucer, son of Telamon, dear head', *Od.*
1.343, Soph. *Ant.* 1. For the fut. part., cf. 1.22n.

75–6 recurres nec ... redibit: a kind of zeugma: 'you will
return to me, and (yet) your sanity will not return (to you)'. *uocata* is
concessive, 'although summoned by Marsian incantations', pre-
sumably those of Canidia's rival (71n.). Some commentators under-
stand *ad me* with *redibit* and take *nec* with *Marsis ... uocibus*: 'your
mind will return (to me) summoned, not by Marsian incantations
(but by a greater spell)'. For the *figura etymologica* with *uocata ... uoci-
bus*, cf. 89, 4.15n.

75 mens 'sanity' (7.16, 17.17, *C.* 1.13.5, 37.14, 2.3.65, 80, 137, 278,
285, 295, *OLD* s.v. 5).

76 Marsis: the Marsi, inhabitants of the region around Lake
Fucinus in Samnium, were prime movers of the Social War (*Bellum
Marsicum*) against Rome (16.3) They claimed descent from a son of
Circe and Ulysses (Plin. *Nat.* 7.15, Gell. 16.11.1), one of their god-
desses, Angitia, was a sister of Medea (Virg. *A.* 7.758–9, Sil. 8.498,
Sol. 2.27–9), and they were famous as snake-charmers, seers, and
sorcerers (17.29, Fordyce on Virg. *A.* 7.750, Bömer on Ov. *F.* 6.142,
Tupet (1976) 176–7, 187–99).

77 maius 'greater' than the nard (59n.).

78 fastidienti: sc. *me*; cf. 12.13, 17.73, Virg. *Ecl.* 2.73 *inuenies
alium, si te hic fastidit, Alexin.*

79–80 Canidia's *adynaton* (appeal to the impossible or unthink-
able) resembles Hdt. 5.92 ('the sky will be below the earth, the earth
above the sky, humans will dwell in the sea, fish where humans
(dwelt) formerly'), but it also sounds like a magic assault on the uni-
verse (45–6n.). For other *adynata*, cf. 15.7–9n., 16.23–24, 17.65–9, N–
H on *C.* 1.2.9, 29.10, 33.7, 3.5.31–4, *Ars* 11–13, 29–30, Kenney on
Lucr. 3.784–5, E. Dutoit, *Le thème de l'adynaton dans la poésie antique*
(Paris 1936). There is a notable example in Archilochus (fr. 122 (App.
1); cf. 16.34n.).

79 inferius: the second *i* is consonantal (2.35n.).

81 amore ... meo 'love for me', the possessive adj. for the
objective gen. Cf. *C.* 1.6.11, 3.10.16, Mankin (1988a) 69.

flagres: cf. *C.* 1.25.13 *flagrans amor et libido*, 2.12.25 *flagrantia ... oscula,*

Cat. 65.25 *mens caeco flagrabat amore*. The subj. shows that this will be Canidia's purpose (cf. *C.* 1.33.6–8 *prius* ... | *iungentur* ... | *quam* ... *Pholoe peccet, OLD* s.v. *priusquam* 2).

82 Canidia's simile comes from witchcraft: *bitumen* (tar) was used to kindle magic fires (Sophron, *Sorceresses* fr. 8, Virg. *Ecl.* 8.82 *fragilis incende bitumine lauros*). For *ater* of 'smoky' fires, cf. *C.* 4.12.26, Virg. *A.* 4.384 (92n.), 8.198, Bömer on Ov. *F.* 2.561.

83–102 The boy speaks, not to beg for mercy, as before, but to curse, threaten, and foretell destruction. His transformation from a frightened child into an almost inhuman force of vengeance may be the ultimate horror (5 intro.).

Curses of this sort (*dirae, arai*) have a long history, as does the belief that victims of premature or violent death can become restless and dangerous ghosts (7.19–20, *C.* 1.28.31–4, Hom. *Od.* 11.72–3, Bömer on Ov. *F.* 5.419, *RE* xvi 2240–64). Cf. 7.19–20, *C.* 1.28.31–4 *fors et* | *debita iura uicesque superbae* [88n.] | *te maneant ipsum: precibus non linquar inultis,* | *teque piacula nulla resoluent* [90n.], Hom. *Od.* 11.72–3 (Elpenor's ghost) 'do not leave me behind unwept and unburied | when you go home, lest I become to you a cause for remembrance by the gods'.

83 sub haec 'after these things'. This use of *sub* with the acc. seems to be colloquial (*S.* 2.8.43, Brink on *Ep.* 2.2.34, *OLD* s.v. 24, LHS II 280), although it does occur a few times in epic (Virg. *A.* 5.394) and in historical prose (Liv. 7.31.5 etc.).

84 lenire: historic infinitive 'used dramatically' (Page) for the imperfect (*S.* 1.5.12, 31, 8.47, 9.66, 2.3.316, 6.113, 8.35, 59, *Ep.* 1.7.61–2, 67, Fordyce on Virg. *A.* 7.15, LHS II 357–8).

85 sed dubius: 'i.e. not knowing with what words to begin in his despair' (Page). Cf. Pease on Virg. *A.* 4.371 (Dido's lament) *quae quibus anteferam?*

rumperet silentium: a poetic expression (Lucr. 4.583, Virg. *A.* 10.63–4 *quid me alta silentia cogis* | *rumpere*, Bömer on Ov. *Met.* 1.208) modelled, perhaps, on Greek *rhēgnumi phōnēn* ('break (into) speech').

86 Thyesteas preces: proverbial of a call for vengeance; cf. Cic. *Pis.* 43 *Thyestea est ista exsecratio*. Thyestes, a Tantalid (17.66), unwittingly ate his own children, then cursed the chef, his brother Atreus. The story figured in Greek tragedy (e.g. Aesch. *Ag.* 1590–62), but was best known to Romans from Ennius' *Thyestes* (Sc. 340–65

Vahlen (*trag.* 349–73 *ROL*); cf. 10.21–4n., N–H on *C.* 1.16.17, Brink on *Ars* 91, 186).

87–8 The meaning seems to be 'enchantments [22n.] can confound [*ualent conuertere* supplied *apo koinou*] great right and wrong, they cannot confound human vengeance [88n.]' (Porph., Lambinus). The *apo koinou* is harsh (Lambinus cites Cic. *Att.* 10.1.4 *istum* [sc. *legatum iri arbitror*] ... *me legatum iri non arbitror*), but may reflect the boy's difficulty in finding words (85). There have been many attempts to emend *magnum* either to a more suitable epithet (*magica* Bentley, *maga* Haupt, *Marsum* (=*Marsorum*) Lenchantin) or to provide a verb (*miscent* E. R. Garnsey (73n.) 30–1, G. Giangrande, *C.Q.* 17 (1967) 327–31, *mactant* E. Paratore, *Phil.* 129 (1985) 73).

For the 'confounding' or 'mixing' of *fas nefasque*, cf. Cat. 64.405 *omnia fanda nefanda malo permixta furore*, Virg. *G.* 1.505 *fas uersum nefasque*, Ov. *Ars* 1.739, *Met.* 6.585–6, *ThLL* vi 295, and H.'s own (*C.* 1.18.10–11) *fas atque nefas exiguo fine libidinum | discernunt auidi*.

88 humanam uicem: the sequel shows that this probably means the 'vengeance' or 'punishment' that pertains to murderous humans, i.e. to be haunted by their dead victims' ghosts, stoned, and left unburied (89–102). Cf. N–H on *C.* 1.28.32 *uicesque superbae*, who compare Greek *amoibai* ('pay-backs'), *C.* 4.14.13 *plus uice simplici*, and *OLD* s.v. *uicis* 5.

89 diris ... dira: *figura etymologica* (75–6, 4.15n.). The substantive *dirae* is first attested of 'evil omens' (Cic. *Div.* 1.29); its use of 'curses' seems to be poetic, and may be modelled on Greek *arai* (*Dirae* 3, Tib. 2.6.53, Prop. 3.25.17, *ThLL* vi 1270, W. Hübner, *Dirae im römischen Epos* (Hildesheim 1970) 5–6; cf. *Dirae = Furiae* (Virg. *A.* 4.473, 12.869)).

detestatio: first here in the sense 'curse' (*ThLL* vi 809); the primary meaning seems to be 'expiation' (Cic. *Dom.* 140). Cf. Paul. *Fest.* p. 184M *obtestatio est cum deus testis in meliorem partem uocatur, detestatio cum in deteriorem*, *C.* 1.1.24–5 *bellaque matribus | detestata*, *OLD* s.v. *detestabilis* 2, *detestor* 1, 2.

90 expiatur: cf. 17.38, N–H on *C.* 1.28.34 (83–102n.). The victims used in expiation (*piaculum*) were usually animals, but there were cases of human sacrifice (Wissowa (1912) 392–4, Fugier (1963) 341–3).

92 nocturnus ... furor: cf. *Ep.* 2.2.209 *nocturnos lemures* and, for the threat, Ap. Rhod. 3.703–4 (Chalciope to Medea) 'may I, having died with my children, | become to you afterwards a hateful Fury [*Erinys*] from Hades', Virg. *A.* 4.384–6 (Dido to Aeneas) *sequar atris ignibus absens | et, cum frigida mors anima seduxerit artus, | omnibus umbra locis adero,* Ov. *Ib.* 141–2 *tum quoque factorum ueniam memor umbra tuorum, | insequar et uultus ossea forma tuos.*

93 curuis unguibus: ghosts and other revenants often have long nails (Bömer on Ov. *F.* 6.134 (of *striges* (20n.)) *unguibus hamus inest*), probably since the nails of corpses, along with their hair and teeth, seem to grow after death 'because the skin shrinks back as it becomes dehydrated' (Barber (1988) 119).

94 deorum ... Manium: the (*di*) *Manes* are the spirits of the dead, capable of helping (*manis = bonus* (E–M s.v.); cf. *immanis*), but also of harming the living. Cf. N–H on *C.* 1.4.16, *CE* 1604.22 *cuius admissi uel Manes uel di caelestes erunt sceleris uindices,* Lattimore (1962) 90–5, Wissowa (1912) 238–40.

95 assidens praecordiis: like a bird (1.19n.), but a malignant one such as the *strix* (20n.) or the eagle that gnawed on Prometheus' liver (17.67n.). *assidens* may also suggest a military siege (R. Lyne, *Lat.* 28 (1969) 694–6; cf. *Ciris* 268, *OLD* s.v. 2, s.v. *aufero* 4b). For *praecordia,* cf. 3.5n.

96 somnos auferam: a frequent threat in H. (*C.* 1.25.3, 2.16.15–16, *S.* 1.5.14–15, *Ep.* 1.10.18, *Ars* 360; cf. 2.28n., *C.* 3.1.21, *Ep.* 1.5.10), but also in real magic (17.24–6n.).

97 uicatim 'street by street' (cf. *uicus*); only here in H., and apparently 'rare and affected' in other Latin (Fedeli (1978) 88). There may be a word play with *uicem* (88). For the poetic *hinc et hinc,* cf. 2.31n.

97 saxis petens: a common form of summary justice in ancient cultures (e.g. Cic. *Ver.* 1.119 *quem iste* [Verres] *conlegam nisi habuisset, lapidibus coopertus esset in foro*).

98 obscenas 'disgusting' (*OLD* s.v. 2), but also 'evil-omened' (s.v. 1). Cf. Virg. *G.* 1.470 *obscenaeque canes importunaeque uolucres,* *A.* 3.241 (Harpies), 12.876 (*Dirae*).

99 post: adverbial, as at *C.* 3.20.3, *S.* 1.2.120, 3.102, 4.88, 6.61, *Ep.* 1.6.43, 18.83, *Ars* 76, 111.

insepulta: an especially terrible threat; cf. 10.21–2, 16.13–14, 17.11–2, Hom. *Il.* 15.349–51, Kroll on Cat. 108.3–6 (of Cominius when he dies) *non equidem dubito quin primum inimica bonorum | lingua* *exsecta auido sit data uulturio,* | *effossos oculos uoret atro gutture coruus,* | *intestina canes, cetera membra lupi,* Virg. *A.* 4.620, Ov. *Ib.* 165–72, and (parody?) Pl. *Cur.* 576 *iam ego te faciam ut hic formicae frustillatim differant.* The cretic-containing *insepultus* occurs in both comedy (Pl. *Mos.* 502) and tragedy (Naev. *praet.* 1 *ROL*).

99 lupi: wolves were found in urban no less than rural areas of Italy (*C.* 3.27.3, Virg. *G.* 1.486, Bömer on Ov. *F.* 4.766), and their taste for human corpses is still a problem in parts of Europe and North Africa (Barber (1988) 92–4).

100 Esquilinae alites: when it was the site of shallow and mass graves (*S.* 1.8.8–13) the Esquiline must have been swarming with carrion birds. Its conversion into gardens (1.8.14–15) was probably earlier than the dramatic date of this poem (App. 2), but the activities of Canidia at the site (17.58) may have brought back the birds, making it poetic justice for them to feed on her corpse. The hiatus here is one of only five in H. (13.3, *C.* 1.28.24, *S.* 1.9.38, 2.2.28), not counting those after interjections (71n.) and in *asynarteta* (11.14, 24 (Intro. 6)).

101 heu mihi: *heu* seems to 'belong chiefly to elevated verse' (Grassman (1966) 99). Cf. 11.7, 21, 15.23, 16.11, 17.14. It occurs 11× in the *Odes*, but only once in the hexameters, in what may be a parody of epic or tragedy (*S.* 2.8.61–2 *heu, fortuna, quis est crudelior in nos* | *te deus?*).

101–2 superstites | effugerit: for *superstes,* cf. 1.15n; for the metrically convenient fut. perf., 1.32n.

EPODE 6

Introduction

A 'dog' shuns wolves and annoys undeserving guests. He should take on H., who resembles bigger and more relentless hounds, or, like the iambists Archilochus and Hipponax, is a 'bull' ready to gore evildoers. If someone provokes him, he will not simply weep like an unavenged boy.

H.'s stance and tone remind some of certain earlier Latin poetry (e.g. Lucil. frr. 87–93 *ROL*, Cat. 15, 16, 21, 23, 25, 37, 40, 98, 108, 116, fr. 3), but the reference to Archilochus and Hipponax appears to

place the epode in the tradition of Archaic Greek *iambus*. The same
may be true of H.'s focus on a stock figure rather than a real person
(1, 13–14nn.), and of the animal comparisons, which seem to recall
both the *ainoi* ('animal fables') of Archilochus (frr. 172–81, 185–7; cf.
Sem. fr. 7 West) and, especially, the beast imagery which is so
prominent in all of the early iambists. It has been suggested that
Epode 6, despite its position in the collection (Intro. 4; cf. Virg. *Ecl.*
6), is a kind of 'programme poem' in which H. indicates his relation
to his predecessors and the nature of his own *iambus* (Buchheit (1961)
520–6, Schmidt (1977) 405–6).

But the poem's 'programme', if it has one, is not immediately
obvious, mainly because of the strange shifts in that same animal
imagery which helps make it 'iambic'. H.'s adversary starts out as a
'dog', then becomes a (human?) 'evil-doer' (11n.), while H. himself at
first also resembles a dog (5–8), then, like Archilochus and Hippo-
nax, a 'bull' (11–12), and, finally, with his denial of the resemblance,
suggests that his enemy at least perceives him as an 'unavenged boy'
(16).

It is possible that the last image provides a clue for the sequence
that precedes it. Since it seems to evoke both the tortured boy of
Epode 5 and the murdered Remus of Epode 7 (16n.), it may suggest
that this poem is also concerned with curses, vengeance, and civil
strife (Porter (1987) 256–7). The 'metamorphoses' both of H.'s adver-
sary and of H. himself – also, therefore, a target of blame (cf. 4
intro.) – might be a kind of symbol for the changes in perception
that lead people (Romans) from recognizing their kinship (all 'dogs')
to seeing each other as members of different and hostile 'species'
('bulls' vs. 'dogs' (or humans); cf. 4.1–10n.), and finally make them
capable of destroying themselves in a way alien to even the wildest
beasts (7.11–12n.).

1 immerentis 'unoffending', in contrast to the wolves (2) and 'evil-
doers' (11). Cf. 7.19, where the meaning is slightly different, and *S.*
2.3.211 *Aiax immeritos cum occidit desipit agnos.*

uexas: dogs are supposed to be wary of strangers, but not in
excess; cf. Sem. fr. 7.18–20 West (a dog-like woman) 'never speaking
sweetly, | not even if she sits among guests, | but she always makes an
idle clamour', Cic. *S. Rosc.* 56–7, Col. 7.12.5 *maxime autem [canes] debent*

*in custodia uigilantes conspici, nec erronei, sed adsidui et circumspecti magis
quam temerarii. nam illi nisi quod certum compererunt, non indicant, hi uano
strepitu et falsa suspicione concitantur.*

canis: a universal term of abuse for the shameless, timid, greedy,
fawning etc. (e.g. *S.* 2.2.55–6, S. Lilja, *Dogs in ancient Greek poetry*
(Helsinki 1976), *ThLL* III 258). Since the dog could also be a symbol
for the blame poet (*S.* 2.1. 84–5, *Ars* 79, Pind. *Pyth.* 2.52–6, Pfeiffer
on Call. fr. 380, Lucil. frr. 3–4 *ROL*, Var. *Men.* 516–18, Watson
(1983) 156–9), H.'s opponent is usually thought to be another iambist
or satirist. But attempts to identify him as Furius Bibaculus (Schol.;
cf. *S.* 1.10.36, 2.5.41), Cassius Severus (titles in some MSS; cf. Tac.
Ann. 1.72, 4.21), or other real person 'start from wrong premisses'
(Fraenkel (1957) 57). Like other villains in *iambus*, he is probably a
stock figure (Intro. 3).

2 aduersum: only here and at *Ep.* 1.1.75 in H., and otherwise,
except for comedy, 'almost alien to poetic diction' (*ThLL* I 851).

For the construction with an adj., cf. Pl. *Epid.* 318 *subdola aduersus
senem*, Liv. 1.25.7 *aduersus singulos ferox*.

lupos: the chief enemies of the flock which the dog guards (4.1n.).
Like *canis*, *lupus* (Greek *lykos*) can be a term of abuse, especially for
the cunning, greedy, and savage (13–14n., *C.* 4.4.50, *Ep.* 2.2.28 (14n.),
ThLL VII 2.1855, Ahl (1985) 69–86, M. Detienne, J. Svenbro, 'The
feast of the wolves', in (edd.) M. Detienne, J.-P. Vernant, *The cuisine
of sacrifice among the Greeks* (trans. P. Wissing, Chicago 1989) 148–63).

It may be significant that the ancients recognized the virtual iden-
tity of wolf and dog, both of the Linnaean genus *Canis*. Cf. *S.* 2.2.64
hac urget lupus, hac canis, aiunt, Aristotle, *H.A.* 8.167, *Rhet. Her.* 4.46,
Cic. *Nat.* 1.97, Plin. *Nat.* 8.148.

3 inanis: probably with *minas* (Lucr. 5.1003 [*mare*] *minas ponebat
inanis*, although it could be felt as nom. with the sense 'foolish' (*S.*
1.4.76–7 *inanis* | *hoc iuuat*, 2.2.14, *OLD* s.v. 10b).

3 si potes 'if you have the guts'; cf. 9.14, *C.* 3.11.31–2 *impiae spon-
sos potuere duro* | *perdere ferro*, *Ep.* 1. 5.1 (to a man used to luxury) *si potes
Archiacis* [*Archias breues lectos fecit* (Porph.)] *conuiua recumbere lectis*, *OLD*
s.v. *possum* 3.

3–4 uertis ... petis: some critics prefer the variants *uerte ... pete*
with the transposition *inanis uerte, si potes, minas* (Fabricius). The indi-
cative makes sense (*OLD* s.v. *quin* A.1a), but the imperative seems

more appropriate to a challenge (e.g. Virg. *Ecl.* 3.52 *quin age, si quid habes*, s.v. A.1b). This is the only place in H. where *quin* introduces a direct question (cf. 5.69–70n.).

4 me remorsurum: an Archilochean posture; cf. fr. 126 (App. 1) 'I know one great thing, | to pay back with terrible ills the one who has treated me ill.' The blame poet as dog and other verbal abusers are often said to 'bite' (IN.; cf. *C.* 4.3.16, *S.* 1.4.81, 6.46), hence the 'black tooth' (15n.). *remordeo* occurs 'almost exclusively in poetry, always of mental anguish' (Kenney on Lucr. 3.827; cf. 4.1135, Virg. *A.* 1.261, 7.402, Juv. 2.35). For the future part., cf. 1.22n.

5–10 It is not clear whether H. likens himself to a sheep dog (Lambinus, Miles, Watson (1983)) or a hunting dog (most commentators). The phrase *amica uis pastoribus* (6) points to the former, as does the reference to snow (7), since Romans seldom used dogs for winter hunting (2.31n.). On the other hand, sheep-dogs were supposed to chase only predators (Var. *R.* 2.9.5, Col. 7.12.8), not 'whatever (kind of) beast' (7–8n.), and to stop their pursuit once the prey was recovered (10n.; cf. Col. 7.12.9 (the sheep dog) *et lupi repellere insidias, et raptorem ferum consequi fugientem, praedam excutere atque auferre debeat*).

5 Molossus ... Lacon: top breeds originally from Molossis (in Epirus) and from Sparta. They were prized both as watchdogs and as hunters (*S.* 2.6.114–15 (Molossian house-dogs), Var. *R.* 2.9.5, Lucr. 5.1063, Mynors on Virg. *G.* 3.405 *uelocis Spartae catulos acremque Molossum*). By giving himself a 'pedigree', H. may imply that his *ignauus* opponent is a 'mongrel' (Miles).

fuluus: a poetic word (*ThLL* VI 1533), only here and perhaps at Grat. 203 of dogs, elsewhere of grander beasts such as sacrificial cattle (*C.* 4.2.60), wolves (Virg. *A.* 1.275, 7.688), and especially lions (*C.* 4.4.14, Lucr. 5.901, Virg. *G.* 4.408). It can indicate anything from 'golden' to 'reddish brown' (André (1949) 132–5); 'sandy' would fit the preference of shepherds for fair-coloured dogs distinguishable in poor light from other animals (Col. 7.12.3).

6 amica uis: probably modelled on Lucr. 6.1222 *fida canum uis* (cf. 4.681 *promissa canum uis*, Virg. *A.* 4.132 *odora canum uis*), which is in turn based on Greek epic periphrases with words for 'might' (*biē, is, menos*); cf. Hom. *Od.* 7.2 *menos hēmionoiin*, 'might of mules', Kenney on Lucr. 3.8 *fortis equi uis*.

7–8 agam ... fera = *agam feram quaecumque praecedet* (2.37n.). The term *fera* can be used of any 'wild beast', whether the predator (wolf, fox, bear) chased off by the sheep-dog, or the game (hare, stag, boar) tracked by the hunting dog (5–10n.). Cf. 7.12n., Var. *L.* 5.80, 100–1.

7 per altas ... niuis 'through deep snows' i.e. even in difficult conditions. Cf. *S.* 1.2.105–6 *leporem uenator ut alta | in niue sectetur.* At *C.* 1.9.1 *alta niue* means 'snow high up (on the mountain)' (J. S. Clay, *C.W.* 83 (1989–90) 103–4).

aure ... sublata: showing excitement; cf. Virg. *A.* 1.152 *silent arrectisque auribus astant (translatio a mutis animalibus, quibus aures mobiles sunt* (Servius)), Prop. 3.6.8 *suspensis auribus ista bibam*, and, for the opposite, *C.* 2.13.33–5 (Cerberus) *carminibus stupens | demittit atras belua centiceps | auris.*

9 complesti: the uncontracted form (*compleuisti*) is not attested (*ThLL* III 2090). For the image, cf. *Ars* 204 *complere sedilia fletu*, and what may be H.'s model, Lucr. 5.1066 (Molossians) *latrant et uocibus omnia complent.*

nemus: since the word can mean trees planted near or within a town (e.g. *C.* 3.10.5–6 *nemus | inter pulcra satum tecta*), H. may imply that his opponent 'barks' from the safety of his own 'yard'.

10 proiectum ... cibum: probably a 'sop' like that used by the Sibyl to quiet Cerberus (Virg. *A.* 6.420–1); cf. Schol. *demonstrat eum pecuniam quaerere maledictis.* But since wolves, not human predators, have been mentioned, this could be a *haedus ereptus lupo* (2.60) which the dog, instead of returning (5–10n.), greedily treats as his own food.

10 odoraris: a *uox propria* of dogs and other animals that hunt by scent (12.4, Pl. *Mil.* 268 *ibo odorans quasi canis uenaticus*, *OLD* s.v.). Except in the form *odoratus* ('fragrant'), *odoror* is rare in verse outside of comedy (Grassman (1966) 74).

11 This is H.'s only trimeter without caesura or tmesis (1.19n.) at pos. 5 or 7 (Intro. 6), unless *nam | que* can be considered tmesis. There is a break at pos. 6 which may be a 'medial caesura' such as is sometimes found in Greek drama (but not in surviving Archaic *iambus*) and in earlier Latin trimeters (e.g. Cat. 29.5 *cinaede Romule haec uidebis et feres*) and choliambs (31.2 *ocelle quascumque in liquentibus stagnis*).

caue caue: although the image is about to change there may be a hint of 'the usual inscription over the door of a Roman house: *caue canem*' (Miles). For the emotive repetition, cf. 4.20n.

malos: including H.'s opponent. His transformation from a 'dog' into an 'evil-doer' is as sudden as that of the 'Horace-hound' into a bull (6 intro.). Some take *mali* here as 'the wicked' in general, as if H. were some kind of crusader; cf. Theocr. *AP* 13.3 (= Hipp. test. 18 Degani) 'the poet Hipponax lies here. | If you are wicked (*ponēros*), do not approach the tomb.' But this would be at odds with the 'tooth for tooth' ethos of the rest of the poem.

asperrimus 'most savage'. *asper* in this sense is used of both beasts and people; cf. *C.* 1.23.9 *tigris ut aspera*, 35.9 (a Dacian), 3.2.10–11 (a metaphorical lion), Virg. *G.* 3.57–8 (a cow) *aspera cornu | et faciem tauro propior*, Fordyce on *A.* 7.505 (Allecto).

12 cornua: cf. 12.17n., *C.* 3.21.18 (wine) *addis cornua pauperi*, *S.* 1.4.34 (the satirist) *faenum habet in cornu, longe fuge*, Hom. *Il.* 2.480–1, 21.237 (Agamemnon and Achilles likened to bulls), Pl. *Ps.* 1021 [*metuo*] *ne ... mihi obuortet cornua.* For the bull as guardian of his herd, cf. Var. *R.* 2.9.2 (dogs are not needed to protect cattle) *cum sciam ... tauros diuersos assistere clunibus continuatos et cornibus facile propulsare lupos.*

Iambus is often characterized as a kind of 'weapon', cf. 17.10n., *C.* 1.16.24–5, *Ars* 79 *Archilochum proprio rabies armauit iambo*, Arist. *Poet.* 1448b32, Call. *Iamb.* 1.3, Cic. *Nat.* 3.91 *quem Hipponactis iambus laeserat aut qui erat Archilochi uersu uulneratus*, Cat. 36.5 *truces uibrare iambos*, 40.2, 54.6, fr. 3 *at non effugies meos iambos*, Ov. *Rem.* 377–8, *Ib.* 51–2, 521, Stat. *Silv.* 2.2.115, *RE* IX 652–3, Gentili (1988) 245.

13–14 Lycambes and Bupalus are the stock enemies of Archilochean and Hipponactean *iambus* (Intro. 3). In Archilochus' 'scenario', Lycambes promises his daughter Neobule to the poet, reneges on the pact, becomes the target of abusive verse and, along with the girl and her sister, hangs himself (*Ep.* 1.19.25–31, Arch. frr. 30–87, 172–81, 196a, 295 West). Bupalus, supposedly a sculptor, mocks Hipponax' ugliness and is likewise blamed into hanging himself (Hipp. test. 7–19 Degani, frr. 1–15, 77, 84, 95, 95a, 120 West). H. seems to play here on the names of these characters (Miles). *Lykambēs*, 'wolf-rhythm' (West (1974) 25–7, Nagy (1979) 243–4) suggests the hostile *lupi* (2), while *Bou-palos*, 'bullfighter' (cf. *palē*, 'wrestling', *antipalos*, 'adversary', *duspalēs*, 'hostile') or 'bull-phallus' (R. Rosen,

T.A.P.A. 118 (1988) 29–41) fits with the image of the iambist as bull (12).

13–14 Lycambae ... Bupalo: the first noun is dat. of agent (16.8, 17.20, *C.* 1.21.4 etc.), the second possibly dat. of 'disadvantage' (LHS II 91–2) either with *acer*, 'an enemy relentless to B.', or with *hostis*, 'a relentless enemy to B.'. But there is no parallel for a dat. with *acer*, and with *hostis* the construction is normally predicate ('is (was) an enemy to X') with a form of *sum* expressed (e.g. Lucil. fr. 1151 *ROL ut si hostes sint omnibus omnes*, *ThLL* VI 3.3058). Kenney suggests *Bupali*, 'a fierce enemy of B.', which could have been corrupted by 'attraction' to *infido*.

14 acer 'relentless' (16.5, *S.* 2.1.1 *sunt quibus in satira uidear nimis acer*), but the epithet may also suggest a 'keen-scented' dog (12.6, Virg. *G.* 3.405 (5n.)) or 'savage' beast (2.31, 12.25, *Ep.* 2.2.28 (a berserk soldier) *uehemens lupus ... ieiunis dentibus acer*; cf. 7.13).

15 an: introducing an indignant question (17.76, *OLD* s.v. 1, LHS II 466).

atro dente: a symbol of malignancy and envy; cf. 5.47n., *C.* 3.20.10, 4.3.16, *S.* 2.1.52, 77–8, *Ep.* 1.18.82, Brink on *Ep.* 2.1.150–1 (victims of *Fescennina licentia*) *doluere cruento | dente lacessiti*, Ov. *Met.* 2.776 (of *Inuidia*) *liuent robigine dentes*, Mart. 5.28.7, *ThLL* VI 1.542. *petiuerit* picks up *petis* (4) and may echo 5.10 *petita ferro belua*. The variant *oppetiuerit*, while not impossible (for the elision, cf. 5.9, 17.49, 74), is probably a gloss (Keller).

16 inultus ... puer: cf. Hom. *Il.* 20.431–2 (Hector to Achilles) 'Son of Peleus, do not expect to frighten me with words as if I were a child.' The simile seems intended to recall the helpless *puer* of Epode 5, and, perhaps, to anticipate the murdered Remus of the next poem (7.19–20). The peculiar word order *inultus ut* probably shows 'that *inultus* belongs equally to the subject of *flebo* and to *puer*' (Naylor; for similar dislocations, cf. 8.5, 8, *C.* 1.15.29, 37.17, 3.15.10, 4.4.57, 12.24, *S.* 1.2.105 (7n.), 3.89, 2.3.246).

EPODE 7

Introduction

Why are the Romans rushing to fight, not against a foreign enemy, but to destroy their own city? Is it madness, the gods, or some fault of their own? They cannot answer, but H. knows the cause: it is the curse arising from the ancient murder of Remus.

The anticipated war is almost certainly that with Antony (Intro. 2), and the dramatic date of H.'s speech may be early in 32 BC (Kraggerud (1984) 65). At the first meeting of the Senate in that year (1 January or 1 February (Reinhold on Dio 50.2.3)) the consul Sosius 'praised Antony and attacked Caesar [Octavian]' (Dio 50.2.4); at the second meeting, Octavian showed up with a bodyguard of soldiers and armed civilians. Soon after the consuls and some 300 of the 1,000 senators left the city to join Antony, and civil war became inevitable (Dio 50.2.4–7; cf. Pelling on Plut. *Ant.* 56–60.1, *MRR* II 417).

Since H. was not a senator (9.3n.), he could not have been present at the actual meetings, but he may be imagined as standing near the Curia (1–14n.) and addressing the senators (cf. 16.1–14n.), both 'Antonian' and 'Caesarian' (below), as they depart. His stance may suggest that of a tribune of the plebs, or of the *haruspex* Spurinna when he warned Julius about the Ides of March in 44 BC (Suet. *Jul.* 81.2), but it is most like that of the early Greek poets when they extended their exhortations and blame from their friends to the community as a whole (1–14, 1–2nn., Intro. 3).

All of the Romans labour under the 'curse of Remus' (20n.), so it seems unlikely that H. is blaming only the 'Antonian' senators (Kraggerud (1984) 50; cf. E. Burck, *Gnomon* 58 (1986) 18). In the 'public' epodes H. may be a friend of Maecenas, but he is not necessarily a 'Caesarian' (1.2n.), and he is capable of expressing anxiety over the conduct of Octavian himself (9.21–6n., 16 intro.). Even in his later works he rarely, if ever (perhaps at *C.* 2.7.9–14 and, allegorically, in *C.* 1.15 and 3.4), assigns blame for the civil wars to one side or the other. What matters most is the death of citizens and the fact that such strife benefits nobody except Rome's external enemies (5–10; cf. 1.11–14, 9.6, 10.11–14, 16.3–10nn.).

1–14 H. addresses the Romans: they are rushing into war, but not a war to defend Italy or expand the empire. Instead, they seem driven to self-destruction in a manner alien even to wild beasts. Is the cause madness, or some external force, or guilt?

H.'s speech here seems more extemporaneous than in Epode 16, where he will address something like an official assembly (16 intro.). Perhaps he is to be thought of as standing near the Curia, the meeting place of the Senate, and reacting to the sight of Octavian's armed supporters and the 300 senators who will soon join Antony (7 intro.). From this site he would be able to point for effect to much of the city (*urbs haec*), including the Sacra Via.

Despite a long tradition at Rome of political verse, H. seems to be the first Latin poet to address, or pretend to address (below), the people with an *iambus* or other type of Greek monody. In this he almost certainly follows Archilochus and other early Greeks (1–2n.). It is often argued that since H. is unlikely to have actually 'delivered' a speech of this sort, he made a 'literary fiction' out of what was a real-life situation for his models (Fraenkel (1957) 42, Fedeli (1978) 114–15). But some Hellenists now believe that the public stance of the early Greek poets was also in some respects a 'fictional' or 'dramatic' construct (Intro. 3).

1–2 A lost poem of Archilochus began with a similar question: 'Erxias, why yet again is the unfortunate army assembling?' (fr. 88 West (App. 1)). Cf. fr. 109 'O wretched citizens, understand my words', Callinus, fr. 1.1, Solon, frr. 4.1–2, 11.1–2 'If you have suffered sorrows because of your wickedness, | do not impute this fate to the gods.'

1 Quo quo: an emotive repetition (4.20n.). *scelesti* anticipates *scelus*, but at first sight could be taken simply as a term of abuse (*C.* 2.4.17, *S.* 2.3.71, 221, Opelt (1965) 160–1) without any religious connotations.

ruitis 'rush heedlessly'. Cf. *C.* 1.3.26, 3.4.58, Virg. *A.* 10.811 *quo moriture ruis*, 12.313 *quo ruitis? quaeue ista repens discordia surgit?*, Tac. *Hist.* 1.46 (soldiers) *ad seditiones et discordias et ad extremum bella ciuilia ruebant.*

2 aptantur: cf. Virg. *A.* 2.671–2 *clipeoque sinistram | insertabam aptans*, 9.364. There may be a play on this sense of *apto* at *C.* 2.12.1–4 *nolis ... bella ... mollibus | aptari citharae modis.* H., like most poets, prefers *ensis* (8 ×) to *gladius* (*S.* 2.3.276 only).

conditi: sc. *in uaginis*, presumably after Philippi or Perusia (Intro. 2), since H. 'goes along' with the pretence that Naulochus was not a civil war (9.7–8n.). This sense of *condo* seems to be poetic; cf. *Saec.* 33

(Apollo) *condito mitis placidusque telo*, Ov. *Rem.* 612 *quae condiderat, tela resumpsit Amor*, *ThLL* IV 149.

3 parumne: with *sanguinis* (partitive gen.); cf. *Ep.* 2.2.111 *parum splendoris*. For *-ne* introducing an indignant or ironic question, cf. 4.7, 11.11, *C.* 3.5.5, and, among many examples in the hexameters, *S.* 2.5.3–5 *iamne [tibi] doloso | non satis est Ithacam reuehi patriosque penatis | adspicere?*

campis atque Neptuno = *terra marique* (2.5–6n.), except that the word *campis* suggests more peaceful uses for 'land'; cf. N–H on *C.* 2.1.29–30 *quis non Latino sanguine pinguior | campus*, Thomas on Virg. *G.* 1.491–2 *nec fuit indignum superis bis sanguine nostro | Emathiam et latos Haemi pinguescere campos.* The metonymy (2.29n., 17.55, *Ep.* 1.11.10, *Ars* 64, Lucr. 2.472, 655, 6.1076) may also be significant, implying that the slaughter offends the gods (17n.); cf. Arch. fr. 12 West (of corpses) 'Let us hide the loathsome gifts of lord Poseidon.' There may even be a reference to Naulochus, the battle against the *Neptunius dux* (9.7–10; cf. AG (1971) 11).

super: both the construction with the abl. and the 'anastrophe' (placement after its nouns) are poetic (LHS II 216, 281; cf. 2.38n., 11.19, 172). Cf. Lucr. 6.1258 [*posses uidere*] *matribus et patribus natos super edere uitam.* Some take *super* here in verse-end tmesis with *fusum est*; cf. *S.* 1.2.62–3 *inter- | est*, 6.58–9, 2.3.117–18, Brink on *Ep.* 2.2.93–4, *Ars* 424, Skutsch on Enn. *Ann.* 105. There is a similar uncertainty at *C.* 2.16.33–4 *te greges centum Siculaeque circum | mugiunt uaccae* (most edd., N–H, but *circum- | mugiunt* L. Mueller, Klingner).

4 Latini sanguinis: cf. Luc. 1.9 *gentibus inuisis Latium praebere cruorem.* In H. 'Latin' and 'Roman' are usually synonymous (the one clear exception is *Saec.* 66), but *Latini* here may be a reminder both of the contributions of allies to Rome's wars and of her early conflicts with the cities of Latium, which were sometimes seen as 'proto' civil wars (Carrubba (1966) 34; cf. Gransden on Virg. *A.* 8.642–5, Liv. 1.23.1 (on the war against Alba Longa (15n.)) *bellum … ciuili similimum bello, prope inter parentes natosque*, Jal (1963) 411). *sanguen* is more poetic than *cruor* (20), but cf. 3.6n. and the *uariatio* at *C.* 2.1.29 (3n.) and 36 *quae caret ora cruore nostro?*

5 superbas: transferred epithet (2.7n.). The Romans were supposed to *debellare superbos* (Virg. *A.* 6.853); cf. *C.* 4.4.70, 15.7, *Saec.* 55.

For Carthaginian *inuidia*, cf. Sall. *Cat.* 10.1 *Carthago aemula imperi Romani ab stirpe interiit.* H. may allude to the idea that the vacuum created by the destruction of Carthage in 146 BC contributed to Rome's internal decline (Miles; cf. Intro. 2, K. Vretska, *Sallust de Catilinae Coniuratione* (Heidelberg 1976) 200–6).

6 arces: poetic plural; cf. N–H on *C.* 2.6.21, Pease on Virg. *A.* 4.234, Man. 4.599 *magnae quondam Carthaginis arces.*

6–7 Romanus … Britannus: 'collective singulars' (LHS II 13; cf. 9.11n., 16.6, *C.* 3.6.2, *S.* 1.4.85, 2.1.37, *Ars* 54 (the Romans), *C.* 1.19.12, 29.4, 35.9, 2.2.11, 6.2, 11.1, 13.18, 20.17–20, 3.3.47, 4.34, 6.14, 8.19, 22, 16.26, 4.5.25, 14.41–2, *Saec.* 54, *S.* 2.1.15, 35, *Ep.* 1.12.26–7 (other peoples)). The distribution of this type of sing. in H. (30× in lyrics, 7× in hexameters) suggests that he considered it poetic; in other Latin 'it seems to have been both archaic and colloquial' (N–H on *C.* 1.19.12; cf. Skutsch on Enn. *Ann.* 560, Cic. *De orat.* 3.168).

7 intactus aut Britannus: the civil war of 50–45 distracted the Romans from following up Caesar's initial attempts on Britain (Tac. *Ag.* 13.2). With the encouragement of H. and other poets (*C.* 1.21.13–16, N–H on *C.* 1.35.30, 3.5.3–4, 4.14.47–8, Virg. *G.* 3.25, Prop. 2.27.5) Octavian contemplated expeditions in 34, 27, and 26 BC (Dio 49.38.2, 53.22.5, 25.2, Kienast (1982) 292–3), but the island was to remain 'untouched' until the reign of Claudius.

7–8 descenderet | … catenatus: as a prisoner on display in a triumphal procession (9.21–6). The Sacra Via (4.7n.) 'descended' from the Velia into the Forum (cf. *C.* 4.2.33–6, Cic. *Att.* 4.3.3 *cum Sacra Via descenderem*). *catenatus* may be a Horatian coinage (*ThLL* III 607; cf. *cinctutis* at *Ars* 50).

9 secundum uota Parthorum: cf. N–H on *C.* 1.2.21–2, 2.1.31–2 *auditumque Medis | Hesperiae sonitum ruinae.* The débâcle of Carrhae (53 BC) was not yet avenged (*C.* 3.5), and after Philippi (42) the Parthians again invaded eastern parts of the empire (*C.* 1.12.53, 21.13–16, 29.3–4, 3.6.9–12). Cf. N–H on *Odes* I, Intro. xxxii–iii, Kienast (1982) 282–6, Pelling on Plut. *Ant.* 37–52. *secundum* occurs only here in H. and otherwise mostly in comedy and prose.

11–12 'Nor was this the norm for wolves or lions, (who are) never [12n.] savage except against something dissimilar.' The 'norm' is civil war or, in animal terms, cannibalism; cf. Sen. *Ep.* 95.31, Juv. 15.159–68, Plin. *Nat.* 7.5 *denique cetera animantia in suo genere probe degunt:*

congregari uidemus et stare contra dissimilia. leonum feritas inter se non dimicat, serpentium morsus non petit serpentis, ne maris quidem beluae ac pisces nisi in diuersa genera saeuiunt: at Hercule homini plurima ex homine sunt mala. All of these exaggerate for rhetorical effect: the ancients knew perfectly well that animals can be quite 'savage' against their own kind. Cf. West on Hes. *Op.* 276–9 (cannibalism among fish, beasts, and birds), Hom. *Il.* 4.471–2, Ael. *N.A.* 7.23 (among wolves).

11 lupis: cf. 6.2n. There may be a reference to the wolf as a foster-mother of Romulus and Remus and as a symbol of Rome (Miles; cf. Ogilvie on Liv. 3.66.4, C. Dulière, *Lupa romana* (Rome 1979)).

fuit: 'gnomic perfect' expressing, in a *sententia* (Greek *gnōmē*), 'what has been and will be'. The usage is probably based on the Greek 'gnomic aorist' (e.g. Hipp. fr. 78.16, Sem. fr. 7.45, Solon 13.28 West) and is first attested in late Republican literature (Kroll on Cat. 62.42, Cic. *Div.* 1.14 (translating Greek), LHS II 318–19). For other examples in H., cf. *C.* 1.28.20, 34.15–16, 3.2.29–32, 23.17–20, 29.16, 4.4.5–16 (?), *S.* 1.9.59–60, 2.3.222–3, *Ep.* 1.2.47–8, 5.19–20, 17.37, 19.48–9, Brink on *Ars* 343, 373.

12 numquam: a Renaissance conjecture accepted by Bentley and most editors after him (cf. Brink (1982) 38). *umquam*, the reading of the MSS and scholia, may have arisen from a misguided attempt to provide a temporal reference for the 'gnomic perfect' *fuit* (11n.). If it is retained (Wickham, Klingner), *hic ... mos* would refer to strife in general rather than civil strife; 'nor was this [i.e. fighting] ever the norm for wolves or lions except against something dissimilar'. The sense is possible, but it is not clear how *feris* would fit in. Despite its position in the sentence some make it attributive with *leonibus* ('wild lions'), while others resort to emendation (*in dispar genus* dett., Lambinus).

in dispar feris: both *dispar* as a neut. sing. substantive and *ferus* with *in* (= *aduersus*) seem to be unparalleled in Classical Latin (*ThLL* v 1.1392, vi 606). But other substantive forms of *dispar* are attested (e.g. *C.* 1.17.25 (fem. sing.), 4.11.31, *S.* 1.7.16 (masc. sing. and pl.), Cic. *Fin.* 2.10 (neut. pl.)), and *in* occurs with words similar in meaning to *ferus* (e.g. 5.4, 6.11, *C.* 1.2.39–40, *S.* 2.8.61; cf. *ThLL* vii 1.750). *dispar* is a *uox propria* of species difference; cf. Cic. *Tusc.* 5.38 *atque earum [bestiarum] quaeque suum tenens munus, cum in disparis animantis uitam transire non possit, manet in lege naturae.*

13–14 As it turns out, the answer is 'all three' (15–20.), but at first sight these alternatives could be taken as mutually exclusive. The *furor* might be caused by disease, not divine wrath (cf. *S.* 2.3.81–2, Brink, Rudd on *Ep.* 2.2.128–40, *Ars* 300), while the *culpa* might be opposed by the other two, since in Roman law 'responsibility' for actions was obviated by both *furor* ('unsoundness of mind'; cf. *RE* VII 380–2) and *uis maior* ('act of god' (13n.); cf. *ThLL* IV 1299).

The phrasing here bears a striking but probably coincidental resemblance to a fragment of Livius Andronicus (*com.* 1 *ROL*) *pulicesne an cimices an pedes? responde mihi.*

13 furorne caecus: *furor*, *rabies*, and *insania* are practically technical terms for civil strife (Jal (1963) 421–3, Opelt (1965) 140–1). Cf. *C.* 3.24.25–6, 4.15.17–19 *custode rerum Caesare non furor | ciuilis aut uis exiget otium, | non ira*, Virg. *A.* 1.150, 294, Luc. 1.8 etc. H.'s phrase seems to be echoed at V. Max. 9.2 *ext.* 5, Sen. *Her. F.* 991, *Thy.* 27 (cf. 339), *Oed.* 590, and Luc. 10.146–7, which makes the otherwise attractive variant *caecos* (Bentley, Brink (1982) 38, Sh. Bailey) unlikely.

uis acrior: probably a poetic equivalent of the legal term *uis maior*, 'act of god (fate, nature) outside of human control' (cf. *OLD* s.v. *uis* 9c). *acrior*, however, suggests anger or sternness (17n.); cf. 6.14, Lucr. 5.87, 6.63 (the gods) *dominos acris*. Some take *uis* here as *uiolentia* (s.v. 4; cf. *C.* 1.16.16, 3.14.15, 4.15.18 (above)), but that would correspond less well to *acerba fata* (17).

14 responsum date: *responsum* can mean an answer to an ordinary question (*OLD* s.v. 1) but here, as in Virgil's famous *hic mihi responsum primus dedit ille petenti* (*Ecl.* 1.44), there may be a suggestion of two other senses, 'legal opinion' (s.v. 2b) and especially 'answer given by an oracle, soothsayer, or sim.' (s.v. 2a; cf. *S.* 1.8.29). The former would fit with the legal or quasi-legal terms in H.'s question (13–14n.), while the latter would anticipate the ending, where the poet is the only one able to 'respond' (15–20n.).

15–20 The Romans cannot answer, and it is left to H. to give his own *responsum*. All of the causes that he suggested (13–14) are at work: *furor* 'smiting their minds' (16), *uis acrior* in the form of 'harsh fates' (17), and *culpa* arising from the ancient and repeated crime of fratricide (15, 18–20).

H. does not say how he knows these things, but it is probably because he is a poet. In early Greek thought poets, usually with the help of the Muses, know more than other mortals about the past and the workings of the gods (Clay (1983) 9–25). This seems to be the case even with the iambist: Archilochus is a 'servant of the Muses' (fr. 1 West; cf. the account of his poetic initiation at test. 4 Tarditi) and speaks with certainty about such matters as the intervention of the gods in battles (frr. 3.2–3, 91.30 (?), 94, 98, 111, 112) and their 'gifts', good or bad, to mortals (13.5–7, 16, 25, 128.7, 130, 131, 230, 298 (?)). Cf. 13.11 (on Chiron's 'song') and 16.66nn. (on the term *uates*). H. does not claim 'vatic' inspiration here, possibly because he can as yet offer no solution to the problem (15n.), even one as desperate as what he will propose in Epode 16.

15 tacent: cf. the Homeric formula (*Il.* 3.95 etc.) 'he spoke, and they were all speechless in silence'. H.'s shift from second (*ruitis, date*) to third person verbs seems to indicate that he no longer speaks directly to the Romans, but has 'withdrawn to the sidelines', perhaps in disgust at his audience's stupidity (16), or in despair at knowing the cause but not the cure for what afflicts them (15–20n.).

H. also shifts from second to third person in Epode 12 and, much later, *C.* 4.13. There seems to be no example of this device in early *iambus*, but it does occur in lyrics of Alcaeus (fr. 42 L–P) and Anacreon (347 *PMG*; cf. 12.9n.), and elsewhere (e.g. Virg. *A.* 4.365–70, Prop. 2.33.35; cf. McKeown on Ov. *Am.* 1.8.35).

albus ... pallor: a sign of strong emotion (17.21n.), including fear (10.16, *S.* 2.8.35, Hom. *Il.* 3.35, Lucr. 3.154, Virg. *A.* 4.499 *pallor simul occupat ora*, Pers. 3.115 *timor albus*), but also guilt; cf. Cic. *Catil.* 3.13 *multo certiora illa* [*indicia sceleris*]: *color, oculi, uultus, taciturnitas. sic enim obstupuerunt, sic terram intuebantur, sic furtim inter se aspiciebant, ut non iam ab aliis indicari, sed indicare se ipsi uiderentur.*

albus is so close in meaning to *pallidus* that it is almost redundant here (André (1949) 28). But H. may be punning on the name of Alba Longa (cf. Virg. *A.* 8.43–8, Ahl (1985) 302–9), the birthplace of Romulus and Remus, later destroyed by the Romans in a 'proto' civil war (4n.). The variant word order (app. crit.) may have arisen from an attempt to simplify the hyperbaton (cf. Schol. *albus palloris epitheton*).

inficit: lit. 'tinges' (*OLD.* s.v. 1b), but H. may hint at the sense 'corrupts' (s.v. 3). Cf. Virg. *A.* 6.742 *infectum eluitur scelus* and (echoing

H.?) Ov. *Met.* 4.486–7 (with the coming of Tisiphone) *postes tremuisse feruntur | Aeolii, pallorque fores infecit acernas.*

16 mentesque … stupent: sc. *furore.* Cf. 5.75n., *S.* 2.3.278 *commotae … mentis.* Despite H.'s phrasing of his question (13–14n.), there does not have to be a contradiction with *acerba fata.* Pious Romans seem to have believed that 'whom the gods would destroy they first make mad' (Cic. *Har.* 39, Liebeschuetz (1979) 93), while sceptics would attribute such frenzy to (irrational) fear of those same gods (cf. *S.* 2.3.295 (of a madwoman) *quone malo mentem concussa? timore deorum,* Lucr. 1.83–101, 3.1011–23 etc.). *percello,* which occurs only here in H., seems to be stronger than *percutio* (11.2n.).

17 sic est = *sine dubio hoc est* (Porph.). Cf. Pl. *Merc.* 268 *nunc hoc profecto sic est: haec illa est capra,* Cic. *Q. Rosc.* 29 *sic est uulgus: ex ueritate pauca, ex opinione multa aestimat.*

acerba fata: for the phrase, cf. Cat. 68.1 (echoed at Virg. *A.* 5.700) *casuque oppressus acerbo,* Virg. *A.* 11.587 (Camilla) *fatis urgetur acerbis,* Hom. *Il.* 16.849 *moir' oloē* ('destructive fate'), *Od.* 11.292 *chalepē … moira* ('harsh fate'), 22.413 (17–18n.). These 'harsh fates', like the *moirai* of Homeric heroes and other early Greeks (13.7n.), are probably to be thought of as 'decreed' (*fari*) by the gods. The civil wars were often seen as either the cause or the result of divine wrath (10.11–14n., 16.63–6, N–H on *C.* 1.2, 35.33–40, 2.1.25–8, 3.6, 24.25–32, Cic. *Har.* 40, Thomas, Mynors on Virg. *G.* 1.463–514, Fantham on Luc. 2.1–66, Jal (1962) and (1963) 238–42, Liebeschuetz (1979) 50–60, 90–5).

17–18 fata … | scelusque: a kind of hendiadys, with the *-que* (sometimes called 'epexegetic') adding a second element 'which explains and enlarges on what precedes' (*OLD* s.v. 6; cf. Kenney on Lucr. 3.346, Mynors on Virg. *G.* 2.192, Norden on *A.* 6.24, LHS II 782–3). There are many examples in H., e.g. 9.37, *C.* 1.17.18 *tristitiam uitaeque labores,* 28.32 *iura uicesque superbae,* 35.33–4 (18n.). *moira* (17n.) from the gods is linked in a similar way with 'crime' at Hom. *Od.* 22.413, where Odysseus explains the destruction of the suitors: 'the fate of the gods [*moira theōn*] and (their own) wicked deeds [*schetlia erga*] overcame these men'.

18 scelusque: both the 'crime' (*OLD* s.v. 2) of fratricide and the 'curse' (s.v. 1) arising from that crime. Some insist on one meaning or the other, but 'the tragedy of Rome's history lies in the fact that the

punishment not only fits the crime but is the crime – for what is civil
war but expanded fratricide?' (Commager (1962) 181). *scelus* is almost
a technical term for civil war; cf. N–H on *C.* 1.2.29, 35.33–4 *cica-
tricum et sceleris pudit | fratrumque*, 3.24.50, Cic. *Lig.* 17–18, Virg. *Ecl.*
4.13, *G.* 1.506, Luc. 1.2, Jal (1962) 172–3.

Unlike the Greeks (Parker (1983) 199–206), the Romans do not
seem to have believed in inherited guilt. But the internal strife fol-
lowing the extirpation of Carthage (5n.) seems to have led to spe-
culation concerning a 'flaw' (Sall. *Hist.* 1. fr. 7 *uitio humani ingeni*) or
'curse' (*C.* 3.6, Virg. *Ecl.* 4.13, 31) coeval with the city (19n.) or even
older (*C.* 3.3, Virg. *G.* 1.501–2 *satis iam pridem sanguine nostro | Laome-
donteae luimus periuria Troae*). Cf. C. Koch, *Religio* (Nuremberg 1960)
170–2, Jal (1963) 402–11, O. Seel, *Römertum und Latinität* (Stuttgart
1964) 99–114 (who suggests that the idea may owe something to Jew-
ish teachings), Liebeschuetz (1979) 90–5.

19 ut = *ex quo*, 'from the time when'. Cf. *C.* 4.4.43, *S.* 2.2.128
OLD s.v. *ut* 27.

immerentis ... Remi: murdered by his brother Romulus while
the two were founding what would become Rome. For the story and
its sources, cf. Ogilvie on Liv. 1.6.3–7.3, *EV* IV 570–4. H. leaves no
doubt here about Romulus' guilt, but in some versions Remus is not
exactly 'blameless' (e.g. Enn. *Ann.* 92–5 Skutsch, Liv. 1.7.3), while in
others the killer is either unknown (Liv. 1.7.2) or an over-zealous fol-
lower of Romulus named Celer (Ov. *F.* 4.837–56, 5.451–84).

It is not clear when Romans began to interpret their foundation
myth as a paradigm of civil strife. There are traces of this view in
Sallust's version of a speech by M. Aemilius Lepidus in 78 BC (*Hist.* I
fr. 55.5 (of Sulla) *scaeuos iste Romulus*), in Cicero (*Off.* 3.41), and per-
haps Lucretius (3.70–3) and Catullus (29.9, 58.5 (20n.), 64.397–9).
Virgil alludes to it (Thomas on *G.* 2.533, *A.* 1.292–3) and it is almost
a commonplace in later writers (e.g. Prop. 2.1.23, 3.9.50, Ov. *F.*
2.143, Luc. 1.93–5). Cf. Jal (1963) 407–10, Cremona (1982) 60–1. In
his later works H. to some extent 'rehabilitates' Romulus (*C.* 2.15.10–
12, 3.3, 4.8.22–4, *Ep.* 2.1.5, Oksala (1973) 154–8). For the identifica-
tion with Quirinus, cf. 16.13n. It may be worth noting that some in
antiquity considered Archilochus a contemporary of Romulus (Cic.
Tusc. 1.3 *fuit ... Archilochus regnante Romulo*).

in terram: the earth itself – perhaps even the goddess Tellus (*C.*

2.12.7, *Saec.* 29, *Ep.* 2.1.143) – is polluted by the crime. Cf. Cat.
64.397 *tellus scelere est imbuta nefando*, Virg. *A.* 3.61 (the blood of Poly-
dorus makes Thrace a *scelerata ... terra*), Fantham on Luc. 2.734–6
(Roman earth spared the taint of Pompey's blood). These passages
may reflect a Roman belief that the site of a homicide required ritual
purification (Fugier (1963) 360–9).

20 sacer 'bringing a curse'; cf. 16.18n. (on *exsecrata*), 17.6, Cat.
14.12 *di magni, horribilem et sacrum libellum*, 71.1, Virg. *A.* 3.57 *auri sacra
fames*. The passive, 'under a curse', seems to be more common (*S.*
2.3.181 *is intestabilis et sacer esto, OLD* s.v. 2). These senses of *sacer*
appear to come from the idea that something made 'sacred' to the
gods, whether for sacrifice or punishment, is off-limits and thus dan-
gerous to humans (Fugier (1963) 224–47, Benveniste (1969) 187–92).

nepotibus: although he had no offspring, Romulus was con-
sidered the *pater* and even *genitor* of the Romans (Enn. *Ann.* 105–9
Skutsch; cf. 16.13, *C.* 1.2.35–6, 4.5.1, *Saec.* 47, Cat. 49.1 etc.). Some
see a reference here to Catullus' puzzling *magnanimi nepotibus Remi*
(58.5; cf. Juv. 10.73 *turba Remi*), but a victim's blood should curse his
murderer's descendants, not his own.

EPODE 8

Introduction

A woman has complained that H. does not respond to her: small
wonder, since she is old and ugly. Her wealth, family, and learning
are to no avail: if she wants to arouse him, she must do it the hard
way.

Women who are old, ugly, or both are targets of verbal abuse
(*aischrologia*) in a wide variety of Greek and Latin literature (Grass-
man (1966) 1–46, Richlin (1992) 105–43), including early *iambus* (6,
9–10, 20, 12.5, 6, 16nn.; cf. Arch. fr. 35, 41–2, 196a.26–31, 205 West).
Sexual activity such as is described here (19–20) is also a common
topic in that genre (e.g. Arch. fr. 34–7, 43–5, 66, 67, 82, 188–91,
196a.48–53, 222, 258; cf. West (1974) 25–6).

There are many theories about the origins and function of this
type of poetry (fertility cult, 'initiation ritual', male 'repression' of
female sexuality). H.'s interest in it, which continues in the *Odes* (*C.*
1.25, 2.8, 3.6, 15, 4.13), may have a personal basis, but here and in

Epode 12, at least, the hag could be a symbolic figure similar or even identical to Canidia (5 intro., App. 2). She may represent 'antiquated literary style' (D. L. Clayman, *C.W.* 69 (1975) 55–61), or a typical young man's dread of impotence (Fitzgerald (1988) 185–6), or she could be a personification of Rome itself, horribly repulsive, yet still strangely fascinating to H. and other *patriae amatores* (App. 2).

1 Rogare: exclamatory infinitive (*infinitivus indignantis*), a colloquial way of expressing anger or surprise (LHS II 369; cf. American 'To ask (say, think) such a thing!'). It is usually introduced by *-ne* or *non* (11.11, *S.* 1.9.72, 2.4.83, 8.67); the omission of the particle here may suggest extraordinary indignation (Grassman (1966) 48).

longo ... saeculo: cf. *C.* 2.16.30 *longa Tithonum minuit senectus*, 4.13.24–5 *parem | cornicis uetulae temporibus Lycen. saeculum* (for *aetas*) is probably hyperbolic; cf. Kenney on Lucr. 3.948 *omnia si perges uiuendo uincere saecla*, Prop. 2.13.46 *Nestoris est uisus post tria saecla cinis*, *Priap.* 57.2 (below).

putidam: lit. 'rotting' (cf. *pus, puteo*), and so of people or things that are 'decrepit' or 'stinking' (*S.* 2.3.75, 7.21, Cat. 42.11 *moecha putida*, *Priap.* 57.2 (a hag) *turba putida facta saeculorum*). As a term of abuse *putidus* seems to be colloquial or even vulgar, more so than its cognate *putris* (8, *C.* 1.36.17, *Ep.* 1.10.49; cf. Grassman (1966) 49–50).

2 eneruet: cf. *nerui* (17). *eneruo* occurs only here in H. and may be colloquial (Grassman (1966) 51), but cf. Cic. *Sen.* 32 *non plane me eneruauit senectus*, Ov. *Rem.* 753 *eneruant animos citharae lotosque lyraeque*, *Met.* 4.286 (the lake) *Salmacis eneruet tactosque remolliat artus*.

3 dens ater: cf. 5.47, 6.14nn. Some take *dens* here as a 'collective singular', but a single tooth makes the woman's mouth more like her 'gaping' *podex* (5n.) and may add to the humour of the final verse (cf. the American term 'gum job'). Cf. Tränkle on [Tib.] *Priap.* 2.26 (= *Priap.* 83 Buecheler; also in *App. Verg.*) *bidens amica Romuli senis memor*, Mart. 3.93.1–2 *cum tibi trecenti consules, Vetustilla, | et tres capilli quattuorque sint dentes*.

3–4 rugis ... exaret: possibly based on Arch. fr. 188.1–2 (App. 1) 'You no longer bloom all over in your soft skin, for it is already drying up | with furrows [cf. *exaret*] and (the lot?) of evil old age destroys (you)'. For the image of ploughing, cf. Virg. *A.* 7.417 (Allecto disguises herself as a hag) *et frontem obscenam rugis arat*, Ov. *Ars* 2.118, *Med.* 45–6, *Pont.* 1.4.2.

uetus | ... senectus: cf. Ter. *Eun.* 688 (of a eunuch) *hic est uietus uetus ueternosus senex*, Tib. 1.8.5 *ueteres ... senes*. The pleonasm is unusual for H.; cf. 7.15n, *S.* 1.6.71 *macro ... agello*, *Ep.* 1.5.2 *modica ... patella*, 7.29 *tenuis uulpecula*, 2.1.12 *supremo fine*, Bo III 349–50.

5 hietque: cf. Cels. 7.29.5 [*uulua*] *hiante*, *Priap.* 12.13 [*cunnus*] *qui tanto patet indecens hiatu*, Mart. 3.72.5 *infinito ... patet inguen hiatu*. But *hio* and *hisco* are normally used either of the mouth (*S.* 1.2.88, 2.2.32, 5.56, *ThLL* VI 2683) or in agricultural contexts (e.g. Virg. *G.* 1.91). H. could be alluding to the topos *os an culus?* (Cat. 33.4, 97.2, Kroll on 98.6, Richlin (1992) 128–9) or continuing the image of *exaret* (3–4n.). Both *natis* (*S.* 1.8.47) and *podex* (only here in H., but cognate with *pedo* (*S.* 1.8.46, 9.70)) seem to be vulgarisms (Grassman (1966) 33–5), although the latter does occur in late medical Latin (Adams (1982) 112).

6 crudae bouis: probably 'quae frustra studet exonerare uentrem' (L. Mueller) rather than 'quae cibum non excoquit ideoque cibum non continet' (Lambinus). Cf. *S.* 1.5.49 *inimicum et ludere crudis*, *Ep.* 1.6.61 *crudi tumidique lauemur*, Var. *R.* 2.4.21 (toasted wheat) *crudum ... soluit aluum*, and for some modern lore about 'cow patties' Henderson (1987) 108. For the comparison with a *bos*, cf. Arch. fr. 35 West (of Neobule?) 'there is a cow (*bous*) in our house', 12.17 (*taurum*), N–H on *C.* 2.5.6 (*iuuenca* = *puella*) and, perhaps, Cicero's use of the epithet *boōpis* ('cow-eyed') for Clodia (*Att.* 2.9.1, 12.2, 14.1, 22.5).

7 pectus et mammae putres: cf. Cat. 64.351 *putrida ... pectora*, Prop. 2.15.21 *necdum inclinatae prohibent te ludere mammae*. For the hendiadys (= *in pectore mammae*), cf. *Mor.* 34 *pectore lata, iacens mammis*, Lucil. fr. 923–4 *ROL*, McKeown on Ov. *Am.* 1.5.20–1, Mart. 3.72.3. *mammae* and *ubera* (8) seem to be anatomical terms, *papillae* an erotic one (Grassman (1966) 55–6).

8 quales: possibly a case of attraction of the pronoun in a defining relative clause to the gender of the antecedent (*mammae*) rather than, what is more usual, the predicate (*ubera*). There seems to be no parallel for this with *qualis*, but cf. Liv. 4.28.5 *necessitate, quae* [for *quod*] *ultimum et maximum telum est*, LHS II 442. The conjecture *qualia* (Madvig, Sh. Bailey) is attractive, but is *lectio facilior* and introduces both a short syllable where H. generally avoids one (Intro. 6) and an elision on a long *u*, a rarity even in H.'s hexameters (8 ×), perhaps without parallel in his lyrics (cf. *C.* 2.11.10 *neque uno* A: *nec uno* B).

9 mollis: for the opposite, cf. Lucil. fr. 923 *ROL hic corpus solidum inuenies*, Ov. *Am.* 1.5.21. The woman's belly could be 'soft' from par-turition (cf. Ov. *Ars* 3.785, Mart. 3.72.4), which would work against the identification with Canidia (5.5–6, 17.50–2nn.). But H. does not anticipate children at her funeral (11–12), where a son would nor-mally give the *laudatio funebris*.

9–10 femur ... additum: Ovid's Corinna has a *iuuenale femur* (*Am.* 1.5.22; cf. *Ars* 3.781, H.'s *S.* 1.2.80–1), H.'s own Phyllis *teretes ... suras* (*C.* 2.4.21), and Archilochus declared that 'a woman thick about the ankles is hateful' (fr. 206 West; cf. Hipp. fr. 135). *tumentibus* suggests oedema, but may also be ironic in light of what is *not* 'tumescent' (18–20; cf. *S.* 1.2.116 *tument tibi cum inguina*). For *additum* (*quasi applicata* ['tacked-on'] *ibi haec aut apposita uideantur* (Porph.)), cf. Ov. *Met.* 5.456 (of a boy turned into a lizard) *cauda est mutatis addita membris*.

11–13 The imperative (*esto*) and the subjunctive (*ducant, sit*) are concessive: 'granted that you are fortunate, and granted that trium-phal images precede your funeral, and that there is no wife who ... struts'. For *esto* in this sense, cf. *S.* 1.6.19, 2.1.83, 2.30, 3.31, 65, *Ep.* 1.1.81, 17.37; for the alternation of imper. with subj., *C.* 3.3.39–44 *regnanto beati;* | *... stet Capitolium* | *... possit* | *Roma ferox dare iura Medis*, LHS II 335–6.

11 beata: for the term, cf. 2 intro. In this case the woman's sup-posed 'happiness' consists of her ancestry (11–12), wealth (13–14), and erudition (15–16). Cf. 15.17–22, Sall. *Cat.* 25 (15–16n.), Prop. 3.20.7–9 *est tibi forma potens, sunt castae Palladis artes,* | *splendidaque a docto fama refulget auo.* | *fortunata domus, modo sit tibi fidus amicus.*

atque: postponed (1.12n.), as at 17.4, *S.* 1.5.4, 6.111, 131, 7.12, 10.28. Some include *C.* 1.25.18, but there *atque* probably = *quam* (N–H *ad loc.*). For *atque* preceding a vowel, cf. 2.40n.

11–12 imagines ... triumphales: i.e. she is descended from *triumphatores* (9.21–6). The funeral of a distinguished Roman would be accompanied by people wearing wax likenesses (*imagines*) of the dead person's more notable ancestors (cf. *S.* 1.6.17, Cic. *De orat.* 2.225 (*imagines* at a woman's funeral), *RE* IX 1097–1104).

12 ducant: the present may suggest that she is already as good as dead; cf. *C.* 3.15.4 (of another old wife) *maturo propior ... funeri*, Pl. *Merc.* 290, *Priap.* 57.1 (a hag) *caries uetusque bustum*, Mart. 3.93.18–19. There may also be humour in the position of *tuum*: H. does not let on until the last word that he means *her* funeral.

13 marita: *maritus = uir* is well attested, but this seems to be the first example of *marita = uxor* (*ThLL* VIII 406), unless it is also a noun at Cat. 67.6 (to a *ianua*) *postquam es porrecto facta marita sene* (*OLD* s.v.; Kroll *ad loc.* takes it as an adj.).

rotundioribus: cf. Plin. *Nat.* 9.112 (of pearls) *dos omnis in candore, magnitudine, orbe* (= *rotunditate*; cf. 27.98), Valg. *poet.* fr. 1 *FPL* (metre uncertain) *situ rugosa, rutunda margarita*. Caesar restricted the wearing of pearls (Suet. *Jul.* 43.1), but it is not clear if this would still be in effect in the thirties. For the six-syllable word, cf. 4.11n.

14 onusta: the word suggests a pack animal (*S.* 1.1.47, *OLD* s.v. 1), a booty-laden soldier (*Ep.* 1.7.18, *OLD* s.v. 2), or a body 'heavy' with food, sleep etc. (*S.* 2.2.77, Lucr. 3.113, *OLD* s.v. 3). Cf. Ov. *Ars* 3.129 *uos quoque non caris aures onerate lapillis*.

ambulet: subj. in a consecutive rel. clause. The unpoetic word (4.5n.) may imply that this wife is less than modest; H. elsewhere complains that *matronae* travel concealed in litters (*S.* 1.2.98).

15–16 The woman is, or pretends to be erudite. In this respect she resembles Sallust's Sempronia (*Cat.* 25.2 *mulier genere atque forma, praeterea uiro liberis satis fortunata fuit; litteris Graecis Latinis docta*) and a certain Caerellia described by Cicero as *studio uidelicet philosophiae flagrans* (*Att.* 13.21.5). Cf. Mart. 2.90.9 *mihi ... sit non doctissima coniunx*, Juv. 6.434–56 (an excessively learned wife). There may be several jokes in the picture of Stoic tracts on her pillows. They would be strange reading for a boudoir; one would expect, if not pornography (*Priap.* 4.2 *Elephantidos libellis*, Griffin (1986) 38), at least love-poetry (cf. *C.* 1.17.19–20, 3.7.17–20, 9.10, 28.9–16, 4.11.34–6, 13.6–8, Cat. 16, Prop. 2.13.11–12 etc.). Yet the hag may have been misled by the reputation of the Stoics for (moral) 'rigidity' (Henderson (1987) 113; cf. 17n., *Ep.* 1.1.17 *uirtutis uerae custos rigidusque satelles*, Sen. *Dial.* 12.12.4 *Stoicorum rigida ac uirilis sapientia*, Juv. 2.64–5). Finally, H. may imply that the woman uses the book scrolls for obscene purposes (Richlin (1992) 111; cf. Juv. 6.337–8 (a penis compared to scrolls), Petr. 138.1 (18n.)).

quid, quod: a rhetorical (and prosaic) transitional formula that can be punctuated and translated in various ways (*OLD* s.v. *quis* 13c; cf. N–H on *C.* 2.18.23, Brink on *Ep.* 2.1.40). With a comma or colon after *amant* (Klingner, Bo) the translation here would be 'What, (just) because ...?'; with a full stop (most edd.), 'What of the fact that ...?'

libelli ... puluillos: the diminutives are probably derisive (11.2n.). Unlike Catullus and, apparently, the other 'Neoterics' (Ross 1969) 22–5), H. and his contemporaries make sparing use of diminutives (Axelson (1945) 38–45, Brink on *Ep.* 2.1.186, Kenney on Lucr. 3.189). In the *Epodes*, except for words diminutive in form but no longer so in meaning (*flagellum* (4.11), *masculus* (5.41), *puella* (3×), *pupula* (5.40), *tabella* (12.2n.)), H. has, besides the two here, only three others (11.2, 23, 16.49). For his other works, cf. Bo III 216–19.

Sericos: until the sixth century AD true silk came only from China, which made it fabulously expensive (*RE* IVA 1724–7). The references to the Chinese (*Seres*) in H. and other late Republican and Augustan poets seem to be the first in Latin (N–H on *C.* 1.12.56, 29.9, 3.29.27, 4.15.23, Thomas, Mynors on Virg. *G.* 2.121, McKeown on Ov. *Am.* 1.14.5–6).

16 iacere ... amant: probably 'are thrilled to lie', as if the books share in the fun. Some take *amant* as simply 'are wont' (= *solent*; cf. Sall. *Jug.* 34.1 with Quint. *Inst.* 9.3.17), but in H.'s other examples of this construction *amo* always has at least something of its true meaning (*C.* 1.2.50, N–H on *C.* 2.3.10, 3.9.24, 16.10, *S.* 1.10.60, 2.3.20, 214, 5.96, *Ep.* 1.14.9, perhaps *Ars* 197 (cf. Brink, Sh. Bailey (app. crit.) *ad loc.*), Grassman (1966) 62–5). *amo* with the active inf. does not occur before H., but is probably based on the analogy of *uolo* and *cupio* rather than, as some argue, Greek *phileō* (LHS II 346–7; cf. H.'s use of *expeto* (11.3), *glorior* (11.24), and *propero* (12.9)).

17 illiterati 'unable to read', and therefore unimpressed by the *libelli*. The epithet goes with both *nerui* and *fascinum*. For the *mentula*'s lack of discrimination, cf. *S.* 1.2.68–71, *Priap.* 68, Mart. 11.19 *quaeris cur nolim te ducere, Galla? diserta es. | saepe soloecismum mentula nostra facit*, and, for its personification, Adams (1982) 29–30, Tränkle on [Tib.] *Priap.* 2, Richlin (1992) 114–19. The cretic-containing *illiteratus* occurs in comedy (Caecil. *com.* 55 *ROL*).

num ... rigent: apparently 'are (my) sinews less frozen', i.e. is his body less paralysed with horror at her ugliness. With this interpretation (Porph., Heinze, Grassman (1966) 65–7) *nerui = uires* (cf. 2, *S.* 2.1.2, *Ars* 26, *OLD* s.v. *neruus* 6), *rigent = frigent* or *torpent* (s.v. *rigeo* 2b; cf. *rigidus* 'unresponsive' at Ov. *Am.* 1.4.36, 2.4.15, *Rem.* 762, *Ep.* 4.73–8). It is true that *neruus* can mean 'penis' (12.19, *OLD* s.v. 1b, Adams (1982) 38), *rigeo* 'have an erection' (s.v. 2b; cf. *rigidus* 3b); cf. Tränkle on [Tib.] *Priap.* 2.42 *rigente neruus excubet libidine.* But if that is their meaning here, there is either an obvious contradiction between lines 17 and 18 or, with *magis* for *minus* in 17 (Heinsius, Sh. Bailey), H. unaccountably says the same thing twice. Housman's *pigrent* ('are sluggish') for *rigent* would eliminate any ambiguity.

18 languet fascinum: cf. 12.14 and, for *fascinum* or *fascinus* (the neuter is first attested here), *Cat.* 13.20, [Tib.] *Priap.* 2.8, Petr. 92.9, Adams (1982) 63–4. The word is also used of a phallus-shaped amulet worn, like the *bulla* (5.12n.), as a charm against evil (Porph.; cf. Plin. *Nat.* 28.39). Petronius (138.1) uses the word of a 'dildo': *profert Oenothea scorteum fascinum, quod ... paulatim coepit inserere ano meo.*

19 prouoces 'call out', 'challenge', as if for a battle. Cf. *S.* 1.4.14 *Crispinus minimo me prouocat.* Outside of comedy and satire, *prouoco* occurs chiefly in prose (Grassman (1966) 69–70), but a few passages suggest that it could have an epic ring; cf. Acc. *trag.* 310 *ROL* (Hector) *primores procerum prouocauit nomine,* Tib. 1.9.62, Ov. *F.* 6.707 (Marsyas) *prouocat et Phoebum.*

19 superbo ... ab inguine: here and at 12.19 *inguen* has its literal sense of 'groin' (cf. *S* 1.2.26, 8.5), but elsewhere it can serve as a euphemism for either the male or female pudenda (*S.* 1.2.116 (9–10n.), Adams (1982) 47–8). For the transferred epithet ('haughty', 'disdainful') cf. 2.7–8n.

20 ore allaborandum est: the passive periphrastic, suggesting 'force and toil' (Thomas on Virg. *G.* 2.397–419), is rare in H.'s lyric (17.63, *C.* 1.7.27, 37.1–2, 2.14.17, 21, 3.24.51–4). For 'work' as a euphemism or metaphor for sexual acts, cf. 12.16, Arch. fr. 42.2 (also of *fellatio*) 'she was toiling with her head down' (*kubda d' ēn poneomenē*), *C.* 3.15.3, *S.* 1.2.37–40, Adams (1982) 156–7. *allaboro* occurs in Classical Latin only here and at *C.* 1.38.5, and may be a Horatian coinage (Bo III 393).

EPODE 9

Introduction

When will H. and Maecenas celebrate Octavian's victory at Actium as they did his victory at Naulochus? Why is there a delay in Octavian's triumph? The enemy has been defeated and is in flight, destination unknown. H. needs more wine to allay the anxiety and fear arising from Octavian's situation.

There is no identifiable model for this epode, but it is reasonable to think that H. drew on Archilochus, many of whose *iambi* were concerned with war and battles (frr. 1–13, 20, 23, 85–115, 214, 218, 228 West). The descriptions of Sextus Pompeius (7–10), the Antonian soldiers (11–16), and Antony himself (27–32) may owe something to iambic invective (e.g. Arch. fr. 114 (a foolish-looking general), 117 West (the silly helmet or haircut of a comrade-in-arms)), and, with the focus on the disgraceful conduct of the enemy as well as on possible mistakes by the victor (below), there can be no question that this is a blame poem (Intro. 3).

There are, however, questions about the 'where' (Actium or Rome) and 'when' (after, before, during the battle) of the poem (Setaioli (1981) 1716–28, Nisbet (1984) 9–17, Kraggerud (1984) 66–128), but it appears likely that the setting is Actium, possibly on board a ship in the Caesarian fleet (3, 17, 19, 35nn.) and that the time depicted is shortly after it has become evident that Antony has been defeated (2, 11–16, 18, 19, 27nn.). The controversy about this is due partly to modern uncertainty about Maecenas' whereabouts in 31 BC (3n.), but mainly, it seems, to the reluctance of commentators to believe that, if H. were (literally or emotionally) on Octavian's 'side' and that side had proved victorious, he would still feel anxiety and fear (37).

The argument here is that H.'s 'qualms' (35n.) arise, not from any further threat posed by Antony (27n.), but from uncertainty as to how Octavian will handle his victory. An ovation (7n.) like that after Naulochus might be appropriate (7–8n.), but now there is expectation of a triumph (21–6n.), despite the fact that the circumstances of Actium, or at least those H. chooses to emphasize (11–16, 17–20, 27–32nn.) make it almost impossible to pretend that Octavian has defeated a foreign, rather than a Roman enemy. Such a triumph might cause resentment and anger, and perhaps lead to yet more civil war (23–6, 33–8nn.).

H.'s forebodings seem to inform several of the remaining poems in the collection, most obviously Epode 16, but also, perhaps, Epode 10, with its apparent 'pharmakos ritual' (10.1, 11–14nn.), Epode 13, where the poet attempts to cheer anxious friends (13.3, 6–7nn.), and Epode 17, whose chilling conclusion may have a symbolic significance (17.58–81n.). The mood scarcely changes in most of the 'political lyrics' of the first book of *Odes* (*C.* 1.2, 12, 14, 21, 34, 35), at least until the 'Cleopatra ode' (*C.* 1.37) finally seems to answer the doubts raised by this 'Actium epode' (1, 21–6nn.).

Because of its 'world-historical' significance, Actium has been the focus of much attention both in ancient and modern times (cf. Woodman on Vell. 2.84–7, Pelling on Plut. *Ant.* 56–69, M. Paladini, *A proposito della tradizione poetica sulla battaglia di Azio* (Brussels 1958), Carter (1970)). H.'s is the first in a series of poetic accounts that include a scene on the shield of Aeneas (Virg. *A.* 8.675–728), elegiac 'hymns' to Apollo (Tib. 2.5, Prop. 4.6), and an epic of uncertain date (Rabirius (?), *Carmen de bello Actiaco* (surviving fragments actually *de bello Aegyptiaco*); cf. Courtney (1993) 334–40).

1–10 When will H. and Maecenas celebrate Caesar's victory as, not long before, they celebrated the defeat of Sextus Pompeius?

H.'s question indirectly establishes the conditions necessary for the 'celebration': there must be Caecuban wine, Octavian must be victorious, H. and Maecenas 'happy' and at the latter's house in Rome (3n.) listening to the proper music, and the whole situation must be parallel to that after Naulochus (7n.). In the course of the poem it becomes evident that two of the conditions have been fulfilled: Octavian has won his battle (27n.) and Caecuban is available (36). Yet H. is still not happy (37), which suggests that he is not yet at Rome (17, 19, 35nn.) and, especially, that the victory over Antony is somehow different from that over Sextus Pompeius (11–16, 21–6, 27–32, 33–8nn.).

1 Quando: the question is finally answered, not in this poem, but wlth *C.* 1.37.1–6 *nunc est bibendum, nunc pede libero | pulsanda tellus, nunc*

Saliaribus | ornare puluinar deorum | tempus erat dapibus, sodales. | antehac nefas depromere Caecubum | cellis auitis.

repostum Caecubum: cf. 36n. Caecuban, from the territory of Fundi in Latium, was considered one of the best Italian wines (Plin. *Nat.* 10.61; cf. N–H on *C.* 1.20.9, 37.5 (above), 2.14.25–6, 3.28.2–3 *reconditum ... Caecubum, S.* 2.8.15). The contracted form *repostum* (2.65n., Lucr. 1.35, 3.346, Virg. *G.* 3.527, Serv. on *A.* 1.26) fits the metre (2.35n.) and is supported by a *testimonium* (Diom. 1.528.27 *GLK*).

festas dapes: cf. 2.48n., *C.* 1.37.4 (above), and, for the phrase, Tib. 2.1.81, Ov. *F.* 6.672.

2 uictore laetus Caesare: the abl. could be either absolute ('now that Caesar is victor') or one of cause ('happy with Caesar as victor'). For the name Caesar of Octavian, cf. 1.3n.

3 sub alta ... domo: on the Esquiline (5.100n.); cf. *C.* 3.29.9–10 (to Maecenas) *desere ... | molem propinquam nubibus arduis,* Suet. *Nero* 38.2, Richardson (1992) 403. The mention of the house has been taken to mean that the poem is set at Rome (Fraenkel (1957) 74, Williams (1968) 218). But besides the indications elsewhere in the poem (17, 19, 35nn.) and the prediction in Epode 1 that he would 'endure Caesar's peril at (his own)' (1.3–4), there is explicit testimony that Maecenas was present at Actium (*Eleg. Maec.* 45–8). This is not contradicted by the evidence that he was back in Rome at the end of 31 BC (Vell. 2.88.2, Dio 51.3.5), unless by Appian (*Civ.* 4.50), who may have confused the Actium with the Alexandrian war (Wistrand (1958) 11–14, Hanslik (1962) 337–9).

(sic Ioui gratum): sc. *est* or *erit.* For the phrase, cf. *C.* 1.33.10 *sic uisum Veneri,* 2.17.15–16 *sic potenti | Iustitiae placitumque Parcis, S.* 2.6.22 *sic dis placitum,* Virg. *A.* 7.110, 11.901, and, for the parenthesis, 11.7, 14.7, 16.14nn.

The word order here suggests that *sic* means specifically 'under (Maecenas') lofty house', but it is not clear why this one detail should be singled out as 'pleasing to Jupiter' (the conjecture *si* (Sh. Bailey) does not resolve this difficulty). Perhaps H. anticipates that the house will be the setting for a feast in honour of the god (Kraggerud (1984) 79–81), who as *Iuppiter Optimus Maximus* presided over Roman victory celebrations (*RE* xviii 1898 (*ouatio*), viiA 495–7, 510 (triumph)). There is no evidence for what was done after an *ouatio* (5–6, 7nn.), but after a triumph banquets were held, one for the Senate in the temple of Jupiter on the Capitoline (Liv. 45.39.13, V. Max. 2.8.6), others for non-senators (such as the *equites* (Intro. 1) H. and Maecenas) at private houses (34n., Liv. 3.29.5, Plut. *Luc.* 37.6, *RE* vɪɪa 510). One of the honours granted Octavian after Naulochus (7–8n.) was an annual banquet at the Capitolium on the date of the victory (Dio 49.15.1), which perhaps repeated an *ouatio* feast.

4 beate: it appears that 'like *laetus* (2), *beate* is tied to the future victory celebration and is not an expression of Maecenas' present happiness' (AG (1968) 75). For the 'proleptic' epithet in the vocative, cf. 3.20n.

5–6 'with the lyre sounding a song mixed with pipes, | with the former (sounding) a Doric (song [6n.]), the latter a barbaric one'. For the combination of instruments, cf. *C.* 3.19.15–20 (at a symposium), 4.1.22–4 (a festival of Venus), 15.2, 30 (a symposium in honour of Augustus), Hom. *Il.* 18.495 (in the peaceful city on the shield of Achilles) 'pipes [*auloi*] and lyres were crying out', Arch. fr. 93a.5 West (men playing (?) the *aulos* and *lyra* on an expedition to Thrace), and, what may be H.'s model, the *synauleia* (mixing of strings and pipes) in Pindaric victory odes (*Ol.* 3.8–9 (5n.), 7.12, 10.94, *P.* 10.39, *N.* 9.8, *I.* 5.27, Comotti (1989) 29). But despite the Greek colouring, H. may refer to the musical accompaniment of an *ouatio* (Kraggerud (1984) 81), which was provided by *tibiae* (Plut. *Marc.* 22.2, cf. Skutsch on Enn. *Ann.* 293) rather than the *tubae* associated with full-scale triumphs (*RE* vɪɪa 503).

5 mixtum tibiis carmen: cf. *C.* 4.1.22–4 (to Venus) *lyraque et Berecyntia delectabere tibia | mixtis carminibus non sine fistula*, 15.29–30 [*canemus*] *duces | Lydis remixto carmine tibiis*, Pind. *Ol.* 3.8–9 (the poet must) 'mingle fittingly [*summeixai prepontōs*] the variously-sounding lyre and the cry of pipes and the placing of words'. For the *tibia* (= Greek *aulos*), a kind of oboe, cf. Rudd on *Ars* 202, Comotti (1989) 67–72.

6 Dorium ... barbarum: H. probably refers, not to the technicalities of 'modes' and 'scales', but to the 'character' (*ēthos*) of Doric (restrained and martial) and 'barbaric' music (below). Cf. *C.* 3.6.21 (lascivious) *motus ... Ionicos*, 4.15.30 (5n.). This seems to be the function of such terms in Pindar (*Ol.* 1.17 ('Dorian lyre'), 102; cf. *Ol.*

3.5, fr. 67, 191 Maehler, Plato, *Rep.* 3.398e–9c, Comotti (1989) index s.v. *ēthos*).

barbarum: cf. Cat. 64.264 *barbaraque horribili stridebat tibia cantu, Ciris* 166 *barbarico Cybeles ... buxo* (= *tibia*). The term here could indicate either of the 'foreign strains' that were part of Greek music, the 'pleasant and peaceful' Phrygian (Plato, *Rep.* 3.399b, but cf. Arist. *Pol.* 8.1339a–42b) or the 'languid' Lydian, suitable to drinking songs (*Rep.* 3.398e). But H. may also hint at the fact that an *ouatio*, not to mention a triumph, was supposed to be celebrated only over a *foreign* enemy (7n.).

7 ut nuper: on 13 November 36 BC, when Octavian celebrated an *ouatio* for his victory over Sextus Pompeius (Intro. 2) at Naulochus (Aug. *Anc.* 4.1, Suet. *Aug.* 22.1, Reinhold on Dio 49.15.1, *MRR* II 400). The *ouatio* was a lesser type of triumph which was held *cum aut* [7–8n.] *bella non rite indicta neque cum iusto hoste gesta sunt, aut* [10, 12nn.] *hostium nomen humile et non idoneum est, ut seruorum piratarumque, aut* [17–20n.] *deditione repente facta impuluerea, ut dici solet, incruentaque uictoria obuenit* (Gell. 5.6.2–12; cf. *RE* XVIII 1892–6). Neither an *ouatio* nor a triumph was supposed to be celebrated after a civil war (Liv. 6.16.5, V. Max 2.8.7, Luc. 1.12 *bella ... nullos habitura triumphos, RE* VIIA 498). Octavian represented the enemy at Naulochus as pirates and slaves (Aug. *Anc.* 25.1, 27.3, Zanker (1990) 40–1), and H. seems to go along with this (7–8, 10nn.). But such pretence could be taken only so far: after his victories in Africa (46 BC) and Spain (45), Julius Caesar aroused great indignation by celebrating triumphs which, although ostensibly over foreigners, included references to his Roman adversaries (App. *Civ.* 2.420, Cic. *Att.* 13.44.1, Gelzer (1968) 284–5, 308, *MRR* II 293, 305).

7–8 actus cum freto ... fugit: there may be 'biting mockery' (Heinze) in the picture of the *Neptunius dux* 'driven from the strait'. The battle (3 September 36 BC) took place off Naulochus, and, when most of his fleet was captured or destroyed (8n.), Sextus fled through the *fretum Siculum* first to Messana, then to Asia Minor, where he became Antony's problem (Vell. 2.79.5, App. *Civ.* 5.118–22, 133–44, Reinhold on Dio 49.8.5–11.1, *MRR* II 399–400). Octavian made no effort to pursue him (App. *Civ.* 5.127) and did not mention him or his Roman supporters (10n.) in connection with the *ouatio* (7n.).

H.'s account of Naulochus seems to follow some sort of 'official

line' (Kraggerud (1984) 78–9, Watson (1987) 123), as he does not
mention, among other things, doubts whether it was a 'just war'
(Tac. *Ann.* 1.10, App. *Civ.* 5.77, Dio 48.45.4, 46.4), Octavian's freeing
of slaves to man his galleys (Suet. *Aug.* 16.1, Dio 49.1.5), defeats –
which H. may have witnessed (Intro. 2) – suffered early on by the
Caesarians, the assistance provided by Antony (App. *Civ.* 5.95), the
prominence of Agrippa (Intro. 2) in the victory, and a dangerous
mutiny shortly after the battle (Vell. 2.81, App. *Civ.* 5.128–9, Rein-
hold on Dio 49.13.1–14.2). It also appears that, despite the supposed
composition of Sextus' force (10n.), there were incidents where
Roman fought Roman (App. *Civ.* 5.120).

Neptunius | dux: cf. 7.3n., Plin. *Nat.* 9.55 *Neptunum patrem adop-*
tante tum [in the Sicilian war] *sibi Sexto Pompeio – tanta erat naualis rei*
gloria, App. *Civ.* 5.100 (after defeats suffered by Octavian (above))
'Pompeius ... sacrificed to Sea and Poseidon and decided to be
called their son ... and it is said that, puffed up by these (successes),
he even exchanged the purple cloak customary for (Roman) com-
manders [27–8n.] for a sea-coloured one, thereby giving himself in
adoption to Poseidon', Dio 48.19.2, 31.5, 48.5. He also put Neptune
and other sea gods and symbols on his coins (Syme (1939) 228,
Zanker (1990) 40).

8 ustis nauibus: cf. Vell. 2.79.5 *paene omnibus exutus nauibus Pom-*
peius, App. *Civ.* 5.121 'twenty-eight ships of Pompeius (were sunk),
and the remainder were burned or captured or, running aground,
were shattered, and only seventeen escaped', Dio 49.11.1.

9 minatus Vrbi uincla: although Sextus cut off the city's food
supply (App. *Civ.* 5.67, 77, Dio 48.17.4, 31.1), there is no evidence that
he ever planned to capture it (cf. App. *Civ.* 5.26 'to Pompeius ... it
seemed best not to attack (Italy) but only to protect himself'). Cleo-
patra is supposed to have made similar 'threats' (N–H on *C.* 1.37.6,
3.6.13–17, Prop. 3.11.39–52, 4.6.41–2, *Eleg. Maec.* 53–4, Ov. *Met.*
15.827–8 *frustraque erit illa minata,* | *seruitura suo Capitolia nostra Canopo*,
Dio 50.5.4). Perhaps in response Octavian would later represent
himself as *libertatis populi Romani uindex* (coin of 28 BC; cf. Aug. *Anc.* 1.1
(in 44 BC) *rem publicam a dominatione factionis oppressam in libertatem uindi-*
caui), but it is not clear exactly what he meant by this (Reinhold on
Dio 50.22.3–4, G. Belloni, *ANRW* II 1 (1973) 1031–3). *uinclum* (17.72,
Ep. 1.7.67) seems to be an older form than *uinculum* (*C.* 4.7.28, *S.*
1.8.50, 2.3.71, 7.84, E–M s.v.).

10 seruis ... perfidis: cf. Aug. *Anc.* 25.1 (of the war against Sextus) *mare pacaui a praedonibus. eo bello seruorum qui fugerant a dominis suis et arma contra rem publicam ceperant triginta fere milia capta dominis ad supplicium sumendum tradidi,* Vell. 2.73.3, Dio 48.19.4. Three of Sextus' commanders, including Pompeius Menas (4 intro.), were ex-slaves, but he also had many free-born Roman supporters (App. *Civ.* 5.25, Dio 47.12.2–13.4, Reinhold on 49.1.3–5, Syme (1939) 227–8).

11–16 Future generations will deny it, but a Roman, enslaved to a woman and her eunuchs, serves as a soldier (in her army), and mosquito nets are draped among (Roman) standards.

H. now turns from past to present (13n.), from Sextus and his slave army to the current enemy, who also seem to be slaves (12n.). But there is an immediate difference: this enemy, despite its degraded state, is still unmistakably Roman (11n.). Furthermore, although it is commanded by eunuchs, as a unit it is isolated from the genuinely foreign contingents, which have deserted to Octavian (17–20n.).

These lines are the most difficult and controversial in the poem, as it is not clear who is being described (11n.), what they (or he) are doing (13n.), or where and when – before, during, or after Actium – they are doing it. The most plausible interpretation (Heinze, Wurzel (1938) 371, AG (1968) 75–7, Kraggerud (1984) 82–9) takes the soldiers (13n.) as Antony's Roman troops, ready to march or fight (13n.) but stranded at their camps by the defection of the Gauls (17–18), by the loss of some of their ships through desertion or treachery (19n.), and, finally, by the flight of their leader (27–32). They would in fact surrender within a few days (Vell. 2.85.6, Plut. *Ant.* 68.3–5, Dio 51.1.4). Other possibilities (cf. Setaioli (1981) 1716–28) include identifying the *miles* as Antony himself and the setting as his camp *before* the battle (13n.).

11 Romanus: either an epithet for *miles* (13) or a substantive with the latter in the predicate, 'as a soldier' (2.5n.). Because there is no obvious transition, the audience might think at first that H. is still talking about Sextus (*qui non bene intellegunt, putant importunum transitum repente a Sexto Pompeio ad Antonium factum* (Porph.)). The sing. has also led some to identify this as Antony (11–16n.), but it is more likely to be collective (7.6–7n.). *Romanus* often has a marked sense of 'Roman as opposed to foreign' (7.6, *C.* 3.6.2, 9.8, 4.3.23, *S.* 1.6.48, 2.1.37, 2.10, 4.10, 7.54, *Ep.* 1.12.25, 18.49, 2.1.29, *Ars* 264, Lucr. 1.40, Virg. *G.* 1.490, 2.172, 176, 3.148, *A.* 6.810 etc.). *eheu* (*C.* 3.2.9, 11.42, *S.* 1.3.66,

2.3.156, v.l. at 15.23, *C.* 1.15.9, 35.33, 2.14.1) seems to be stronger than *heu* (5.101n.).

(posteri negabitis!): cf. *C.* 2.19.2 *credite posteri*, Arch. fr. 122.1–6 West (App. 1), Pind. *Paean* 7b.45 Maehler 'I fear (I am saying) things that are unbelievable [*apista*]', [Tib.] 3.7.11 *neget ne longior aetas*, Stat. *Silv.* 5.2.88–9 *excidat illa dies aeuo nec postera credant | saecula.* H.'s apostrophe (2.21–2n.) emphasizes the horror of the situation (*tam foeda sunt haec, ut non uideantur ab ullo Romano admitti potuisse* (Porph.)), but may also call attention to his role as a poet. Although poetry is capable of lies (Hes. *Th.* 27, Solon, fr. 29 West), one of its functions, especially in contexts of praise or blame (Intro. 3), is to 'contrive that the unbelievable (*apiston*) be often believable (*piston*)' (Pind. *Ol.* 1.31–2; cf. *C.* 2.18.9, Brink on *Ars* 119, 144, 151, 338, Norden on Virg. *A.* 6.14, M. Detienne, *Les maîtres de vérité dans la Grèce archaique* (Paris 1967) index s.v. *peithō, pistos*).

12 emancipatus: cf. Pl. *Bac.* 92–3 *mulier, tibi me emancipo: | tuos sum, tibi dedo operam,* Cic. *Phil.* 2.51 (to the Senate) *tum iste* [Antony] *uenditum atque emancipatum tribunatum consiliis uestris opposuit. emancipo,* a rare and probably technical term, is used literally of the transfer by sale of property (including slaves) from one citizen to another (R. Brophy, *T.A.P.A.* 105 (1975) 1–11). If, as seems likely (11–16n.), the *Romanus* represents Antony's troops, then the phrase may suggest that their commander has 'sold them down the river' (Brophy 7; cf. Kraggerud (1984) 84). If it is Antony, then H. would seem to refer to the *seruitium amoris* (11.25n.), here compounded because the 'buyer' is not even a Roman citizen. For Antony as Cleopatra's 'slave', cf. Prop. 3.11.29–32, Plut. *Ant.* 28.1, App. *Civ.* 5.8, Reinhold on Dio 51.9.5, Griffin (1986) 32–47.

feminae: late Republican and Augustan poets do not name Cleopatra but refer to her as *femina* or *mulier* (*C.* 1.37.32, Prop. 3.11.30, 49, 58, 4.6.22, 57, 65, *Eleg. Maec.* 53, Man. 1.917), *Aegyptia coniunx* (Virg. *A.* 8.688, Ov. *Met.* 15.826), or *regina* (*C.* 1.37.7, *A.* 8.696, 707, Prop. 3.11.39). Here H. seems to allude to Antony's supposed placement of Roman troops under her command (Serv. on Virg. *A.* 8.696 *Augustus in commemoratione uitae suae refert Antonium iussisse ut legiones suae apud Cleopatram excubarent eiusque nutu et iussu parerent,* Reinhold on Dio 50.5.1, 25.1).

13 fert uallum: since the *uallus* ('stake') is not planted in a palisade but being carried, 'this description is much better suited to the picture of an army marching [11–16n.] than to that of regular camp service' (Kraggerud (1984) 85). Cf. Cic. *Tusc.* 2.37 *qui labor quantus agminis* ['an army on the march' (*OLD* s.v. 5)] ... *ferre uallum*, Liv. 33.6.1 *uallum secum ferente milite ut paratus omni loco castris ponendis esset.* If this is a description of the camp before the battle (11–16n.), then either the present tense verbs here are 'historical' (5.17n.) or those in the lines on Antony are 'prophetic' (27–32n.).

13–14 spadonibus ... rugosis: eunuchs often look like old women (Ter. *Eun.* 231, 357 *inhonestum hominem ... senem mulierem*, 688 (8.3–4n.), *RE* Supp. III 453). For Cleopatra's eunuchs, cf. *C.* 1.37.9–10 *contaminato cum grege turpium | morbo uirorum*, Plut. *Ant.* 60.1 (in his declaration of war against Cleopatra (27n.) Octavian alleged) 'that since Antony was influenced by drugs and not master of himself, the enemies [of Rome] were Mardian the eunuch and Pothinus [another eunuch] and Iras and Charmian, the handmaids of Cleopatra, in whom was vested the most authority'. Most Romans seem to have regarded eunuchs with loathing (*RE* Supp. III 451); an exception, ironically, was Maecenas (Watson (1987) 123), who was attended by such creatures both in private (Porph. on *S.* 1.1.105) and in public (Sen. *Ep.* 114.6 *cui tunc maxime ciuilibus bellis et sollicitata urbe et armata comitatus hic fuerit in publica: spadones duo, magis tamen uiri quam ipse*). There may be a eunuch among the attendants of Maecenas' friend Nasidienus (*S.* 2.8.15 *Alcon ... maris* [from *mas*] *expers*; cf. Housman (1972) 861).

H.'s phrasing here, although more direct than in his 'lyric version' (above), does not appear to be vulgar. *spado* is a Greek word (E. Maass, *Rh.M.* 74 (1925) 439–41) but occurs in standard Latin prose and even in other verse (*Priap.*, Mart., Juv.; cf. *ThLL* v 2.1050), while *rugosus*, one of H.'s more exotic -*osus* forms (3.16n., Ernout (1949) 26), may be poetic (Lucil. fr. 590 *ROL rugosi passique senes*, Valg. *poet.* fr. 1 *FPL* (8.13n.), [Tib.] 3.5.25, Ov. *Am.* 1.8.112 etc.).

14 seruire ... potest: since it echoes *seruis* (9), *seruire* here probably has its primary sense of 'serve as a slave' (*OLD* s.v. 1). For *potest*, 'brings himself to', cf. 6.3n.

15 signa ... militaria: the Roman legionary standard was not only a rallying-point but an object of religious veneration which (like the American flag) could be 'defiled' (Tac. *Ann.* 1.39, G. Watson, *The Roman soldier* (Ithaca NY 1969) 127–31).

16 Sol aspicit: because he 'sees everything' (*Saec.* 11–12, Hom. *Il.* 3.277 etc.), the Sun is often 'witness' to or even 'polluted' by horrible sights (16.13n., West on Hes. *Op.* 727, Eur. *Med.* 1251–4 (= Enn. *Sc.* 284–6 Vahlen *summe Sol, qui res omnis aspicis,... inspice hoc facinus*), Cic. *Off.* 2.28 (of a triumph held over a former ally of Rome) *multa praeterea commemorarem nefaria in socios, si hoc uno quicquam Sol uidisset indignius*, Pease on Virg. *A.* 4.607).

conopium: *quasi retis genus sit ad culices* [Greek *kōnōpes*] *prohibendos, quo maxime Alexandrini utuntur, qui ibi ex Nilo culices abundant* (Porph.); cf. Prop. 3.11.45 (Cleopatra sought) *foedaque Tarpeio conopia tendere saxo.* The area around Actium was probably mosquito-ridden, and there may have been malaria in Antony's camp (Watson (1987) 122–3), but bug-nets were considered inappropriate even for women in Rome (Var. *R.* 2.10.8, *RE* xi 1341–2), let alone soldiers in the field (cf. the US Army's ban on umbrellas). Some take the *conopium* as evidence of Cleopatra's (and Antony's) presence in the camp (11–16n.), but it could belong, if not to Romans 'gone native', then to their eunuch commanders (13–14).

17–20 In contrast to these debased Romans, Antony's foreign cavalry (17–18) and fleet (19–20n.) have deserted him.

Despite its 'world-historical' importance, the battle of Actium is extremely difficult to reconstruct (Carter (1970) 215–27, Woodman on Vell. 2.84–7, Pelling on Plut. *Ant.* 63–5, Reinhold on Dio 51.31.1–35.6). H. singles out and connects (19n.) two events, perhaps because they were in fact decisive for Octavian's victory (18, 21–6, 27nn.), but also, it seems, both because they involved little, if any, fighting (21–6n.), and because they resulted in the isolation of the Antonian troops and of Antony himself (27–32) from the non-Roman elements which might have disguised this as something other than a civil war (21–6n.).

17 at huc 'but hither', i.e. to the Caesarian side (Heinze, Wistrand (1958) 25). Cf. Vell. 2.84.1 *hinc ad Antonium nemo, illinc ad Caesarem quotidie aliquis transfugiebat*, Plut. *Ant.* 63.5 'there were desertions of kings, of Amyntas [18n.] and Deioterus to Caesar [*pros Kaisara*]', Serv. on Virg. *A.* 6.612 (18n.). If, as elsewhere in H. (33, 4.9, 6.3, 16.57, 59 etc.), *huc* is to be taken in a more narrow, 'local' sense, then it might mean 'towards the open sea' or 'towards Octavian's camp' (19, 35nn.).

The *at* here is probably necessary (*comparatio Romanorum et Gallorum particulam aduersitiuam postulat* (Klingner, app. crit.), Wistrand (1958) 24–6), but the conjectures *hinc* (Cunningham), 'from Antony's side', and *nunc* (Housman (1971) 7–8) merit consideration. The other MS readings (app. crit.), if not simply palaeographical variants (*ad* often written for *at*), could have arisen from connecting this passage, not with 11–16, but with 21–2 ('so far (*adhuc*) there have been desertions: do you, Triumph, still delay?'), or from an attempt to give the Galli someone (*ad hunc*) to 'turn the horses' or 'grumble' against (below). For other interpretations and conjectures, cf. Bartels (1973) 292–3, Setaioli (1981) 1717–28.

frementis ... equos: cf. *C.* 4.14.23–4 *frementem* | *mittere equuum*, Virg. *G.* 1.12, *A.* 11.496, 599, 607, 12.82 *equos ... frementis*, all based, perhaps, on Homeric (*Il.* 4.226–7, 16.506) *hippous phusioōntas* ('snorting horses'). Some who read *at hoc* (sc. *conopium*) or *ad hunc* (*ad hoc* Bentley) take *frementes* (app. crit.) with *Galli*, 'the Galatians grumbling at (or against) the net (or Antony)' (Porph., Lambinus, Bentley), but this would probably violate the 'two-epithet rule' (1.26n.). For the scansion *uerterunt*, cf. *S.* 1.10.45 *adnuerunt*, *Ep.* 1.4.7 *dederunt*, Williams on Virg. *A.* 3.48, LHS I 607–8. Elsewhere H. has only the standard *-ēre* (82×) and *-ērunt* (14×).

bis mille: this is the only evidence for the strength of the Galatian cavalry (18n.). The combination of a numerical adverb with a cardinal, rather than a distributive number, seems to be poetic (Brink on *Ep.* 2.1.24 *bis quinque uiri*, Skutsch on Enn. *Ann.* 311 *bis sex*, Sil. 8.613 *ter mille uiros*, ThLL II 2008, LHS II 213).

18 Galli: i.e. 'Galatians' (Liv. 33.18.3 etc.), although H. may wish to evoke the name of Rome's inveterate enemies (16.6n.; cf. Liv. 38.17.2–4). The leader of this Galatian cavalry, Amyntas, had been an ally of Brutus and Cassius but deserted them after the first battle of Philippi (Dio 47.48.2) as he now deserted Antony (Vell. 2.84.2, Plut. *Ant.* 61.3, 63.5, Dio 50.13.8). Because H. mentions it (17–20n.), this has been taken, rightly or wrongly, as a crucial phase in the war; cf. Serv. on Virg. *A.* 6.612 *nam transierunt ad eum* [Octavian] *ab Antonio duo milia equitum, per quos est uictoriam consecutus: Horatius, Ad hunc* [v.l. *adhuc*] ... *Caesarem*, Kraggerud (1984) 90–2, Watson (1987) 123–4.

canentes Caesarem: in some sort of 'marching song'; cf. Virg. *A.* 7.698 (the troops of Messapus) *ibant aequati numero regemque canebant*, Tac. *Ger.* 3.1 (Germans) *fuisse apud eos et Herculem memorant, primumque omnium uirorum fortium ituri in proelia canunt*, and the *carmina* sung by the Romans themselves during triumphs (Liv. 3.29.5, 4.20.2, *FPL* pp. 119–20, Courtney (1993) 483–5, *RE* VIIA 509–10).

19 hostiliumque nauium: the epithet (27n.) suggests that these ships, like most in the Antonian fleet (Pelling on Plut. *Ant.* 62.1, 64.3, Dio 50.11.1), were manned by non-Romans, the -*que* that their action is parallel to the desertion of the Galatians. But otherwise it is not at all clear what H. is describing. The most plausible explanation (Bentley, Kraggerud (1984) 94, Pelling on Plut. *Ant.* 63.5, 68.1, *C.Q.* 36 (1986) 177–81) is that the ships, a significant part of Antony's right wing, withdrew before the battle into the straits leading to the gulf of Ambracia (below), a movement which someone in the Caesarian fleet (35n.) would see as 'towards the left' (*sinistrorsum*) and, perhaps, interpret as a sign of widespread treachery or panic among the enemy. Other possibilities (cf. AG (1968) 78–81, Bartels (1973) 293–8, Setaioli (1981) 1728–9), none of which particularly fit H.'s words here or in *C.* 1.37, include taking the ships as Cleopatra's personal contingent, which during the battle sailed off towards the south ('to the left' for someone on land) heading for the 'port' of Alexandria (Plut. *Ant.* 66.5, Reinhold on Dio 50.33.1–2; cf. Porph. *sinistrorsum citae autem quid dixerit, manifestum est Alexandriam uersus esse*), or as the bulk of the fleet, which surrendered, probably without much of a fight (Pelling on Plut. *Ant.* 68.1–2), after Antony fled (27n.).

portu latent: if the ships returned to their harbour in the gulf of Ambracia, they would probably be 'hidden' from the opposing wing as soon as they 'turned left' in preparation for rounding the promontory of Actium. But they would still be visible from the Caesarian camp, which commanded a view of the entire gulf (Dio 50.12.2–8).

20 puppes ... citae: this seems to be a rendering of the Greek idiom *prumnas krouesthai* (Bentley), lit. 'strike the sterns' = 'row in reverse', 'back water' (*LSJ* s.v. *krouō* 9). *citae* is almost certainly participial (17.7n.); cf. Virg. *A.* 8.642–3 *citae Mettum in diuersa quadrigae* | *distulerant*, perhaps Ov. *Ars* 1.3 *arte citae ueloque rates remoque mouentur*, and the use of *concitus* (Ov. *Am.* 2.4.8 *rapida concita puppis aqua*, *Met.* 4.706, 7.491–2 *pleno concita uelo* | *Attica puppis adest in portusque intrat* *amicos*) and *citatus* (Sen. *Phaed.* 1049, Luc. 8.456–7 *Cyproque citatas | immisere rates*). 'If there is an ironic reference to the conventional "swift ships" [*C.* 1.37.24 *classe cita*, Hom. *Il.* 1.12 etc., Cat. 64.6 *cita decurrere puppe*], it can only be secondary' (Nisbet (1984) 13).

sinistrorsum: it seems best to take this rare word in its literal sense (19n.; cf. *S.* 2.3.50 *ille sinistrorsum, hic dextrorsum abit, OLD* s.v.) rather than as a nautical term for 'to port' (Nisbet (1984) 13–14), or as a 'gloss' on Homeric *ep' aristera*, which may mean 'in flight' (Cairns (1983) 90–1, but cf. Janko on *Il.* 13.675), or even as a 'moral' comment (also with Greek colouring; cf. *C.* 3.27.15, *S.* 2.4.4, *Ars* 301, 452, Pease on Cic. *Div.* 1.12, 2.82), 'to the wrong (and at the same time unlucky) side' (Wurzel (1938) 374).

21–6 Why does Triumph delay his procession? He did not bring back such a leader either from the Jugurthine or the Third Punic War.

H.'s impatient apostrophe (21n.) suggests that he considers Octavian's victory a foregone conclusion (17–21, 27nn.), but it is somewhat surprising, since up to this point he has anticipated an *ouatio*, not a full-scale triumph (5–6, 7nn.). With the 'slave enemy' (12n.) in a desperate position (11–16n.), and their leader, like Sextus Pompeius (7–8n.), in flight (27–32), it would seem that the conditions for an *ouatio* had been fulfilled. A triumph, on the other hand, would require (7n.) a 'bloody victory' rather than one attained through treachery or surrender (17–20n.), a worthier enemy, and, possibly, the death or capture of the opposing commander (23–6n.). Yet as things stand – and this must be the reason for the 'delay' and also, perhaps, for H.'s 'anxiety and fear' (33–8n.) – the only enemies still in arms and thus available for bloodshed or capture are fellow Romans (11–16, 17–20nn.).

When Octavian finally celebrated his 'triple triumph' (13–15 August 29 BC) he included Actium, but the focus was on his Illyrian campaigns and, especially, on the conquest of Egypt (30 BC), which he depicted as a war against Cleopatra and other foreigners (Aug. *Anc.* 4.1, Virg. *A.* 8.714–28, Prop. 3.11.49–54, Suet. *Aug.* 22, Reinhold on Dio 51.21.5–9). This is probably the context for *C.* 1.37 (A. Hardie, *P.L.C.S.* 1 (1976) 113–40) which, among other things, celebrates the fact of a non-Roman enemy after so many civil wars.

21 io Triumphe: *quasi deum inuocat Triumphum* (Porph.); cf. *C.*

4.2.49–50 *teque, dum procedis, io Triumphe,* | *non semel dicemus, io Trium-*
phe, Ov. *Am.* 2.12.16 *o cura parte Triumphe mea.* It may be that *Triumphe*
was originally a vocative (cf. the *carmen Aruale* (*FPL* p. 5)), but it is
usually represented as the ritual cry of the soldiers accompanying a
triumphal procession (Var. *L.* 6.68, Tib. 2.5.118, Ov. *Tr.* 4.2.51–2,
Met. 1.560, Liv. 21.62.2, 45.38.12). The word was thought to come
from Greek *thriambos,* the ritual hymn and sometime epithet of Dio-
nysus (Var. *L.* 6.68, Plin. *Nat.* 7.191, H. Versnel, *Triumphus* (Leiden
1970) 20–38), and H. may allude ironically to the special association
of that god with Antony (cf. 38, Pelling on Plut. *Ant.* 24.4, 33.6–34.1,
50.6, 75.4–5, Griffin (1986) 43).

21–2 tu moraris ... boues?: the *tu* seems to be emphatic, per-
haps with the force 'it is the triumph-god himself who delays the
procession, all else is ready' (Wickham). For the question without an
interrogative pronoun or particle, cf. 5.58n., *C.* 3.28.5–8 *inclinare*
meridiem | sentis et ... | parcis deripere ... amphoram?

aureos | currus: poetic pl. (*C.* 1.15.12, *ThLL* IV 1520), unless H.
anticipates something like the 'triple triumph' (21–6n.). The first of
Julius Caesar's disturbing triumphs (7n.) involved four separate pro-
cessions. The gilded chariot in which the *triumphator* stood during his
procession from the Campus Martius to the temple of Jupiter Cap-
itolinus was one of the features that distinguished a triumph from an
ouatio, where the victor went on foot or rode a horse (*RE* VIIA 503–4,
xviii 1898–9).

22 intactas: *id est indomitae* (Porph.); cf. Virg. *G.* 4.540 *intacta ...*
ceruice iuuencas, A. 6.38 *grege de intacto septem mactare iuuencos,* Hom. *Il.*
10.293–4 (= *Od.* 3.383–4) 'To you [Athene] I will sacrifice a one-
year-old broad-fronted cow, | unbroken [*admētēn*], which a man has
not yet led under the yoke.' As might be expected (2.59n.), the *boues*
triumphales, which were sacrificed to Jupiter (3n.), were usually male
(*C.* 4.2.53, Virg. *G.* 2.146–8, *RE* VIIA 503). It is not clear why H.
makes them female, unless for the sake of euphony (Porph.).

23–6 At first sight, H.'s purpose in these lines seems to be to
magnify the victory by comparing Octavian to earlier Roman con-
querors of parts of Africa (23–4n.). But in the present circumstances
the two parallels are somewhat disconcerting, since both Marius
(23–4n.) and Scipio (25–6n.) paraded their opponents in their tri-
umphs and, later, despite their great achievements over foreign

enemies, would be remembered as an instigator (Marius) and as a possible victim (Scipio) of civil strife.

23-4 nec ... parem | ... ducem: i.e. Marius (but cf. 24n.). His victory in the Jugurthine War (below) was the first of many *bene-facta* (Prop. 2.1.24) for Rome, but his reputation was diminished by his murderous civil war with Sulla (16.7n; cf. Vell. 2.11.1 (Marius) *quantum bello optimus, tantum pace pessimus*, 23.1 *uir in bello hostibus, in otio ciuibus infestissimus*, T. Carney, *A biography of Gaius Marius*, *P.A.C.A.* Supp. 1 (1962) 4–5). Octavian would eventually attempt to 'rehabili-tate' Marius by including him (and Sulla as well) among the *summi uiri* whose statues and *elogia* were placed in the Forum Augustum (Zanker (1990) 210–13, Richardson (1992) 160–1; cf. *CIL* 1 ii p. 195 (the *elogium* of Marius)), but this was long after Actium (16 BC).

Iugurthino ... bello: like the Third Punic War, the last stages of the Second (25n.), and, eventually, Octavian's 'Alexandrian War', this took place in Africa. Jugurtha, a one-time ally of Rome, attempted to unite Numidia under his rule; he was opposed, with scandalous failure, by several Roman commanders until Marius and his then subordinate Sulla captured him through treachery (Sall. *Jug.*, Scullard (1982) 46–51). He was brought to Rome and, as was customary when an enemy had been captured (N–H on *C.* 1.37.32, 4.2.33–6, *Ep.* 1.17.33, Aug. *Anc.* 4.3, *RE* VIIA 503), paraded in Marius' triumph (1 January 104 BC), then executed (Sall. *Jug.* 114.3, Vell. 2.12.1, Plut. *Mar.* 12.2–5, *Sulla* 3.3, *MRR* 1 558). Cf. Prop. 4.6.65–6 (regretting that Cleopatra escaped) *di melius! quantum mulier foret una triumphus*, | *ductus erat per quas ante Iugurtha uias*.

It is possible that H. alludes to Sallust's *Bellum Jugurthinum* (for the title, cf. *Jug.* 19.7, 77.2, 100.5, Quint. *Inst.* 3.8.9), in which Marius is portrayed sympathetically (Kraggerud (1984) 103–4, Nisbet (1984) 15), but the epithet *Iugurthinus* is attested outside of this work (e.g. Lucil. fr. 450 *ROL*, Cic. *Nat.* 3.74), and there are other references to Jugurtha which may be independent of it (*C.* 2.1.25–8, Prop. 3.5.15–16, 4.6.66 (above), Ov. *Pont.* 4.3.45).

24 reportasti = *reportauisti*. In the first conj. perf. H. prefers the contracted (41×) to the uncontracted forms (17×). *reporto* probably means 'repatriate' (Cic. *Red. sen.* 28 (of his return from exile) *non reducti sumus in patriam ita, ut nonnulli clarissimi ciues, sed equis insignibus et curru aurato reportati, OLD* s.v. 2). But there may be a play on the sense 'carry back spoils of war' (s.v. 3) through which the audience would at first take *ducem* to mean Jugurtha (cf. *dux* (8) of Sextus Pompeius), who was not the 'equal' of Antony either as a general or, what is especially cogent, in nationality (Plüsz (1881) 330–9). It seems less likely that the ambiguity extends to *Africanum* (25n.).

25 neque Africanum: sc. *reportasti* [*ut*] *parem* [*Caesari*]. The slight zeugma may have generated the variant *Africano* (sc. *bello*), which has its supporters (Lambinus, Plüsz (1881) 334) but would be a difficult antecedent for the rel. clause. Another possibility (Madvig, Kiessling) is *Africani*, also sc. *bello*, 'from the war of Africanus'.

Since the rel. clause seems to refer to the destruction of Carthage (25–6n.), H. probably means the 'second' Africanus, Scipio Aemilianus, who accomplished this in the Third Punic War of 149–146 BC (Lambinus, Bentley, Kraggerud (1984) 104–6). The leader of the Carthaginians, Hasdrubal, begged for his life and was paraded in Scipio's triumph (Liv. *Per.* 52, App. *Lib.* 131, *MRR* I 467). His wife (a 'model' for Cleopatra? (*C.* 1.37.25–32)) chose to kill herself and their children (Polyb. 38.20, Liv. *Per.* 51, V. Max. 3.2.8). Scipio himself would later (129 BC) die mysteriously, the victim, it was suspected, of followers of Ti. Gracchus and C. Carbo, whose 'revolutionary' programme he opposed (Cic. *Rep.* 6.12 etc., *MRR* I 505).

If, as some argue (Heinze; cf. Kraggerud (1984) 104–5), H. means the 'first' Africanus, the victor in the Second Punic War, or has conflated both *Scipiadae* (Cairns (1983) 83–4; cf. *C.* 4.8.13–20, Lucr. 3.1034, Virg. *G.* 2.170, *A.* 6.843), then the *exemplum* might suggest a happier outcome (23–6n.), in which Antony, like the older Scipio's enemy Hannibal (cf. Liv. 30.35.4), would escape the disgrace of a triumph. It is also possible that, with the ambiguity of *reportasti* (24n.), the 'African' might be taken as Hasdrubal or Hannibal (Plüsz (1881) 330–9), although *Africanus* does not appear to be used elsewhere of a Carthaginian (*ThLL* I 1260–3, but cf. *Afer* (*C.* 2.1.26, 16.35, 4.4.42, *ThLL* I 1253) and *Africus* (I 1255)).

25–6 cui ... condidit 'whose valour placed a tomb over Carthage', i.e. turned the city into a cemetery. Cf. Polyb. 39.2 (Hasdrubal said that) 'for those well-disposed toward their country this fire [burning Carthage in 146 BC] is a lovely shroud', Cat. 68.89 *Troia (nefas) commune sepulcrum Asiae Europaeque*, Cic. *Catil.* 4.11 *cerno animo sepulta in patria miseros atque insepultos aceruos ciuium*, Tac. *Hist.* 3.35

sepultae urbis ruinis. The phrase has been interpreted even more meta-
phorically, 'whose valour made a monument (for him) over (or sur-
passing) Carthage' (Lambinus, Bentley, Bartels (1973) 300). If *sepul-
crum* by itself can = *monumentum* (the supposed parallels (Thuc. 2.43.2,
Vell. 1.12.5 (26n.), V. Max. 1.73, Stat. *Silv.* 2.7.71–2, *Ap.* 7.73, 235–7)
are not compelling), then this could be taken of either Africanus
(25n.) and, possibly, refer to or even quote (*cui ... condidit* forms a
trochaic septenarius (Heinze)) the 'poetic monument' to the older
one, Ennius' *Scipio* (Bentley, Cairns (1983) 84); cf. fr. 8 Vahlen of that
poem (= Cic. *De orat.* 3.167) *testes* [of Scipio's greatness] *sunt Campi
Magni* (near Utica, site of a Roman victory in 203 BC (Liv. 30.8.3)). It
seems most unlikely that H. is thinking of Octavian's own *sepulcrum*
(Kraggerud (1984) 106–7).

26 uirtus: cf. *S.* 2.1.72 *uirtus Scipiadae* ('epic periphrasis' (6.6n.)
for Aemilianus), Vell. 1.12.5 (Aemilianus) *eamque urbem* [Carthage] ...
funditus sustulit fecitque suae uirtutis monumentum, quod fuerat aui eius [the
first Africanus] *clementiae.* Aemilianus built a temple to Virtus (Plut.
De fort. Rom. 5, Richardson (1992) 431), perhaps after the destruction
of Carthage (A. Astin, *Scipio Aemilianus* (Oxford 1967) 79).

27–32 Utterly defeated, the enemy is fleeing towards Crete, or
Cyrene, or parts unknown.

Although Antony (27n.) in fact escaped the battle on Cleopatra's
ship (Vell. 2.85.3, Plut. *Ant.* 67.1, Dio 51.5.3), H. depicts him as alone
and thus isolated from his foreign allies. This may reflect con-
temporary uncertainty about Antony's means of escape, but it also
creates the impression that the only *hostis* Octavian could capture for
his triumph would be a fellow Roman (21–6n.).

Those who interpret the epode as set before Actium (9 intro.) take
this passage as a 'fantasy' or 'prophecy' by 'the poet ... trying to
cheer himself with glowing anticipation' (Housman (1971) 8; cf. Wis-
trand (1958) 24–33). Yet even if, as seems unlikely (Bartels (1973)
302–3, Setaioli (1981) 1721–2), the verbs here could be 'present for
future' or 'prophetic presents', one might expect a 'fantasy' with
Antony (and Cleopatra) not at large, but captured or dead. Even less
likely is the suggestion (Cairns (1983) 85–90) that the *hostis* here is
Hannibal (!).

27 terra marique uictus: this seems to be a 'formula' meaning
'totally defeated' (*Saec.* 53, Cic. *Catil.* 2.29 *omnibus hostium copiis terra*

marique superatis, A. Momigliano, *J.R.S.* 32 (1942) 62–4, Setaioli (1981) 1729–30), but it could also refer specifically to the desertions of the Galatians 'by land' and of the fleet 'by sea' (17–20). The absence of a connecting particle (*nunc, nam*) may be the reason why some MSS and scholia begin a new poem here (app. crit.).

After Actium Antony and Cleopatra still had resources to continue the fight, but the débâcle seems to have completely demoralized them and their supporters (*C.* 1.37.13–17, Plut. *Ant.* 69–75, Dio 51.5.1–10.9, Huzar (1978) 223–6). Octavian's delay of several months before resuming operations and the change of theatre from Greece, a part of the empire, to Egypt, still an independent country, would enable him to depict what was essentially a 'mop-up' as a separate 'Alexandrian War' (21–6n.).

hostis: Antony, as would probably be clear from the reference to the cloak (27–8n.). The war had been declared against Cleopatra alone, and it is not certain if Antony was ever officially designated *patriae hostis* (Pelling on Plut. *Ant.* 60.1, Reinhold on Dio 50.4.3–4, Suet. *Aug.* 17.2, App. *Civ.* 4.45) as he had been twice earlier in his career (49 BC (*MMR* II 258), 43 (*ibid.* 343)). But *hostis*, although primarily indicating a foreign enemy, could be used of a private *inimicus* (5.53, 6.14) and of a *ciuis seditiosus* (*ThLL* VI 3.3057–8) even without a decree; cf. *C.* 1.6.1 (Agrippa's civil war 'enemies'), 2.7.13 (Caesarians at Philippi), *Ep.* 1.18.62 (boys 'playing Actium' *hostili more*), Cic. *Phil.* 2.2, 3.14 (Antony a *hostis* before the *senatus consultum* declaring him that (43 BC)).

There was a *damnatio memoriae* (removal of statues, of names from inscriptions and coins, reversal of official acts) on Antony, although it is not certain whether it was decreed before or after his suicide on 1 August 30 BC (Reinhold on Dio 51.19.3–5, Pelling on Plut. *Ant.* 86.9; cf. Plut. *Cic.* 49.4). Either way, it was not effective: his name remains on inscriptions, including the consular Fasti restored by Octavian himself (cf. Reinhold), in historical works, and in 'Augustan' poetry (*S.* 1.5.33, Virg. *A.* 8.685, Prop. 3.9.56, Ov. *Pont.* 1.1.23). H. would later recall Antony with a reference to his widow Octavia (*C.* 3.14.7; cf. Mankin (1992) 381) and address a poem to his son Iulus Antonius (*C.* 4.2). For his 'afterlife' in other literature, cf. Huzar (1978) 242–52, Pelling on Plut. *Ant.* intro. 4, 5.

27–8 punico | ... sagum 'substituted [1.28n.] a mournful (soldier's) cloak for his purple (general's cloak)'. Similar actions are recorded of Pompey after his defeat at Pharsalus (Caes. *Civ.* 3.96.3, Plut. *Caes.* 45.8), of Sextus Pompeius (7n.) after Naulochus (App. *Civ.* 5.122), and of the *triumuir* Lepidus when his troops deserted him for Octavian, also in 36 BC (Vell. 2.80.4; cf. *MRR* II 400). Antony seems to have been given to gestures involving his clothing (Plut. *Ant.* 4.3, 5.9, 10.8, 14.2, 18.2, 22.7, 29.2, 33.7, 44.3).

A number of editors (K–H, Klingner; cf. Wistrand (1958) 27, 46–8) place a comma rather than a colon or period (Bentley, Borzsak, Sh. Bailey) after *sagum*, but this would create an 'exceeding harsh anacoluthon' (Brink (1982) 48). If this passage were a 'prophecy' (27–32.), one might expect *mutabit* (Lachmann) for *mutauit*.

punico: sc. *sago*, the purple cloak of a Roman *imperator* (Skutsch on Enn. *Ann.* 529–30, *B. Afr.* 57.5, Liv. 30.17.13, *RE* IA 1755), such as Antony placed over the dead Brutus after Philippi (Plut. *Ant.* 22.7). H. may also (*Punicus* = Carthaginian) continue the parallel with Hasdrubal or Hannibal (25n.) and, perhaps (*punicus* being the colour of the stripe on a magistrate's toga (5.7n.)), hint at the fact that Antony was supposed to be consul for 31 BC (Cairns (1983) 86–7; cf. *MRR* II 419–20).

29–32 H.'s uncertainty about the enemy's destination is again (27–32n.) appropriate to the aftermath of the battle. In fact Antony and Cleopatra sailed to Paraetonium, a place much closer to Alexandria than to Cyrene (Pelling on Plut. *Ant.* 69.1–2). But the possibility of his reaching Crete or Cyrene might be particularly unsettling, since he had a Roman army stationed in the latter (31n.), and both were Roman provinces, in which any fighting would mean a continuation of civil war (27n.).

29 aut ille ... Cretam: sc. *petit* (31), although *Cretam* might be the object of *iturus* (16.35–6n.). The *ille* is 'resumptive' (12.9, *C.* 1.12.19, 53, 2.2.7 etc., *OLD* s.v. 2, 11) but may also serve to emphasize that the fugitive is the male Roman, not the female Egyptian.

Under the terms of the pact of Brundisium (40 BC; cf. Intro. 2) Crete, a Roman province since 67 BC, and Cyrene (since 74) were included in Antony's eastern share of the empire (*MRR* II 379). Both were probably stops on his supply route to Actium (Huzar (1978) 216), but unlike Cyrene (31n.), Crete does not appear to have been a base for Roman troops.

centum ... urbibus: a poetic phrase (*C.* 3.27.33–4, Hom. *Il.* 2.649 'Crete of a hundred cities' (cf. *Od.* 19.174 'ninety cities'), Virg. *A.* 3.106, Ov. *Met.* 13.706–8) which eventually found its way into prose (Mela 2.212, Plin. *Nat.* 4.58). Here it may add a touch of grandeur to Antony's flight, although the Latinized form *Cretam* (cf. *Creten* at *C.* 3.27.34) could be a reminder that the island was now a part of Rome (above).

30 uentis ... non suis: *non optatis, non prosperis* (Schol.); cf. Virg. *A.* 5.832 *ferunt sua flamina classem*, Sen. *Ep.* 71.3 *ignoranti quem portum petat nullus suus uentus est, OLD* s.v. *suus* 13b. *iturus* has been taken to mark this whole passage as a 'prophecy' (27–32n.), but the fut. part. is often used to express likelihood (1.21n.) or purpose (1.9n.) in present contexts (6.4, *C.* 1.22.2–6, 2.3.27–8, 4.2.3–4, 4.15–16, *S.* 1.5.86–7 *hinc rapimur ... raedis | mansuri oppidulo, Ars* 475–6).

31 exercitatas ... Noto: the south wind is especially stormy in the autumn (10.4n.). For the phrase, cf. *C.* 4.14.20–1 *indomitas ... undas | exercet Auster*, Ov. *Met.* 8.166 (a river) *incertas exercet aquas*. With its cretic *exercitatus* is excluded from dactylic verse, but it is also rare in other types (Ter. *Hec.* 407) and may be prosaic (*ThLL* v 2 1387–9).

Syrtes: the dangerous shallows off the coast of ancient Cyrene (N–H on *C.* 1.22.5 *Syrtes ... aestuosas*, 2.6.3, 20.15). Antony had stationed four Roman legions in Cyrene, a part of his 'eastern empire' (29n.), but after Actium their commander refused to bring them to Paraetonium (29–32n.) and eventually turned them over to Octavian's aide (the poet) Cornelius Gallus (Pelling on Plut. *Ant.* 69.3, 74.1, Reinhold on Dio 51.5.6, 9.1).

32 fertur: the verb seems to suggest that he is helpless; cf. 10.11, 11.20, 17.34, *C.* 4.2.11, *S.* 1.4.31 *fertur uti puluis collectus turbine*, Virg. *A.* 3.11 (Aeneas) *feror exsul in altum*, Austin on 4.110 (Dido) *fatis incerta feror.*

incerto mari: from H.'s perspective this could mean 'in an unknown (part of the) sea' (*OLD* s.v. *incertus* 7); from Antony's, either 'in a dangerous sea' (s.v. 5) or, with the epithet transferred (11.20), 'in a sea without direction' (s.v. 10; cf. Porph. *anaphora ad ipsum, id est: ipse fertur incertus animi*).

33–8 H. calls for larger cups and either Greek wines or Caecuban, a cure for nausea: drinking can ease the anxiety and fear arising from Caesar's situation.

It now becomes evident that H. and Maecenas are already drinking (33n.), but despite the Caecuban (36n.), this is not the celebration anticipated at the beginning of the poem (1–10n.). The symposium seems to be taking place on board a ship (35n.), not in the house of Maecenas (3n.), and rather than 'elation' (4n.), there is 'anxiety and fear' (37). Since victory is assured (2, 27n.), these emotions cannot arise from a military threat, but would seem to have something to do with the uncertainty about the fate of Antony. A wrong move by Octavian, killing or capturing Romans and, especially, emphasizing them in his triumph (21–6, 27–32nn.) might, as had happened with Caesar (7n.), arouse resentment and anger or even, perhaps, lead to another wave of civil strife.

Other interpretations of these lines take H.'s 'anxiety and fear' as (1) the result of undefined 'qualms' about Octavian (E. T. Salmon, *Phoen.* 1 (1946) 7–14) or about the decisiveness of the victory (most commentators); (2) a kind of 'hangover' from the tension of the battle (Kraggerud (1984) 113–14); (3) evidence that the poem is set before the battle (9 intro., 11–16, 13, 27–32nn.); (4) little more than a 'convention' of sympotic poetry (Williams (1968) 217, Bartels (1973) 308–11; cf. 37–8n.).

33 capaciores ... scyphos: the comp. probably indicates that they have already been drinking (Fraenkel (1957) 73; cf. *C.* 1.9.6–7, 3.21.8, *S.* 2.8.35 (wine has been served (14–16) when a guest) *calices poscit maiores*, Hom. *Il.* 9.203–3, Eur. *Ion* 1178–80, Cic. *Ver.* 2.66, Cat. 27.1–2 *puer | inger mi calices amariores*, Petr. 65.8 (well into the *cena*, Trimalchio) *capaciorem poposcit scyphum*). But it might 'simply mean "larger than usual"' (Nisbet (1984) 17; cf. Schol. *pro laetitia maiores*), as at Sen. *Dial.* 5.14.2 (Cambyses) *bibit deinde liberalius quam alias capacioribus scyphis*. The *scyphus*, a large, stemless goblet (N–H on *C.* 1.27.1, D–S IV 1159–61) was often associated with the bibulous Hercules (Fordyce on Virg. *A.* 8.278), who was supposed to be an ancestor, protector, and 'model' for Antony (Pelling on Plut. *Ant.* 4.1–3, Zanker (1990) 45–6, 59; cf. Plin. *Nat.* 21.12 (*scyphi* at one of Cleopatra's banquets)).

puer: the slave who pours the wine is a conventional figure in sympotic poetry (N–H on *C.* 1.29.8, 38.1, 2.3.14, 11.18, 3.14.17, Hipp. fr. 13.2 West, Alcaeus, fr. 362.2 L–P, Anacr. 356, 396 *PMG*, Cat. 27.1 (above), Bartels (1973) 308), but his presence here is not inconsistent with a setting at Actium, since Romans often brought private attendants (*calones*) on campaign with them (N. Rouland, *Les esclaves romains en temps de guerre* (Brussels 1977) 28–40).

34 Chia ... Lesbia: first-rate Greek wines (N–H on *C.* 1.17.21, 3.19.5, *S.* 1.10.24, 2.3.115, 8.15 (Chian with Caecuban), 48), often mentioned together (Call. fr. 399 Pf., Pl. *Poen.* 699, Virg. *G.* 2.90–8, Plin. *Nat.* 14.73). H.'s audience might recall that Chian and Lesbian were among the wines served at a huge public banquet following Caesar's 'multiple triumph' of 46 BC (Plin. *Nat.* 14.97; cf. 7, 21–2nn.).

35 uel 'or rather', introducing an alternative distinct from what was mentioned previously (2.17, 59, 12.13, *S.* 1.1.54–5, 2.7.95, LHS II 501). The Italian Caecuban was 'un vin fort', the Greek Chian and Lesbian 'vins légers et doux' (Plessis).

quod ... coerceat: either a rel. clause of purpose (1.33–4n.), 'in order to quell nausea', perhaps implying that someone is already sick, or a potential rel., 'which might quell nausea (if it arises)'. *coerceo* is not an unpoetic word (*C.* 1.10.18, 2.18.38, 19.19, 5× in hexameters, *ThLL* III 1433), but H. seems to use it here in a technical, medical sense (Cels. 3.6.15 etc., Plin. *Nat.* 23.50 (doctors prescribe wine) *ut sudorem coerceant*, *ThLL* III 1435).

fluentem nauseam: in medical contexts *fluens* can be a technical term for ailments 'accompanied by a flux' (Cels. 1 pr. 55, 56, 68, *OLD* s.v. *fluo* 5b). Since these include seasickness (Cels. 1.3.11), the epithet makes it likely that H. means *nausea* (from Greek *naus* = *nauis*) in its literal sense (cf. *Ep.* 1.1.92–3 *nauigio ... nauseat*, Plin. *Nat.* 27.52 [*absinthium*] *nauseam maris arcet in nauigationibus potum*). It thus seems to be another (3, 19nn.) and possibly decisive indication that the poem is set on a ship in the Caesarian fleet (F. Buecheler, *Kleine Schriften* II (Leipzig 1927) 320 (orig. publ. 1878), Heinze, AG (1968) 85–9, Nisbet (1984) 16–17). Octavian himself spent the night following the battle on his ship (Suet. *Aug.* 17.2, Oros. *Hist.* 19.10), and it would not be surprising if his friends did the same (cf. 1.1–4). A poem of Archilochus (fr. 4 West (App. 1)) describes a shipboard symposium, also, it appears, in wartime (cf. 8–9 'we will not be able to be sober on this guard duty').

On the other hand, the *nausea* here might simply be 'upset stomach' (*OLD* s.v. 2) caused by excessive drinking (Fraenkel (1957) 73) or 'queasiness' (s.v. 3) arising from 'anxiety and fear' (Salmon (33–5n.))

or, perhaps, from the thought of Antony's stormy flight (29–34; cf. AG (1968) 83–4).

36 metire ... Caecubum: *metire inquit quia cyatho* ['ladle'] *hauriebatur ex cratere* ['mixing bowl'] *uinum* (Porph.; cf. N–H on *C.* 2.11.19, 3.19.11–12). But *metior* may also suggest wartime (35n.), since it is often used of 'rationing' supplies to troops (Caes. *Gal.* 1.16.5 etc., *ThLL* VIII 883).

If H. and Maecenas (*nobis*) are at Actium, this cannot be the same Caecuban mentioned at the beginning (1). But it is unlikely that the repetition is casual (Fraenkel (1957) 73) or an error (Campbell suggests *faeculam*). Besides completing a 'ring structure', it may add a certain poignancy: wine once reserved for peacetime celebration is now (so to speak) 'pressed into service' as a battlefield ration (above). Cf. the American Civil War song 'Goober Peas' (peanuts) 'Lying in the shadows, underneath the trees, | Goodness how delicious, eating goober peas | ... I wish the war was over, when free from rags and fleas, | We'd kiss our wives and sweethearts and gobble goober peas.'

37–8 curam ... soluere: a traditional function of wine (e.g. 13.17, *C.* 1.7.17–19, N–H on 18.4, 2.7.21–2, 11.17–18, 3.1.41–4, 8.17, 12.1–2, 21.14–17, 29.2, 4.12.19–20, *Ep.* 1.5.16–18, Alcaeus, fr. 346 L–P), although this hardly explains why the poem ends on such a sombre note (33–8n.).

37 curam metumque Caesaris rerum: a vague and perhaps deliberately ambiguous phrase. Since *cura* with gen. usually means 'anxiety *on behalf of* x' (*ThLL* IV 1469), *metus* 'fear *arising from* x' (VIII 909; cf. *C.* 1.23.4, 35.37, 2.20.17, 3.24.7, *S.* 1.3.111, 4.127), 'Caesar's situation' (below) could be both the 'source' and the 'cause' of this 'anxiety and fear'.

The combination *curam metumque* seems to be 'formulaic' (Cic. *Dom.* 141 (the gods) *mentem cura metuque terrebant, Fin.* 1.49 *sine cura metuque uiuamus, Div.* 2.150 *plurimae curae metusque, Rep.* 3.26, Lucr. 2.18–19 *mens ... cura semota metuque,* 3.461, 826, cf. *C.* 3.14.13–15, *ThLL* IV 1470).

Caesaris rerum 'the situation, affairs, fortunes of Caesar [Octavian]' (*C.* 1.2.25–6 *ruentis | imperi rebus,* 4.6.22–3 *diuum pater adnuisset | rebus Aeneae,* Virg. *A.* 3.54 *res Agamemnonias,* 5.690 *Teucrum res, OLD* s.v. *res* 17). For the 'double gen.', cf. *C.* 4.6.43–4 *modorum | uatis Horati.*

38 Lyaeo soluere: 'alludit ad Graecum nomen Lyaei, id est Bacchi, quod ductum est a uerbo "luein", id est "soluere"' (Lambinus; cf. 11.16n., N–H on *C.* 1.7.22, Pind. fr. 248 Maehler 'Lyaeus loosening [*luonti*] the cord of grievous cares', Virg. *G.* 2.228–9 (soil) *fauet ... rarissima* [= *soluta*] *quaeque Lyaeo*). The metonymy (2.29n.) wine-god = wine occurs in Greek (Eur. *Ba.* 280–5, *Cyc.* 519–28) but is especially common in Latin (*C.* 2.11.17, 3.16.34, 21.16, 4.12.14, *S.* 1.4.89, Andr. *fab. inc.* 31 *ROL*, Pl. *St.* 661, Ter. *Eu.* 732, Lucr. 2.656, 3.221, Virg. *Ecl.* 5.69, *G.* 1.344 etc.).

EPODE 10

Introduction

A ship is carrying off Mevius: may the wind gods assault it with a storm as terrible as that sent by Pallas against Ajax. If they leave the corpse on the shore as prey for birds, they will receive a sacrifice of a goat and a lamb.

H.'s model is usually identified as the 'first Strasbourg epode' (Hipp. fr. 115 West = 194 Degani; text can be found in App. 2), a poem rediscovered in 1899 (R. Reitzenstein, *S.B. Berlin* 45 (1899) 857–64) and attributed to either Archilochus or, what seems more plausible, Hipponax (cf. Degani *ad loc.*). Like Epode 10, it can be characterized as a 'reverse *propempticon*' (1–10n.). But unlike H., the Greek poet explains why he wishes disaster on his target (Hipp. fr. 115.15–16 West), and there is nothing in the Greek text corresponding to H.'s prayer to the winds (3–8, 21–4) and mythic *exemplum* (11–14).

These differences, which seem to make H.'s 'version' less direct and 'personal', have been interpreted as symptomatic of the distinction between a poem based on 'real life' and a 'literary exercise' (cf. Fraenkel (1957) 29–36, Fedeli (1978) 117). But the 'realism' of the Greek epode has been over-emphasized: nearly every word in it is epic, rather than 'conversational' Greek, and there is no certainty that its unnamed target is an actual oathbreaker and not an 'exemplary figure' (Intro. 3) symbolizing the seriousness of this crime in early Greek society (cf. West on Hes. *Th.* 231).

Nevertheless, H.'s 'alterations' of his apparent model may still be significant, not, however, for generalizing about the supposed gap between early Greek and Horatian *iambus*, but for determining the meaning of Epode 10. The vagueness about what 'Mevius' has done could suggest that he is a *pharmakos* (1, 2nn.), the prayer and sacrifice to the winds, that his expulsion is a matter of great urgency, and the myth, that the 'ritual' is intended to avert the anger of the gods from Rome (11–14n.). Interpreted in this way, the poem is a fitting sequel to Epode 9, with its anxiety about further civil strife (9 intro.), and it would also seem to anticipate Epode 16, in which it becomes evident that the attempt at 'purification' has failed.

1–10 In both the opening and closing lines (21–4n.) H. seems to 'invert' what later antiquity would call a *propempticon*, a 'bon-voyage' poem (N–H on *C.* 1.3, Fraenkel (1957) 35, Cairns (1972) 130 and index s.v.). Such a poem would normally include a prayer for a safe journey (e.g. *C.* 1.3.2–4 (3–8n.), Sappho, fr. 5 L–P, Theognis 691–2 West, Call. fr. 400 Pf., Theocr. *Id.* 7.52–4), here turned into a curse, and a vow for a celebration if the traveller returns safely, here replaced by a 'banquet' for the gulls (21–4n.). H.'s use of the *propempticon* is sometimes thought to indicate the influence of Hellenistic or neoteric poetry, including the *Propempticon Pollionis* of Cinna (fifties BC), which apparently mentioned Actium and Leucas (19–20n.) as places to visit (fr. 5 *FPL*; cf. Courtney (1993) 217). But there are early Greek examples (above), and Hipp. fr. 115 West (10 intro.) may already be an 'inversion' of the genre (Cairns (1972) 55–6).

1 Mala ... alite: an 'inversion' (1–10n.) of the favourable signs that are normally hoped for at the start of a journey (16.24, *C.* 4.6.24). Cf. N–H on *C.* 1.15.5–6 (Nereus to Paris) *mala ducis aui domum | quam* [Helen] *multo repetet Graecia milite*, 3.3.61 *alite lugubri*. Bird omens (*auspicia*) were important in Roman divination (16.24n.), but they also figure in early Greek poetry (e.g. Hom. *Il.* 13.821–3; cf. Burkert (1985) 112), and it may be that a 'bird' was mentioned in the lost opening of Hipp. fr. 115 West. In some versions of the Ajax story (11–14n.) the 'bird diviner' (cf. *Il.* 1.69, 13.70) Calchas warns the Greeks not to leave Troy until they have averted Athene's wrath (Apollodorus, *Epit.* 5.23).

exit: sc. *ex portu*, perhaps that at Actium (10 intro.; cf. 9.19). H. says nothing about the ship's destination (cf., by contrast, Hipp. fr.

115.5–6 West, *C.* 1.3.6–7, and other *propemptica* (1–10n.)), as if the only thing that matters is the removal of Mevius. In this respect Mevius seems to resemble what the Greeks called a *pharmakos* (Plüsz (1904) 71), an individual ritually expelled in order to carry away with him divine anger, curses, plagues, or other ills that afflict the community (Parker (1983) 258–80, Burkert (1985) 82–4). Hipponax compared an enemy to a *pharmakos* (frr. 5–10 (App. 1); cf. 118 E, 128 (21n.) West, S. R. Slings in Bremer (1987) 89–91), and the ritual figures in a number of myths, including some connected with Ajax (14n.).

2 olentem: sc. *male*; cf. *C.* 1.17.7 (23n.), *S.* 1.2.30 *olenti in fornice*, Pl. *Men.* 864 *leonem … olentem*, Virg. *G.* 3.564–5 *olentia … membra*.

Meuium: Mevius (the more common form in inscriptions) or Maeuius is an actual name (*RE* XIV 283, XV 1508–11), but it is also used in legal texts (*OLD* s.v.) of fictitious persons (cf. 'John Doe'). This would make it appropriate for a stock figure (Intro. 3) and, perhaps, for a *pharmakos* (1n.), since it appears that such people were sometimes given false names or titles (Burkert (1985) 83).

Real-life Mevii from the late Republic include a centurion in Octavian's army at Alexandria in 30 BC (V. Max. 3.8.8), another 'Caesarian' who is supposed to have killed himself after he unwittingly slew his 'Antonian' brother at Actium (*Anth.* 460–1 Sh. Bailey), and a poet mentioned at Virg. *Ecl.* 3.90 *qui Bauium non odit, amet tua carmina, Maeui.* This last is identified as H.'s target by the scholia (Porph. (cf. on *S.* 2.3.239), Schol., Servius on *Ecl.* 3.90 (cf. Servius Auctus on *G.* 1.120)) and by many modern commentators. But there seems to be nothing in the epode to suggest that Meuius is a poet (Fraenkel (1957) 27), unless his unpleasant features symbolize his 'smelly' (2; cf. Schol. *cuius carmina puteant*), 'effete' (17), and 'flabby' (21) verses (Buechner (1970) 54–5, Miles). Cf. 8 intro.

3–8 Storms in the Mediterranean often involve more than one wind (*RE* VIIIA 2241, 2265–7), and this is reflected in poetry from Homer on (e.g. *Il.* 9.4–7, 16.765–9, *Od.* 5.291–6); cf. N–H on *C.* 1.3.13, 9.10–11, Enn. *Ann.* 432–4 Skutsch, Virg. *A.* 1.81–91, 2.416–18 (a simile that may suggest that storm that would destroy the Greek fleet (11–14nn.)) *aduersi rupto ceu quondam turbine uenti | confligunt, Zephyrusque Notusque et laetus Eois | Eurus equis.* In *propemptica* (1–10n.) it was conventional to pray that, *obstrictis aliis*, only a favourable wind should blow (N–H on *C.* 1.3.4; cf. Hom. *Od.* 10.19–26). By mentioning only dangerous winds H. may be 'inverting' this topos, although for trips across the Adriatic no wind is favourable in November (10n.).

3–4 ut ... uerberes ... memento: the final clause (rather than inf.) with *memento* is unusual (Pl. *Cas.* 823–4 *ut uiro subdola sis,* | *precor, memento, ThLL* VIII 654), and some take *ut* (= *utinam*) ... *uerberes* as an optative with *memento* parenthetical. *memento* does not seem to be a normal term in Roman prayers (but cf. Ov. *Met.* 14.729–30 *o superi ... este mei memores*), and H. may be imitating Greek use of *mnē-sai* (imper. of *mimnēskomai*, 'remember'); cf. Hom. *Il.* 15.375 (to Zeus) 'remember (the offerings I have made) and avert, Olympian one, the day of doom', *Od.* 4.765, Callinus, fr. 2a West.

  horridis ... fluctibus: cf. 13.1, *C.* 3.24.40–1, Acc. *trag.* 402 *ROL mare cum horreret fluctibus*, Cat. 64.205–6 *horrida contremuerunt* | *aequora.* The enclosing word order seems to 'reflect' the image of an assault from both sides.

  3 uerberes latus: cf. Lucr. 1.271–2 *uenti uis uerberat incita pontum* | *ingentisque ruit nauis et nubila differt.* Although *latus* is a technical term (*C.* 1.14.4 *nudum remigio latus*, Cic. *De orat.* 3.180, *OLD* s.v. 6a), the image of 'beating the flank' (cf. 4.3) may suggest the flogging of a *pharmakos* (1n.); cf. Hipp. fr. 6 West (App. 1) 'striking (him) during the winter (or in a storm?) and beating (him) | with branches and squills, just like a *pharmakos*'.

  4 Auster: the south wind is singled out with an apostrophe (2.21–2n.), probably because it is the most dangerous of those which disturb the Adriatic, especially in the late autumn (10n.). Cf. N–H on *C.* 1.3.15–16 (Notus) *quo non arbiter Hadriae* | *maior,* 28.21–2, 3.3.4–5 *Auster,* | *dux inquieti turbidus Hadriae,* 7.5–8, 27.17–24, 4.14.20–2, *S.* 1.1.6, *Ep.* 1.11.15. Except in this poem (20n.), H. seems to alternate the Greek name *Notus* (9.31, 16.22, 4× in *Odes*) with Italian *Auster* (4× in *Odes*, 5× in dactyls) according to metrical need.

  5 niger ... Eurus: for the east wind in the Adriatic (Ionian), cf. Virg. *G.* 2.107–8 *ubi nauigiis uiolentior incidit Eurus,* | *... quot Ionii ueniant ad litora fluctus.* It is 'black' with storm clouds (N–H on *C.* 1.5.7 *nigris ... uentis,* Hom. *Il.* 12.375 *eremnēi lailapi* ('dark gust'); cf. (the opposite) *C.* 1.7.15–16 *albus ... Notus,* 3.7.1–2, 27.19–20). *Eurus* is the Greek name but more common, even in prose, than Latin *Volturnus* (Lucr. 5.745; cf. *RE* VIIIA 2323).

5-6 inuerso ... mari ... differat: cf. Virg. *A.* 1.43 (Pallas destroying the Greek fleet) *disiecitque rates euertitque aequora uentis*, 2.419 (3-8n.) *imo Nereus ciet aequora fundo*. The sea is often 'inverted' in poetic storms (e.g. Solon, fr. 13.19-20 West, Acc. *trag.* 390-2 *ROL*, Virg. *A.* 1.106-7, Ov. *Ep.* 7.42 *euersas concitet Eurus aquas*), but it is possible that both H. and Virgil echo an account of the death of Ajax, perhaps that in the cyclic *Nostoi* (11-14n.).

7 insurgat Aquilo: cf. 13.3n., Virg. *A.* 3.285 (north winds blowing at Actium in the time of Aeneas). *surgo* seems to be a technical term for winds 'rising' (*OLD* s.v. 10), but *insurgo* is not attested in this sense before H. and may be a poetic use of compound for simple verb (cf. Bo III 389). H. prefers the Latin name *Aquilo* (9×) to Greek *Boreas* (*C.* 3.24.38), although the latter is common in other Latin verse from Catullus on (26.3, Virg. *Ecl.* 7.51, *G.* 1.93 etc.).

7-8 quantus ... ilices: cf. *C.* 2.9.6-7 *Aquilonibus | querqueta Gargani laborant*, Hes. *Op.* 509-10 (in winter Boreas) 'striking many high, leafy oaks and broad firs | in mountain glens pushes them to the much-nourishing earth', Virg. *G.* 2.404 (11.6n.), 440-1. The comparison may imply that Aquilo is to 'smash' the mast, a kind of 'tree' (*OLD* s.v. *arbor* 4b, LSJ s.v. *doru*); cf. Hom. *Od.* 9.70-1 (in the same storm that hit Ajax (11-14n.) the ships of Odysseus) 'were carried sideways, and their masts | the force of the wind [Boreas; cf. 67] scattered in three and four pieces'. The 'trembling' of the proverbially sturdy *ilices* (*C.* 4.4.57-60, Pind. *P.* 4.263-9) seems to anticipate the panic of Mevius and his crew (Miles).

8 frangit: cf. *fractos* (6); the repetition may be a kind of emphatic *figura etymologica* (4.15n.), although it is difficult to see its point. *plangit* (Wakefield) is an attractive alternative; Kenney compares Ov. *Ep.* 19.121 *quanto planguntur litora fluctu*; cf. *Ep.* 7.169 *freta ... Afrum plangentia* [Heinsius; *frangentia* codd.] *litus*.

9 nec sidus ... amicum appareat: cf. *C.* 2.16.2-4 (a sailor in the Aegean panics) *simul atra nubes | condidit lunam neque certa fulgent | sidera nautis*, Ap. Rhod. 2.1102-4 (Boreas) 'at night rushed monstrous onto the sea, and lifted the waves | shrieking with his blasts. A black mist covered the heavens, | nor anywhere did the bright stars appear to be seen.' This seems to be the first instance of *amicus* used of a star or constellation (cf. *C.* 3.6.43-4 *amicum | tempus*, Virg. *A.* 2.255 *amica silentia Lunae*, Man. 2.300).

atra nocte: not just the literal 'night' but the 'darkness' (5n.) of the storm. Cf. Hom. *Od.* 5.294, 9.69 ('night (*nux*) arising' in storms), Virg. *A.* 1.89 *ponto nox incubat atra.*

10 qua ... Orion cadit: *qua* is either the rel. adverb, 'in which part (of the sky)' (*OLD* s.v. 4) or has *nocte* as its antecedent (Porph.). The 'setting' (*OLD* s.v. *cado* 6, West, 'Excursus II' to Hes. *Op.*) of Orion in early November was associated throughout antiquity with the most dangerous storms (15.7, N–H on *C.* 1.28.21–2, 3.27.17–18, West on Hes. *Op.* 619, Gow on Theocr. *Id.* 7.53, Ap. Rhod. 1.1201–4, Pease on Virg. *A.* 4.52),

tristis Orion: cf. *C.* 1.3.14 (another sign of autumn storms) *tristes Hyadas,* Virg. *G.* 4.235 [*Pleas*] *tristior hibernas caelo descendit in undas.* This sense of *tristis* seems to belong to the language of divination (*OLD* s.v. 5b), but it is possible that H. alludes to Orion's *tristitia* as a lover (15.7n.) in order to suggest a parallel with Mevius (Schmidt (1977) 410–11). The forms $\bar{O}r\bar{\imath}on$ (*C.* 1.28.21, 2.13.39, 3.4.71, 27.18) and $\bar{O}\breve{a}r\breve{\imath}on$ (e.g. Cat. 66.94) are the normal ones in most Greek and Latin verse (West on Hes. *Op.* 598), but H. also has $\breve{O}r\bar{\imath}on$ (15.7n.).

11–14 The sea should be no calmer for Mevius than it was for the victorious Greeks when Pallas (Minerva) turned her wrath from Troy and directed it against Ajax.

The 'impiety' of Ajax occurred during the sack of Troy, when he defiled the temple of Pallas Athene (14n.). Although they were warned (11n.), the Greeks failed to punish him, and when they sailed for home, the goddess attacked not only Ajax but the whole fleet with a terrible storm. This story was popular in poetry and art (e.g. Hom. *Od.* 1.326–7, 3.130–85, 4.496–511, 5.105–11, cyclic epic (*Iliupersis, Nostoi*), Eur. *Tro.* 48–97, Call. fr. 35 Pf., Lyc. *Alex.* 357–97 (21–2n.), Virg. *A.* 1.39–45, 2.402–19 (3–8n.), Ov. *Ib.* 337–40 (echoing H.?), *RE* I 936–9, Roscher I 135–7). Archilochus probably alludes to it in connection with a 'political storm' (fr. 105 West (13.1–3n.); cf. J. S. Clay, *A.J.Ph.* 103 (1982) 201–4), and Alcaeus (fr. 298 L–P) uses the failure of the Greeks to punish Ajax to warn his countrymen not to make the same mistake with the tyrant Pittacus (H. Lloyd-Jones, *G.R.B.S.* 9 (1968) 125–39). Here 'the scene of the heroic world serves to ennoble [H.'s] fierce curses' (Fraenkel (1957) 24), but it may also have a function not unlike that in Alcaeus. It could suggest that Mevius, like Ajax (or Alcaeus' Pittacus), is guilty of some act of impiety (Schmidt (1977) 407–9) and, as often in Latin verse (13.13, 16.10nn.), Troy, her 'mother city', may be a symbol of Rome. Perhaps H. hopes that, even if it might be too late (*usto* ... *Ilio* 13), the gods will once again turn their *uis acrior* and *acerba fata* (7.13, 17) from his community onto an enemy.

11 quietiore ... aequore: cf. Virg. *A.* 5.848 *fluctusque quietos*, and, for postponed *nec* (*neque*), 1.12n., 16.33, 55, 60, *C.* 1.8.6, 3.4.77, 18.6, 4.5.14, 7.25, *Ep.* 1.18.37.

12 Graia ... manus: both the epithet for noun (cf. 16.4, Enn. *Ann.* 229 Skutsch *Marsa manus*, Virg. *A.* 7.43, 11.597, *ThLL* viii 366) and the form *Graius* instead of *Graecus* (N–H on *C.* 2.4.12) seem to be poetic.

uictorum: they owed their victory to Pallas (*C.* 4.6.13–16, Hom. *Od.* 8.520 etc.), who was their chief ally and Troy's worst enemy until Ajax's impiety (Eur. *Tro.* 65–73).

13 Pallas ... uertit iram: the phrase suggests an *apopompē* (5.49–6on.). For Athene's 'wrath', cf. Hom. *Od.* 3.134–5 (11–14n.) 'many [Greeks] met an evil fate | because of the baneful wrath [*mēnis*] of [Athene] the grey-eyed daughter of a mighty father'. *Pallas*, originally an epithet of the goddess, is first attested as a name in Greek lyric (e.g. Alcaeus, fr. 298.17 L–P, Pind. *Ol.* 2.26), and in Republican Latin occurs almost exclusively in poetry (*C.* 1.6.15, 7.5, 12.20, 15.11, 3.4.57, Cic. *Arat.* 302, Lucr. 6.750–3, Virg. *Ecl.* 2.61 etc.).

usto ... ab Ilio: cf. 14.14n., *C.* 1.15.35–6 *uret Achaicus | ignis Iliacas domos*, 4.4.53 *cremato ... ab Ilio*, *Saec.* 41, Hom. *Il.* 20.316–17 (=21.375–6) 'when all of Troy with devouring flames is kindled | and burning'.

14 in impiam ... ratem: the jingle *in im-* is most unusual for H. (12.19; cf. *S.* 1.5.72) and other Latin poets (e.g. Enn. *Ann.* 84 Skutsch, Tränkle on [Tib.] 3.3.38, 7.19, Prop. 2.26.36, 4.2.28, Ov. *Met.* 12.419, *F.* 6.435, *Tr.* 1.2.31). For the transferred epithet, cf. 3.1n., *C.* 1.3.23–4 *impiae ... rates*.

Aiacis: 'lesser' Ajax, the son of Oileus and king of Locris in Greece. He chased Cassandra into the temple of Athene at Troy and either dragged her and the cult statue from the sanctuary (*Iliupersis*, Eur. *Tro.* 70) or raped her in front of the statue (Call. fr. 35 Pf., Lyc. *Alex.* 348–64, perhaps Alcaeus, fr. 298.22 L–P (text uncertain)). As someone whose punishment might have averted disaster from his people, Ajax fits the pattern of a *pharmakos* (1n.), and even in histor-

ical times the Locrians atoned for his crime with *pharmakos*-like rit-
uals, burning a black ship (Tzetzes on Lyc. *Alex.* 365) and sending
two maidens to Troy, where they were killed or became servants of
Athene (Pfeiffer on Call. fr. 35, Burkert (1985) 84).

15–16 The immediate return to third person narrative (17–24,
but cf. 22n.) suggests that this is not a formal address to Mevius
(16n.) but an apostrophe (4n.) showing H.'s almost 'subjective' par-
ticipation in the disaster. Cf. Hipp. fr. 115.14 West 'I would wish to
witness these things', and Aeneas' apostrophes at Virg. *A.* 8.537–40
*heu quantae miseris caedes Laurentibus instant! | quas poenas mihi, Turne,
dabis! quam multa sub undas | scuta ... uolues, | Thybri pater!*

15 o quantus ... sudor: cf. *C.* 1.15.9–11 (1n.) *heu heu quantus
equis, quantus adest uiris | sudor, quanta moues funera Dardanae | genti*, Virg.
A. 8.537 (15–16n.), and, for *o* in such exclamations, *S.* 1.5.43, Lucil.
fr. 2 *ROL*, Virg. *Ecl.* 3.72, *ThLL* IX 2.7. The *sudor* here is the 'sweat'
of fear (*S.* 1.9.10–11, Enn. *Ann.* 417 Skutsch *tunc timido manat ex omni
corpore sudor*, Lucr. 3.154–5 (when the mind is frightened) *sudoresque ita
palloremque exsistere toto | corpore*, Virg. *A.* 3.175, 7.457–8). *instat* goes
also with *eiulatio* (17) and, with a slight zeugma, *preces* (18).

nauitis ... tuis: 'it is well known that, if there is one bad man
among the passengers, the gods are prepared to let the whole ship
sink' (Fraenkel (1957) 33). Cf. *C.* 3.2.26–30, Aesch. *Sept.* 602–8, Eur.
El. 1354–5, Parker (1983) 9. The archaic form *nauita* (5× in *Odes*)
seems to be more poetic than *nauta* (15.7, 16.59, 17.20, 4× in *Odes*,
4× in *Sat.*).

16 tibique: a vocative (*Meui*) has to be supplied from the oblique
case of the second person pronoun. There is no parallel for this in
H., but there seem to be examples in early *iambus* and elegy (Arch.
fr. 25.5, Hipp. fr. 19.1, 117.7, 10, Theognis 413–14, 465–6, 1363–4,
1381–5, Sem. fr. 7.108 West), and it was to become a favoured tech-
nique of Propertius (2.9.15, 12.17, Fedeli on 3.4.4, 7.11, 4.11.42).

pallor luteus 'a yellowish-green pallor'. Since there is no paral-
lel for *lutum* as a colour of 'fear', which is usually 'green' (Hom. *Il.*
7.479 etc.) or 'white' (7.15n.), the epithet here may suggest seasick-
ness (9.35n.); cf. Tib. 1.8.52 *nimius luto corpora tingit amor*, Pers. 3.95 (a
sick man) *surgit tacite tibi lutea pellis*.

17 illa ... eiulatio: *non gemitus, qui uirilis est, sed eiulatio, quae fem-
inea est. nam eiulatio est mulierum siue infantum, clamor et gemitus uirorum*

(Schol.; cf. 16.39, Cic. *Tusc.* 2.55, *Leg.* 2.59). *illa* here could mean 'that great' (*OLD* s.v. *ille* 8) or 'that infamous' (s.v. 4); the latter might suggest that Mevius is given to such outbursts (Orelli).

18 preces et: the *et* is postponed (1.12n.). For these kinds of *preces*, cf. *C.* 2.16.1–2, 3.29.57–9, Lucr. 5.1229–30 (the commander of a fleet caught in a storm) *non diuum pacem uotis adit ac prece quaesit | uentorum pauidus paces animasque secundas?*

auersum ad Iouem: cf. *C.* 3.23.19 *auersos Penates*, Virg. *A.* 1.482 (Minerva) *diua ... auersa*, 2.170, Liv. 7.3.2 *auersis ... dis*. As the supreme weather god (13.2), Jupiter (Zeus) is often blamed for storms whether or not he sent them (e.g. Hom. *Od.* 3.288, 9.67–9 (Zeus blamed for Athene's storm (11–14n.)), Hes. *Op.* 667–8).

19–20 Ionius udo ... sinus | Noto: both epithets may be felt *apo koinou* with both nouns (cf. app. crit.). The adj. *Ionius* can be used of any part of the southern Adriatic (Plin. *Nat.* 3.100, 150, Fantham on Luc. 2.624), including the waters off Actium (Prop. 4.6.15–17 *est Phoebi fugiens Athamana ad litora* [in Epirus] *portus, | qua sinus Ioniae murmura condit aquae, | Actia Iuleae pelagus monumenta carinae*). The most conspicuous island in this area, Leucas, was the site of a *pharmakos* ritual (Strab. 10.452, Burkert (1985) 83).

19 remugiens: cf. *C.* 3.10.5–7 *quo strepitu ... nemus | ... remugiat | uentis*, 3.29.57–8 *si mugiat Africis | malus procellis*.

20 Noto: instrumental abl. It is not clear why H. now uses the Greek name for the south wind (4n.), especially since the metre would allow *Austro*. Perhaps Notus figured in an account of the death of Ajax (11–14n.); cf. Virg. *A.* 2.417 (3–8n.).

carinam ruperit: the 'last straw', as a ship might survive broken oars and mast (5–8), but not a shattered 'keel'. This would also eliminate a means of escape; cf. Hom. *Od.* 12.420–4, where Odysseus makes a 'life raft' out of the intact keel of his ship.

21–4 In *propemptica* (1–10n.) and other contexts safe arrivals are celebrated with sacrifice and a meal (N–H on *C.* 1.36, 2.7.17, Hom. *Od.* 9.85–7, Theocr. *Id.* 7.62–89, Enn. *Sc.* 362–5 Vahlen (topos 'inverted' in curse of Thyestes (5.86n.)), Virg. *A.* 1.210–15, 3.219–24, Ov. *Am.* 2.11.45–52). Here, however, Mevius *is* the meal, and the sacrifice will be payment for calamity rather than safety. Cf. Hipp. fr. 115 West, where the poet's enemy eats, not a thanksgiving feast, but 'the bread of slavery' (8), and 'reclines', not at a banquet, but 'like a dog' on the shore (11–12; cf. 22n. below). In the *pharmakos* ritual the victim was given an elaborate last meal (Hipp. fr. 8 West; cf. 5.33n.).

21 opima ... praeda: cf. Hom. *Od.* 3.270–1, 24.291–2 (of Odysseus) 'him either the fish ate in the sea, or on the shore | he was prey [*helōr*] for beasts and birds', Lyc. *Alex.* 381–400 (Ajax and other dead Greeks (11–14n.) described as stranded fish), Cat. 64.153–4 (Ariadne) *dilaceranda feris dabor alitibusque | praeda.* If *praeda* refers to Mevius alone (22n.), *opima* might suggest that he is a 'choice' (sacrificial) victim (*OLD* s.v. 2) or that he is 'fat' (s.v. 3; cf. Porph. *ex quo apparet et pinguem fuisse, Ep.* 2.1.181); if to his crew as well, then it could mean 'plentiful' (*S.* 2.7.103 *cenis ... opimis,* s.v. 4). For *quodsi,* cf. 2.39n.

curuo litore: a poetic phrase (*C.* 4.5.14, Acc. *trag.* 573 *ROL,* Cat. 64.74, Virg. *A.* 3.16, 223, 11.184). The wretch in Hipp. fr. 115 West ends up 'along the edge of the surf' (14), and another of the poet's enemies, perhaps a *pharmakos* (1n.), 'dies by the stoning (or by lot) a shameful death | at the command of the people beside the shore of the barren sea' (fr. 128.3–4 (App. 1)).

22 porrecta: lit. 'lying prostrate' (*C.* 3.10.3 *porrectum ante fores*), but the word might also suggest food 'spread' on a plate (*S.* 2.2.39 (a mullet) *porrectum magno magnum ... catino,* 8.42–3) or a diner 'reclining' at a feast (Miles; cf. *S.* 2.6.88–9 (the 'city mouse') *pater ipse domus ... porrectus ... | esset,* 106). If Mevius is a *pharmakos* (1n.), there may be a play on *porrecta* from *porricio,* 'offer as a sacrifice'.

mergos: the *mergus,* a type of gull or cormorant (W. G. Arnott, *C.Q.* 14 (1964) 249–62), is not only insatiable (Lucil. fr. 1159 *ROL*), but indiscriminate enough to eat even 'stinking Mevius' (Plin. *Nat.* 10.130 *mergi soliti auide uorare quae ceterae [aues] reddunt*).

iuuerit: cf. 2.49. The third person verb fits the narrative style of most of the poem (15–16n., Fraenkel (1957) 32–3) but makes it uncertain whether the *praeda* consists of Mevius alone or the sailors as well (21n.). For this reason many scholars (Lambinus, Bentley, Brink (1982) 40–1, Sh. Bailey) prefer the early conjecture *iuueris.*

23 libidinosus ... caper: there appears to be no parallel for such an offering to the *Tempestates* (24n.), but goats (Greek *aiges*) were associated with Athene (13), the 'bearer of the *aigis*' (*aigiphoros*) and sacrificed to her each year at Athens (Var. *R.* 1.2.20). In certain other rites they seem to be 'substitutes' for human victims (cf. Gell. 5.12.12 (to Veiouis) *immolaturque ritu humano capra,* W. Burkert, *Homo* *necans* (Berkeley 1983) 65–7, 152–3), and it is possible that the *caper* here 'stands for' Mevius (*similitudine impudici et petulantis poetae* [2n.] *animal comparat immolandum* (Schol.), Plüsz (1904) 64, Schmidt (1977) 409). Besides being 'lustful' (like Ajax? (14n.)), goats are notoriously 'olent' (12.5n., *C.* 1.17.8 *olentis ... mariti*, *Ep.* 1.5.29). *libidinosus* (only here in H.) is not in general suited to verse (*Priap.* 47.6) but is otherwise a 'normal' -*osus* form (3.16n., Ernout (1949) 63).

24 agna Tempestatibus: this seems to be the usual offering (Ar. *Ran.* 847–8, Virg. *A.* 3.120, 5.772–3). The cult of the winds, of great antiquity among the Greeks (Hom. *Il.* 23.194, West on Hes. *Th.* 378, Burkert (1985) 175), was established at Rome in 259 BC when the consul L. Cornelius Scipio built them a shrine after surviving a storm (*ROL* IV p. 4 (= *CIL* I 9) *dedet Tempestatebus aide meretod*; cf. Pease on Cic. *Nat.* 3.51, Ov. *F.* 6.193–4, Richardson (1992) 379). Octavian sacrificed to the winds in 36 BC at the beginning of the war against Sextus Pompeius (App. *Civ.* 5.98), and they would later be depicted on his Ara Pacis (Zanker (1990) 174).

EPODE 11

Introduction

Pettius should know that H. is in love again and that, just like the last time, he is unable to cure himself by writing poetry. It was three years ago that he finally got over Inachia, but not before he had become a laughing stock, vexed his friends, disrupted a banquet, and humiliated himself at the girl's door. Now it is Lyciscus who possesses him, and his only hope of release is to transfer his desire to another girl or boy.

The setting seems to be a *conuiuium*, but there is no clue as to the place or date, unless *December* (5) is meant to suggest that this poem, like Epode 13 (13 intro.), may take place around the time of H.'s birthday (13.6n.), perhaps at Octavian's headquarters late in 31 BC (5n.). If so, then H.'s lament, although not without serious implications (below), might be imagined as a kind of 'diversion' for his anxious comrades-in-arms (1n.; cf. 12 intro., 13.3–10).

The subject matter of the epode and a number of its topoi (1, 6, 11, 12, 20–2, 27nn.) have led some to argue that it is based on Roman

elegy, or at least on two of that genre's apparent models, comedy
and epigram (Leo (1900) 9–16, G. Luck, *I.C.S.* 1 (1976) 122–6). But
love, and especially frustrated love, was also a subject in early Greek
iambus (1–2, 6, 8, 12, 13–14, 16, 20–2, 24nn.), and it is now evident
that Archilochus and probably Hipponax as well composed *iambi*
which, like this one, were essentially narrative in structure (5 intro.,
Intro. 3).

The best preserved of these 'blame narratives' is the 'Cologne
Epode' of Archilochus (fr. 196a West), a poem whose metre (Intro. 6)
and opening lines (1–2n.) seem to have influenced Epode 11 (cf. 8,
20nn.). It, too, contains an account of a past sexual episode, and
seems to show its speaker, whether Archilochus or not (cf. Nagy
(1979) 251–2), behaving in a manner (seducing or raping a virgin)
likely to make him a *fabula* throughout his *urbs* (Gentili (1988) 187–
8).

H.'s 'misconduct', however, is quite different, and seems to be
more closely related to thematic concerns of other epodes than to
anything in Archilochus. He is caught in a kind of 'vicious cycle',
rushing from one 'flame' to another and each time being driven to
shameful and disruptive acts. This may make him like any other wild
youth, but it is also ominously similar to what is happening to his
city in its seemingly endless repetition of the 'crime of Romulus'
(Fitzgerald (1988) 189). Both individual and society are impelled by
'madness' (6n., 7.13), and the 'advice and reproaches' of H.'s friends
have no more effect on him (25–6) than his own exhortations have
on his fellow citizens (7.15–16).

1–2 The opening seems to be based in part on Arch fr. 196 (eleg-
iambic) 'but, my friend, limb-loosing desire is conquering me'
(App. 1), which is now thought to be the second verse of 196a, the
Cologne Epode (11 intro.). Some join it with fr. 215 (trimeter) 'and
(or even) for me there is care neither for *iambi* nor for enter-
tainments' (App. 1). But the source which preserves this (cf. West)
cites it as the poet's response, not to a failed love affair, but to the
death of a brother-in-law in a shipwreck.

1 Petti: evidently the host of the *conuiuia* (8, 20) and a close friend
(12, 19) and, perhaps, a comrade-in-arms (cf. Porph. *Pettium Con-
tubernalem alloquitur*, 11 intro.), although H. does not mention him

elsewhere and nothing else is known about him. The name Pettius seems to be Oscan and is attested for magistrates in various towns, especially in Campania, but not at Rome (*RE* xix 1381). Perhaps this Pettius was a 'provincial on the rise' who withdrew from public life or died before he could make his mark.

The unadorned vocative as first word of the poem may be a device from early Greek monody, in which such openings seem to be relatively common (Arch. frr. 15, 88, 105, 168, 172, Hipp. frr. 1, 28, 118, Theognis 19, 39 etc. West, Alcaeus, frr. 45, 69, Sappho, frr. 5, 104, 131, 133b L–P). In the *Odes* there are ten of these (*C.* 1.1, 8, 10, 29, 30, 33, 2.6, 3.11, 17, 18) as opposed to only three in the hexameters (*Ep.* 1.3, 4, 2.2). It may be significant that there are more in Catullus' lyric 'polymetrics' (13 of 57 poems = 22%) than in his epigrams (4 of 48 = 8%), and that they are practically absent from Latin elegy (Tib. 2.5, Prop. 2.28, 3.9, 12, Ov. *Pont.* 1.2, 2.3, 4.11).

nihil me ... iuuat: here poetry fails to 'help' (cf. 16–17n., *S.* 1.2.109–10 (2n.), Arch. frr. 11, 215 (1–2n.), Cat. 65.1–4, 68.1–40, Virg. *Ecl.* 10.62–3 (of Gallus), Prop. 2.16.34). But it is more often cited as the single best 'remedy' for grief (13.9–10, 17–18, 14.11–12, N–H on *C.* 1.32.14–15, 2.13.37–40, 3.4.37–40, 4.11.35–6, Brink on *Ep.* 2.1.131, West on Hes. *Th.* 55, 98–103, perhaps Arch. fr. 253 (cf. West's app. crit.), Theocr. *Id.* 11.1–6 (= *HA* 493–8), Thomas on Virg. *G.* 4.464). In elegy it has this function (e.g. Prop. 1.7.13–14) and is also a means of 'winning the girl' (Prop. 1.8.39–40).

sicut antea: sc. *nihil iuuit*. 'Scribbling verses' was no more helpful to H. when he was in love with Inachia (5–6) than now, when he is in love with Lyciscus (23–4). Some supply only *iuuit*, with the sense that writing was in fact helpful in Inachia's day (Watson (1983a) 230). But there is no indication of this in the 'flashback' (5–22) and it runs contrary to the idea that H. is caught in a 'vicious circle' (11 intro.). *antea* occurs only here in H.; even in the *Odes*, where metre might allow it, he prefers adverbial *ante* (cf. 5.83, LHS II 223).

2 uersiculos: the diminutive is probably contemptuous (8.15–16n.): 'poetry [is] trifling in the face of the power of love' (Giarratano). Cf. *S.* 1.2.109–10 (of Call. *Ep.* 31 Pf.) *hiscine uersiculis speras tibi posse dolores | atque aestus curasque grauis e pectore pelli?*, 10.32, 58, Cic. *Orat.* 67, *Pis.* 75, Cat. 16.3. H. appears to mean poetry in general (Watson (1983) 231), although some take this as a rejection of *iambi* in particular in favour of other genres (Schmidt (1977) 414–15; cf. 14.6–8).

percussum: cf. Arch. fr. 196 West (1–2n.), Anacr. fr. 413 *PMG* 'again love struck me like a smith with a big | hammer'. H. may also echo Lucr. 1.922–3 *sed acri | percussit thyrso laudis spes magna meum cor*, and perhaps, Virg. *G.* 2.476 [*Musae*] *quarum sacra fero ingenti percussus amore* (cf. *A.* 1.513, 8.121, 9.197). If so, the point could be that 'H. is "smitten" with the wrong kind of inspiration; love is obstructing his poetic mission' (Kenney). In three of the Virgil passages, as here, the MSS offer the variant *perculsus*. This seems to be a stronger word (7.16) and may be excessive of a blow from *amor* rather than something more material (Bentley; cf. N–H on *C.* 1.7.11).

3 amore: an emotive repetition (4.20n.). *expeto* seems normally to be used of people or gods rather than feelings or things (*OLD*), but in light of line 24 *amor* here, like *pothos* in Arch. fr. 196 (cf. *erōs* in fr. 191 (14.1–2n.)) is probably 'only on the verge of personification' (Heinze). Cf. 16.31, 17.57n. For the unpoetic *praeter omnis*, cf. 3.9n.

3–4 me ... expetit ... urere 'seeks me out ... to burn (me)'. For the construction, cf. Pl. *Cur.* 107–8 *ipsum* [wine] *expeto | tangere, inuergere in me liquores tuos*. The infinitive with *expeto* (probably final or epexegetic (LHS II 346, Grassman (1966) 92–3)) is rare outside of Plautus (13×) and then much later Latin, and may be colloquial (Ruckdeschel (1911) 32).

4 in pueris aut in puellis: cf. *C.* 1.17.19–20 *dices laborantis in uno | Penelopen uitreamque Circen*. This use of *in* after verbs of emotion, especially in love, seem to be related to the abl. of origin or cause ('in the case of', 'because of'; cf. Ter. *Eun.* 567 *in hac* [sc. *puella*] *commotus sum*). It occurs mostly in poetry, although seldom, at least until the Empire, in higher poetry (*ThLL* VII 1.781; cf. McKeown on Ov. *Am.* 1.9.33–4).

For the alternatives 'boys or girls', cf. 27–8, *C.* 4.1.29, *S.* 1.2.116–17, 4.27, 2.3.325, *Ep.* 1.18.74–5, Lucr. 4.1053–4 (a man 'wounded' by Venus) *siue puer membris muliebribus hunc iaculatur | seu mulier toto iactans e corpore amorem*, Virg. *Ecl.* 10.37, McKeown on Ov. *Am.* 1.1.20. H.'s affection for boys (Lilja (1983) 70–4), in so far as it is a 'literary pose', is sometimes attributed to the influence of Hellenistic poetry (Fedeli (1978) 118). But pederasty is already a theme in Greek monody (e.g. Solon, fr. 25 West, Theognis, Alcaeus (24n.), Anacreon (14.10)), although not, it seems, in early *iambus* (K. J. Dover, *Greek homo-sexuality* (New York 1978) 9–10, 57–9).

urere: cf. 14.13, *C.* 1.6.19 etc., Virg. *Ecl.* 2.68 *me tamen urit amor,* Ov. *Met.* 7.21–2 *quid in hospite, regia uirgo,* | *ureris?* From early Greek poetry on (e.g. Sappho, frr. 38, 48 L–P) 'fire' is one of the most common metaphors for love (5.24n., 81, 14.4, 9, 13, 17.30n., N–H on *C.* 1.13.8 (9–10n.), Pease on Virg. *A.* 4.2).

5 hic tertius December: cf. Pl. *St.* 29–30 *uiri nostri domo ut abierunt* | *hic tertius annus,* Men. 234, *Merc.* 533–5, Mart. 3.36.7 *hoc per triginta merui, Fabiane, Decembres,* 12.18.7 *multos ... post Decembres.* It is not clear why H. specifies December; perhaps his misery is supposed to coincide with his birthday (8 December (13.6n.)) or to intrude on the pleasures of Saturnalia (17–23 December). But the name of the month could also be a hint that his poem, like Epode 13, is set in the aftermath of Actium (13 intro., Intro. 4). For the hepthemimeral cae-sura (pos. 7), cf. Intro. 6. There are four of these in the trimeters of the Cologne Epode (Arch. fr. 196a.27, 30, 33, 36 West).

ex quo: H.'s use of a rel. clause to introduce his 'narrative' (11 intro.) may suggest the style of early Greek epic and lyric (e.g. Hom. *Il.* 5.60, 24.765–6, *Od.* 2.89–90, Arch. fr. 89.5 West (?)). Cf. 14.11, 17.9, *C.* 1.12.27, 15.29, 20.2, 36.4, 37.21, 2.5.21, 12.17, 3.27.33, 4.4.41, *Saec.* 41, *S.* 2.6.40–2, West on Hes. *Th.* 22, Cat. 64.12, Virg. *A.* 5.46–8, W. Slater, *C.A.* 2 (1983) 118.

6 Inachia: abl. of cause (LHS II 133), as if the girl were not a person, but a thing or force. Cf. 12.14, 14.9, *C.* 1.4.19 (Lycidas) *quo calet iuuentus, S.* 1.4.49 *meretrice nepos insanus amica.* Inachia does not appear to be a real name, but occurs frequently as an epithet of Io (the daughter of Inachus), whom Zeus turned into a heifer (cf. Thomas on Virg. *G.* 3.153 *Inachiae Iuno pestem meditata iuuencae*). H. may imply that the girl, like the heroine, has bovine qualities (8.6, 12.14nn.), and his switch from her to the 'wolf' Lyciscus (24n.) could recall the animal images of other Epodes (4.1, 6.13–14nn.).

furere: the near-rhyme with *urere* (4) may serve to equate love's 'burning and churning'. Cf. Thomas on Virg. *G.* 3.244 *in furias ignem-que ruunt: amor omnibus idem.* 'Madness' is another ancient metaphor for love (5.75, 17.45n., *C.* 1.13.11, 25.14, 3.27.36, *S.* 2.3.239–71, Hom. *Il.* 14.294, Hes. *Th.* 121–2, Arch. fr. 191.3 (14.1–2n.), Campbell (1983) 1–27). It is common in Latin poetry from the late Republic on (e.g.

Cat. 64.54, 94, 124 (first instance of *furo = amo*), Lucr. 4.1058–1170), and its prominence in both Virgil (*Ecl.* 10.22, 60, Pease on *A.* 4.8) and in elegy (e.g. Prop. 1.1.7) may indicate that it was a theme in Gallus (Grassman (1966) 96–7). With *brevis in longo* at this position in the *asynarteton* (cf. 10, 26, 13.8, 10, 14), as with hiatus (14, 24), H. is almost certainly imitating Archilochus (Intro. 6).

siluis honorem decutit: cf. Virg. *G.* 2.404 *frigidus et siluis Aquilo decussit honorem*, which Servius identifies as a 'verse of Varro (of Atax)' (=fr. 6 *FPL*), who in turn seems to have imitated Ap. Rhod. 2.1100. It is not clear which of these, if any, is H.'s model, and the image could go back to Archilochus, on whom Apollonius wrote some kind of treatise (Ath. 10 451d, cf. 3.9n.). This use of *honor* seems to be poetic; cf. 17.18, N–H on *C.* 1.17.16. *decutio*, on the other hand, may be a technical term from agriculture (*ThLL* v 1.249).

7 heu me: first here for the usual *heu me miserum* or *infelicem* (*OLD* s.v. *heu* 1b). The phrase may be (mock-)tragic; cf. Sen. *Phaed.* 898, 997, 1173.

(nam ... mali): H. is fond of *nam* introducing an explanatory parenthesis (17.45, *C.* 3.11.1, 30, *S.* 1.1.33, 2.96, 4.142, 2.6.51, *Ep.* 1.15.2, 16). In this case the clause gives the reason either for H.'s *heu me* (Porph.) or, what seems more likely, for his being a *fabula* (Orelli). The tenses of *pudet* and *paenitet* (8) probably indicate that even after all this time H. still feels shame and regret. The genitive with these verbs (*C.* 1.35.33, 3.24.50, *S.* 1.6.89) appears to be rare in verse between comedy and Ovid, and may be prosaic or colloquial (*ThLL* xi 58–60).

8 fabula quanta fui 'how great a (source of) rumour I was'. Cf. *Ep.* 1.13.9, Caecil. fr. 150 *ROL* (=Gell. 2.23.10) *differar sermone misere*, Tib. 1.4.83 *parce ... ne turpis fabula fiam*, 2.3.31–2, Prop. 2.24.1, Ov. *Am.* 3.1.21, *Ars* 2.630. The examples from elegy may indicate that a phrase of this sort occurred in Gallus. But H. could also be echoing Arch. fr. 196a.33–4 'having such a woman | I will be a source of ridicule [*charma*] to my neighbours' (cf. 172.3–6 (App. 1), A. Henrichs, *Z.P.E.* 39 (1980) 17). In both contexts the 'tables are turned' on the blame poet (cf. 17.59n.).

conuiuiorum: a traditional setting for *iambus* and other poetry (Intro. 3), but also for people to make fools of themselves. Cf. *C.* 1.4.17–20, 18.8–16, 27.9–24, 3.6.25–32, 19.22–8, 4.1.33–6, Hom. *Od.*

14.463–6, Arch. fr. 124b (13–14n.), Campbell (1983) 28–53 (other early lyric), Call. *Ep.* 43 Pf. (9–10n.), Prop. 3.25.1–2, McKeown on Ov. *Am.* 1.4. For the postponed *et*, cf. 1.12n. Bentley's *ut* (exclamatory; cf. 2.19n.) is attractive.

9 quis = *quibus* (*S.* 1.1.75, 3.96, 4.72, 130, 5.42, 9.27, 2.8.18). The form seems to be an archaism (Grassman (1966) 100).

9–10 amantem ... | arguit 'bore witness that I was a lover'. The phrase has a legalistic ring (*OLD* s.v. *arguo* 3, 4, *ThLL* II 552–3). Cf. *C.* 1.13.6–8 *umor* [of tears] ... *arguens | quam lentis penitus macerer ignibus*, *Ep.* 1.19.6, Ov. *Ars* 1.733 (of lovers) *arguat et macies animum*. For the 'symptoms' or 'evidence' of love-sickness, cf. Lucr. 4.1121, Cat. 58b.9 (lassitude), *C.* 4.1.35–6, Sappho, fr. 31.9 L–P (silence), *C.* 3.7.10, Call. *Ep.* 43.1–2 Pf. (*HA* 1590–1) 'the stranger was not letting on that he had a wound [17n.], | but did you see how painful the breath which he dragged through his chest?', Pl. *Cis.* 55–6 (10n.), Cat. 64.98, Prop. 1.16.32 (sighing) and, in general, Kenney on Apul. *Met.* 5.25.5.

10 latere ... imo: cf. Virg. *A.* 1.371 *suspirans imoque trahens a pectore uocem*, Ov. *Met.* 10.402–3 *Myrrha ... suspiria duxit ab imo | pectore*. H.'s *latere* fits his metre, but may also be more vivid (22n.). *imus* seems to be rare in most verse outside of dactyls, where it is more convenient than *infimus* (Axelson (1945) 33–4). It is not clear why, but H. prefers it (6×) to *infimus* (2×) even in his non-dactylic poetry.

petitus ... spiritus: cf. Pl. *Cis.* 55–6 (a lover) *petiuit | suspirium alte*, Ov. *Met.* 2.621–2 *gemitus ... alto de corde petitos*. H. and Propertius (1.16.32) seem to be the first to use *spiritus* for *suspiritus* or *suspirium*. The effect may again be greater vividness, as impaired *spiritus* can be a symptom of physical suffering or disease (17.26; cf. Lucr. 6.1186, Virg. *G.* 3.505–6 (plague victims)).

11 contrane ... ualere: exclamatory infinitive, here introduced by *-ne* (8.1n.). The attachment of *-ne* to a preposition is unusual; the grammars cite no other example, nor can one be found in H.'s predecessors and contemporaries. But this klnd of tmesis is not uncommon with the other enclitics *-que* (v.l. here) and *-ue* (e.g. *S.* 1.4.74), especially with disyllabic prepositions (LHS II 217, 398–9, Marouzeau (1949) 37–44). For *ualere* in the sense 'avail', cf. 5.62n.

lucrum: either Inachia's insatiable 'desire for gain' (*C.* 3.16.12, *Ep.* 1.12.14, *OLD* s.v. *lucrum* 3) or the 'profit' (*C.* 1.9.14 etc., *OLD* s.v.

1, 2) she receives from another lover. Both the greedy woman (or boy) and the wealthy rival are stock figures in love poetry (14.15, N–H on *C.* 2.4.19, Brown on Lucr. 4.1124–30, McKeown on Ov. *Am.* 1.3.10). H. scans *lŭcrum* here and in his hexameters, but *lūcrum* in the *Odes*.

11–12 candidum ... ingenium: the epithet, ironically echoed at 27, probably means 'sincere' or 'well-meaning' (14.5, *C.* 1.18.11 (13n.), *S.* 1.5.41, 10.86, *Ep.* 1.4.1, 6.68, ThLL III 244). The meaning of *ingenium* is less certain; it could be H.'s 'character' (Porph.; cf. *S.* 1.3.33, 2.1.67, 8.73–4, *OLD* s.v. 1) or his 'poetic talent' (Schol., Watson (1983a) 233–4; cf. *C.* 1.6.12 etc., s.v. 5). But it could also be both, as often in elegy, where the lover/poet 'is what he writes' (e.g. Prop. 1.7.7–14, 2.1.3–4; cf. S. Commager, *Prolegomenon to Propertius* (Cincinnati 1974) 6–7).

12 pauperis: the term seems to be relative, indicating, not that H. is actually impoverished (cf. 17.47, Intro. 1), but either (11n.) that he has been 'beggared' by Inachia or is 'poor' in comparison with his rival. Some see a reference here to Call. *Iamb.* 3, where an impoverished poet laments the greed of his (male) beloved. But the *pauper amator* is yet another stock figure (N–H on *C.* 2.18.10, 4.11.21–4, Anacr. fr. 384 *PMG*, McKeown on Ov. *Am.* 1.3.7–10, Griffin (1986) 116–17). Poverty, actual or relative, is a common topic in Hipponax (frr. 3a, 32, 34, 36, 38, 39 West; cf. West (1974) 28–30).

querebar: cf. 2.26n., 5.11. The verb may suggest that H.'s 'complaint' took the form of a poem; cf. N–H on *C.* 2.9.17–18 (the poet Valgius' *querellae*), 2.13.24–5, 3.21.2. In Tibullus (e.g. 1.2.9) and Propertius (1.7.8) *queror* and its cognates are almost technical terms for *elegia*, which was itself thought to mean 'lament' (Brink on *Ars* 75, West (1974) 6–9). *ploro* also occurs in amatory contexts (*S.* 2.3.253, Tib. 2.5.103 etc.), but *apploro* is first attested here and may be a Horatian coinage (Bo III 393). The dat. seems to be analogous to that with *arrideo* (e.g. *S.* 1.10.89).

13–14 It is commonplace that wine causes people to talk too much (N–H on *C.* 1.18.16, 3.21.1–4, 15–16, *S.* 1.4.88–9, 2.8.36–9, *Ep.* 1.5.16–20, 15.20, 18.38, *Ars* 435, Campbell (1983) 28–53 (Greek lyric), Tib. 1.5.25–6), but H. may refer to Arch. fr. 124b West (App. 1) 'drinking much unmixed wine, | not having brought a share, ... | not invited ... you came as a friend, | but your belly led astray your mind and wits | into shamelessness'. Cf. Hipp. fr. 67 West 'they have little sense who have drunk unmixed wine'.

13 simul calentis: *simul* goes with *promorat*, *calentis* (possessive gen.) with *arcana*. But the hyperbaton may suggest that they are also to be taken together, with the gen. equivalent to an ethical dat. (Naylor) or even a Greek genitive absolute ('as soon as I was getting warm'). Cf. 5.33, *C.* 2.8.1, 3.4.77. *calentis* and *feruidiore*, while referring literally to the wine, may hint as well at H.'s amatory turmoil (Grassman (1966) 103–4). Cf. Ov. *Ars* 1.525–6 *Liber ... quoque amantis* | *adiuuat et flammae, qua calet ipse, fauet,* Apul. *Met.* 5.13.3 (Psyche to Cupid) *per pectus nescio quo calore feruidum.*

inuerecundus deus: the wine god Liber (Bacchus) is 'shameless' because he induces shameful behaviour (7–8, 17). There seems to be no exact parallel for the epithet, but cf. Hom *Il.* 5.593 (personified) 'Panic, shameless (*anaidēs*) in battle', *H. Merc.* 156 (Hermes' *anaideia*), Meleager, *AP* 12.119.5 (14n.), *C.* 1.18.11 *candide Bassareu,* where H. may refer to the god's 'candour' (11n.) as well as his beauty (27, 3.9n.), *S.* 1.4.89 *uerax ... Liber,* Ov. *Pont.* 1.10.29 *immodico ... Lyaeo.* In a different context Bacchus is *uerecundus* (*C.* 1.27.3). Dionysus figures in Archilochus (frr. 120, 194, 251 West), and may have been a patron deity of *iambus* (West (1974) 23–5). Although not suited to dactyls, *inuerecundus* does not seem to be unpoetic (*inc. trag.* 85 *ROL*).

14 arcana: cf. 5.52n., *C.* 1.18.16, 3.21.15–16 (a wine-jar) *arcanum iocoso* | *consilium retegis Lyaeo.* There may be a play on the idea of Bacchus' 'mysteries'; cf. Meleager, *AP* 12.119.5–6 (to Dionysus) 'you are born a traitor and untrustworthy, ordering (me) to conceal your mysteries [*orgia*], | and yet eager to reveal mine'. This could be H.'s model (Grassman (1966) 105), although a common source in Archilochus is also possible.

promorat = *promouerat* (cf. *S.* 1.9.48 *summosses,* 2.1.45 *commorit,* 71 *remorant*). For the sense 'coax forth' (*OLD* s.v. 1d), cf. *C.* 4.4.33.

15–18 'But if (my) anger should boil free in my vitals, so that it scatters to the winds these unpleasant (or vain, or unappreciated) applications [16–17n.] in no way easing (my) awful wound, then (the cause of my) shame [18n.], having been removed, will cease to struggle with (those who are my) inferiors [18n.].' The passage is 'vexed and elliptical' (Watson (1983a) 235), perhaps in order to suggest that H.'s tirade was a drunken babble inappropriate to the 'sober' tone in which it was delivered (19).

15 quodsi ... inaestuet: for the caesura *in* | *aestuet*, cf. 1.19n. *quodsi* introduces the climax (2.39n.) of H.'s complaint. The sentence begins as an ideal, 'less vivid' condition but ends, as if to show H.'s resolve, with a 'more vivid' future (*desinet*). There are similar mixed conditions at *C.* 2.17.13–15, 3.3.7–8, *S.* 1.6.42–3, 2.3.66–7, *Ep.* 2.2.53–4, *Ars* 461–4. *inaestuo* seems to be another Horatian coinage (Bo III 393), but *aestuo* is not uncommon in this sense of 'seething' (*OLD* s.v. 5; cf. *S.* 1.2.110 (the *aestus* of desire)). *praecordiis* (3.5n.) is probably locative, although some take it as dative.

16 libera bilis: for the adj., cf. 26, 4.10n. There may be a play on Liber (13n.), as at Naev. *inc.* 27 *ROL libera lingua loquemur Liberalibus*, Pl. *Cist.* 127–8 etc. (*ThLL* v 2.1289; cf. 9.38n.). 'Bile' secreted by the liver (5.37–8n.) was thought to cause anger and similar emotions (N–H on *C.* 1.13.4, Brink on *Ars* 302). Cf. Arch. fr. 234 West (a reproach?) 'for you do not have bile (*cholē*) in your liver'. The word *bilis* is rare in verse outside of comedy and satire, and may be prosaic or even vulgar (*ThLL* II 1187–8).

16–17 haec ingrata ... fomenta: the 'bandages' are evidently H.'s (poetic) complaints, which were 'unpleasant' (*OLD* s.v. *ingratus* 3) to his friends, 'ineffectual' (s.v. 1c) in healing his 'wound', and, possibly, 'unappreciated' (s.v. 2) by Inachia. *fomenta* (the pl. is the usual form) seems to be a prosaic technical term introduced to verse by H. (*S.* 1.1.82, *Ep.* 1.2.52, 3.26; cf. Ov. *Pont.* 1.3.44, 2.3.94, *ThLL* VI 1018–20). But the topos *remedium amoris* is, of course, a familiar one (1, 17nn.). There is no parallel in Arch. for the monosyllable (*haec*) at the end of a hemiepes (Intro. 6), but there are examples of this in the pentameter (= two hemiepe) of elegy both Greek (e.g. Theognis 4, 34, Solon, fr. 13.58, 60 West) and Latin (Cat. 70.2, 72.4, 6 etc.).

uentis diuidat: a peculiar fate for 'bandages', but traditional for words, especially vain prayers and promises (N–H on *C.* 1.26.3, Hom. *Od.* 8.408–9, Cat. 30.10, 64.59, 142, McKeown on Ov. *Am.* 1.4.11–12, Otto (1890) 364).

17 uolnus: another traditional metaphor for the effects of love (*C.* 1.27.12, Arch. fr. 193 West (14.1–2n.), Call. *Ep.* 43.1 (9–10n.), Pl. *Pers.* 24, Lucr. 4.1048–9, 1068–72, Pease on Virg. *A.* 4.2, Kenney on Apul. *Met.* 4.32.4).

18 imparibus: possibly 'those (lovers) who are insuitable for me' (Turnebus, Grassman (1966) 107–8; cf. 15.14, *C.* 1.17.25, 33.10, 4.11.31, *ThLL* VII 1.519). This interpretation fits the context, but

requires *certo* with the dat. to mean 'quarrel with' (= *rixor*), for which
there seems to be no parallel earlier than Silius (e.g. 4.707; cf. *ThLL*
III 891). If it has its usual meaning of 'compete with' (= *aemulor*), then
the *impares* would seem to be H.'s 'rivals' (11n.), who are his 'infer-
iors' in *ingenium*, if not in *lucrum* (K–H, Watson (1983a) 236). There
may also be a play on *imparibus* (instrumental abl.) in the sense *uersi-
bus impariter iunctis* (*Ars* 75; cf. Ov. *Am.* 2.17.21, 3.1.37, *Ars* 1.264, *Tr.*
2.220, *Pont.* 4.16.11, 36), here meaning not elegy, but H.'s own epodic
verse, which he will cease to use as a 'weapon' (6.12n.) in his amatory
'wars'.

summotus pudor: a difficult phrase. *summotus* is probably pro-
leptic ('once *pudor* is eliminated'), but it is not clear what *pudor*
means. Some take it as a (misguided) 'sense of decency' (*OLD* s.v. 2a)
which keeps H. from giving up on Inachia (Heinze; cf. *S.* 2.3.39, *Ep.*
1.9.12 *depositum ... pudorem*, 16.24, 18.77), others as the 'cause of (H.'s
shame' (*OLD* s.v. 4a), i.e. of his foolish behaviour (Lambinus, Wat-
son (1983a) 235–6). Yet after *pudet tanti mali* (7) one might expect *pudor*
to be something good, perhaps (genuine) 'shame', which would help
H., not by its 'removal', but by coming into play (cf. *dolor* at 15.16).
commotus ('aroused') for *summotus* (Sh. Bailey) would give the required
sense; another possibility might be *furor* (cf. 6n.) for *pudor*.

19 ubi ... laudaueram 'when I had praised these things [*bilis,
summotus pudor*] in a serious manner'. H.'s seriousness not only seems
at odds with his drunkeness (cf. *Ep.* 1.19.9 *siccis ... seueris*, Cat. 27.6–
7), but, since *seuerus* can mean 'prude' or 'kill-joy' (*C.* 3.8.28, *Ep.*
1.18.42, Cic. *Cael.* 30, 48, Cat. 5.2 *senum seueriorum*, Ov. *Am.* 2.1.3 etc.),
it may explain why he was expelled from the party (20). *laudo* (only
here in the *Epodes*) may be ironic in an *iambus* (Intro. 3) where H. has
been *blaming* Inachia and himself. This seems to be the first instance
of *palam* as a preposition (*ThLL* x 108).

20–2 After his expulsion H. went to the house of Inachia, where
he behaved like a typical *exclusus amator*. This figure was familiar
from lyric (e.g. Alcaeus, fr. 374 L–P), epigram, comedy, elegy, novel,
and, no doubt, real life (N–H on *C.* 1.25, 3.7, 10, 26, *S.* 1.2.67, 4.48–
52, 2.3.259–64, Brown on Lucr. 4.1177–84, McKeown on Ov. *Am.*
1.6, Copley (1956), Cairns (1972) index s.v. *kōmos*). The topos may
have occurred in Archilochus; cf. fr. 47 West 'the maidens drove
(me?) away from the doors'. Although H. does not do so here, it was

conventional for the *amator* to serenade his beloved or her locked door (*paraclausithyron*), and it appears that the songs could sometimes be iambic invectives (West (1974) 27–8).

20 abire domum: a colloquial dismissal (*C.* 3.14.24, 4.1.7, *Ep.* 1.7.53, Brink on *Ep.* 2.2.205, 215, *ThLL* I 66). Cf. Pl. *Poen.* 309 *abi domum ac suspende te.* There may be an echo of Archilochus' equally colloquial 'to the crows with her' (fr. 196a.39; cf. Henrichs (8n.) 17).

ferebar incerto pede: for *feror* 'carried away (helplessly)' cf. 9.32n. H.'s unsteady foot is probably due both to his drinking (14) and his passion. Cf. Prop. 1.3.9–14 *ebria cum multo traherem uestigia Baccho | ... et ... duplici correptum ardore iuberent | hac Amor, hac Liber, durus uterque deus.* The elegists enjoy depicting themselves or other lovers on the way to humiliation (Smith on Tib. 2.6.13–14 *iuraui quotiens rediturum ad limina numquam! | cum bene iuraui, pes tamen ipse redit,* Prop. 2.25.19–20 etc.).

21–2 non amicos ... postes ... | limina dura: the epithets are 'transferred' from Inachia (2.7–8, 5.30nn.; cf. *C.* 3.10.2–3 *asperas ... ante foris*). The door and its parts are often the targets of the complaints and frustration of the 'excluded lover'; cf. Lucr. 4.1177–9 *et lacrimans exclusus amator limina saepe | floribus et sertis operit postisque superbos | unguit amaracino et foribus miser oscula figit* (22n.), McKeown on Ov. *Am.* 1.6.73–4, Copley (1956) 28–42. The doubled exclamation *heu ... heu* is especially emotive or maudlin (5.71, 15.23), and the enjambment following the second *heu* may provide further emphasis (cf. *C.* 4.6.17–18 *heu nefas, heu | nescios fari pueros*). It is one of only two monosyllables at verse end in H.'s trimeters (17.63, Intro. 6).

22 quibus ... latus: H. may be describing an obscene act (Grassman (1966) 112–15; cf. Ar. *Eccl.* 707–9), a 'logical extreme' of the kisses placed on the door by the lover in Lucretius (21–2n.) and elsewhere (Copley (1956) 34). Both *lumbi* and *latus* can be euphemisms for the male privates (Adams (1982) 48–9), while *infringo* here may be equivalent to *rumpo* (12.12n.). *quibus* is probably dat. (cf. 5.69), although an instrumental abl. might be more vivid.

23–4 gloriantis ... amor Lycisci: the hyperbaton may suggest that H. is reluctant to give the name of his latest *amor.* Cf. *C.* 1.27.10–20, where he has to coax a friend to reveal *quo beatus | uolnere, qua pereat sagitta* (11–12). The language in this couplet is remarkably unpoetic: *glorior* (only here in H.) and *mollities* (*S.* 2.2.87) seem to be prosaic (*ThLL* s.vv.), while *quilibet* (2× in *Odes*, 7× in hexameters) and *muliercula* (only here in H.) are probably colloquial (LHS ii 202, Grassman (1966) 115–16). The last is another 'contemptuous' diminutive (in.). For the scansion *muljerculam*, cf. 2.35n.

24 uincere mollitie: the inf. goes with *gloriantis (ThLL* vi 2.2094). *uincere* here could mean either (or perhaps both) 'surpass' (15.22) or 'seduce' (e.g. Tib. 1.8.49 *neu Marathum torque: puero quae gloria uicto est?*). *mollities* was a quality as attractive in catamites (4) as it was reprehensible in grown men (1.10n.).

Lycisci: a name from real life (*RE* xiii 2295–6) and from comedy (Alexis, frr. 149–50 Kock, Pl. fr. 149 Lindsay). But the important thing here could be its meaning, 'little wolf', which may suggest that H.'s new love is even more 'predatory' than his old one. Cf. the names Lycambes (6.13–14n.), Lycidas (*C.* 1.4.19), Lyce (*C.* 3.10.1, 4.13.1), Alcaeus' boy-friend Lycus (N–H on *C* 1.32.11), and Gallus' Lycoris (Virg. *Ecl.* 10.2, Courtney (1993) 160–2; cf. *C.* 1.33.5). When she set up shop as a prostitute the empress Messalina took the name Lycisca (Juv. 6.123).

25 expedire non ... queant: with the image of 'release' H. may allude to still another familiar topos, that of *seruitium amoris* (9.12n.). This was a favourite of the elegists including, it seems, Gallus (fr. 4.2 *FPL* (Lycoris?) *domina ... mea*); cf. N–H on *C.* 1.33.14 (to Tibullus) *grata detinuit compede Myrtale*, McKeown on Ov. *Am.* 1.3.5–6. But it also occurred in earlier Greek poetry (e.g. Theognis 1379–80, Eur. *Tro.* 949–50). H. has *queo* or *nequeo* only here in his lyrics, as opposed to 16 examples in his hexameters. It is not clear whether they were felt to be archaic or colloquial (Grassman (1966) 116–17).

26 contumeliae graues: cf. Cic. *Tusc.* 4.77 *grauissimae contumeliae*. The 'insults' probably come from H.'s friends once their (milder) *consilia* go unheeded. It is less likely that H. means the 'abuses' he suffers from Lyciscus (Porph.), but cf. Pl. *Merc.* 30, Ter. *Eun.* 47–9 *an potius ita me comparem | non perpeti meretricum contumelias? | exclusit; reuocat; redeam? non si me obsecret*, Pac. *trag.* 181, 304 *ROL*.

27 alius ardor: a time-honoured *remedium amoris*; cf. Pl. *Epid.* 135, Cic. *Tusc.* 4.75 *etiam nouo quidam amore ueterem amorem tamquam clauo clauum eiiciendum putant*, Brown on Lucr. 4.1068–72, Tib. 1.5.39, Ov. *Rem.* 441–86.

puellae candidae: this could turn out to be Inachia, who is mentioned again in the next poem (12.14–15). For *candidus*, cf. 12, 3.9n.

28 teretis: apparently *teretia crura aut bracchia habentis* (Porph.). This and *S.* 2.7.86 (the wise man) *teres atque rotundus* seem to be the first instances of *teres* used of a person rather than an object (e.g. *C.* 1.1.28) or a body part (*C.* 2.4.21 *bracchia et uoltum teretesque suras*, Cic. *Arat.* 58 *tereti ceruice* (cf. Lucr. 1.35), Cat. 61.174 *brachiolum teres*).

renodantis: since *renodo* is first attested here (Bo III 394) it is not clear whether the prefix indicates repetition ('knot up again') or reversal ('unknot'). For the former, cf. N–H on *C.* 2.11.23–4 *incomptum Lacaenae | more comae* [v.l. *comam*] *religata nodum*; for the latter, V. Fl. 5.380 (the only other example of the verb in Classical Latin) *renodatum pharetris ac pace fruentem*. It may be significant that handsome boys are often depicted with their hair in disarray (N–H on *C.* 1.29.8, 2.5.23, 3.20.14, 4.10.3); cf. 15.9. *coma*, like *crinis*, seems to be a poetic word (5.16n.).

EPODE 12

Introduction

H. asks a hag why she wastes her gifts and love letters on a man who can smell her and see how disgusting she is when she is 'on heat' or when she rails at his miserable performance, blaming him for being more responsive to Inachia and for not appreciating her gifts but instead fleeing her as if she were a wild beast.

The mention of 'drinking companions' (23) may identify this as yet another sympotic poem with which H. diverts his friends at his own expense, perhaps under the same grim circumstances as in Epodes 11 and 13 (cf. 11, 13 intro.). The form, narrative with 'enclosed invective', also resembles that of Epode 11 and its possible antecedents in early *iambus*, and by 'allowing' the hag to complain about him, H. seems to work an amusing variation on the iambic theme of 'saying the worst things about oneself' (Intro. 3).

This poem is often paired with Epode 8, especially in being omitted from 'expurgated' editions (e.g. Wickham's), but also in featuring an old woman who may be identifiable as Canidia and thus as a symbolic figure (8 intro., App. 2). The 'news' here, possibly significant for Epode 17 (17.15–18n.), is that H. has not only seen this creature naked (8.6–10), but 'worked on her' (12.15–16n.), presumably after she had completed her own 'labours' (8.20).

1 Quid tibi uis: a formula indicating surprise and impatience (*S.* 1.2.69, 2.6.29, Pl. *Mil.* 1050 *quid nunc tibi uis, mulier?*, Prop. 1.5.3 *quid tibi uis, insane?*). *mulier* is H.'s regular term for woman (2.39n.).

nigris ... barris: the implications seem to be that the woman is herself 'swarthy' (2.41, 11.27; cf. Brown on Lucr. 4.1160, *Priap.* 46.1 *o non candidior puella Mauro*) and that she has a 'mammoth' sexual appetite (11, 17nn.; cf. Courtney on Juv. 6.333–4 (a woman with a jackass)). H. may also refer to the (false) notion that elephants copulate rear-end to rear-end (Arist. *H.A.* 5.2.539b, Plin. *Nat.* 10.173), *ex quo uidetur poeta dicere cum his eam concumbere debere, quia illam non uideant* (Porph.). *barrus*, which may be an Indian word (Isid. *Orig.* 12.2.14), is first attested here in Latin, but cf. the proper name Barrus (*S.* 1.6.30, 7.8, v.l. at 4.110).

2 munera ... tabellas: a kind of 'role reversal', as it is usually the man who sends 'gifts and love letters' (11.11). Messages and other occasional writings were often scratched with a *stilus* on *tabellae*, waxcoated wooden 'tablets' (*S.* 2.6.38, Pl. *Bac.* 715 etc.). They are an important 'prop' in Roman elegy (e.g. Prop. 3.23, Tib. 2.6.45, [Tib.] 3.13.7, Ov. *Am.* 1.11, 12, *Ars* 1.437–8; cf. *Met.* 9.521–9). In H. the words *tabella* and *tabula* alternate according to metrical need, and neither seems to be felt as a diminutive (8.15n.; cf. A. S. F. Gow, *C.Q.* 26 (1932) 153).

3 nec firmo iuueni: as she herself complains (15–16); cf. 1.16n. (on *firmus parum*). At the time of Actium H. was 34 years old and still, by Roman reckoning, a *iuuenis*; cf. 13.4, 6, 17.21, *C.* 1.16.22–5. Since *nec firmo* is probably litotes (5.8n.) for *molli* (16), the variant word order *nec iuueni firmo* is unlikely, although it creates a metrical sequence, dactyl in the second foot, spondee in the third, that is especially common in Latin hexameters (Intro. 6).

naris obesae: gen. of quality (4.8n.), in effect an adjectival phrase parallel to *firmo* (cf. 5.41–2, 16.9, *S.* 1.4.7–8 *facetus, | emunctae naris*, 7.7, 2.4.13, 7.52, *Ep.* 1.20.24). For *obesus = obtusus*, cf. Calp. *Ecl.* 4.148 *carmina ... obesis auribus apta*, *S.* 1.3.38 (*pinguis = stupidus*), and perhaps *S.* 2.2.3 *rusticus, abnormis sapiens crassaque Minerua. naris*, especially in the sing., seems to be more poetic than *nasus* (Grassman (1966) 73).

4 unus 'one above all others' (*OLD* s.v. 8). This use of *unus* seems to be colloquial (LHS II 193, Grassman (1966) 74). It is rare with comparative adjectives or adverbs (Fordyce on Cat. 10.17, Virg. *A.* 1.15–16), more common with superlatives (e.g. *A.* 2.426) and positives (*S.* 2.3.24–5, 6.57–8, *Ep.* 1.9.1–2). For *sagax, odoror*, and *acer* (6, 25) of dogs, cf. 5.25, 6.10, 14nn.

5 polypus: sea creatures are proverbial for their stench (Lilja (1972) 104–5, 149–50); cf. Mart. 4.4.3–4, 11 [*redolet*] *piscinae uetus aura quod marinae*, | *quod pressa piger hircus in capella*, | ... *mallem quam quod oles olere, Bassa*. For the odour of the octopus, cf. Plin. *Nat.* 9.89, 92–3, 10.194. Porph. and others take *polypus* here as a 'polyp' disfiguring the woman (cf. *S.* 1.3.40, Mart. 12.37.2, Cels. 6.8.1–2). But such a thing would 'lurk' in her nose, not in her armpits.

grauis ... in alis: the enclosing word order is of the type found in a so-called 'golden line' (cf. 13, 2.15n.); and H. may intend both epithets to be felt *apo koinou* with both nouns (i.e. the goat is 'shaggy', the armpits are 'offensive'). This is H.'s only lyric hexameter with a fourth-foot rather than a third-foot caesura (Intro. 6).

hirsutus: women were supposed to remove excessive body hair (Ov. *Ars* 3.193–4, *Priap.* 46.4, Lilja (1972) 134, Richlin (1992) 123). *hirsutus* (only here in H.) is normally used of animals and plants and may be abusive when applied to humans or their parts (e.g. Virg. *Ecl.* 8.33–4 *tibi est odio* ... | *hirsutumque supercilium*, Prop. 4.9.49 (Hercules) *mollis et hirsutum cepit mihi fascia pectus*). There may be a play on the sound of the word, which seems to contain both *HIRcus* and *Svs* (6).

hircus: the goat (*hircus, caper*, Greek *tragos*; cf. *grasos*, 'goat-reek') is a metaphor for body odour from at least Old Comedy on (Ar. *Pax* 814, *Ach.* 852; cf. *S.* 1.2.27 (=4.92), *Ep.* 1.5.29, Pl. *Ps.* 738, Cat. 69.5–6 *tibi fertur* | *ualle sub alarum trux habitare caper*, 71.1, Lilja (1972) 132–7, 151–2). It may have occurred in early *iambus*; cf. Hipp. fr. 78.5 (a poem about impotence) 'just as the [...] of a goat', and 117.8 'a thief reeking of [...]', where Diehl supplies *tragou*, Wilamowitz *grasou*.

6 sus: a dog should track an *aper* (2.32n.), not a *sus*, which is normally a domestic pig (Benveniste (1964) 27–36). In other cases, where *sus* seems to equal *aper* it may be 'ironical' or 'contemptuous'

(Mynors on Virg. *G.* 3.255; cf. Lucr. 5.25, Var. *Men.* 361). *sus* and other words for 'pig' can be terms of abuse (Pl. *St.* 64; cf. the 'sow-woman' at Sem. fr. 7.2–6 West). H. may also refer to the Greek use of *choiros* ('piglet'), *delphax* ('mature pig'), and *hus* (= *sus*) as slang for the *cunnus* (e.g. Ar. *Lys.* 684, perhaps Hipp. fr. 114b West 'flesh from a baby pig'; cf. Henderson (1991) 131–2). It appears that *porcus*, if not other terms, was used in this way in Latin; cf. Var. *R.* 2.4.10 *nostrae mulieres, maxime nutrices, naturam qua feminae sunt in uirginibus appellant porcum, et [ut?] Graecae choeron,* Adams (1982) 82. For the monosyllable at verse end, cf. Intro. 6.

7 qui: cf. *C.* 2.1.33 *qui gurges.* The variant *quis* is probably *lectio facilior,* since that is the preferred form in H. and most other Classical Latin (LHS II 540–1). H. may be trying to avoid too many *s* sounds, but cf. *C.* 4.7.17 *quis scit.*

uietis ... membris: probably locative (*C.* 3.16.35–6) or abl. of origin (*OLD* s.v. *cresco* 2b), although some take the phrase as dative. For the 'synizesis' of *uietis* (pronounced *ujetis*), cf. 2.35n. *membra* can apparently be used of female as well as male genitalia (perhaps Lucr. 3.346; otherwise in later Latin (*ThLL* VIII 636, Adams (1982) 46, 93)), but *undique* seems to indicate that H. means the woman's 'limbs' (5.99, 17.17).

8 crescit: this seems to be the first place where *cresco* is used of perspiration or odor (*ThLL* IV 1179). The image may be of a wind or river 'rising' (*OLD* s.v. 3a, 5), of a disease 'festering' (*C.* 2.2.13 *crescit ... dirus hydrops*) or, ironically, of a male member 'growing erect' (*Priap.* 80.2 [*mentula*] *quam si tactes, crescere posse putes*). For the stench when sweat mixes with cosmetics, cf. Pl. *Most.* 274–8, Lilja (1972) 131–7.

pene soluto: instrumental abl. with *sedare* (9). *soluto* anticipates the woman's complaints (15–16). Cf. Virg. *G.* 4.198–9 (bees) *neque concubitu indulgent, nec corpora segnes | in uenerem soluunt,* Ov. *Am.* 2.10.36 (15–16n.), Cels. 1.1.4 *rarus* [*concubitus*] *corpus excitat, frequens soluit,* Petr. 140.6. The word *penis* (only here in H.) seems to have been considered obscene (Cic. *Fam.* 9.22.2), although less so than *mentula* (Adams (1982) 35–6, Tränkle on [Tib.] *Priap.* 2.4).

9 properat: for the shift to third person verbs, cf. 7.15n. There may be an even closer parallel in a lyric of Anacreon (347 *PMG*), where the poet likewise addresses a woman (1–10), then describes and quotes her (11–18). Some take this as two separate poems, but there seems to be no division in the papyrus which preserves it (*P. Oxy.* 2322 fr. 1).

rabiem 'lust'; cf. Ter. *Eun.* 301, Lucr. 4.1083, 1115–17 (of lovers) *tandem ubi se erupit neruis collecta cupido, | parua fit ardoris uiolenti pausa parumper. | inde redit rabies eadem et furor ille reuisit.*

10–11 There is a similar scene at Petr. 23.4–5 when an effeminate *cinaedus* tries to arouse Encolpius: *mox et super lectum uenit ... super inguina mea diu multumque frustra moluit. perfluebant per frontem sudantis acaciae* [balsam hair-tonic] *riui, et inter rugas malarum tantum erat cretae, ut putares detectum parietem nimbo laborare.*

creta ... | stercore fucatus crocodili: the 'chalk' imparted a fair complexion (Ov. *Ars* 3.199), while the crocodile dung was supposed to remove blemishes and 'redden the cheeks' (Plin. *Nat.* 28.109, 184). *stercus* seems to be a prosaic and technical term (Adams (1982) 234–7; cf. Norden on Virg. *A.* 6.5–8). H. also uses the vulgar *caco* and *merda* (*S.* 1.8.37–8). *fuco* (*fucatus*) and *fucus*, on the other hand, are not alien even to higher poetry (*ThLL* VI 1460–1).

11 subando: gerund, one of only two in the *Epodes* (14.5). By H.'s time the abl. of the gerund seems to have been something of an archaism (N–H on *C.* 2.2.9, Brink on *Ep.* 2.1.155, LHS II 363). *subo* is a rare word; cf. Lucr. 4.1199–1200 *illarum* [female animals] *subat ardet abundans | natura*, where *ardet* serves as a kind of 'gloss'. H. seems to be the only Classical author to use it of a woman rather than a beast 'on heat' (Grassman (1966) 79; cf. Aed. *poet.* 1.4 *FPL* (of a man), Brown on Lucr. 4.1199). There may be an etymological connection with *sus* (6n.); cf. Porph. (*ad loc.*) *subare proprie sues dicuntur cum libidinantur*, Fest. p. 310M (based on H.?) *ut opprobrium mulieribus inde* [sc. *ex suibus*] *tractum sit, cum subare dicuntur.*

12 tenta cubilia: poetic plural (5.69n.). One type of Roman bed consisted of a mattress (*cubile*) 'stretched' (*tentum*) or 'supported' (*subtentum*) on straps (*lora, restes*). Cf. Cato, *Agr.* 10.5 *lectos loris subtentos*, Lucil. fr. 284 *ROL tres a Deucalione grabati* ['cots'] *restibus tenti*, D–S III 1020–3. There may be a play here on *tenta* (fem. nom. sing.) in the sense 'sexually aroused' (*S.* 1.2.118 (below), Kroll on Cat. 80.6, *Priap.* 20.6, 27.6, Juv. 6.129 (Messalina) *ardens rigidae tentigine uoluae,*

Adams (1982) 21, 103). Cf. Schol.'s paraphrase, *dum cales ergo tu, ait, tenta libidine rumpis stratum. rumpo* also has a sexual connotation (*S.* 1.2.116–18 *tument tibi cum inguina, num ... malis tentigine rumpi?,* Cat. 11.20, 80.7, Adams (1982) 150–1).

tectaque: usually interpreted as a 'canopy' (*aulaeum, uelum;* cf. *RE* I 2156), although there seems to be no parallel for the use of *tectum* in this sense. Perhaps H. means that in her frenzy the woman 'hits the roof'. Cf. his own desperate act in the preceding poem (11.22).

13 uel ... cum ... agitat 'or again when she attacks ...' The clause 'formally continues *cum properat* (8) without being exactly parallel in content: it merely describes another scene equally revolting to the poet' (Heinze). There seems to be a similar use of *uel cum* at Virg. *A.* 11.406 (Gransden *ad loc.,* LHS II 501–2). The 'golden' word order (5n.) may suggest that H.'s *fastidia* are also *saeua,* and, on another level, that the woman's words are in a sense his own (*mea*), since she is a character in his poem.

14 Inachia: for the 'instrumental' abl. and the name, cf. 11.6n. The reference to Io, the 'Inachian heifer', is more pointed here with H. about to be described as a 'bull' (17).

ac: cf. 1.16n. H. seems to be the first to use *ac* and *atque* in positive as well as negative comparisons (LHS II 478).

15 ter nocte potes: three times seems to be the usual number (Enk on Prop. 2.33.22 *ter faciamus iter*); more than that is, at least by convention, 'sheer exaggeration' (Kroll on Cat. 32.8 *nouem continuas fututiones;* cf. Ov. *Am.* 3.7.25–6, Philodemus, *AP* 11.30). With *potes* there is a euphemistic ellipse of *futuere* or the like; cf. Mart. 3.32.1, 76.4, 11.97.1–2 *una nocte quater possum: sed quattuor annis | si possum, peream, te, Telesilla, semel,* and the parallel use of *dunamai* in Greek (e.g. Strato, *AP* 12.11.1, 213.2, perhaps Arch. fr. 254 West).

15–16 ad unum | mollis opus: *ad* here indicates purpose (*OLD* s.v. 42). Cf. Virg. *A.* 8.472–3 *nobis ad belli auxilium ... | exiguae uires.* For *mollis,* cf. 1.10n. *opus* is another euphemism (8.20n.); cf. Pl. *As.* 873, Caecil. fr. 161 *ROL properatim in tenebris istuc confectum est opus,* Ov. *Am.* 2.10.36 *cum moriar, medium soluar et inter opus,* Adams (1982) 157.

16 pereat male: a standard and perhaps colloquial imprecation (*S.* 2.1.6, *OLD* s.v. *male* 10). Cf. Arch. fr. 196a.31 (11.20n.).

16–17 te ... inertem: the hyperbaton seems to mirror her disappointment as she became aware of his sluggishness ('you ... (I thought) a bull ... (but) ... impotent'). *iners* in this sense seems to be euphemistic; cf. 14.1, Cat. 67.26 *iners sterili semine natus erat*, Ov. *Am.* 3.7.15 *truncus iners iacui*, *Rem.* 780, [Tib.] *Priap.* 2.5, 38, Adams (1982) 46.

17 Lesbia: supposedly the *lena*, professional or amateur, who introduced H. to the woman (Schol., most commentators). Yet the introduction of another female character seems unmotivated, and it may be that *Lesbia* is not a name, but an epithet for Inachia. It would correspond to *Cous* for Amyntas (18n.), and explain why Inachia is able to arouse H. (14–15): she is like the women of Lesbos in her mastery of erotic arts, especially *fellatio*. This seems to have been the primary connotation of the term 'Lesbian' in the Greek world (Gentili (1988) 95–6, 266, Henderson (1991) 183–4) and it was almost certainly known to the Romans. Cf. Catullus' 'Lesbia' (e.g. 58.5) and 'Lesbius' (79), Mart. 1.34, 6.23, 10.39, 11.62, 99, perhaps Petr. 133.3 (mention of Lesbos in 'hymn' to Priapus), *RE* XIII 2100–2.

quaerenti taurum: sc. *mihi* 'when I was looking for a bull'. H.'s *dignissima barris* (1) may be a sarcastic exaggeration of the hag's words, as the elephant was sometimes called *Luca bos* (Var. *L.* 7.39). For *taurus* as a symbol of 'stud-like' virility, cf. N–H on *C.* 2.5.3, Greek *ataurotos* ('without a bull') of women without husbands (Ar. *Lys.* 217 etc.), Petr. 25.6, [Ov.] *Am.* 3.5.15–16. In Greek *tauros* can be a metaphor for the *phallus* (Henderson (1991) 127, 202–3). There may also be an ironic reference to H.'s self-presentation as a 'bull' at 6.11–12.

18 Cous ... Amyntas: there is an 'Amyntas' at Theocr. *Id.* 7.2 (set on Cos) and the name occurs 10× in Virgil's *Eclogues*. H. may be referring to these texts, although his purpose is not clear. On the other hand, Amyntas is a real-life name (*RE* I 2025–8), and it appears that *Cous*, somewhat like *Lesbius* (17n.), could mean 'handsome' or 'lascivious'. Cf. Cael. *Orat.* fr. 23 (= Quint. *Inst.* 8.6.53) *in triclinia Coam, in cubiculo Nolam* (evidently of Clodia, with a pun on *nolam*, 'I won't'), Damoxenos, fr. 3.1–3 *PCG* 'a certain youth ... about 17 years old, | a (real) Coan. For that island seems to produce gods'. The second meaning seems to come from Coan 'bombyx', a kind of fake silk made into robes that were almost transparent (*C.* 4.13.13, *S.* 1.2.101–2, Griffin (1986) 10, *RE* IV 127).

19–20 The simile may be a parody of Hom. *Il.* 12.131–4 (two

warriors) 'stood before the high gates | as when high-crowned oaks
stand in the mountains, | which endure wind and rain for ever, |
secured by their huge, far-spreading roots'. Cf. *C.* 3.10.17 (Lyce) *nec
rigida mollior aesculo*, Thomas on Virg. *G.* 2.291–7, Pease on *A.* 4.441–5
*uelut annoso ualidam cum robore quercum | Alpini Boreae ... | eruere ... certant
... | ipsa* [sc. *arbor*] *haeret scopulis.*

19 in indomito ... neruus: both epithets may be again (5n.)
felt with both nouns. *indomitus* makes Amyntas' 'parts' a match for
the woman's 'lust' (9), while *constantior* 'stands' (as it were) in contrast
to *soluto* (8). For the unusual jingle *in indomito*, cf. 10.14n., for *ner-
uus = mentula*, 8.17n.

20 noua ... arbor: in her enthusiasm for Amyntas' youth (*noua*)
the woman forgets her arboriculture: older trees with well-estab-
lished roots are in fact 'more steadfast'. Cf. the oaks in Homer and
Virgil (19–20n.).

21 muricibus ... lanae: the *munera* (2) turn out to be 'fleeces of
wool dyed twice with Tyrian purple'. Purple cloth (2.20, 9.27) was
even more expensive if it was 'double-dyed' (*dibaphus*). But it could
also have a fishy odour such as might remind H. of the woman (5n.).
Cf. N–H on *C.* 2.16.35–7, Mart. 4.4.6 (Bassa stinks) *quod bis murice
uellus inquinatum*, Lilja (1972) 136, 166.

iteratae: first here in this sense, but it could be a technical term
for the dye industry. Cf. Stat. *Silv.* 3.2.139–40 *purpura fuco | Sidoniis
iterata cadis*, N–H on *C.* 1.7.32 (*itero* an agricultural term), 2.19.12
(possibly a bee-keeping term). The phrase *uellera lanae* may come
from Lucr. 6.504 (clouds) *ueluti pendentia uellera lanae*; cf. Var. At. *poet.*
21 *FPL*, Thomas on Virg. *G.* 1.397.

22 properabantur: the imperfect (see app. crit) is required by
the sequence of tenses (23–4) and the sense (she has already sent the
fleeces (2)). In Classical Latin *propero* is normally intransitive (9, 2.62,
etc.); the transitive use seems to be archaic and poetic (Grassman
(1966) 84; cf. *C.* 3.24.62, *Ep.* 1.3.28, N–H on *C.* 2.7.24 (*deproperare*),
Sall. *Jug.* 37.3, Virg. *G.* 1.196, 260, 4.171, *A.* 8.454). *nempe* occurs only
here in H.'s lyric, as opposed to 9× in the hexameters. The dis-
tribution suggests that it might have a colloquial or prosaic cast, but
it is found even in elevated verse (Lucr. (6×), Virg. *G.* 3.259, Ov.
Met. 2.664, etc.; cf. Brink on *Ep.* 2.2.156).

23 foret: only here in the *Epodes*. The form is a 'convenient metrical stand-by for *esset*' (Brink on *Ars* 289), especially in dactylic verse (13× in H.'s), but also in Aeolic-type lyric with its choriambs (*C.* 3.4.13, 4.8.22).

aequalis inter conuiua: the participants in a *conuiuium* (11.8n.), like the *hetairoi* of a Greek symposium, were often 'equals' in age and status (*C.* 1.8.6, Ter. *An.* 453–4, Cic. *Cael.* 39 *aequalium . . . conuiuium*, *ThLL* I 993–4). For the position of *inter*, cf. 2.38n. The word *conuiua* is more common in comedy, satire, and epigram than in higher poetry (*ThLL* IV 879–80). H. has it only here and at *C.* 1.28.7 in his lyric, but 16× in his hexameters.

24 quam te: sc. *mulier tua diligeret*. There may be an echo of Cat. 70.1–2 *nulli se dicit mulier mea nubere malle | quam mihi*.

25–6 The similes may echo Hom. *Il.* 11.383 (Paris to Diomedes) 'they [the Trojans] fear you as bleating goats a lion' and Theocr. *Id.* 11.24 (Polyphemus to Galatea) 'you flee me as an ewe who has seen a wolf', although the latter could be drawing on a common source, perhaps Archilochus (cf. 13.4n.). On the other hand, both images seem to be proverbial; cf. 15.7n., *C.* 1.23, 33.7–9 (26n.), 3.18.13, 4.4.13–16, Virg. *Ecl.* 2.63–5, *A.* 10.723–8, Ov. *Met.* 1.505–6 (Apollo to Daphne) *nympha, mane! sic agna lupum, sic cerua leonem, | sic aquilam . . . fugiunt . . . columbae*, Otto (1890) s.v. *leo, lupus*.

25 o ego non felix: for the hiatus, cf. 5.71n. *o* with the nom. is rare (10.15–16n.), and even rarer with *ego* (Brink on *Ars* 301 *o ego laeuus*, *Ciris* 424 *o ego crudelis*). *felix* is a common term in Latin *makarismoi* (2 intro., 16.53, Mynors on Virg. *G.* 2.490). It seems to be first used of those 'lucky in love' at Cat. 100.8 *sis felix, Caeli, sis in amore potens* (Grassman (1966) 85, *ThLL* VI 1.442; cf. 15.17, *C.* 1.13.17, 3.27.13, 4.13.21). *paueo* appears to be a poetic word (*ThLL* x 1.806; cf. 2.35n.).

26 agna . . . leones: more 'role reversal', with the female animals corresponding to H., the males to the woman. The word order may suggest that the wolves are enemies of the *capreae* as well as the *agna*; cf. *C.* 1.33.7–9 *prius Apulis | iungentur capreae lupis | . . . Pholoe peccet adultero*.

EPODE 13

Introduction

A storm is raging, alarming the poet's companions. He exhorts them
to make the bad weather an occasion for easing their troubles with a
drinking party. The centaur Chiron gave Achilles similar advice for
the hero's time of grief at Troy.

The setting is not made explicit, but the winter storm, the refer-
ence to H.'s birthday in December (6n.), the anxiety of his com-
panions, the parallel, even if incomplete (below) with Achilles, and
the position of the epode in the book (Intro. 4) suggest the time of
uncertainty after Actium and before the Alexandrian war (Intro. 2;
cf. 3, 6–7n.). It seems less likely that the date is before Philippi in 42
BC (Kilpatrick (1970); cf. 6–7n.) or prior to Actium (Wilkinson (1951)
128), or that the context is simply a 'generic symposium' (Commager
(1962) 173, Davis (1991) 146–50).

The poem's affinity with certain early Greek lyric (e.g. Alcaeus,
frr. 38A, 50, 58, 335, 338 (1–2n.), 362 (9n.) L–P) and with H.'s own
'convivial' *Odes* (*C.* 1.4, 7, 9, 11, 27, 36, 2.3, 7, 11, 3.8, 14, 17, 19, 21,
28, 29, 4.7, 11, 12) has led to doubts whether it is an *iambus* in any-
thing but metre. But the symposium is an important context for
early *iambus* (Intro. 3), and iambic blame is often directed, as here, at
'friends' (*philoi*) who behave in an inappropriate manner (3 intro.).
H.'s description of the storm (1n.) and his exhortation (3–10n.) may
also owe something to Archilochus, and the same may be true of the
technique, if not the details (11n.), of the mythical *exemplum* (3.9–
14n.).

As for the myth, the parallel between H.'s and Chiron's exhorta-
tions is not complete, but the differences may be as important as the
similarities (Mankin (1989) 138–40). They suggest that the present
company, as ordinary humans, are more fortunate than the great
hero of myth. The storm is not attacking them, as the rivers of Troy
would attack Achilles; in their ignorance of the future they still have
hope of a good outcome, something Chiron's prophecy and his own
decision to kill Hector would take away from the hero. H. and his
friends can console each other in a true *con-uiuium*; at the time pre-
dicted by Chiron, Achilles would be isolated from other men. If the

Centaur could urge his embattled, doomed, and lonely 'fosterling' to ease the 'whole evil' with wine and song, H.'s *amici* ought to be able to do the same.

1 tempestas: there seems to be a play on several senses of this word (Babcock (1978) 111–12). To H.'s friends the almost supernaturally violent 'storm' (*OLD* s.v. 3) is a cause of mental 'turmoil' (s.v. 4), perhaps because they view it as an evil omen (cf. Cic. *Div.* 2.42) or as a kind of symbol of some 'disturbance' (s.v. 4) in the human world (cf. N–H on *C.* 1.14 ('shipwreck of state' allegory), Brink on *Ep.* 2.2.85, Arch. fr. 105 West (other 'political storms'), Gentili (1988) 197–215). But to H. himself it is simply an 'occasion' (s.v. 1) for a party at which they can forget those 'other things' which disturb them.

    caelum contraxit: *'caelum' pro nubibus accipe, et 'contraxit' [pro] in unum coegit, ac per hoc 'densas fecit' intellegendum* (Porph.). Cf. Lucr. 6.211–13 (of clouds) *hasce igitur cum uentus agens contrusit in unum | compressitque locum cogens, expressa profundunt | semina quae faciunt flammae fulgere colores.* There may be a hint at the expression *frontem contraho* ('frown'; cf. *S.* 2.2.125 *explicuit uino contractae seria frontis*), as if the sky 'mirrored' the unhappy faces of H.'s friends (5n.).

    1–2 imbres | niuesque deducunt Iouem: an ominous image: *deducunt* may suggest either military triumph (*C.* 1.37.31), as if Jupiter had been defeated in a battle of the gods and giants (*C.* 3.4.42–80), or magical entrapment, as if a witch had pulled him from the sky (5.45–6, 17.5, 78nn.; cf. Ov. *F.* 3.285–348). Supposed parallels (Alcaeus, fr. 338 L–P, Virg. *Ecl.* 7.60), where 'Zeus' and 'Jupiter', metonymies for 'sky' and 'rain' (2.29n.), 'descend' of their own accord, underline the violence of H.'s expression.

    2 nunc ... nunc: picked up in line 8 to emphasize the urgency of the *occasio*, suggest its connection with the storm (1n.), and prepare for a contrast with *illic* (17n.). Cf., among many passages in H. (*nunc* is a favourite word), *C.* 1.4.9–12, 9.18–24, 37.1–4.

    siluae: pronounced *silüae* (vocalic diaeresis); cf. 16.32n., N–H on *C.* 1.23.4, 2.15.17, *S.* 1.8.17, LHS I 133.

    3 Threicio Aquilone: for *Aquilo*, cf. 10.7n. Greeks from Hesiod on (*Op.* 553) describe the north wind as coming from Thrace, and the epithet here, which would not be appropriate to an Italian wind (cf.

N–H on *C.* 1.25.11), may suggest a Greek setting, perhaps the island of Samos, which Octavian (6n.) made his headquarters after Actium (9.27n.). At the end of 31 BC (6n.) he was called to Italy to settle a mutiny of his veterans (Plut. *Ant.* 73.6, Reinhold on Dio 51.4.2–8). His journey was vexed by bad weather (Suet. *Aug.* 17.3: cf. Dio 51.5.2), and at that time of year it would not be surprising if a storm had alarmed him and his friends before his departure.

The form and scansion *Threicio* (first here in Latin) are epic (Hom. *Il.* 13.13, 23.230, Virg. *A.* 3.51 etc.), and the same may be true of the hiatus without shortening of the first vowel (cf. 5.100n., N–H on *C.* 1.28.24, Arch. fr. 120.1 West (trochaic tetrameter) *Dionusou anaktos*, Hom. *Il.* 1.30 etc., Coleman on Virg. *Ecl.* 2.24, 3.6, Cic. *Orat.* 152).

3–10 H.'s exhortation seems to anticipate many *Odes* (13 intro.), but it may be Archilochean; cf. frr. 4 (9.35n.), 111 'encourage the young men; the boundaries of victory are with the gods', and especially fr. 13 West (App. 1), where the poet rebukes a friend and his fellow citizens (6–7n.) for being overcome by grief from a shipwreck and not 'rejoicing in revels'.

3 amici: vocative and emphatic: H.'s companions should heed his *libera consilia* (11.26) because he speaks as a friend to friends.

The shift from pl. to sing. addressee (6n.) has led some to take *amici* as nom. ('let us (you and I) as friends ...'), others to write *amice* (Bentley), which at least preserves the emphasis on friendship, or *Amici*, the voc. of the proper name Amicius (Housman (1972) 1087, Sh. Bailey).

4 occasionem de die: probably 'from this particular (rainy) day' (cf. *C.* 3.8.27 *dona praesentis cape laetus horae*), although H. might mean 'from early in the day', i.e. before the usual evening starting-time for a symposium (Porph.; cf. Fordyce on Cat. 47.5–7 *uos conuiuia lauta sumptuosa | de die facitis; mei sodales | quaerunt in triuio uocationes*, Cic. *Phil.* 2.87). The cretic-containing (Intro. 5) *occasio* occurs in both comedy (Pl. *As.* 945 etc.) and tragedy (Acc. *trag.* 78 *ROL*).

uirent genua: unless H. anticipates a dance (cf. *C.* 1.9.16), the reference to 'knees' seems odd for a symposium, where the drinkers reclined, and it could hint at a coming battle (13 intro.) from which strong legs might provide escape (N. Rudd, *A.J.Ph.* 81 (1960) 385; cf. 14n., Arch. fr. 233 West). A similar phrase at Theocr. *Id.* 14.70 'do

what is fitting, since (your) knee is green', may point to a source in
Archilochus, also a model for Theocritus (cf. *Epigr.* 21, A. Henrichs,
Z.P.E. 39 (1980) 7–27). For 'green' of youthful vigour, cf. 17.33n., *C.*
1.9.17, 25.17, 4.13.6.

H.'s reminder of his friends' age and what befits it suggests a
number of *Odes* (*C.* 1.4, 9, 23, 2.11, 3.14, 3.27, 4.1) but with a differ-
ence: here he includes himself among the young men (*rapiamus*). At
C. 2.7.5–8 an older H. reminisces about occasions of this sort: *Pompei,
meorum prime sodalium, | cum quo morantem saepe diem mero | fregi coronatus
nitentis | malabathro Syrio capillos.*

5 obducta ... fronte: abl. of separation. For the thought, cf. *C.*
3.29.16, *S.* 2.2.125 (1n.). Since *obduco* can be used of gloomy weather
(*OLD* s.v. 5c), it may be, in a sense, 'exchanged' with *contraxit* (1n.) in
order to emphasize the connection between the storm and the
unhappiness of H.'s friends.

senectus: only here, it seems, in the sense 'gloom', a common
meaning of *senium* (*OLD* s.v. 3). The word may be meant to suggest
that H.'s friends, unlike Achilles in the *exemplum* (18n.), can at least
hope to survive to 'old age'. Cf. Virg. *A.* 10.549 (when Anxur went to
war) *canitiemque sibi et longos promiserat annos.*

6–7 tu ... loqui: the shift from group (*amici*) to individual (*tu*) is
not without parallel (*C.* 1.27.10, 3.14.17, Arch. fr. 13.10 West (App. 1)),
but the absence of a name is puzzling (3n.). In certain other cases an
unnamed addressee can be plausibly identified from various clues,
one of which is the poet's reluctance to reveal the name (N–H on *C.*
2.18.17 (Maecenas), 3.24.3 (Augustus), Mankin (1988a) on Virg. *Ecl.*
8.5–13 (Octavian)). The individual here is enjoined to see to the
wine, which could indicate that he is the host (6n.), and to 'stop talk-
ing (about) the other things', which may imply that he is someone
whose words are likely to influence the mood of the company (7n.).
Both of these things suggest an authoritative figure, perhaps a mili-
tary commander whom H. would be shy of rebuking by name. If, as
seems likely, the setting is some time after Actium (13 intro.), then
the man could be Octavian; if it is before Philippi, then he could be
Brutus (Intro. 1) or Cassius (Kilpatrick (1970) 137–41).

6 Torquato ... pressa meo: i.e. in 65 BC (Intro. 1). It was cus-
tomary to date wine jars (N–H on *C.* 1.20.3, 3.8.12, 14.18, 21.1

(below), *Ep.* 1.5.4, *ROL* IV pp. 208–11 (= *CIL* I ii 653, 699– 702)). For *meus = natalis*, cf. Cic. *Att.* 13.42.2 *diem meum scis esse II Non. Ian.* [3 January]; *aderis igitur.*

The reference to H.'s birth may provide a date for the poem (8 December 31 BC (13 intro.)), but its main function seems to be to anticipate the *exemplum* by identifying H. as an ordinary, adult Roman, that is, no centaur or *puer* from mythical times (11, 12nn.).

moue: apparently 'dislodge' the wine (poetic pl.) from its container or storage place. But *moueo* seems to be used in connection with wine only here and at *C.* 3.21.6 (a *testa* also containing 'Torquatan') *moueri digna bono die*, where there is a play on the meaning 'entreat' (17.3n.; the ode is a parody of a hymn (Commager (1962) 126–7)). There may be a similar play here (anticipating *deus*): 'entreat the wine – not the god'.

It seems to have been 'proper etiquette for a guest to specify the vintage to his host' (Kilpatrick (1970) 136); cf. *C.* 3.21.7–8, *S.* 2.8.16–17, Petr. 48.1.

7 cetera mitte loqui: cf. *C.* 1.9.9 *permitte diuis cetera*, and, for the construction, N–H on *C.* 1.38.3 *mitte sectari*, Pl. *Per.* 207 *mitte male loqui*, Ter. *An.* 873, 904, Lucr. 6.1056 *mirari mitte.* The 'other things' here are what cause 'dire anxieties'; H.'s friend may have been expressing his fears about the apparent ill omen of the storm (1n.).

deus: H. does not know which god (5.1, 14.6n., *C.* 1.5.6, 2.1.25, 3.16.43, 27.50, *S.* 2.3.16, 7.24, *Ep.* 1.11.22; cf. Arch. fr. 24.15 (to a friend who escaped disaster) 'but now (some?) god has rescued you', 210 West, Clay (1983) 21–5 (on the Greek expressions *theos tis, daimōn tis*)). His ignorance, that of an ordinary human (6n.; cf. *C.* 3.29.29–32), tempers somewhat the optimism of his encouraging words, but it will contrast favourably with Achilles' fatal certainty (15–16).

haec: apparently both the elements disturbed by the storm and the *cetera* that concern H.'s friend.

fortasse: the etymology (from *fors*; cf. 16.15n., *C.* 2.16.31) may be important: if things turn out well, 'some god' (above) could be responsible, but to H. and his friends, ignorant of divine plans and actions, it will seem the result of 'chance'. Cf. Arch. fr. 16 West (App. 1) 'chance [*tychē*] and fate [*moira*], Pericles, give all things to a man', which appears to mean (Treu (1959) 192) that what is 'chance' from a human perspective is 'fate' from a divine one. *fortasse* seems to be less poetic than other *fors* compounds (Axelson (1945) 31, Blok (1961) 83).

7–8 benigna ... uice: the epithet, conventional with *deus* (cf. *C.* 4.2.52, 4.74) is 'transferred' to *uice*, perhaps to emphasize again (7n.) H.'s ignorance. Mortals can know that a 'turn of events' (*C.* 1.4.1, *OLD* s.v. *uicis* 7) is 'favourable', but they cannot know the disposition of the gods. *uice* is *brevis in longo* (10, 14; cf. 11.6n.).

8 reducet in sedem 'bring back to (their proper) place'. Cf. Lucr. 6.573–4 (the earth is not destroyed when buffeted by winds) *inclinatur enim retroque recellit | et recipit prolapsa suas in pondere sedes*, Aug. *ap.* Suet. *Aug.* 28.2 *ita mihi saluam ac sospitem rem publicam sistere in sua sede liceat.* H. may play on *reduco* in the sense 'bring home' (*C.* 4.2.17, *OLD* s.v. 1b) and on *sedes* in the sense 'home' (*C.* 2.6.6, s.v. 4) in order to suggest that the 'god' might grant him and his friends a 'home-coming', something denied by the Fates to Achilles (15–16).

8–9 Achaemenio | ... nardo 'balsam fit for an Achaemenes', the ancestor of the great Persian kings (Cyrus, Darius, Xerxes) who were symbols of power and 'oriental luxury' (N–H on *C.* 2.12.21 *diues Achaemenes*, 3.1.44 *Achaemeniumque costum*). Their empire had once included Syria, which produced an especially prized variety of *nardus* (*C.* 2.11.16, Plin. *Nat.* 12.45). In H. nard and other perfumes are usually associated with convivial drinking (*C.* 1.5.2, 2.3.13, 7.8, 22–3, 3.14.17, 20.14, 29.4, 4.12.16–17; cf. *C.* 1.38.1 ('Persian junk' inappropriate to a solitary drink)). Its absence from the drinking scene in the *exemplum* may be another sign of Achilles' solitude (18n.).

9 fide Cyllenaea: Mount Cyllene in Arcadia was the birthplace of Hermes (Mercury), the inventor of the lyre (*C.* 1.10.6, 21.12, 3.11.1–6). The epithet may be meant to evoke the *Homeric hymn to Hermes*, where the lyre is characterized as 'the companion of the feast' (31) and Hermes' first song on it is compared to when 'young men tease each other at banquets ... in comradely friendship' (55–8), which sounds very much like a context for *iambus* (13 intro.; cf. Clay (1989) 108–9). Archilochus received a lyre from the Muses in his 'poetic initiation' (test. 4 Tarditi) and he was supposed to be an innovator in the use of that instrument (test. 71 Tarditi, Gentili (1988) 183). It is possible that Hermes figured in his *iambi* (cf. app. crit. at Arch. fr. 95 West) as he does in those of Hipponax (frr. 3, 3a, 32, 35, 47, 79 West).

$\overline{Cyll\bar{e}na\bar{e}a}$ makes for a spondaic hexameter, one of four in H.'s lyric
(16.17, 29, C. 1.28.21), all involving proper names; the sole example
in the hexameters, Ars 476, does not, and has been suspected (Brink
ad loc.). 'Spondiazontes' (Cic. Att. 7.2.1) are relatively frequent in Hel-
lenistic Greek verse, and are supposed to be a Neoteric 'affectation'
in Latin (Fordyce on Virg. A. 7.631), but they occur in earlier Greek,
including Archaic elegy (e.g. Theognis 7, Solon, fr. 17 West). The
spelling -aea is preserved only in the lemma of Porph., but is the
proper Latin form for an adj. from a Greek noun of the first declen-
sion (Housman (1972) 514–18, 887–902; cf. Arat. Phaen. 597, app.
crit. to Hipp. fr. 32.1 West ($Kull\bar{e}nie$ C : -$ai\bar{e}$ Meineke)).

10 leuare: here with the acc. of the thing 'lightened' and abl. (of
separation) of the cause of the distress (cf. 17.26, S. 2.5.99 cum te ser-
uitio longo curaque leuarit, OLD s.v. 6). The change in construction in
the exemplum may be significant (17n.).

diris: 'a very strong word' (Heinze); the anxieties are not merely
'unpleasant' (so with duris (dett., Bentley, Sh. Bailey)), but 'danger-
ous' (5.89, Lucr. 4.1046 dira lubido, Virg. A. 2.519 mens tam dira), per-
haps because they might sap the courage of H.'s friends when they
need it most (13 intro.).

sollicitudinibus: cf. Cic. Tusc. 4.18 sollicitudo [is] aegritudo cum
cogitatione. H.'s other uses of this prosaic word (C. 1.18.4, S. 2.8.68; cf.
Blok (1961) 86) and of sollicitus (e.g. C. 3.29.26) and sollicito (3.1.26) fit
this definition, and make it likely that it is not simply 'fear' of the
storm which afflicts his friends (that would be timor (Cic. Tusc. 4.19)),
but 'distress with brooding' about the future.

The long word (4.11n.) fills the hemiepes of the asynarteton (Intro. 6)
as, perhaps, the anxieties of H.'s friends 'fill' their thoughts. There
are no seven-syllable words in surviving Greek epodic verse, but sev-
eral occur in the hemiepe of early Greek elegy (Callinus, fr. 1.2,
Demodocus, fr. 5.6, Mimn. fr. 6.2, Solon, fr. 20.4, Theognis, fr.
1058, Tyrt. fr. 4.6 West). The one Republican Latin example of this,
at Cat. 68.112 Amphitryoniades, can hardly be H.'s model, and he may
be imitating something in a lost epode (or elegy) of Archilochus.

11–18 Chiron's exhortation parallels that of H. in being linked to
a specific context (below) and in calling for wine and song to
'lighten' trouble. But it differs in being a prophecy (11n.) of a future
time and place (17n.). The Centaur knew things that an ordinary

Roman (6n.) could not (7n.); by imparting them to his 'fosterling', he removed uncertainty, but also hope.

The speech consists of an address to Achilles (12), a description of Troy (13–16), and an exhortation (17–18). The three parts are closely linked (*inuicte ... nate ... te manet ... tellus quam ... unde ... illic*), with the first two providing details which indicate the precise context of the third. Achilles' grief will come when he has proved 'unconquered' (12n.) in battle against the rivers of Troy (13–14n.) at the point when his return home has been 'shattered' (15n.). All of this suggests the time (depicted in Hom. *Il.* 23–4) after the deaths of Patroclus and Hector and just before Achilles' own death.

11 nobilis ... alumno: a 'golden line' (2.15n.) which 'lifts the thirteenth Epode from the contemporary atmosphere of the beginning to that of the Heroic Age' (Wilkinson (1951) 147). The variant *cecinit grandi* would spoil the effect, and may have arisen because it produces a pattern for the first four feet D(actyl)DS(pondee)S that is more common (13×) in H.'s epodic hexameters than that with *grandi cecinit* (DSDS (7×)).

nobilis ... Centaurus: cf. Hom. *Il.* 11.832 'Chiron the most just (*dikaiotatos*) of the Centaurs', Pind. *P.* 3.63 'the moderate [*sōphrōn*] Chiron', 4.199, *N.* 3.53, Bacch. *Dith.* 27.34 Maehler, all distinguishing Chiron from the rest of a breed usually characterized as the opposite of 'noble', 'just', and 'moderate' (N–H on *C.* 1.18.8). His special status may derive from the fact that, as a son of Cronus and Philyra, he was a 'demigod' rather than a 'demihuman' and also a half-brother of Zeus. He is portrayed as foster-father and tutor to many heroes (West on Hes. *Th.* 1001) but especially to Achilles (Hes. fr. 204.87–9 M–W, Hom. *Il.* 11.831–2, Pind. *P.* 6.21–3, *N.* 3.43–53). There was a collection of his supposed 'teachings' addressed to Achilles ([Hes.] frr. 283–5), and he is said to have prophesied that hero's birth and exploits (Bacch. *Dith.* 27.34–45 Maehler, Eur. *I.A.* 1062–75) although not, it seems, except here, his death (but cf. Fraenkel (1957) 65).

ut cecinit: picking up on *iuuat* (9): 'it is helpful ... (just) as the Centaur sang to his ... fosterling'. For *ut = sicut* or *uelut*, cf. 1.19, 12.25, *C.* 1.8.13–14 *quid latet, ut marinae | filium dicunt Thetidis*, 4.4.57. *cecinit* seems at first to suggest that in the *exemplum* Chiron 'stands for' the poet (H.), but it soon becomes evident that the Centaur was not 'singing' but 'prophesying' (*Saec.* 25 *ueraces cecinisse Parcae*, Cat. 64.383

(15n.) *carmina diuino cecinerunt pectore Parcae*, *OLD* s.v. *cano* 8, Davis (1991) 14), something that is beyond H.'s powers here (7n., but cf. 7.15–20, 16.66nn.).

grandi ... alumno: in Republican Latin *grandis* is normally applied to beasts and things rather than humans, and here it may recall Homeric *pelōrios* ('huge', 'monstrous'), used twice of Achilles during his most furious battle (*Il.* 21.527, 22.92). But there may also be something pathetic about the idea of a 'huge fosterling', who is 'superhuman' in size but still a *puer* (12). Juvenal (7.210–12) turns the pathos into comedy: *metuens uirgae iam grandis Achilles | cantabat patriis in montibus et cui non tunc | eliceret risum citharoedi cauda magistri.*

There is no mention of Achilles in surviving *iambus*, but he is prominent in other early lyric (e.g. Ibyc. fr. 282 *PMG*, Stes. 115–20 *SLG*, Sappho 105, Alcaeus 44, 283 L–P, Simonides, frr. 10–17 West, Pind. *Ol.* 9.70–9 etc.) and elsewhere in H. (1.5, 4.1–2, 17.8–14nn., *C.* 1.6.5–6, 8.13–16, 15.34, 2.4–24, 16.29, 4.6.3–24, *S.* 1.7.11–15, 2.3.193, *Ep.* 1.2.11–14, *Ars* 120–2). Cf. K. King, *Achilles: a paradigm of a war hero from Homer to the Middle Ages* (Berkeley (1987)).

12 inuicte: since Achilles is still a 'child', the epithet is proleptic (3.20n.) or, rather, prophetic (11n). For most of the Trojan war he will be 'undefeated' (*OLD* s.v. *inuictus* 1) and 'invincible' (s.v. 2); he will be 'resolute' (s.v. 4) in his wrath and then his desire for vengeance, and as the 'best of the Achaeans' (Hom. *Il.* 1.244 etc.) he will always be 'matchless' (s.v. 5).

mortalis ... Thetide: 'the alternation of words ... suggests Achilles' double nature, half human, half divine, and the dilemma that was his tragedy' (Wilkinson (1951) 147); the phrase might stand as an epigraph to the *Iliad*. For *mortalis*, cf. 2.2n. and, for Achilles as 'the mortal hero', Schein (1984) 92–6.

dea: abl. of source or origin without a preposition, as often, especially in elevated verse, with participles meaning 'born of' (N–H on *C.* 1.12.50 *orte Saturno*, 2.4.5 *Aiacem Telamone natum*, *S.* 2.6.5, Enn. *Ann.* 28 Skutsch (13n.)).

13 manet: cf. 16.41 and the more sinister *C.* 1.28.15 *sed omnis una manet nox*. Achilles would be buried in the 'land of Assaracus' (*C.* 4.6.9–12, Hom. *Il.* 23.91–2, 243–8, *Od.* 24.76–84).

Assaraci: a son of Tros, seldom mentioned except as the ancestor of Aeneas (*Il.* 20.231–40; cf. Skutsch on Enn. *Ann.* 28–9 *Assaraco natus Capys optimus isque pium ex se | Anchisen generat*, Virg. *G.* 3.35). The *tellus* is thus the ancestral land of H. and his friends (10.11–14n.), yet another difference between them and Achilles, the invader of that land (cf. *C.* 4.6.3–24).

13–14 What is ostensibly a description of the Trojan landscape serves to prophesy the *machē parapotamios*, Achilles' battle along and against the rivers of Troy (Hom. *Il.* 21.211–381). Reference to this battle amplifies the differences between Achilles and H. and his friends in several ways. The attacking rivers, natural forces as well as gods hostile to Achilles (14n.), contrast with the storm which, however frightening, is not directed at H. and his friends (1n.). The *machē* comes at a point where Achilles has made his decision to kill Hector and thus forfeit his return home (15n.). It, and the surrounding episodes, show Achilles at his most heroic and most inhuman (Schein (1984) 146–50) and thus least like ordinary men (6n.).

frigida ... flumina: there may be a reference to Hom. *Il.* 22.151–2 (a spring of Scamander near the Trojan wall) 'in summer flows like hail | or cold snow or ice from water', but cf. on *parui* (13n.). *flumina* is poetic pl. (Cat. 64.89 *Eurotae ... flumina*, Virg. *Ecl.* 6.64, *G.* 4.278 *curua ... flumina Mellae*, *ThLL* VI 958).

13 parui: the epithet is peculiar, since the Scamander was in fact 'great and deep-eddying' (Hom. *Il.* 20.73; cf. Plin. *Nat.* 5.124 *Scamander amnis nauigabilis*; Luc. 9.974–5 *in sicco serpentem puluere riuum | ... qui Xanthus* [below] *erat* seems to be fantasy). There may be a contrast between the (relative) 'smallness' of the river while it 'awaits' Achilles and the swollen flood it will become when it attacks him (Heinze; cf. *Il.* 21.234–41); *frigida* likewise would anticipate the time when Hephaestus will save Achilles by 'boiling' the river (21.348–82). Others see a reference to Scamander's complaint that his stream is 'narrowed' by the corpses thrown into it by Achilles (*Il.* 21.219–20; cf. Alcaeus, fr. 395 L–P, O. Vox, *Rh.M.* 136 (1993) 190–1), or 'a faint verbal antithesis to *grandi* ... to emphasize the "smallness" of [Achilles'] lot' (Wickham), or an adaptation of the epic scenery to the smaller 'dimensions of a lyric landscape' (Davis (1991) 15). The reading *praui*, even if a genuine variant (it occurs only in the least valuable part of the Schol. (Intro. 7)), is not much of an improvement; conjectures include *flaui* (N. Heinsius; cf. the river's 'divine name' (*Il.* 20.74) *Xanthus*, 'yellow'), *proni* (Bentley), and *curui* (Sh. Bailey; cf. Virg. *G.* 4.278 (13–14n.)).

14 lubricus et Simois: the other river of Troy, summoned by Scamander to join the attack on Achilles (Hom. *Il.* 21.307–23). *lubricus* here probably means 'gliding' (Lucr. 5.949–50 *fluenta* | *lubrica*, Ov. *Am.* 3.6.81 *lubricus amnis*, *F.* 4.337, 6.238; cf. Virg. *A.* 5.261 *rapidum Simoenta*), but there may be a hint of the sense 'slippery' (*OLD* s.v. 1). During the 'battle with the rivers' (13–14n.) Achilles, 'swift-footed' though he is, cannot outrun the river (Scamander, but presumably Simois would offer the same threat) or keep his footing without divine help (Hom. *Il.* 21.240–92, esp. 263–4). For postponed *et*, cf. 1.12n.

15 reditum: the warrior's *nostos*, 'homecoming' (cf. 16.35, *Ep.* 1.2.21 (Ulysses) *dum sibi, dum sociis reditum parat* (= Hom. *Od.* 1.5), *Ars* 146 *reditum Diomedis*). The other heroes in Homer can hope for and, in some cases, achieve a *nostos* (cf. the Cyclic epic *Nostoi*), but by killing Hector, Achilles forfeits his, as he is reminded by his mother (*Il.* 18.95–6), his horses (19.408–17), and Hector himself (22.358–60).

certo subtemine: instrumental abl., 'broke off (your) homecoming with (their) unerring thread', although the phrase might also be felt as an abl. of quality, 'the Fates of unerring thread' (Bentley; cf. *C.* 1.7.28 *certus enim promisit Apollo*). The *subtemen* ('woof') is the transverse thread which the weaver feeds under the *stamen*, the vertical thread ('warp'); cf. Var. *L.* 5.113 *stamen a stando, quod eo stat omne in tela* ['loom'] *uelamentum, subtemen, quod subit stamini*. It is not clear why both here and at Cat. 64.327 (below) Achilles' fate is woven with this 'subordinate strand'.

The metaphor of the 'thread' of human life is at least as old as Homer (*Il.* 20.127–8, 24.209–10, 525–6, *Od.* 7.197–8), where the 'spinners' or 'weavers' are the gods and certain *Klōthes*. The *Moirai* (below) dispense the thread beginning with Hesiod (*Th.* 904–6) and early lyric (e.g. Callinus, fr. 1.9 West; cf. Lattimore (1962) 159–60, Burkert (1985) 129).

Parcae: originally Roman birth goddesses (*C.* 2.16.39, Gell. 3.16.11), later identified in both literature and real life with the Greek *Moirai*, 'Fates' (7n.; cf. *C.* 2.6.9, 17.16, *Saec.* 25 (11n.), Cic. *Nat.* 3.44, Cat. 64.306, Virg. *Ecl.* 4.47, *ThLL* x 1.324–5). The *Moirai* joined most of the other gods as guests at the wedding of Thetis and

Peleus, where they 'sang' (11n.) Achilles' destiny (cf. the 'François vase' (*c.* 570 BC), probably based on the Cyclic epic *Cypria*, Cat. 64.303–81, R. Reitzenstein, *Hermes* 35 (1900) 73–105).

16 nec ... te reuehet: cf. 8n., Hom. *Il.* 18.59–60 (Thetis, when she realizes that Achilles plans to kill Hector) 'him I shall not again receive | when he has completed his homecoming to the house of Peleus', 330–2.

caerula: the colour of the sea (*OLD* s.v. 2), suggesting that Thetis, like the Trojan rivers (13–14n.), is both a divinity and a natural force (*per matrem Thetiden atque ex hoc metōnymicōs mare intellegendum* (Porph.)). Achilles' 'affinity' with such things distinguishes him from ordinary humans (1n.).

17 illic: 'Unlike the addressee of the poem, to whom the injunction is to act here and now (2n.), Achilles is advised for a future time and place' (Babcock (1978) 109). Since Chiron died before the Trojan war, he would not be able to offer comfort in person, although there was a story that his ghost returned 'in order to furnish Achilles some easement of sorrow' (Paus. 5.19.9, describing a scene on the ancient 'Chest of Cypselus' (*OCD* s.v.)).

omne malum 'the whole trouble' of Achilles' mortality, foreknowledge, and isolation (18n.). For the phrase, cf. Aesch. *Pers.* 353 *tou pantou kakou* ('the whole evil'), Cic. *Tusc.* 5.73 *cum sit omne et bonum eius et malum in potestate fortunae*, Virg. *A.* 6.736. Some take *omne* to mean 'every' and Chiron's advice to apply to any time when Achilles would be unhappy, but the details of the prophecy seem to point to a single, specific occasion (11–18, 13–14nn.).

uino cantuque: like H. and his friends, but cf. 8–9n. and on *leuato* (below). There was a tradition that Chiron was Achilles' music teacher (e.g. *Orph. Argonautica* 399, Ov. *F.* 5.385–6, Juv. 7.210–12 (11n.), *LIMC* s.v. 'Achilleus').

The embassy sent to persuade Achilles to return to battle finds him playing the lyre, singing, and drinking (Hom. *Il.* 9.186–204). Some have argued that this is the scene prophesied by Chiron, but it takes place well before Achilles has lost the possibility of returning home (15n.; cf. 9.410–16).

leuato: fut. imperative for a command that will be carried out at a later time (above; cf. *C.* 3.3.39, 14.24, 27.69, 29.44, *Ep.* 1.13.7, *Ars* 427). But by the late Republic the fut. imp., except where there is no present (*esto* (8.11), *memento* (10.4)) occurs chiefly in poetic and archaizing contexts. H. uses the present where strict usage would require the future (e.g. *S.* 2.2.15), the fut. in place of the pres. (*S.* 1.4.85, 2.5.88, *Ep.* 1.18.68, *Ars* 99–100), and the two together with no apparent difference in meaning (*S.* 2.1.8–10, 3.161, 7.44).

The change in construction of *leuo* (cf. 10n.) is suggestive: while H.'s friends can 'lift' their hearts *away from* (abl. of separation) their 'anxieties', Achilles will only 'mitigate' (*OLD* s.v. *leuo* 5) his 'trouble', not escape it.

18 deformis ... alloquiis 'with sweet consolations of ugly suffering'. The phrase is in apposition to *uino cantuque* (17). There seems to be no parallel for *alloquium* governing an objective gen., but cf. the construction with *solacium* (*OLD* s.v. 1b) and Greek *paramuthion* (e.g. Soph. *El.* 130 *kamatōn paramuthion*, 'distraction of troubles'). Some construe *aegrimoniae* with *omne malum*, but even if such a hyperbaton were possible, the alliterative pattern here (*d-, a-, d-, a-*) seems to suggest that the four words should be taken together (Kenney).

deformis: active, as 'causing ugliness'; cf. *C.* 2.20.22 *luctusque turpes*, Luc. 8.81–2 *deformis ... dolor*. In his grief for Patroclus, Achilles 'poured dust on his head and made ugly his handsome face' (Hom. *Il.* 18.24–5). *deformis* is often used of old age (Lucil. fr. 354 *ROL deformis senex*, Var. *L.* 5.5, Cic. *Ver.* 5.64; cf. Mimn. fr. 5.5–6 West *amorphon | geras* ('ugly old age')), and it may suggest here that Achilles' sorrow, like that of H.'s friends (5n.), would bring a kind of premature *senectus*. But unlike them, he would have no hope of survival into a real old age (*Il.* 1.352, 417, 505, 9.410–16, 18.95, 458, 21.277–8). Cf. what may be a word play at Acc. *trag.* 304 *ROL* (Achilles speaking?) *mors amici; quod mi est senium multo acerrimum.*

aegrimoniae: a rare word (17.73, Pl. *Rud.* 1190, *St.* 406, Cic. *Att.* 12.38.2), chosen, perhaps, to recall Lucretius' *mortalibus aegris* (6.1; cf. Virg. *G.* 1.237, *A.* 2.268 etc.) and its model, Homer's *deiloi brotoi* ('suffering mortals'; cf. *Il.* 21.463–4, 22.31, 76, 24.525).

alloquiis: first here in extant Latin. The etymology (from *alloquor*) and later use of the word suggest that this type of 'consolation' ought to involve 'conversation' (cf. Var. *L.* 6.57 *hinc 'adlocutum' mulieres ire aiunt cum eunt ad aliquam locutum consolandi causa*, V. Fl. 1.250–1 *hanc uero, socii, uenientem litore laeti | dulcibus alloquiis ludoque educite noctem*, Babcock (1978) 116–17). But at the time which Chiron seems to predict (13–14, 17nn.) Achilles will have lost Patroclus, the one person with whom he shared 'sweet conversation'; cf. the lament of Patroclus' ghost (Hom. *Il.* 23.77–8): 'Achilles, not again in life, sitting apart from | our companions, shall we (two) plan our plans'. For Achilles' isolation, cf. *Il.* 23.59–60, 217–32, 24.1–22, 120–4, 472–4, Schein (1984) 153–63.

EPODE 14

Introduction

Since Maecenas is 'killing' H. to find out the cause of his lethargy, he will state it: it is a god who prevents him from finishing his book of *iambi*. Anacreon suffered in the same way, and Maecenas, who is also 'aflame' with love, should know the feeling. But he is luckier than H., whose tormenter is Phryne, an ex-slave with a roving eye.

Like the previous epode (13 intro.), this one is often seen as less iambic than 'lyric' (cf. *C.* 1.13, 19, 27, 33, 2.12, 3.10, 26, 4.1, 10), and it is possible that H. is 'looking ahead' to the *Odes* (9–12n.; cf. Davis (1991) 71–4). But in its brevity, address to Maecenas, and focus on another situation where Maecenas 'threatens' his friend (5), Epode 14 seems to be a kind of 'sequel' to Epode 3, one of the most 'iambic' poems in the collection.

This time, however, the cause of the quarrel is not garlic but *iambus* itself, as if the darker side of this type of poetry (6 intro.) now threatens to disrupt a friendship that exemplifies the 'like-minded-ness' which it is meant to affirm and preserve (1 intro., Intro. 3). The failure of *iambus* at this 'stage' in the collection could simply warn H.'s audience that he is tiring of the genre (above), but, like the 'collapse' of bucolic in the last three of Virgil's *Eclogues* (cf. J. Solodow, *Lat.* 36 (1977) 757–71, Mankin (1988a) 76), it may have deeper implications. It seems to anticipate H.'s failures in the poems that bring the book to its uneasy conclusion, where he 'gives up' on Neaera (Epode 15) and, in his public stance, on saving Rome (16), and is forced to surrender to Canidia (17).

1–2 The opening couplet may be based on either Arch. fr. 193 West or, what seems more likely, fr. 191 (App. 1) 'for so great a desire for intimacy coiled-up under my heart | poured much mist over my eyes,

| having stolen the softened wits from my breast'. There is no clue as to the fragment's context, but perhaps Archilochus was also 'saying the worst things about himself' (Intro. 3) while apologizing for a failure of some sort.

1 Mollis inertia: for *mollis*, cf. 1.10n. To the Romans *inertia* was almost a cardinal sin (*C.* 4.9.29, *Ep.* 1.11.28, Cic. *Off.* 1.28, Sall. *Cat.* 52.22, 28, Opelt (1966) s.v.). There may be some irony in Maecenas, of all people, reproaching H. with 'effeminate indolence' (Intro. 1).

diffuderit: perf. subj. dependent (indirect question) on *rogando* (5). The image of 'pouring forgetfulness' anticipates the simile (3-4) but also suggests the ancient idea of sleep and other sensory inhibitors – including love (16n.) – as liquids (5.69-70, Arch. fr. 191.2 (1-2n.), Hom. *Il.* 2.19, 14.164 etc., Skutsch on Enn. *Ann.* 499, Lucr. 4.907-8).

1-2 imis ... sensibus: cf. 11.10, Virg. *Ecl.* 3.54 *sensibus haec imis – res est non parua – reponas.*

3 pocula ... ducentia somnos: cf. *C.* 3.1.21 *somnum reducent,* Tib. 1.2.79-80 *soporem | ... ducere. pocula* is H.'s word for Canidia's potions (5.38n.) and may here imply that he is the victim of magic (cf. 3.7-8).

Lethaeos: cf. *C.* 4.7.27-8 *Lethaea ... uincula,* Call. *Hymn* 4.234 'sleep on Lethaean wing', Cat. 65.5 (first instance of *Lethaeus* in Latin), Virg. *G.* 1.78 *Lethaeo perfusa papauera somno.* In Greek tradition *lēthē* ('forgetfulness') is personified (Hes. *Th.* 227) and, later, thought of as a place of oblivion or source of 'forgetful water' in the underworld (Theognis 705, 1215 West, Ar. *Ran.* 186, Plato, *Rep.* 10.621a). Cf. Virg. *A.* 6.714-15 (the dead) *Lethaei ad fluminis undam | securos latices et longa obliuia potant,* M. P. Nilsson, *Opuscula selecta* III (Lund 1960) 85-92.

4 arente ... traxerim: the subj. verb may show that this simile was part of Maecenas' original question. The whole phrase appears to be poetic: *areo* occurs only in verse in Classical Latin (*ThLL* II 504-5), while this seems to be the first use of the 'poetic singular' *fauce* (VI 392; cf. 2.64n.). *traho* in the sense *bibo* may also be an innovation (*OLD* s.v. 7); cf. Greek *helkō* (lit. 'drag') of drinking (e.g. Eur. *Ion* 1200).

5 candide 'sincere', 'well-meaning' (11.11-12n.). Cf. *S.* 1.10.86

(one of H.'s 'ideal readers') *candide Furni, Ep.* 1.4.1 *Albi, nostrorum sermonum candide iudex.*

occidis saepe rogando: a comic hyperbole; cf. *C.* 1.8.2–3 *amando | perdere,* 2.17.1 (also to Maecenas) *cur me querelis exanimas tuis?,* Brink on *Ars* 475 *occiditque legendo,* Pl. *Ps.* 931 *occidis me quom istuc rogitas,* Ter. *Eun.* 554 *rogitando obtundat enicet. occido* (only here in the lyrics, 9× in the hexameters) is rare in both elevated prose and verse and may be colloquial (Axelson (1945) 65–7). For the gerund, cf. 12.11n.

6 deus, deus: an emotive repetition (4.20n.) or, perhaps, a prayer-like *anadiplosis* (5.5n., 9.21). Cf. Lucr. 5.8 *deus ille fuit, deus,* Virg. *Ecl.* 5.64, Norden on *A.* 6.46, Arch. fr. 177.1 (App. 1). The *nam* is postponed *metri causa* (1.12n.) but also, it seems, to add emphasis to the word preceding it (17.45, *C.* 1.18.3, 4.14.9, *S.* 2.3.20, 41, 302, 6.78, *Ep.* 2.1.186, Marouzeau (1949) 107).

The *deus* here may be Amor (most commentators; cf. 11.1–3, Prop. 2.13.3 (below), Ov. *Am.* 2.18.13–18) or, what seems less likely, Jupiter (Schmidt (1977) 417–19). But, as in the previous poem (13.7n.), the fact that the god is not named may be more important than his identity. It may suggest that H. has lost the help of the Muses, the source of a poet's knowledge of the divine and, as daughters of Memory, the antithesis of the *obliuio* that afflicts him (7.15–20n.).

uetat: the verb often occurs in *recusationes* (9–12n.); cf. *C.* 1.6.9–10 *pudor | imbellisque lyrae Musa potens uetat, S.* 1.10.32, Prop. 2.13.3 *[Amor] me tam gracilis uetuit contemnere Musas,* 4.1.134.

7 A rare example in H. of 'parenthetic' or 'inserted apposition' of the type *raucae, tua cura, palumbes* (Virg. *Ecl.* 1.57). Cf. Brink on *Ep.* 2.1.234 and, for variations on the pattern, *C.* 1.1.29, 20.5, 3.24.42, 4.8.31. The figure is poetic and, it seems, 'very mannered' (Brink), and its popularity with H.'s contemporaries may reflect the influence of Hellenistic poetry or of Gallus (cf. Virg. *Ecl.* 1.69, 74 etc., Thomas on *G.* 2.146–7, Prop. 1.11.30, McKeown on Ov. *Am.* 1.12.7, J. B. Solodow, *H.S.C.Ph.* 90 (1986) 129–53). But here at least H. could be imitating something in Archilochus; cf. fr. 196a.49–50 West (the first known instance of the figure) *neon, | hēbēs epēlusin, chroa* ('her fresh skin, an enchantment of youth').

inceptos olim ... iambos: the whole collection, whose title would be *Iambi* or *Iamborum Liber* (Intro. 4). *olim* is too vague a word

(*OLD* s.v. 1) to help decide when H. actually began writing (Intro. 4). Since it is at the caesura it probably goes with *inceptos* but may also be felt with *promissum* (*apo koinou*).

promissum carmen: for the participle, cf. *S.* 2.3.6, Brink on *Ep.* 2.1.52, *Ars* 45 *promissi carminis*, where it seems to mean not just 'promised' but 'eagerly awaited' (i.e. 'promising'). Since this phrase is in apposition (above) to the plural *iambos*, *carmen* here probably means 'poetry' (e.g. *C.* 4.6.30, 11.36, *Ars* 408) or 'collection of poetry' (*C.* 3.30.13 *Aeolium carmen* = the *Odes*) rather than, as some take it, '(individual) poem'. H. can use *carmen* as a technical term for 'lyric' as opposed to other types of verse (9.5, *Ep.* 2.2.59), but cf. *Ep.* 1.19.27 (*carminis artem* of 'Parian *Iambi*'), 31 (*famoso carmine* of an *iambus*), *C.* 1.6.2, *Ars* 129 (*carmen* = *epos*), *S.* 2.1.63 (*carmina* = *satira*).

8 ad umbilicum: i.e. 'to the end'; cf. Sen. *Suas.* 6.27 *ut librum uelitis usque ad umbilicum reuoluere*, Mart. 4.89.1–2 *ohe, iam satis est, ohe, libelle,* | *iam peruenimus usque ad umbilicos*. The *umbilicus* is either the rod on which the papyrus roll was wound (Porph., Tränkle on [Tib.] 3.1.13) or an ornamental knob attached to the end of that rod (Kenney (1982) 16). The word occurs at Cat. 22.7 but also, in a different sense, in tragedy (*inc. trag.* 13 *ROL*).

9–12 Anacreon of Teos (late sixth century BC) was most famous for his lyric poetry, but he also wrote *iambi*, including epodes (frr. 5–7 West). Some take lines 11–12 here to mean that, when he was in love, he could only compose the former; this would in turn suggest that Epode 14 is a kind of *recusatio*, with H. claiming that his current inspiration is likewise suited, not to *iambi*, but to lyric (Davis (1991) 71–4). But it is not clear how the phrase *non elaboratum ad pedem* could refer to the complex metres of lyric (12n.), and it may be that the surprising point of the *exemplum* is that it refers as much to Maecenas as to H. (9, 13nn.).

9 non aliter: cf. *C.* 3.5.50, 25.8–9 *non secus in iugis* | *exsomnis stupet Euhias*. This type of litotes occurs in similes in comedy (e.g. Pl. *Am.* 1078, *Rud.* 410) but especially in Virgil (*G.* 1.201, 3.346, 4.176, *A.* 2.382 etc.) and later epic (*ThLL* I 1655, VI 2.2561).

Samio ... Bathyllo: abl. of cause (11.6n.). The epithet may recall Anacreon's rivalry over Bathyllus (test. 5 Campbell) or another boy (fr. 414 *PMG*) with Polycrates, tyrant of Samos, or, since Samos was the homeland of Pythagoras (15.21n.), it may hint at 'reincarnation' (below). Bathyllus is mentioned as a lover of Anacreon by later authors (test. 11) and in the *Anacreonta* (4, 10 etc.), but not in the surviving fragments of the poet himself. This is probably coincidence, although it may indicate that the boy was known only from 'report' (*dicunt*), as if Anacreon sang of him *ex tempore* and 'not for publication' (K–H). On the other hand, H. and others appeal to 'tradition' (*dicunt, fertur, ut fama est*, etc.) even in contexts where there is clearly a poetic source (N–H on *C.* 1.7.23, Norden on Virg. *A.* 6.14). The device is favoured by Hellenistic poets and their followers, but also occurs in early Greek (e.g. Hom. *Il.* 2.783, 24.615, Sappho, fr. 166 L–P, Theognis 1287 West). It may be relevant that Maecenas was supposed to have loved a pantomime named Bathyllus (Tac. *Ann.* 1.54, Dio 54.17.5, cf. Juv. 6.63–4).

10 Anacreonta: Greek acc. sing.; cf. 9.29n., *Ilion* (14 below), and *Nirea* (15.22). Anacreon was the most famous 'product' of Teos, an Ionian city in Asia Minor. Cf. *C.* 1.17.18 *fide Teia*, Critias (Intro. 3, n. 35) fr. 8.2–3 Diehl (= Ath. 13 600d–e) 'Teos brought into Greece sweet Anacreon, | the spur of drinking parties, the seducer of women, | the rival of the pipes, the lyre-lover, sweet, painless', Ov. *Ars* 3.330 (cf. *Rem.* 762, *Tr.* 2.364) *Teia Musa*.

11 persaepe ... fleuit amorem: cf. Dioscorides (late third century BC) *AP* 7.31.3–4 'Anacreon, alas, for Bathyllus | you often pour a liquid tear in the wine cups.' *persaepe* (only here in H.'s lyric, 3× in the hexameters), like many compounds with *per*, seems to be colloquial and unpoetic (Brink on *Ars* 349, Axelson (1945) 37–8). For *fleo* in the sense 'lament with song', cf. *C.* 2.9.9 *flebilibus modis*, *Epitaph. Naeuii* 2 (*FPL* p. 40) *flerent diuae Camenae Naeuium poetam*, Cat. 96.4, *OLD* s.v. 2a, and Greek *klaiō* (e.g. Arch. fr. 11.1 West).

There seems to be a connection between this verse and Virg. *G.* 4.464 (Orpheus) *ipse caua solans aegrum testudine amorem*. But it is not clear if one poet echoes the other, or whether they share a common source. One possibility, as always, is Gallus, who was thought to have influenced the part of the *Georgics*, the 'Aristaeus epyllion', in which Virgil's line occurs (cf. Thomas on *G.* 4.315–558).

caua testudine: cf. the 'hollow lyre' (*phorminx glaphyrē*) of Greek epic (Hom. *Od.* 8.257, *H. Merc.* 64 etc.). H. and others call the lyre a 'tortoise' (*testudo*, Greek *chelys*) because its sounding box was sometimes made from the shell of that creature (N–H on *C.* 1.32.14,

3.11.3, 4.3.17, *Ars* 395, *H. Merc.* 31–61 (13.9n.), 153, 242, Sappho, fr. 118 L–P, D–S v 157–8).

12 non elaboratum ad pedem: apparently 'to the rhythm of [*OLD* s.v. *ad* 39] a (metrical) foot that was not perfectly worked out'. In his sorrow, Anacreon, like H. (1–8), could not put the 'finishing touches' to his verse (K–H; cf. 9n.). Other interpretations, all of which seem less suited to the context, are (1) that in his Bathyllus poems Anacreon used metres 'less complex' (*OLD* s.v. *elaboratus*) than in his *iambi* (9–12n.), although it is hard to imagine what lyric measure would fit this description, or (2) that in general Anacreon's versification, like that of Pindar (*C.* 4.2.11–12), lacked discipline (Schol., Grassman (1966) 134–5), or (3) that his lament included something about Bathyllus' (literal) foot (J. Pohl, *Z.G.* 33 (1879) 582).

13 ureris ipse miser: for *uro* of love's 'fire', cf. 11.4n. *miser*, which is almost a 'perpetual epithet' for the Roman lover (e.g. *C.* 1.5.12), seems to be explained here by line 14 with its suggestion that Maecenas' *ignis* is destructive as well as beautiful (below).

quodsi: adversative, 'but if no lovelier flame set fire to besieged Troy, rejoice in your lot'. In H. *quodsi* usually introduces a climax (2.39n.), but cf. *S.* 2.4.6, *Ep.* 1.3.25, 7.10, 20.9, 2.1.241.

non pulchrior ignis: probably Helen, who both 'aroused' the Trojans (*OLD* s.v. *accendo* 4a; cf. Hom. *Il.* 3.154–60) and, in some accounts of Troy's fall, 'kindled' (s.v. 1) a (signal) fire for the Greeks (Austin on Virg. *A.* 6.518). But H. could mean Paris, who was also 'beautiful' (*C.* 1.15.13–14, Hom. *Il.* 3.44 etc., *Ilias* 282 *pulcher Alexander*) and whose mother Hecuba dreamed she gave birth to a torch that set fire to Troy (possibly in the *Cypria* (*RE* xv 1489)). Cf. Ov. *Ep.* 16.49–50 (Paris to Helen) *arsurum Paridis uates canit Ilion igni: | pectoris, ut nunc est, fax fuit illa mei.*

The comparison appears meant as a compliment to Maecenas, yet it is a peculiar one. The 'flame', however lovely, did destroy Troy, Rome's 'mother city' (10.11–14n.). If it is Helen, then Maecenas would seem to correspond to Paris, an adulterer; if it is Paris, the implication might be that his beloved is a handsome male such as Bathyllus (9n.).

ignis: the metonymy 'flame' (*ignis, flamma, fax*) = 'beloved' seems to be less common and thus more vivid in Latin than in English (*C.* 1.27.20, Ter. *Eun.* 85, Virg. *Ecl.* 3.66 *meus ignis Amyntas*, Ov. *Am.*

2.16.11, *ThLL* VI 867, VII 2.295). For the shift from metaphorical to literal 'fire', cf. N–H on *C.* 2.4.7, Lucr. 1.473–5 (without matter and void) *numquam Tyndaridis formae conflatus amore | ignis, Alexandri Phrygio sub pectore gliscens, | clara accendisset saeui certamina belli,* Ov. *Ep.* 16.49–50 (above).

14 accendit ... Ilion: cf. Andr. *trag.* 2–3 *ROL Pergama | accensa.* H. seems to be the first in Latin to use the fem. *Ilios* (cf. *C.* 4.9.18–19 *Ilios | uexata,* Ov. *Ars* 1.363, *Ep.* 1.48, *Met.* 14.466–7 *cremata ... Ilion* (v.l. *Ilios*)). This is the normal form in early Greek epic, but later authors prefer the neut. *Ilion* or *Ilium* (10.13 etc.; the gender is not indicated at *C.* 1.15.33, 3.3.37).

15–16 libertina nec uno | contenta: H. may imply that his friend's beloved is the opposite of these things, i.e. *ingenua et uno contenta* (Orelli, Grassman (1966) 141). If so, the 'flame' might be a *matrona* (below), perhaps even Maecenas' own wife Terentia (Porph.), although this would seem at odds with the hints of pederasty and adultery in the similes (9, 13–14nn.).

libertina: cf. *C.* 1.33.13–15 *ipsum me melior cum peteret Venus, | grata detinuit compede Myrtale | libertina.* In *S.* 1.2 H. recommends *libertinae* as 'safer' than married women or slaves (cf. 47–8 *tutior at quanto merx est in classe secunda, | libertinarum dico*). But here he seems to be 'the victim of his own advice' (Christes (1990) 349). Except in H. (9×, 4× of his father (Intro. 1)) *libertinus* (*-a*) is rare in verse, even in comedy and satire (*ThLL* VII 2.1319). It can be a term of abuse (*S.* 2.7.12, Pl. *Mil.* 962, Lucil. fr. 652 *ROL*), although the sense 'libertine' does not seem to be earlier than the sixteenth century AD (*OED*).

nec uno | contenta: cf. Ter. *Eun.* 122 (to the *meretrix* Thais) *neque tu uno eras contenta,* Cat. 68.135 (Lesbia) *uno non est contento Catullo.* All of these seem to invert the traditional praise for a Roman wife who was *uniuira* (*C.* 3.14.5, Pl. *Merc.* 824 *uxor contenta est quae bona est uno uiro,* Cat. 111.1–2, S. Dixon, *The Roman family* (Baltimore 1992) 89–90).

16 Phryne: probably a stock figure (Intro. 3). The name occurs in verse (Lucil. fr. 290 *ROL*, Prop. 2.6.6 (both of the historical Phryne), Tib. 2.6.45 (a typical *lena*)), but does not seem to have been current in real life in Rome (*RE* xx 893–4). The original Phryne was called that either because of a dark complexion (**phrynos* cognate with 'brown'; cf. 12.1n., Ath. 13 583b) or because of a 'snub nose' (*phrynē* a kind of toad; cf. 5.19n.). She was an Athenian courtesan so beautiful that she modelled for statues of Aphrodite and so wealthy that when Alexander had razed Thebes (335 BC) she was able to offer to pay for its rebuilding (*RE* xx 894–907). H. may imply a contrast between his Phryne and Helen (or Paris), the destroyer of a city (O. Harnecker, *Z.G.* 36 (1882) 431).

macerat 'torments' (Pl. *Cist.* 71, Lucr. 3.75, 826, *OLD* s.v. 3), although the lit. meaning of *macero*, 'soak', 'drench' (s.v. 1) may also be felt here as a contrast to the earlier fire imagery (9, 13). Cf. *C.* 1.13.8 (oxymoron?) *macerer ignibus, Ciris* 244 *amor noto te macerat igni.* H. could also be alluding to the idea of love as something 'liquid' or 'liquefying' (1n.; cf. 5.40n., N–H on *C.* 1.36.17–18, West on Hes. *Th.* 910, Brown on Lucr. 4.1060, Onians (1954) 201–2).

EPODE 15

Introduction

Neaera swore to share her love with H. for ever, but now she has proved false and must beware of his vengeance. As for her new lover, he may consider himself fortunate, but he too will weep when Neaera finds someone else, and H. will have the last laugh.

Like the other 'erotic Epodes' (8, 11, 12, 14), this poem contains or alludes to a number of familiar amatory topoi, and it too has been seen as closer in spirit to Roman elegy, Hellenistic epigram, or even to Catullus than to early Greek *iambus* (Grassman (1966) 145–67, Fedeli, *R.C.C.M.* 19 (1977) 373–81). But some, at least, of the topoi can be found in Archilochus and Hipponax (7–9, 12, 20, 24nn.), and the crucial event, Neaera's breaking of her oath, would seem to recall the similar misconduct of Lycambes and Neobule (6.13–14n., Intro. 3).

Neaera and her new lover are H.'s targets, but as in so many other Epodes (Intro. 3), he himself seems vulnerable to ridicule and blame. His threats are not very convincing, especially since they depend on this 'Flaccus' somehow becoming a 'man' (11, 12nn.). Despite his vaunting, he seems to be no more in control of the present situation than he was of the past, when the very terms of the oath he dictated (4n.) betrayed his doubts about its fulfilment (7–9n.). The 'last laugh' has a 'hollow ring', since his rival's sufferings will not change the fact that he has been duped and has failed to win the 'mutual love' that he sought.

H.'s failure seems to connect this essentially humorous poem with the more serious Epodes which precede and follow it (14 intro.). The oath, the appeal to 'manhood', and the suggestion in the final verses of a 'vicious cycle' make it especially close in theme to Epode 16 (Fitzgerald (1988) 177–9), as if H. is meant to be seen as a kind of 'microcosm' of the impotence and despair that civil war has brought on the 'macrocosm' of the Roman state.

1–2 The opening couplet is remarkable in that it suggests at least five distinct ways in which the poem might develop (Kuhn (1973) 42–51). As it turns out, the night sky was a kind of 'witness' to Neaera's perjury (1n. on *caelo ... sereno*), but it could have served as a point of comparison for her beauty (2n.), or as a setting for magic (cf. 5.51–6), or for a love scene (1n. on *luna*), or even an account of the sack of Troy (1n. on *nox erat*).

1 Nox erat: this seems to be the first example of what would become a popular phrase in Latin poetry (Virg. *A.* 3.147, Pease on 4.522, 8.26, Prop. 3.15.26, [Ov.] *Am.* 3.5.1). It may go back to Gallus (Tränkle (1960) 24) or Ap. Rhod. 3.744 (5.55–6n.), but the nearest parallel to H.'s line (Grassman (1966) 145) seems to be *Ilias parua* fr. 9 *PEG* (Sinon prepares his signal for the Greek assault on Troy) 'it was midnight, and the shining moon was rising'.

caelo ... sereno: cf. *S.* 2.4.51 *Massica si caelo suppones uina sereno.* H. may allude to the invocation of the moon and especially the stars as 'witnesses' to oaths, curses, and the like (Porph.; cf. Pease on Virg. *A.* 4.519–20 (Dido) *testatur ... deos et conscia fati | sidera*). It is not clear if this was a real-life custom in Republican Rome, where the normal divine *testes* were Jupiter, Hercules, and the Dioscuri (3n.; cf. *RE* x 1253). But it was customary among the Greeks (*RE* v 2076–7, Burkert (1985) 250–1), and it became a topos in connection with the oaths of lovers (N–H on *C.* 2.8.11, Meleager, *AP* 5.8, 165, Prop. 2.9.41, 3.20.18, Grassman (1966) 45).

luna: moon and stars figure in magic (5.45–6n.) but also, whether invoked or not (above), as 'spies' on nocturnal doings such as lovers' trysts (e.g. Meleager, *AP* 5.191, Philodemus, *AP* 5.123 (= *HA* 1622–7), Cat. 7.7–8, Prop. 1.3.31–2, 10.8).

2 minora: H. may hint at the topos of beautiful women (or boys) 'outshining' their companions as the moon the stars (Kuhn (1973) 48–50); cf. N–H on *C.* 1.12.48, 2.5.19–20, 3.15.5–6, *S.* 1.7.24–5, Sappho, frr. 34, 96.6–9 L–P 'now she stands out among Lydian | maidens as when the sun | has set the rose-fingered moon | surpasses all the stars', Ov. *Ep.* 18.71–4, Sen. *Phaed.* 741–60.

3–4 cum ... iurabas: an 'inverted *cum*-clause' (*cum inversum*), grammatically subordinate, but containing the main idea of the sentence. Cf. *S.* 1.5.20–1, 8.1–3, 2.6.100–2 *iamque tenebat | nox medium caeli spatium, cum ponit uterque | in locuplete domo uestigia*, 111–12. H. seldom uses the imperf. ind. in temporal clauses (*C.* 1.37.6–8, 3.9.1, 5–6) and it is rare with *cum inversum* even in other authors (K–S II 338–40; cf. Virg. *G.* 4.429–30, *A.* 3.301–3, Williams on *A.* 5.84–5). Here it may suggest that Neaera never actually finished reciting the oath ('when you were starting (or trying) to swear ...') and thus might not consider herself bound by it.

3 magnorum ... deorum: cf. *S.* 1.7.33–4 *per magnos, Brute, deos te oro*. By *di magni* H. probably means Jupiter and other more 'powerful' gods in the pantheon (cf. Virg. *A.* 10.6 *caelicolae magni*, *OLD* s.v. *magnus* 12b). But in some contexts the term seems to be used specifically of the Penates or the Dioscuri (1n.) or, perhaps, of both (Skutsch on Enn. *Ann.* 190 *uolentibus cum magnis dis*, Virg. *A.* 3.12 (cf. Servius *ad loc.*), Gransden on 8.679, *RE* XIX 453–4).

numen laesura: the fut. part. indicating purpose (1.9n.) *ad euentum refert ... quasi, cum* [Neaera] *iuraret, iam perfidiam fallendi in animo haberet* (Porph.). 'Wounding' the power (*numen*) of a god with an immoral or otherwise objectionable act was normally a serious matter (17.3n.; cf. Cic. *Dom.* 140, Lucr. 2.614–15, Virg. *A.* 1.8, 2.183, *RE* XVII 1277–8). But it was a commonplace that the gods tended to forgive perjury when it was committed by lovers (N–H on *C.* 2.8, Hes. fr. 124 M–W, Call. *Ep.* 25 Pf. (= *HA* 1596–1601), Pl. *Cis.* 472, Cat. 70 etc.). Cf. 11, 24nn.

4 in uerba ... mea: i.e. H. dictated the terms of the oath. Cf. 16.25, *Ep.* 1.1.14 *nullius addictus iurare in uerba magistri*, and Hom. *Od.* 10.337–47, where Odysseus makes Circe (17.17n.) swear an oath not to 'unman' him if he goes to bed with her. The expression *in uerba (alicuius) iuro* is often used of soldiers swearing to a formula set by their commander (*OLD* s.v. *iuro* 5a). H. may evoke the topos *militia amoris* (Grassman (1966) 147–8; cf. N–H on *C.* 1.6.17, Kenney on

Apul. *Met.* 5.21.5), although the amatory *miles* is usually an 'enlisted man', not an officer.

5–6 artius atque ... ilex ... adhaerens: the participle is in apposition to *cum tu* [Neaera] *iurabas*, but also seems to modify *ilex* (6n.). This and other ambiguities (5n.) may give special force to the simile (Kuhn (1973) 60–73, Miles), which is otherwise conventional (N–H on *C.* 1.36.20). It may also be relevant that ivy can be harmful to its 'host' tree (Babcock (1966) 408; cf. Plin. *Nat.* 16.151, 243, 17.239). For *atque* = *quam* in comparisons, cf. 12.14n.

5 procera: probably with *ilex* (*C.* 3.25.16 *proceras ... fraxinos*, Enn. *Ann.* 178 Skutsch (*pinus*), Cat. 64.289 (*laurus*), Virg. *Ecl.* 6.63 (*alnos*)). But the rare elision (Intro. 6) may allow the epithet to be felt with both nouns, as if the plants, equals in height, symbolized H.'s hope that Neaera would prove his 'equal' in love (14).

astringitur ilex: from the parallels (5–6n.) one might expect the tree to symbolize H., the male partner (cf. 12.19–20). But the syntax of *adhaerens* seems to suggest that the *ilex* corresponds to Neaera (5–6n.), and it is she who is 'bound' by the oath (*OLD* s.v. *astringo* 8; cf. Cic. *Off.* 3.111 *nullum ... uinculum ad astringendam fidem iure iurando ... artius*).

6 lentis ... bracchiis: another ambiguous phrase. It seems to continue the plant image (*OLD* s.v. *bracchium* 4) but actually refers to Neaera (5–6n.); it could be dat. (the girl 'clinging to (H.'s) arms') or abl. ('clinging with (her own) arms'), and *lentis* could suggest 'pliancy' and 'tenacity' (*OLD* s.v. 1, 3, Cat. 61.102–5; cf. *C.* 1.13.8, 3.19.28 *lentus ... amor*) or, more pessimistically, 'frigidity' (s.v. 8). The last sense is especially common in love elegy; cf. Prop. 1.6.12 *a pereat, si quis lentus amare potest*, 15.4, 2.14.14, Tib. 2.6.36, Pichon (1902) 186.

7–9 dum ... capillos: 'id est, semper' (Lambinus). This kind of expression, especially in a negative form (a type of *adynaton* (5.79–80, 16.25–34nn.)), is not uncommon in Greek and Latin poetry (*C.* 3.30.7–8, Hom. *Il.* 1.233–9, Virg. *Ecl.* 5.76–8, *A.* 1.607–8, Smith on Tib. 1.4.65–6). But H.'s examples of recurring phenomena are somewhat peculiar. The first two, with their emphasis on hostility (*infestus*), and the third, with what may be a suggestion of promiscuity (9n.), seem at odds with a pledge of 'mutual love', as if H. sensed even when he dictated the words of the oath (4n.) that Neaera would betray him (Babcock (1966) 408–9, Kuhn (1973) 90–100).

It has been suggested that these lines were 'inspired by a passage in the *Iamboi* of Callimachus' (Fraenkel (1957) 67; cf. Intro. 3), fr. 202 (= *Iamb.* 12). 69–70 Pf. (Apollo promises a baby girl that her fame will endure) 'while my chin is clean of hair | and rapacious wolves delight in (?) kids' (App. 1). But Call.'s phrasing, metre (trochaic trimeter catalectic), and context are different, and the one real similarity, the mention of wolves, could be due to a common model in Archilochus (4.1n.).

7 dum pecori lupus: sc. *infestus turbaret*. But since a wolf could not 'stir up the sea', it seems necessary either to supply an object such as *ouilia* (Wickham) or, through a zeugma, to take *turbaret* first as intransitive ('runs amok'; cf. Virg. *A.* 9.339 *leo per ouilia turbans*, *OLD* s.v. 1), then (with Orion) as transitive (Postgate, *C.R.* (1905) 217). Another possibility, involving a harsher but not unparalleled zeugma (cf. *S.* 2.2.11–13, Kenney on Lucr. 3.614, Virg. *G.* 1.92–3), is to infer a different phrase for *lupus*, '*terreret ouilia*, or what you will' (Housman (1972) 545).

lupus: a symbol of hostility (4.1n.) but also, in amatory contexts, of 'incompatibility' (12.25–6n.) and of 'predatory' desire (Kuhn (1973) 94–5); cf. Plato, *Phaedr.* 241d, Theocr. *Id.* 10.30–1, Virg. *Ecl.* 2.63–5 *torua leaena lupum sequitur, lupus ipse capellam* | ... | *te Corydon, o Alexi: trahit sua quemque uoluptas*.

Orion: the harbinger of winter storms (10.10n.). H. may also refer here to both 'the notable bad luck Orion had as a lover' (Babcock (1966) 408; cf. *C.* 3.4.70–2, Hes. *Op.* 619–20, *RE* xviii 1072–5) and to the stormy sea as a metaphor for unhappy love (Kuhn (1973) 96, N–H on *C.* 1.5.16; cf. Sem. fr. 7.37–40 West (a woman who is like the sea)). The scansion *Ŏrīŏn* (10.10n.), although well-suited to hexameter end, seems not to be attested before H. (only here) and Virgil (*A.* 1.535, Pease on 4.52, 10.763; cf. Prop. 2.16.51, Ov. *Ars* 1.731, Bömer on *F.* 5.493).

9 intonsosque ... capillos: a typical feature of Apollo, emblematic of youth and beauty (N–H on *C.* 1.21.2, 3.4.62, 4.6.26, *LIMC* ii 185). Here it may hint at a younger and more handsome rival for H. (Carrubba (1969) 79; cf. 11.28n.), although its movement in the breeze could also suggest the god is attacking someone; cf. Arch. fr. 26.5–6 and Hipp. fr. 25 West, where Apollo is asked to 'destroy' (*ollumi*, *apollumi*) evil-doers. It seems less likely that the breeze recalls the winds to which lovers vainly entrust their words (Kuhn (1973) 97; cf. 11.17–18n.), or that, as in Callimachus (7–9n.), H. invokes Apollo as a god of poetry who will immortalize Neaera's perfidy (S. Lieberman, *C.W.* 62 (1968–9) 219). For the prosaic *capillus*, cf. 5.16n.; *aura*, on the other hand, occurs chiefly in poetry (*ThLL* II 1471).

Apollinis: his limited role in the *Epodes* (only here) and hexameters (*S.* 1.9.77, 2.5.60, *Ep.* 1.3.17, 2.1.216, *Ars* 407) is striking, given his importance for the *Odes* (especially books 1 and 4), for the poetry of H.'s contemporaries, and for 'Augustan ideology' even prior to Actium (Kienast (1982) 192–200, Zanker (1990) 49–53).

10 mutuum: H. himself (4n.) probably meant *mutuus* in the sense 'reciprocal' (*OLD* s.v. 2; cf. N–H on *C.* 2.12.15, 3.9.13, 4.1.30, Cat. 45.20 *mutuis animis amant amantur*, Pichon (1902) 211). But Neaera's conduct suggests that she may have taken it, or pretended to take it, in the sense 'on (temporary) loan' (Babcock (1966) 409; cf. *OLD* s.v. 1, *Ep.* 1.7.80 and, for a similar pun, Pl. *Curc.* 46–8).

11 o dolitura ... multum: cf. 5.74n., and, for the threat, *C.* 1.25.9–10 *inuicem moechos anus arrogantis | flebis*, Cat. 8.14 *at tu dolebis, cum rogaberis nulla*, Prop. 1.15.27–8 (Cynthia) *audax a, nimium nostro dolitura periclo, | si quid forte tibi durius inciderit.*

mea ... uirtute: 'there seems to be an intended play in *uirtute ... uiri* [12]' (Wickham); cf. 16.39, Cic. *Tusc.* 2.43 *appellata est enim ex uiro uirtus*. H. has to rely on his own 'manhood', such as it is (12n.), presumably because the gods will overlook Neaera's falsehood (3n.).

Neaera: a Greek name meaning 'young girl' (LSJ s.v. *nearos*) or, perhaps, 'belly' (s.v. *ne(i)aira*); cf. 5.42n. and Postgate, *C.Q.* 8 (1914) 121–2. Neaera is also the name of a young girl at *C.* 3.14.21, of several nymphs in Greek myth (*RE* XVI 2104), some *meretrices* in comedy (Gell. 13.23.16), a *hetaera* in a speech attributed to Demosthenes (*Or.* 59), and the girl-friend of the elegiac poet (or character) 'Lygdamus' ([Tib.] 3.1.6 etc.).

12 Flacco: this was certainly H.'s cognomen (Intro. 1), but there may be a humorous contrast between its literal meaning, 'flaccid', 'weak', and the poet's boasts of *uirtus* and *constantia* (L. Mueller, Babcock (1966) 413–14). There seem to be similar puns at *S.* 2.1.18–19

Flacci | uerba per attentam non ibunt Caesaris aurem (cf. *S.* 1.9.20, Rudd (1966) 125) and at Mart. 11.27.1 *ferreus es, si stare potest tibi mentula, Flacce.*

It is not unusual for a poet or character to refer to himself by name (Austin on Virg. *A.* 6.510), but H. may here imitate Hipponax, who seems to have done this often (frr. 32.4, 37, 79.9, 117.4 West; cf. Call. fr. 191 (= *Iamb.* 1).1 Pf.). The device can have 'various nuances' (Austin) from grandiloquence (e.g. *C.* 1.7.27, *S.* 2.2.53, *Ep.* 1.5.27, 14.5, West on Hes. *Th.* 22, Hom. *Il.* 1.240, Virg. *A.* 12.11) to pathos (*C.* 3.9.6, *S.* 2.1.18 (above), Cat. 8.12 etc.).

si quid ... uiri est: cf. Ter. *Eun.* 66 [*puella*] *sentiet qui uir siem,* Cic. *Fam.* 5.18.1 *oro te colligas uirumque praebeas, OLD* s.v. *uir* 3. H. may also hint at *uir* as a euphemism for *membrum uirile* or *testes* (Kroll on cat. 63.6 *membra sine uiro,* Adams (1982) 70).

13 non feret: cf. Tib. 2.6.35 (an angry ghost) *non feret usque suum te propter flere clientem.* The acc. + inf. with this sense of *fero* (= *sustineo*) seems to be rare before Ovid and Livy (*ThLL* VI 538; cf. Fedeli on Prop. 3.7.47).

assiduas ... noctes: apparently 'uninterrupted nights' (Lucr. 5.252 (2.41n.) *solibus adsiduis, Ciris* 417 *uincta tot assiduas pendebo ex ordine luces;* cf. Prop. 2.16.14 *rumpat ut assiduis membra libidinibus, ThLL* II 884). The phrase *dare noctes* may be a slur on Neaera, as it is often used of *meretrices* 'providing services' (Pl. *As.* 194, 736, *Trin.* 250, *Truc.* 32, 279, McKeown on Ov. *Am.* 1.8.67, Adams (1982) 178).

potiori 'a favoured rival' (Page); cf. *C.* 3.9.2, *S.* 2.5.76, *Ep.* 1.5.27. *potior* (*potissimus*) in this sense occurs in comedy (Pl. *Men.* 359, Ter. *Ph.* 533) but only once in elegy (Tib. 1.5.69 (17n.), which prefers *riualis* (Pichon (1902) 254), a term avoided by H. (*Ars* 444 only).

14 parem: i.e. someone with whom *amor* can be truly *mutuus* (10). Cf. 11.18n.

15 semel offensi ... constantia 'the resolution of (me) once wronged'. For the ellipse of *mei*, cf. 11.13. *offensi* was conjectured by H. Gogavius (1567) and later found in some of the 'Pseudacronian' scholia (Intro. 7; cf. Brink (1982) 42). The rest of the scholia and the MSS know only *offensae,* which seems to be acceptable Latin, although H. does not elsewhere use *offensus* in the active sense 'hateful' (*OLD* s.v. 2). Yet here it is not Neaera's *forma* that 'offends', but her 'conduct, depravity, inconstancy, and perfidy' (Bentley), things which, in the tradition of love poetry, would in no way lessen her physical charms (*C.* 2.8.1–8, Ov. *Am.* 3.3.1–12). The word *constantia* is rare in verse (Prop. 2.26.27, 3× in Ov.) and may be prosaic (*ThLL* iv 504).

16 si … dolor: the clause is usually taken to mean 'if a sure (cause of) grief shall have come', i.e. if it can be proved that Neaera has been unfaithful. This would suggest that the matter is still in doubt and, perhaps, that despite his 'bravado … H.'s resolution is less reliable than Neaera's oath' (Carrubba (1969) 76). But it is possible that *si* here is concessive (= *etsi*; cf. *C.* 4.9.5, *S.* 2.3.319, *OLD* s.v. 9), that *dolor* = *cupido* (*S.* 1.2.109 (11.2n.), Cat. 27, 50.17, Pichon (1902) 132) and that the meaning is 'my resolution will not give way (even) if persistent desire (for Neaera) shall have come (upon me)'. For this sense of *certus*, cf. Lucr. 4.1067 [*amoris*] *curam certumque dolorem*, Prop. 3.8.18 *has didici certo saepe in amore notas*, Ov. *Am.* 3.6.29–30 *Alpheon … currere … certus adegit amor.*

intrarit = *intrauerit* (fut. perf.). The image of *dolor* 'entering' or 'attacking' or 'invading' is not uncommon, even in prose (e.g. Cic. *Ver.* 3.95 *dolor insideret, ThLL* vi 1845).

17 et tu = *etiam tu*, 'you also' (17.45, *OLD* s.v. *et* 5a); cf. Prop. 2.25.21–2 *tu quoque, qui pleno fastus assumis amore, | credule, nulla diu femina pondus habet.* For similar addresses to rivals, cf. *C.* 1.5.12–13, Tib. 1.2.89–90 (24n.), 5.69 (echoing H.?) *at tu, qui potior nunc es, mea furta timeto,* 9.53–74, 2.3.33 (below), Cairns (1972) 81. The presence of *at* in many of these passages has persuaded some editors to print it here, but it is weakly attested (app. crit.) and would jar with the ensuing *ast* (24).

quicumque es: the indefinite pronoun may suggest that H. does not know for sure that there is a rival (K–H), or it may be contemptuous 'whoever the hell you are' (cf. N–H on *C.* 2.13.2, *S.* 1.4.36, 2.4.62, 7.49, *Ep.* 1.18.31, *Ars* 188, Tib. 2.3.33 (a rival) *at tu, quisquis is es,* Ov. *Ib.* 9). This is one of only two elisions at the caesura in H.'s lyric hexameters (cf. *C.* 1.7.13) and the only instance in the lyrics of prodelided *es* (5× in the hexameters; cf. Soubiran (1966) 175–9).

felicior: the term *felix*, like *beatus*, can introduce a *makarismos* (2 intro., 8.11, 12.25n.), and what follows (19–22) is a kind of midget version of that topos.

17–18 meo nunc | superbus ... malo 'rendered proud by my mishap' (Page). The position of *nunc* between adj. and noun (cf. Cat. 3.17 *tua nunc opera*) and as a monosyllable at verse end (Intro. 6) seems to give it special emphasis, perhaps 'mine now (but yours later)'; cf. *uicissim* (24).

18 incedis: probably not simply 'enter' but 'parade' or even, like *ambulo* (4.5n.), 'strut'. Cf. *S.* 1.6.112, Virg. *A.* 5.67–8 [*miles*] *qui uiribus audax | aut iaculo incedit melior*, N. Horsfall, *Glotta* 49–50 (1971–2) 145–7.

19 sis ... licebit: cf. 4.5n. The form *licebit* is convenient at hexameter end and can be used even where there is no sense of futurity (*C.* 1.28.35, *S.* 2.2.59, 3.192, *Ep.* 1.5.10, Prop. 2.11.1, *ThLL* VII 2.1364).

diues: like Alfius in his dreams (2.9–38n.), the upstart (4.13), the hag (8.13–14), and, perhaps, Inachia's new lover (11.11n.), but unlike H. himself (1.25–8, 11.12n.).

20 Pactolus: a gold-producing river in Lydia, the 'Klondike' of the ancient world (Soph. *Phil.* 394, Hdt. 5.101, Bacch. 3.44–5 Maehler, Var. *Men.* 234.1, Virg. *A.* 10.142, Prop. 1.14.11, 3.18.28 (22n.)). It is mentioned by Callimachus (fr. 194(= *Iamb.* 4).106 Pf.), but, given their interest in the kings of Lydia, it may also have figured in Archilochus (cf. fr. 19 west (App. 1), Clay (1986) 11–12) and Hipponax (frr. 42.1–2, 104.22). H. may suggest a parallel between his rival and the most famous of those kings, Croesus, who was a prime example of 'happiness' (19n.) turned into misfortune (Hdt. 1.30–4, 86–90, Cic. *Fin.* 2.87).

21 nec te ... fallant: probably 'the secrets do not escape your understanding' (3.7, 5.68, *Ep.* 2.2.127, *OLD* s.v. *fallo* 6), although the meaning could be 'they do not fool you (into believing them)' (16.45, *C.* 2.5.22, etc., s.v. 3). If the former, then H. may imply that his rival is not only a philosopher (cf. 8.15–16n.), but a magician who has bewitched Neaera (below).

Pythagorae ... renati: Pythagoras of Samos (14.9n.), later of Croton in Italy, was a philosopher of the sixth century who taught, among other things, that after death souls passed into new bodies ('metempsychosis'). He himself claimed to be the reincarnation of the Homeric warrior Euphorbus (N–H on *C.* 1.28.10). His doctrines were popular at Rome, where they influenced Ennius (Skutsch on *Ann.* 3) and Virgil (Norden on *A.* 6.706–51), but H., like Lucretius (e.g. 1.115–26, 3.713–83), seems to have been sceptical of them (*C.* 1.28.9–16, *S.* 2.4.1–3, 6.63, *Ep.* 2.1.52). In the late Republic some 'Pythagoreans' were suspected of being sorcerers who sacrificed children (cf. L. Ferraro, *Storia del Pitagorismo nel mondo romano* (Turin 1955) 293, 308, Hierche (1974) 26–42).

22 formaque uincas: cf. 11.24n., Hom. *Il.* 9.130, 272 (girls from Lesbos) 'who in beauty surpassed (*enikōn*) the races of women'. Nireus was a Greek warrior 'who came to Ilium as the most handsome man | of all the Danaans after blameless Achilles. | But he was feeble, and few men followed him' (*Il.* 2.673–5). Cf. *C.* 3.20.15 (a handsome boy) *qualis ... Nireus fuit*, Prop. 3.18.27–8 (from death) *Nirea non facies, non uis exemit Achillem,* | *Croesum aut, Pactoli quas parit humor, opes,* Ov. *Ars* 2.109 (looks are not enough) *sis licet antiquo Nireus adamatus Homero.*

23 heu heu ... maerebis: cf. *C.* 1.5.5–6 (Pyrrha's new lover) *heu quotiens fidem* | *mutatosque deos flebit.* In both places the tragic exclamation (5.101n.) seems to be 'a touch of pathos or, rather, bathos, at the rival's expense' (Miles).

translatos alio: the phrase seems to be conventional (Ter. *Hau.* 390, *Hec.* 169–70 *huc transtulit* | *amores,* Prop. 2.15.35 *alio transferre calores*). But there may be a joking reference to Pythagoreanism (Miles); cf. Cic. *Tim.* 45, where *transfero* is used of metempsychosis: *eum secundus ortus in figuram muliebrem transferet ...* [and, in future lives] *in ... figuras pecudum et ferarum transferetur.*

24 ast ... risero: this 'compact last clause ... has the true ring of Archilochus' (Fraenkel (1957) 67; cf. frr. 13.7–9, 172.4 West (App. 1). *uicissim* suggests payback ('ut tu, felicior riualis, me nunc, derides' (Orelli)), but H.'s laughter may also echo that of the gods at perjured lovers (3n.). Cf. N–H on *C.* 2.8.13 *ridet hoc* [Barine's perfidy] ... *Venus,* Ov. *Ars.* 1.633 *Iuppiter ex alto periuria ridet amantum.* Both *ast* and *risero* seem to be *metri causa,* the latter for *ridebo* (1.32n.), the former for *at* (cf. Tib. 1.2.89–90 *at tu, qui laetus rides mala nostra, caueto* | *mox tibi*; 5.69 (17n.)). This use of *ast,* originally a correlative for *si* (LHS II 489), is common in hexameter verse (*S.* 1.6.125, 8.6, Austin on Virg. *A.* 1.46, 2.467, and may go back to Ennius (Skutsch on *Ann.* 93).

EPODE 16

Introduction

Rome is destroying itself with civil war; its citizens, or the 'better part' of them, should follow the example of the Phocaeans and abandon their city. They should sail off to the west, to the 'happy fields and fortunate islands' where Jupiter preserved the golden age when he contaminated the rest of the world with bronze and iron. H., as *uates*, will show them the way.

The setting of H.'s speech is probably the Roman forum, his audience the Roman people in a *contio* (1–14n.). It is more difficult to pinpoint a date (cf. Setaioli (1981) 1757–61); proposals include just before Actium, Naulochus (36 BC), and even Philippi (42 BC). But the poem's place in the Epode book would seem to suggest a time after Actium (Intro. 4; cf. Kraggerud (1984) 136), perhaps on the eve of the 'Alexandrian War' (9.21–6, 27, 13.3nn.).

It is not, as some claim, 'unrealistic' for H. to present himself addressing a public assembly, although his stance does seem to owe less to Roman forensic practice (but cf. 15, 17, 23, 25–6, 37nn.) than to early Greek *iambus* and elegy (7.1–14n.; cf. Arch. frr. 13 (39n.), 88, 94, 98, 106, 109, 111, 112, Solon, frr. 4, 11, 32–7, Tyrtaeus, frr. 1–4 West). He draws on other sources as well, including – it seems – Homer (below), the 'Sibylline Oracles' (10n.), Herodotus (17n.), Sallust (43n.), and a variety of 'ethnographic' and 'utopian' texts (41–50n.).

The relation of Epode 16 to Virgil's Eclogue 4 has especially interested scholars, with some arguing for H.'s, most for Virgil's priority (B. Snell, *Hermes* 73 (1938) 237–42, Setaioli (1981) 1754–61). If the Eclogue is in fact earlier (cf. 33, 41–2, 49, 57–6onn.), then the Epode would seem to be a kind of 'answer' to its 'optimism', although Virgil's poem is itself not entirely free from anxiety about the future (A. J. Boyle, *The Chaonian dove* (Leiden 1986) 23–4).

Virgil seems to predict that the 'golden age' will return to Rome (cf. 41–6on.); according to H., it can only be found in the remote 'happy fields'. His proposal for a migration to these fields is not entirely implausible (15–4on.), but his account of what his followers might find there is disturbingly similar to the absurd fantasies of Alfius in Epode 2 (41–2, 44, 48, 49nn.), and even if the place does exist, it would not appear to be a likely haven for 'accursed' Romans (63–6n.).

Some have attempted to mitigate H.'s pessimism by interpreting his proposal symbolically, as a brief either for an 'intellectual retreat' into poetry and philosophy (Klingner (1961) 355, AG (1971) 90–101, Setaioli (1981) 1745–6) or for the Romans to 'reverse' somehow his advice and bring the 'golden age' to Rome rather than look for it elsewhere (Kraggerud (1984) 129–56). A more compelling suggestion (Kukula (1911) 5–40) is that H.'s speech, like that of Agamemnon to the Greek army in Homer (*Il.* 2.110–41), is meant as a 'test' of his fellow citizens. H. does not indicate their response, which may allow some room for hope. But the nature of their alternatives, to stay and perish or to flee to a place that cannot exist, still makes this a profoundly pessimistic poem.

1–14 Civil war is destroying another generation and Rome, which survived the assaults of external enemies, is collapsing from her own might.

The opening lines have the ring of an early Greek *iambus* or elegy (7.1–2n.); cf. Solon, fr. 4.1–8 West 'Our city is not being destroyed in accordance with Zeus's | plan or the will of the blessed immortal gods,... but the citizens themselves in their folly, | swayed by greed, wish to destroy a great city, | and the unjust mind of the leaders of the mob, who are sure | to suffer many griefs from their great arrogance.'

If H.'s audience in Epode 7 seemed to be the Senate (7.1–14n.), here he appears to 'take his case to the people', possibly in a *contio* (discussion of proposals) of the sort that normally preceded full meetings of the *comitia* (17, 33nn.; cf. Fraenkel (1957) 45). In the late Republic *contiones* were held at the Circus Flaminius or, more commonly, in the Forum at the Rostra or Temple of Castor in sight of the Comitium (13n.), their ancient setting (Taylor (1966) 20–8). It has been argued that someone like H., the son of a *libertus* (Intro. 1), could not be imagined as addressing such a meeting (Fraenkel (1957) 42–7), at which most of the speaking was done by the presiding magistrates. But private persons were also invited to speak, and although they were usually prominent citizens, there are examples of foreigners and even *liberti* and women being granted the privilege

(G. W. Botsford, *The Roman assemblies* (New York 1909) 145–51, Taylor (1966) 18, 118 n. 6).

1 Altera ... aetas: *aetas* here could mean either (or both?) 'generation' (9n.) or 'era' (*C.* 4.15.4, *OLD* s.v. 8a). If the first, then the generation 'prior' to this *altera* would seem to be that of Pompey and Caesar (Schol., AG (1971) 20–3); if the second, then H. might be thinking of two 'ages' of civil strife, the earlier in the time of Marius, Sulla, Cinna, and Lepidus (88–77 BC), the next beginning with Caesar's crossing of the Rubicon in 50 BC and extending to the present (Orelli). For the various ancient views on the number, names, and sequence of the Roman civil wars, cf. Jal (1963) 43–55.

teritur: the verb seems to fit either sense of *aetas* (above), since it can mean both 'spend (time)' (*OLD* s.v. 6) and 'wear (people) down' (s.v. 7). There may be a similar ambiguity at Virg. *A.* 9.609 *omne aeuum ferro teritur.*

2 suis ... uiribus ruit: cf. 7.10, Cic. *Rep.* 5.2 *nostris enim uitiis, non casu aliquo, rem publicam uerbo retinemus, re ipsa uero iampridem amisimus,* Fedeli on Prop. 3.13.60 *frangitur ipsa suis Roma superba bonis,* Liv. 1. *praef.* 4 (Rome) *iam magnitudine laboret sua.* The idea of states collapsing under the 'weight' of their own power or vices is a commonplace of Greek political thought (Solon, fr. 4 West (1–14n.), J. de Romilly, *The rise and fall of states according to Greek authors* (Ann Arbor 1977) 60). The juxtaposition *Roma uiribus* may be meant to suggest the Greek derivation of *Roma* from *rhōmē*, 'power', 'might' (C. MacLeod, *C.Q.* 29 (1979) 220–1; cf. Lyrophron, *Alex.* 1233 (of Aeneas' offspring) 'a race surpassing in *rhōmē*', Prop. 4.10.17 (Romulus) *urbis uirtutisque parens*).

et: the first of some ten postponed particles (1.12n.) in the poem (cf. 4, 5, 29, 33, 40n., 42, 45, 55, 60), a remarkable number for H. (Marouzeau (1949) 85).

3–10 For his list H. 'selects wars which were waged in Italy or at her borders and therefore directly endangered Rome, not in chronological order, but starting from neighbours [Marsi, Porsena, Capua, Spartacus (5n.)] ... and concluding with the most terrible enemies [Gauls (6n.), Germans, Hannibal] who invaded Italy from outside' (K–H). It may be significant that these threats came from every direction except the west, which will be H.'s 'escape route'

(21–2, 39–40). This passage seems to be echoed at Virg. *A.* 2.196–8 and Tac. *Hist.* 3.72.

3 finitimi ... Marsi: cf. 5.76n. The Marsi took the lead among those of Rome's allies who turned on her in the 'Social' or 'Marsian' War (90–88 BC, cf. *C.* 3.14.18 *Marsi ... duelli*). This conflict has been seen as a kind of 'proto-civil war' (*Marsi ... qui primi mouerunt bella ciuilia, id est sociale* (Schol.); cf. Flor. *Epit.* 2.6.1, Jal (1963) 26). But H.'s point may be that the Romans prevailed in it despite internal dissensions which would soon erupt in a 'real' civil war, that between Marius and Sulla (1n.).

4 minacis ... Porsenae: cf. *C.* 2.12.12 *minacum ... regum.* Like many adjectives in *-ax* (2.24n.), *minax* occurs chiefly in verse (*ThLL* VIII 995). Lars Porsen(n)a (or Porsin(n)a; cf. app. crit., *RE* XXI 315–16) of Clusium in Etruria attacked Rome in an attempt to reinstate the exiled Tarquin the Proud (509 BC). Ancient opinion was divided as to whether or not the city was captured (Scullard (1981) 75), but H. clearly refers to the version in which it was not. He may also wish his audience to recall that one of Rome's saviours was a Horatius (Cocles), the famous 'Horatius at the bridge' (Enn. *Ann.* 123 (but cf. Skutsch), Cic. *Off.* 1.61, *Leg.* 2.10, Virg. *A.* 8.646–51, Liv. 2.10). Cf. Cicero's joking reference to the king Servius Tullius as his 'kinsman' (*Tusc.* 1.38) and the comparisons of M. Brutus to the Brutus who expelled Tarquin (e.g. *S.* 1.7.33–5, Cic. *Brut.* 53).

5 aemula nec uirtus Capuae: cf. 7.5 and, for the periphrasis *uirtus Capuae*, 'the valiant Capuans', 6.6n., *S.* 2.1.72 (9.26n.), Virg. *A.* 10.410 *socium uirtus coit omnis in unum.* From the third century BC on, Capua was the 'second city' of Italy (cf. Cic. *Phil.* 12.7 (43 BC) *Capua ... quae temporibus his Roma altera est*). Her ambition of becoming the 'first' led her to join Hannibal (8) after his victory at Cannae in 216 BC (Cic. *Agr.* 2.87, Liv. 23.2–10, esp. 10.2 (Hannibal) *pollicitus breui caput Italiae omni Capuam fore*).

Spartacus: cf. *C.* 3.14.19. Spartacus was a Thracian gladiator who led a slave revolt that defeated three Roman armies (73–72 BC) before it was crushed by Crassus and Pompey (71 BC). He may be a kind of 'transition figure' in H.'s list, since his war arose within Italy (at Capua, in fact), but his army consisted of non-Italian slaves and allies.

6 infidelis Allobrox: collective sing. (7.6–7n.). The Allobroges
were a Gallic tribe in what is now Switzerland. Like Capua, they
supported Hannibal, but H. probably alludes here to their war with
Rome in 121 BC, at the height of the 'revolution' (*nouisque rebus*) of C.
Gracchus (for the chronology, see *MRR* I 516–21). *infidelis* (5.50) sug-
gests that for a time, at least, they had been allies, although there
seems to be no other evidence for this (*RE* I 1587–8). Some see a
reference here to a later 'perfidy', when a few Allobroges defected
from Caesar's army to join Pompey (48 BC; cf. Caes. *Civ.* 3.59–61).
Another possibility (Lambinus) is that they represent all of the Gauls,
Rome's inveterate enemies (11–14, 9.17nn.) and a people *in consiliis
capiendis mobiles et [qui] nouis plerumque rebus student* (Caes. *Gal.* 4.5.1).
Least likely is a reference to the Catilinarian conspiracy (Schol.),
since in that crisis they were in fact 'faithful' to the Senate. It may be
significant for the 'logic' of H.'s list that their name was thought to
mean 'outlanders' (*RE* I 1587).

7 A 'golden line' (12.5n.; cf. 33, 55). The Germanic Teutones and
Cimbri defeated Roman armies in Gaul and were on the verge of
overrunning Italy when they were destroyed by the legions of Marius
(102–101 BC). It was considered a sad irony that Marius himself
would later come close to destroying Rome in his civil war with Sulla
(Cic. *Tusc.* 5.56; cf. Luc. 2.67–133).

  caerulea ... pube: the epithet probably means 'blue-eyed'
(Porph.; cf. Tac. *Ger.* 4 (Germans have) *truces et caerulei oculi*, Juv.
13.164). There seems to be no parallel for *caeruleus = caeruleis oculis*,
but other colour terms are used in this way (cf. *rauus* (33n.), André
(1949) index s.v. 'yeux'). If the phrase has to mean 'blue youth(s)',
then H. may imagine them wearing war-paint (Lambinus, R. Edge-
worth, *Glotta* 67 (1989) 229–32), although ancient sources associate
this practice with Britons (Caes. *Gal.* 5.14) not Germans. *pubes* in the
sense 'young men' (*C.* 1.25.17, 2.8.17, 3.5.18, 4.4.46) occurs chiefly in
poetry and seems to be an archaism (Fordyce on Virg. *A.* 7.105).

8 parentibusque abominatus: cf. *C.* 1.1.24–5 *bellaque matribus |
detestata*. The 'parents' could be those of the soldiers who died in the
Hannibalic war (9.25–6), or 'ancestors' (*OLD* s.v. *parens* 2) of H.'s
audience, or members of that audience for whom Hannibal was still
a 'nursery bogey-man' (Horsfall (1973) 138). This seems to be the first
instance of *abominatus* as a passive (rather than deponent) participle

(*ThLL* I 122; cf. 18, 5.39nn.). In either voice the form is rarer and thus *difficilior* than *abominandus* (app. crit.). For the caesura at the prefix (*ab* | *ominatus*), cf. 1.19n.

9 impia ... aetas: here *aetas* almost certainly means 'generation' (1n.; cf. *C.* 1.35.34–5 *quid nos dura refugimus* | *aetas*, 3.6.46 (63–6n.), *OLD* s.v. 3). *impius* (3.1n.) is often used both of the participants in civil war and of the wars themselves (*C.* 2.1.30, 3.24.25, Cic. *Catil.* 1.23 etc., Virg. *Ecl.* 1.70, *G.* 1.468, 511, *A.* 6.613, Fantham on Luc. 2.63 (on the brink of civil war) *pietas peritura*). For the 'double motivation' (as Homerists would say) of impiety and a curse, cf. 7.17–18n.

perdemus: the implied object is *eam* or *hanc* (7.10) supplied from *Roma ... quam* (2–3). For the repetition *perdere ... perdemus*, cf. 1.10–11, *S.* 1.4.102–3 *promittere ... promitto*, 2.3.63–4 *insanire ... insanit*, Bo III 403. Here it makes for a kind of archaic Greek-sounding 'ring structure', the first of several in this poem (cf. 15–37, 18–36, 25–35).

deuoti sanguinis: gen. of quality (4.8n.). *sanguis* here probably means 'ancestry' (*C.* 2.20.6, 3.27.65, 4.2.14, *Saec.* 50, *Ars* 292), but there is almost certainly a reference to the (literal) 'blood of Remus' (7.19–20). *deuotus* in the sense 'accursed' seems to be rare and poetic (*C.* 3.4.27, Cat. 64.135, *ThLL* v 1.883–4).

10 ferisque ... solum: cf. 20n., *C.* 3.3.40–2 *dum Priami Paridisque busto* | *insultet armentum et catulos ferae* | *celent inultae*, Hom. *Od.* 9.123–4 (an island abandoned by the Phaeacians (J. S. Clay, *C.Q.* 30 (1980) 261–4)) 'unsown and unploughed for all days | it is bereft of men and provides (only) for bleating goats', Virg. *A.* 3.10–11 (Aeneas) *portusque relinquo* | *et campos ubi Troia fuit*, 10.59–60, Luc. 9.966–9 (Troy). The parallel with the *Odes* passage and those from Virgil and Lucan suggest that H. may allude to an account of the sack of Troy, Rome's 'mother city' (10.11–14n.), perhaps from the cyclic *Iliupersis* (cf. 15.1n.).

It has been suggested that H. also drew on the 'Sibylline oracles', a collection of Greek hexameter prophecies attributed to the Cumaean and other Sibyls and consulted during various crises of Roman history (A. Kurfess, *Phil. Woch.* 59 (1939) 701–2, McLeod (2n.); cf. Coleman on Virg. *Ecl.* 4.4, *EV* IV 828–31, H. W. Parke, *Sibyls and Sibylline prophecy in classical antiquity* (London 1988) 144–51). Cf. *Orac. Sib.* 8.40 Kurfess (when Rome is destroyed) 'wolves and foxes will inhabit your foundations'.

rursus: i.e. the site will be reduced to its primitive state. For descriptions of 'pre-Romulan' Rome, cf. Virg. *A.* 8.360–1, Tib. 2.5.25, Prop. 3.9.49, 4.1.1–4, Ov. *Ars* 3.119–20, Bömer on *F.* 1.243. Most of these have a 'golden age' quality lacking here, and the occupants are usually harmless cattle rather than wild beasts. H.'s *ferae*, besides anticipating the *adynata* later in the poem (30–4, 51–2), may recall his comparison of the Romans to wolves and lions (7.11– 12).

11–14 The scene may be intended to recall the Gallic sack of Rome (390 BC) and perhaps also the aftermath of that calamity, when the Romans supposedly considered abandoning the ruins and migrating to Veii (21–2n.). They were deterred by an omen (23–4n.) and by a speech of Camillus who, unlike H., could find reasons for them to stay and rebuild (Liv. 5.49–55, Plut. *Cam.* 31). It has been argued that this story was invented in the late Republic as a patriotic counter to proposals like that of H. (Ogilvie on Liv. 5.51–4), but there seems to be no reason to doubt its antiquity, even if its historicity is questionable (Fraenkel (1957) 268).

11 barbarus: cf. 9.6n. Any number of 'barbarians' were eager to destroy Rome, including contemporary Gauls (1.11–14n.) and the Parthians (7.9n.), both noted for their cavalry (9.17, *C.* 1.2.51, 19.11– 12 etc.). Since the poem is probably set after Actium (16 intro.), it is unlikely that H. means the foreign contingents of Antony's army (Kraggerud (1984) 139), but cf. *C.* 1.37.6–8 (of Cleopatra) *Capitolio | regina dementis ruinas | funus et imperio parabat* and *C.* 3.6.13–16.

cineres: probably those of the devastated city (Cic. *Catil.* 4.12 (the Catilinarians tried to destroy Rome) *ut gentem Allobrogum* [6n.] *in uestigiis huius urbis atque in cinere deflagrati imperi conlocarent*). But H. could also mean human remains like those of Quirinus (13–14); cf. Ov. *Pont.* 1.2.107–10 (echoing H.?) *si moriar ... | nec male compositos, ut scilicet exule dignum, | Bistonii cineres ungula pulset equi.*

11–12 Vrbem | ... ungula: an epic-sounding phrase; cf. Enn. *Ann.* 263 Skutsch [*equitatus*] *consequitur, summo sonitu quatit ungula terram*, 431 *it eques et plausu caua concutit ungula terram*, Virg. *G.* 3.88, *A.* 8.596, 11.875.

12 eques: probably in apposition to *uictor* (11), 'and, on horse-back' (cf. 17.74), although some take the *eques* as a separate figure. Either way it seems odd both here and at Enn. *Ann.* 431 (11–12n.) for

rider rather than horse to 'strike with resounding hoof'; hence the
v.l. *equi* (cf. Ov. *Pont.* 1.2.110 (11n.), Virg. *A.* 10.892–3 *quadripes et cal-
cibus auras | uerberat*). Despite ancient testimony (e.g. Gell. 18.5.7–9)
the idea that *eques* can mean *equus* seems 'absurd' (Skutsch on Enn.
Ann. 236). It is possible that *ungula* is synecdoche for the horse (Orelli;
cf. *S.* 1.1.114, Mart. 12.50.5), or perhaps H. and Ennius intentionally
conflate human and equine (cf. Thomas on Virg. *G.* 3.116–17) to
suggest something monstrous, like a centaur.

   13 carent ... solibus: cf. 16, *C.* 3.19.8, 29.23, Virg. *G.* 1.435
(days) *pluuia uentisque carebunt*. By *solibus* H. may mean both the heat
of the sun (2.41) and the 'light of day' (9.16n.) which might be pol-
luted by the sight (14) of the bones. Cf. Pseudophocylides, *Gnomai*
99–101 Diehl 'do not open up a tomb of the dead and show things
not to be looked at [*atheata*] to the sun and (thus) arouse divine
anger'. Greek and Roman epitaphs sometimes call on Helios (Sol) to
protect the tomb (Lattimore (1962) 110, 122). It appears that Hanni-
bal (8) violated Roman tombs (Liv. 26.13.13), and his ally Philip V of
Macedon shocked both Greeks and Romans by doing this at Athens
in 200 BC (31.24.18, 26.9, 30.5; cf. Hdt. 4.127.3).

   ossa Quirini: i.e. of Romulus (7.19n.). The name may be para-
doxical, as when it is used elsewhere of Romulus it generally means
'the deified Romulus', not his corpse (N–H on *C.* 1.2.46, 3.3.15–
16, *S.* 1.10.32, Virg. *G.* 3.27, *A.* 1.292, Austin on 6.859). Quirinus,
originally a (Sabine?) god distinct from Romulus, began to be iden-
tified with him, perhaps before Ennius or, more likely, in the late
Republic (Skutsch on *Ann.* 99–100, G. Radke, D. Porte, *ANRW* II
17.1 (1981) 276–342). Despite this identification and a tradition that
he was torn into unrecoverable shreds by the Senate (Cic. *Rep.* 2.20,
Liv. 1.16.4), Romulus seems to have had a *sepulcrum* at Rome (scholia
on this passage, citing Varro; cf. Dion. Hal. 1.87.2, 3.1.2, Fest. p.
184M) which might have been visible from several of the places
where H. could be standing (1–14n.). Archaeology has discovered a
Lapis Niger in the right place which, if not a tomb, might have been
taken for one (Richardson (1992) 267–8, 358–9).

   14 (nefas uidere!): an emotive parenthesis; cf. *C.* 3.24.30, 4.6.17
heu nefas and, for the phrase, *C.* 1.11.1 *scire nefas*, 4.4.22, Cic. *Har.* 8
(the rites of Bona Dea) *quae uiri oculis ne imprudentis quidem aspici fas est*,
Ov. *Met.* 11.70 (transformations) *quae uidere nefas*, Tyrtaeus, fr. 10.26

West (the corpses of old men) 'disgusting to the eyes and shameful to see (*nemesēton idein*)'.

insolens: cf. App. 3, *C.* 1.16.20–1 *imprimeretque muris | hostile aratrum exercitus insolens, inc. trag.* 56 *ROL uictor insolens,* Liv. 5.48.9 (when the Romans were weighing out gold to ransom the city in 390 (11–14n.)) *additus ab insolente Gallo ponderi gladius, auditaque intoleranda Romanis uox, Vae uictis.*

15–40 H. has a plan: to abandon Rome as the Phocaeans long ago abandoned their city and, like them, to swear an oath not to return unless the natural order of things should reverse itself.

Since it is keyed to a historical precedent, H.'s proposal might, on first hearing, seem to at least part of his audience (17n.) not only feasible but acceptable. There were other precedents: the aftermath of the Gallic sack (11–14n.), recent mass migrations such as that of the Helvetii into Gaul (Caes. *Gal.* 1.2–5), and the smaller-scale movements of Roman citizens, especially veterans, to colonies in all directions, including some in the east (21–2n.) which Octavian established immediately after Actium (Reinhold on Dio 51.4.2–8, Kienast (1982) 397–9).

15–16 '(If) perhaps something would help (you), do you all together or the better part (actually) seek to be free from dire sufferings?' Before he reveals his plan H. has to make sure that his countrymen are not so far gone that *nec uitia nostra nec remedia pati possumus* (Liv. 1. *praef.* 9).

The syntax and punctuation of this couplet are most uncertain (Fraenkel (1957) 53–6, W. Schmid, *Phil.* 102 (1958) 93–102, AG (1971) 31–5, Setaioli (1981) 1752–3, Kraggerud (1984) 156–66, W. Batstone, *A.J.Ph.* 106 (1985) 237–40). The interpretation accepted here (that of Fea) assumes, probably rashly, that *forte quid* can = *si forte quid* (15n.) and that the words *communiter ... laboribus,* although lacking an interrogative, can be read as a question (Porph.; cf. 5.58n.). Other suggestions include: (1) taking *forte* (=*fortasse*) with *quaeritis,* the phrase *quid expediat* as an indirect question, and *carere* as an object or consecutive inf. dependent on *expediat* ('perhaps you ask what will help (us) to be free ...'). But even if *carere* can be separated from *quaeritis,* there seems to be no parallel for a construction of this sort with *expedit,* which normally takes a subject inf. (i.e. 'what being free ... will avail us'; cf. LHS II 348). (2) A zeugma (15.7n.), with *quaeritis* governing both indirect quest. and inf. ('perhaps (you ask) all together what will help or, the better part, you seek to be free ...'). This requires breaking up the phrase *communiter ... pars* (15n.) and introduces a distinction between 'expediency' and 'freedom from troubles' which seems extraneous to the context. (3) Making *forte* the neut. sing. of *fortis*, *quid* an indef. pronoun, and *expediat* a hortatory or optative subj. ('let something strong (or bold) help us!'). But *quid = aliquid*, although possible in a subordinate clause (15n.), seems most unlikely in an independent sentence (Fraenkel (1957) 54). (4) Emending to *quod expediat* (dett., Bentley, AG), which would be in apposition to *carere* either as a defining rel. clause ('what would help, to be free ...') or as a parenthetical wish ('which (thing), may it help!'). But such a clause seems redundant here, and it is not clear how the reading *quid* could have arisen. If there is corruption, it may lie in *carere*, which could have arisen from *carent* (13) and supplanted either another finite verb (e.g. *leuetque*) parallel with *expediat* (cf. interpretation (1) above) or an acc. object for *expediat* (Kenney).

15 forte quid: possibly = *si forte quid*. There seems to be no exact parallel (*ThLL* VI 1130–6) except perhaps Virg. *A.* 5.291–2 *hic, qui [= si qui?] forte uelint rapido contendere cursu, | inuitat pretiis animos et praemia ponit*, where the text may be unfinished (Williams *ad loc.*). But ellipse of *si* is quite common (LHS II 656–7) and there are many examples in H. (*C.* 4.4.65, more than 40 in the hexameters (Bo III 295)), including two in which *quis*, like *quid* here, serves as an indefinite pronoun (*S.* 1.3.56, 63; cf. Smith on Tib. 1.10.13, LHS II 194). The alternatives, that *forte* is from *fortis*, or that it = *fortasse*, create other difficulties (15–16n.), although the latter has some support from parallels (Vitr. 5.5.7, 6 pr. 4, then later Latin (*ThLL* VI 1131)). The position of *forte* at the beginning of the phrase is also unusual (*Ep.* 1.7.29, 20.26, Brink on 2.2.34) and H. may give it emphasis in order to suggest the 'chanciness' of his proposal (AG (1971) 36; cf. 13.7n.).

expediat: probably intr., 'would help (you, the state)' (*OLD* s.v. 8; cf. Scipio Nasica, *orat.* 38.3 (= V. Max 3.7.3) *quid expediat rei publicae intelligo*), although it could be trans. with *uos ... laboribus* supplied from the next clause, 'would release (you from troubles)' (*OLD* s.v. 2b; cf. 11.25, *C.* 3.24.8, Ter. *Hec.* 288 *citius qui te expedias his aerumnis reperias*).

communiter ... pars: the restatement at 36–7 shows that the adverb = *omnis ciuitas*. At that point H. will qualify *melior pars* (37n.), but here the audience might take it as 'the greater number' (Porph; cf. *C.* 4.2.46, *S.* 1.1.61 *bona pars hominum*, Brink on *Ars* 297, Virg. *A.* 9.156 *melior ... pars acta diei*). *communiter* is rare in verse, although it does not seem to be unpoetic (*Ep.* 1.2.13, Cic. *Arat.* 16, Ov. *Met.* 6.262, Luc. 9.417). For the monosyllable at verse end, cf. Intro. 6.

17 potior sententia: cf. *Ep.* 1.17.16–17 *audi* | *cur sit Aristippi potior sententia*, Virg. *A.* 4.287 *haec alternanti potior sententia uisa est.* The terms *sententia* and *sic placet* (23) were often used of 'opinions' given in the Senate (Fraenkel (1957) 44–5), but they also occur in connection with popular assemblies (*OLD* s.v. *sententia* 4, s.v. *placeo* 5b; cf. Cic. *Dom.* 53 *populo ... placeat, Phil.* 11.18 *rogatus est populus quem id bellum gerere placeret*).

Phocaeorum: for the spondaic hexameter, cf. 29, 13.9n. Phocaea, an Ionian city in Asia Minor, was besieged by a Persian army (540 BC). Rather than surrender, the Phocaeans abandoned their city, taking with them the more valuable statues and offerings from their temples. They decided to head for Corsica, but first 'they put powerful curses on anyone who abandoned their expedition. They also threw into the sea an iron ingot and swore not to return to Phocaea before this ingot should reappear. But as they were setting out for Corsica longing and pity for their city and the surroundings of their country seized more than half of them, and becoming forswearers (of the oath) they sailed back to Phocaea' (Hdt. 1.165). The story became proverbial (Pfeiffer on Call. fr. 388.9, *RE* xx 444–8), but it seems likely that H.'s source is Herodotus (AG (1971) 37–40). There are, however, some differences (19, 25–6, 35–6nn.), and H. has omitted certain details which might, if known to his audience, raise doubts about the validity of the precedent. The Phocaeans were trying to escape, not civil war, but a foreign enemy, and the direction of their flight, from the east towards the Etruscan sea (Corsica), was almost the reverse of that proposed for the Romans.

18 profugit exsecrata: it is not clear which of these governs *agros ... patrios* (19). If *profugit* is trans. (*OLD* s.v. 2), then *exsecrata* would seem to be passive here (but cf. 36) and mean 'bound by a curse' (cf. *OLD* s.v. *exsecratio* 2). This would cohere with Herodotus' account (17n.), where the Phocaeans 'put curses', not on their territory, but on 'anyone who abandoned the expedition'. The non-deponent use (8n.) of *exsecror* is not common (Cato, *Hist.* 90, Afran. *com.* 192, Titin. *com.* 47, Plin. *Nat.* 28.27), but there are examples in Cicero's speeches (*Phil.* 1.5, 2.65).

ciuitas: cf. 36. Despite leaving their *urbs* in a condition similar to that which H. predicts for Rome (10), the Phocaeans were still a state (cf. *C.* 4.4.53–6, Virg. *A.* 7.295–6 (Trojans survive the burning of Troy)). For the distinction between *ciuitas* ('citizenry') and *urbs* ('physical site'), cf. Cic. *Sest.* 91 *tum conuenticula hominum, quae postea ciuitates nominatae sunt, tum domicilia coniuncta, quas urbes dicimus, Tusc.* 5.57, *Ac.* 2.137, Caes. *Gal.* 1.2.1 *Orgetorix* [a leader of the Helvetii (15–40n.)] *... ciuitati persuasit ut de finibus suis cum omnibus copiis exirent.* Despite its form, *ciuitas* does not seem to be unpoetic (*C.* 3.29.25, 4.2.51, Enn. *Sc.* 291 Vahlen, Pac. *trag.* 49 *ROL*).

19 Lares: probably metonymy (2.29n.) for *domos* (*C.* 1.12.44 etc. although the mention of Lares, who were Latin gods, seems to 'Romanize' the Phocaeans. Cf. *Saec.* 39 (40n.), *S.* 2.5.14 (Lares in Ulysses' Ithaca), Pl. *Aul.* 2 (at Athens), Cic. *Ver.* 3.27, 125 (among Sicilian Greeks), Thomas on Virg. *G.* 3.344 (Libyans), 4.43 (bees), *A.* 5.744, 9.259 (Trojans), 8.543 (Evander's Arcadians), Roscher II 1878–9.

19–20 habitandaque ... lupis: cf. 10n. 'The poet is apparently urging his audience to escape from civil war by taking action that will have identical results to civil war' (Miles). H.'s elaboration of Herodotus (17n.) may anticipate the *adynata* (25–34), especially since in Republican Latin *habito* is normally used of humans or gods, not beasts (*ThLL* v 3.2476, but cf. Pl. *St.* 64, Cat. 69.6, Var. *R.* 3.17.18, Virg. *G.* 3.430, *A.* 6.599).

20 rapacibus lupis: cf. *C.* 4.4.50 *cerui, luporum praeda rapacium,* Hom. *Il.* 16.156–7 *lukoi hōs | ōmophagoi* ('like ravenous wolves').

21–2 pedes ... per undas: i.e. 'by land or sea'. There is no hint yet of 'happy fields', and the audience might take the former to mean a place like Veii (11–14n.), the latter a colony in the eastern Mediterranean (15–40n.), the goal of ships driven by the south (Notus) and south-west (Africus) winds.

21 ire: dependent on *sententia* (17); cf. *Rhet. Her.* 3.40 *te hortari non est sententia,* Cic. *Off.* 3.116 *honestatem tueri ac retinere sententia est,* LHS II 351.

pedes ... ferent: cf. 58. There are many parallels for this phrase (e.g. *C.* 3.11.49, Hom. *Il.* 18.148, Gow on Theocr. *Id.* 13.70, Virg. *Ecl.* 9.1), but one in Phoenix of Colophon (fr. 2.5 Powell *hokoi podes pherōsin*), an imitator of early *iambus*, may indicate that H. is echoing Archilochus or Hipponax.

22 uocabit ... Africus: cf. Cat. 4.19–20 *laeua siue dextera | uocaret aura*. The epithet *proteruus*, 'violent' (*C.* 1.26.2), may be a hint as to the time of year, since Africus, like other winds (9.31, 10.3–4, 13.3), was at its worst in winter (*C.* 1.1.15, 3.12, 14.5, 3.29.57–8, Plin. *Nat.* 2.119).

23 melius ... habet suadere: the inf. with *habeo* is not attested before Cicero (e.g. *Balb.* 33 *quid habes igitur dicere*) and may be a Graecism (LHS II 314–15). H.'s request seems to recall the procedure of Roman assemblies (*OLD* s.v. *suadere* 2, Fraenkel (1957) 45), but he may also echo Hom. *Il.* 14.107–8 (Agamemnon, after he has suggested – this time for real (16 intro.) – that the Greeks return home) 'Now if there be someone who might speak a plan better than this one, | whether he is young or old, I would be delighted.'

23–4 secunda | ... alite: cf. 66, 10.1n., Enn. *Ann.* 74–5 Skutsch *Remus ... secundum | solus auem seruat*, Cic. *Div.* 2.79 *aues euentus significant aut aduersos aut secundos*. In 390 BC (11–14n.) an omen persuaded the Romans not to abandon the city (Liv. 5.55.1–2). The *uates* (66n.) was not, technically, a 'bird-watcher' (*auspex*), but would sometimes usurp this function (Cic. *Div.* 2.56, Liv. 2.42.10).

24 ratem occupare: they should 'occupy' (*OLD* s.v. *occupo* 11, 12) the ships before the land is 'occupied by wild beasts' (10). *ratem* is probably collective sing. (cf. Skutsch on Enn. *Ann.* 378), although H. may imply that the *melior pars* (37n.) will fill only a single boat.

25–34 The starting-point for H.'s oath appears to be that of the Phocaeans (25n.), but he elaborates with three pairs of *adynata* (5.78–9n.), the first suggesting the destruction of Italy (17–19), the second a perversion (30–2), the third an inversion (33–4) of nature. All of this adds up to an emphatic 'never' (cf. 15.7–9n.), yet some of the *adynata* resemble the kind of 'prodigies' that might be observed by a *uates* (28, 30–2, 30nn.), while another is oddly similar to something in the 'happy fields' (33, 51nn.).

25 in haec: sc. *mea uerba* (15.4n.).

25–6 'As soon as stones shall have swum up raised from the deepest sea, let it not be forbidden to return.' The prefix in *renarint* (first here) is probably meant to complement *redire*, 'when the stones come back, we will come back too' (Kenney). But it could imply that the stones would first be thrown into the water, although it is strange that H. does not say this and that he has substituted *saxa* for the 'iron ingot' of the Phocaeans (17n.). Perhaps he drew on a source other than Herodotus or adjusted the details to cohere with the other *adynata*, which are all from the natural world (M. Hubbard, *C.Q.* 27 (1977) 356–7). It may be relevant that oaths at Rome were sometimes sworn on a rock, *per Iouem lapidem* (*RE* x 1255).

imis ... | uadis: cf. Virg. *A.* 1.125–6 *imis | stagna refusa uadis*. The phrase may be an oxymoron, since *uadum* normally means 'shallow water' or even 'ford' (*C.* 1.3.24, *OLD* s.v. 1), although at times 'poetic freedom ... made it a synonym for *undae* and *aequora*' (Fordyce on Virg. *A.* 7.24; cf. Acc. *inc.* 12–13 *ROL*, Cat. 64.6, 58).

27 conuersa domum ... lintea: the language is properly nautical except that *linteum* in the sense 'sail' seems to be poetic (*ThLL* VII 2.1467). *piget* occurs only here in H. but is not alien even to elevated verse (Enn. *Sc.* 60 Vahlen, Virg. *A.* 4.335, 5.678, 7.233).

28 Padus ... lauerit: H. seems to amplify the proverb 'when rivers run backwards' (N–H on *C.* 1.29.10, Eur. *Med.* 410, Pease on Cic. *Div.* 1.78 (as a prodigy)) into a great catastrophe, with the Po in NE Italy exceeding its usual floods (Virg. *G.* 4.371–3) to inundate the country down to the SE coast. A real flood by the Po was thought to be an omen of Caesar's assassination (Virg. *G.* 1.481–2; cf. Pease on Cic. *Div.* 1.100), but the image may also recall the deluge which blotted out evil humanity in the time of Deucalion and Pyrrha (*C.* 1.2.5–12, Virg. *Ecl.* 6.41, Ov. *Met.* 1.262–323; cf. 34n.). For *lauo* cf. *C.* 2.3.18 [*uilla*] *flauus quam Tiberis lauit*, Lucr. 5.949–50 *umori' fluenta | lubrica proluuie larga lauere umida saxa*. It appears (*ThLL* VII 2.1047) that *lauere* (11× in H.) is more poetic than *lauare* (4× – all in the hexameters).

Matina ... cacumina: it is not certain where or what Matinus was. The few other references suggest a coastal region of Calabria or Apulia, although there are no notable 'mountain peaks' in this area (N–H on *C.* 1.28.3; cf. 4.2.27, Luc. 9.185). Perhaps *cacumina* (only here in H.) means 'tree-tops' (*ThLL* III 10–12). The contexts in which it has this sense usually include a mention of trees or leaves, but cf. Ov. *Met.* 6.705–6 (Boreas) *puluereamque trahens per summa cacumina pallam | uerrit humum*, 7.804–5, 9.93–4.

29 in mare ... Appenninus 'till the Apennines, which run down the middle of Italy, push their chain out into the sea' (Wickham). *procurro* seems to be a technical term for a feature 'projecting' from the coast (Virg. *A.* 5.204, Ov. *F.* 4.419, Plin. *Nat.* 4.86, Tac. *Ag.* 10.3, 11.2). For *Appenninus* in a spondaic hexameter (17n.), cf. Ov. *Met.* 2.226, Petr. 124.279, Pers. 1.95, Quint. *Inst.* 9.4.65. The Romans normally spoke of the 'Apennines' (Ital. 'Appennini') as a single mountain (e.g. Cic. *Sest.* 12, Virg. *A.* 12.703, Plin. *Nat.* 3.48).

seu 'or if' (*OLD* s.v. *siue* 1). Postponed (2n.) *seu* or *siue* is especially rare (Virg. *A.* 9.680, 11.779, Marouzeau (1949) 83–4).

30–2 Unnatural matings often figure in *adynata* (N–H on *C.* 1.33.7–9, *Ars* 12–13 (31n.), Ar. *Pax* 1075–6 'this is not dear to the blessed gods, | to end the war: sooner would a wolf marry a ewe', Lucr. 3.748–53, Virg. *Ecl.* 8.27–8). They were also a concern of diviners: (the Etruscans take omens) *etiam ex hominum pecudumque conceptu et sata* (Cic. *Div.* 1.93; cf. 36 (mule foaling), 98 (*ortus androgyni*), 121 (woman giving birth to a lion).

30–1 nouaque ... | mirus: cf. Lucr. 5.97 *res noua miraque menti*, Thomas on Virg. *G.* 2.82 (46n.). For *libido* (prosaic), cf. 5.41n.; for *mirus amor*, Virg. *A.* 7.57 (Amata's 'strange love' for Turnus).

30 monstra iunxerit: the noun is predicative: 'the animals will become *monstra* ... by mating with other than their own species' (Wickham). Cf. Ter. *Hec.* 798 *unaque nos sibi opera amicos iunget* ('will join (as) friends'), Virg. *A.* 3.169 *iunge pares* ('join (oxen as) pairs'). 'Monsters' figure in certain Greek oaths such as that taken by members of the Amphictyonic League (Aeschines 3.109–11): 'If anyone ... goes back on this oath, he is under a curse ... and the curse is that for them neither does the earth produce fruits nor do their wives bear children like their parents, but monsters [*terata*], nor do their oxen produce natural offspring.'

31 tigres ... ceruis: cf. *Ars* 12–13 (artists have 'licence') *sed non ut placidis coeant immitia, non ut | serpentes auibus geminentur, tigribus agni.* Despite numerous references (*C.* 1.23.9, 3.3.14, 11.13, 27.56, *Ars* 393, 9× in Virgil), in H.'s day the tiger was still an almost fabulous beast (Var. *L.* 5.100 (forties BC) *tigris ... qui uiuus capi adhuc non potuit*, Virg.

A. 2.151, Pease on *A.* 4.367, Plin. *Nat.* 8.65 (first live specimen at Rome in 11 BC)).

subsidere: cf. Lucr. 4.1197–8 (because of *amore*) *uolucres armenta feraeque | et pecudes et equae maribus subsidere possent.* There may be a play on *subsido* in the sense 'wait in ambush' (*OLD* s.v. 2), a more natural 'position' for a tigress *vis-à-vis* a stag.

32 adulteretur ... miluo: this may be a 'double *adynaton*' (K–H), since not only is the kite a natural enemy of the dove (Phaed. 1.31.3), but the latter was thought to be averse to any kind of 'adultery' (Prop. 2.15.27–8, Plin. *Nat.* 10.104). In Republican Latin *miluus* is always a trisyllable.

33 credula ... leones: this item would not be out of place in the description of the 'happy fields' (51n.). It seems likely (16 intro.) that H. is echoing Virg. *Ecl.* 4.22 (when the golden age returns) *nec magnos metuent armenta leones.* For *credula,* cf. Ov. *Met.* 8.857–8 (to an angler) *sit tibi piscis in unda | credulus.* The word may continue the erotic imagery here, since it can be used of 'gullible' lovers (*C.* 3.7.13, 4.1.30, Tib. 1.9.38, Pichon (1902) 115).

rauos ... leones: cf. *C.* 3.27.3 *raua ... lupa,* Var. *R.* 2.9.3 (dog), Hom. *Il.* 20.172, *Od.* 11.611 ('green-' and 'grey-eyed' lions), Cat. 45.7 *caesio ... leoni. rauus* seems to indicate a 'yellowish grey' eye colour (André (1949) 69–70). The word is not common, and the variants (app. crit.) are likely to be glosses or interpolations, although some editors accept *flauos* (cf. Stat. *Theb.* 4.154) or *fuluos* (cf. Lucr. 5.901 *corpora fulua leonum,* Virg. *G.* 4.408).

34 amatque ... aequora 'enjoy the salt water'; cf. 2.57n., Virg. *Ecl.* 5.76 *dum iuga montis aper, fluuios dum piscis amabit,* and, for the image, *Ars* 30, Arch. fr. 122.6–9 West (App. 1) 'let none of you be surprised | even if beasts receive a sea dwelling from dolphins, and to them [the beasts] the echoing waves | become dearer than land, while to those [the dolphins] the wooded mountain (becomes dear)', Hdt. 5.92 (5.79–80n.), Virg. *Ecl.* 1.59–60, Prop. 2.3.5–6. This particular *adynaton* becomes reality with 'Deucalion's flood' (28n.; cf. N–H on *C.* 1.2.9, Lycophron 83–5, Ov. *Met.* 1.296–308). *salsa* seems to be a poetic epithet (Enn. *Ann.* 370, 453 Skutsch, *Sc.* 367 Vahlen, Kenney on Lucr. 3.493).

leuis: the goat would exchange its normal shagginess for the 'smooth' skin of a fish or dolphin (Plin. *Nat.* 9.40 *alia* (sea creatures) *corio et pilo integuntur . . . alia corio tantum, ut delphini*). Cf. the *adynaton* at Pl. *Men.* 918 *esse* [from *edo*] *auis squamossas, piscis pennatos.* There are also strange goats in the 'happy fields' (49).

35–6 haec ... | eamus ... exsecrata: *haec* seems to be an internal acc. (1.23–4n.) with *exsecrata*, which is here deponent (18n.), 'having cursed these (curses)' (cf. Enn. *Sc.* 401 Vahlen *cui quod in me est exsecrabor*, Liv. 10.28.18 *haec exsecratus in se hostesque*). Another possibility is that *exsecrata* is passive (18n.) and that *haec* (sc. *aequora* 34) goes with *eamus* as an acc. of local object without preposition, 'let the whole state, bound by a curse, go (to) these waters [i.e. the Etruscan sea (40)] and (to) whatever waters [i.e. Ocean (41)] ...' (Kukula (1911) 7). This construction normally involves place-names (9.29, LHS II 49) or terms such as *domum* (e.g. 27, 2.62, 11.20, 13.16) and *rus* (*S.* 1.6.102, *Ep.* 1.7.76), but cf. Lucr. 6.742 (birds) *ea ... loca cum uenere uolantes*, Virg. *G.* 4.364–5 *lacus ... lucosque sonantis | ibat*, Fedeli on Prop. 1.1.18 *ire uias*.

35 reditus ... dulcis: cf. 13.15n., Arch. fr. 8.2 West (App. 1), Hom. *Od.* 22.223 *glukeron noston* ('sweet homecoming'), [Tib.] 3.3.27 *pro dulci reditu.*

37 aut pars ... melior: H. now qualifies *melior pars* (15n.): it is not the 'majority', but a 'part' – possibly even a minority (*grex* (*C.* 1.24.18, 37.9, *S.* 2.3.44, *Ep.* 1.4.16) suggests a large, if not larger number) – which proves 'more excellent' because it is not 'intractable' and because of its 'courage' (39). In the late Republic *pars melior* could be a 'loaded term' (Ogilvie on Liv. 2.44.3) when used by 'partisans' of their 'faction' (*ThLL* XI 474–5, *RE* XVIII 773–98).

mollis et exspes: the 'part' or individual who proves 'effeminate' (cf. 39, 1.10n.) and 'defeatist'. The variant *expers*, although not impossible (*expersque uirtutis* (Porph.)), is probably *lectio facilior*, as *exspes* is a rarer and more poetic word (Brink on *Ars* 20, *ThLL* V 2.13).

38 inominata ... cubilia: the beds are 'ill-omened' either because they are in a doomed city (9–14) or (transferred epithet) because their occupants, like many of the Phocaeans (17n.), will be 'accursed' for having violated the oath to leave. Both *inominata* (only here in Classical Latin) and *perpremo* (Ov. *Ars* 1.394, Sen. *Ep.* 99.18; cf. Prop. 1.3.12 *impresso ... toro*, 2.29.35 *toro ... presso*) may be Horatian coinages.

39 muliebrem ... luctum: probably an echo of Arch. fr. 13.10 West (App. 1), where, after a shipwreck, the poet urges his fellow citizens to 'endure, pushing aside womanish grief'. For *muliebris*, cf. 2.39n., *C.* 1.37.22–3, *inc. trag.* 33 *ROL uos enim iuuenes animum geritis muliebrem*, Hom. *Il.* 2.235–6 (Thersites seconds Agamemnon's proposal (16 intro.)) 'Achaean women, no longer Achaean men, | let us go home with our ships'; for *tollo*, *Ep.* 1.12.3 *tolle querelas*, Cic. *S. Rosc.* 6 *metum ... tollatis*.

40 Etrusca ... litora: it is not clear if this means the west bank of the Tiber (cf. N–H on *C.* 1.2.14 *litore Etrusco*), 'the shores of Etruria' (i.e. towards Ocean *via* a NW route), or, what seems most likely, 'the shores of the Etruscan sea' (a SW route). With the last the Romans would be departing along the course by which their Trojan ancestors arrived in Italy (*C.* 4.4.53–4, *Saec.* 37–9 *Iliaeque | litus Etruscum tenuere turmae, | iussa pars mutare Lares et urbem*).

praeter et uolate: probably tmesis (7.3n.) for *praeteruolate*; cf. *S.* 1.1.86 *argento post omnia ponas*, Skutsch on Enn. *Ann.* 376 *uolat super impetus undas*. The alternative is for *praeter* to govern *Etrusca ... litora* with *et* postponed (2n.) to the third position (Virg. *A.* 12.381, Marouzeau (1949) 80). The metaphor of ships 'flying' is common in both Greek and Latin (e.g. *C.* 1.37.16, 4.5.19, Hom. *Od.* 11.125, West on Hes. *Op.* 628).

41–60 H. at last reveals the destination: certain 'happy fields' or 'wealthy islands' where there is no need for toil (43–50), no danger from predators or bad climate (51–6), and no 'contamination' from the outside world (57–60). Up to this point his plan has been at least somewhat plausible (15–40n.), but this seems less likely for his talk of 'happy fields'. Even if his audience allowed themselves to believe that such a place could exist, they would probably be disappointed by the finale, where it becomes apparent that this wonderful land is not for the likes of them (63–6n.).

H.'s description of the place may owe something to an incident in 81 BC, when the rebel Q. Sertorius tried vainly to escape from Spain to certain 'Atlantic islands' (the Canaries?) which were supposed to be 'ten thousand stades from Libya [Africa] and called Islands of the Blest [41–2n.]. With moderate rain ... and soft winds [63–4], they not only have soil good and rich for ploughing and sowing, but even bear self-produced fruit [43–6] ... that could feed without toils or

trouble an idle people. And an air that is healthy [61–2] because of
moderate seasons and weather [56] covers the islands ... Therefore
a strong belief has spread even to the barbarians that here indeed is
the "Elysian plain", the dwelling-place of the blest, of which Homer
sang' (Plut. *Sert.* 8, probably based on Sallust (43n.)). But 'utopias'
figure in the legends of many peoples and in the Graeco-Roman
tradition as early as Homer and Hesiod (Gatz (1967) 189–214). The
gods live for ever in such a place (Hom. *Od.* 6.42–6, Lucr. 3.18–24)
and, long ago, so did the 'golden race' (64n.) of humans (Hes. *Op.*
109–26). Some imagine a return of this 'golden life' (Virg. *Ecl.* 4, *A.*
1.286–96, 6.792–4; cf. *C.* 4.2.39–40), but in H.'s time it could only
be found on the far side of the grave (63n., N–H on *C.* 2.13.23,
4.8.27, Pind. *Ol.* 2.61–75, Norden, Austin on Virg. *A.* 6.637–78) or in
remote and isolated parts of the earth (Thomas (1982) 21–2, Romm
(1992) 45–67, 156–71) like the 'Atlantic islands' (above), Scythia
and other northern areas (e.g. *C.* 3.24), Homer's 'Elysian plain' (*Od.*
4.563–8), Phaeacia (7.85–132), and the land of the Cyclopes (9.105–
15; cf. Theocr. *Id.* 11 (= *HA* 493–573)), and Hesiod's 'islands of the
blest' (63n.). Ironically, Italy herself was once such an 'outpost' of
the golden age (Virg. *G.* 2.536–40, *A.* 8.319–27); Archilochus (fr. 22
West (App. 1)) knew of a place 'by the streams of the Siris' (on the
gulf of Tarentum) which was more 'lovely, alluring, and desirable'
than his own Thasos.

41 Oceanus circumuagus: the epithet (first here) may be based
on Greek *apsorrhoos*, 'flowing back (into itself)', used of Ocean in
Homer (*Il.* 18.399, *Od.* 20.65) and Hesiod (*Th.* 776); cf. Aesch. *Prom.*
138–9, Ov. *Met.* 1.30 *circumfluus umor.* It seems less likely that *circum* is
in tmesis (*ordo est: Oceanus circum arua beata uagus* (Porph.); cf. app.
crit., Brink (1982) 42–4).

Even in Roman times the Atlantic and Indian 'oceans' and Cas-
pian Sea were usually thought to be branches of a single *Oceanus* en-
circling the known parts of Europe, Africa, and Asia (Cic. *Rep.* 6.22,
Cat. 64.30, Virg. *A.* 7.100–1, Romm (1992) 12–20, 121–40). Sertorius'
islands were supposed to be in the Atlantic (41–60n.), the 'isles of
the blest' lay 'beside deep-eddying ocean' (Hes. *Op.* 171), and in
Elysium 'Oceanus always stirs the breezes of clear-blowing Zephyr
[the west wind]' (Hom. *Od.* 4.567–8). The western Ocean can also be

a setting for the land of the dead (Hom. *Od.* 11.14–22, 24.11–14, West on Hes. *Th.* 720–819, Pind. *Ol.* 2.71–2).

41–2 arua beata | ... arua: *beatus* and its synonyms (2.1n.) are standard terms for 'utopias' (42, 53nn.; cf. West on Hes. *Op.* 171, Virg. *A.* 6.638–9, 743–4 *per amplum | mittimur Elysium et pauci laeta arua tenemus*). The repetition (64–5, 4.20n.) of *arua* may emphasize that the place, like Alfius' dream land (Epode 2), is a *rus* with no trace of an *urbs* and its ills (1–14). Cities, towns, and even houses are absent from many 'utopias'; cf. Hes. *Op.* 131, 150 (first houses among the silver and bronze races), Lucr. 5.1108 (cities 'corrupt' primitive life), Virg. *Ecl.* 4.31–3 (just before the return of the golden age) *pauca tamen suberunt priscae uestigia fraudis, | quae temptare Thetin ratibus* [57–60n.], *quae cingere muris | oppida, quae iubeant telluri infindere sulcos* [43n.], Thomas on *G.* 2.495–540, Gatz (1967) 144–64.

42 diuites et insulas: 'hendiadys' (5.16n.) for (*arua*) *diuitum insularum*. 'Utopias' (41–6on.) are often islands (e.g. Pl. *Trin.* 549 *fortunatorum ... insulas*, Cic. *Fin.* 5.53 *beatorum insulis*), to be reached only by ship, if at all (57–60n.). The sequel shows that *diuites* here means 'bountiful' (=*felices* (2.14n.) or *feraces*, both unmetrical; cf. *S.* 1.2.74, Virg. *G.* 2.224 *talem* [*agrum*] *diues arat Capua*, *A.* 7.262, *ThLL* v 1.1490). But when used of places *diues* (*dis*) often indicates more material 'riches' (e.g. 2.65, *C.* 1.7.9, 3.24.2, *S.* 1.7.19), and H.'s followers might think at first that he is leading them to 'treasure islands'. It appears that the *uates* was supposed to be able to find hidden *diuitiae* (Enn. *Sc.* 322–3 Vahlen (66n.)), a belief that may also inform *C.* 4.8.25–6 (the power of *uates*) *Aeacum ... diuitibus consecrat insulis*.

43 tellus inarata: cf. Hes. *Op.* 117–18 (for the gold race) 'the life-giving land produced fruit | of its own accord in abundance and unstintingly', Hom. *Od.* 9.108–11 (the Cyclopes) 'neither sow seed with their hands nor plough, | but all things grow unsown and unploughed (*anērota*), | wheat, barley, and vines which produce | a grape-rich wine', Sall. *Hist.* 1.100 Reynolds *quas insulas* [i.e. those sought by Sertorius (41–6on.)] *... constabat suopte ingenio alimenta mortalibus gignere*, Virg. *Ecl.* 4.33, 39–41, Thomas on *G.* 1.127–8, Gatz (1967) 229. *inaratus* (first here and at Virg. *G.* 1.83) may be modelled on Homer's *anērotos* (AG (1971) 70).

Cererem =*fruges*, a common metonymy (2.29n., *C.* 3.24.13, Ter.

Eun. 732, Cic. *Nat.* 3.41, Lucr. 2.655–6, Cat. 63.36, Virg. *G.* 1.297, 2.229, Fordyce on *A.* 7.113). Greek uses *Demeter* in this way (e.g. Hdt. 7.141 (an oracle from 481 BC)) but much less frequently (Roscher II 1321).

44 imputata ... uinea: cf. Hom. *Od.* 9.110–11 (43n.), Virg. *Ecl.* 4.29 *incultisque rubens pendebit sentibus uua, G.* 1.132, and, for the labour normally required for viticulture, 2.9–10n. *imputatus* seems to be a technical term (*OLD*).

45 germinat ... termes: sc. *quotannis* (43); in Italy the olive normally produced fruit only in alternate years (Var. *R.* 1.55.3). Both *germino* and *termes* seem to be rare technical terms (*OLD*).

numquam ... fallentis: cf. *C.* 3.1.30 *fundusque mendax*, 16.30 *segetis certa fides, Ep.* 1.7.87 *spem mentita seges*, Thomas on Virg. *G.* 2.467 [*agricolarum*] *nescia fallere uita*, Tib. 2.1.19, Ov. *Ars* 1.401. In ancient, as in modern times, the olive could be a symbol of peace (Virg. *G.* 2.425 (2.55–6n.), Fordyce on *A.* 7.154, *RE* XVII 2020).

46 suamque ... arborem: i.e. not grafted (2.13–14n.) onto a tree of another type. Like Virgil, H. may imply that the act of grafting is somehow immoral; cf. Thomas on *G.* 2.82 [*arbos*] *miratastque nouas frondes et non sua poma.* The rare word *pulla* could indicate either ripeness (Porph.; cf. N–H on *C.* 1.25.18 *pulla ... myrto*) or a particular variety of fig (Hipp. fr. 48 West, Plin. *Nat.* 15.70). There were fig trees in the wondrous garden of Alcinous in Phaeacia (Hom. *Od.* 7.114–21).

47 mella ... ex ilice: the honey comes from wild, not artificial hives (cf. Thomas on Virg. *G.* 2.452–3). Abundance of honey is a common feature of 'utopian' landscapes (N–H on *C.* 2.19.10–12, West on Hes. *Op.* 233, Virg. *Ecl.* 4.30 *durae quercus sudabunt roscida mella*, Ov. *Met.* 1.112, Gatz (1967) 229).

48 leuis ... lympha desilit: the point seems to be that there is abundant fresh water (cf. Hom. *Od.* 7.129–30 (springs in Phaeacia), Pind. *Ol.* 2.73 (on the 'island of the blest')), although the image also suggests a *locus amoenus* (2.23–8n.); cf. *C.* 3.13.15–16, Theocr. *Id.* 11.47–8 (in the land of the Cyclopes) 'there is cool water, which for me many-treed Aetna | casts from its white snow as an ambrosial drink'. *leuis* is probably felt with *pede* (*C.* 1.1.31 *leues ... chori*) as *crepante* (below) with *lympha*.

crepante ... pede: cf. Lucr. 5.270–2 (= 6.636–8) *materies umoris ... super terras fluit agmine dulci | qua uia secta semel liquido pede detulit undas*, Virg. *A.* 9.125 *reuocatque pedem Tiberinus*. The variant *nympha* may have arisen from unfamiliarity with this conceit. There seems to be no parallel in Classical Latin for *crepo* of the sound of water, but cf. Virg. *G.* 1.449, *A.* 11.299 (*crepito*), Ov. *Tr.* 1.4.24 (*increpo*).

49 iniussae ... capellae: for domestic animals functioning without supervision, cf. 1.26, 2.12nn., Hom. *Od.* 9.447–52 (the Cyclops Polyphemus' ram), Theocr. *Id.* 11.12–13 (his sheep), Virg. *Ecl.* 4.21–2 (cf. 2.46n.) *ipsae lacte domum referent distenta capellae | ubera*, Thomas on Virg. *G.* 3.3.16–17 ('golden age' goats), Petr. 45.4 (parody) *dices hic porcos coctos ambulare*, Gatz (1967) 229. In some 'happy' times and places there are no domestic animals at all (2.59–60n.).

ueniunt ad mulctra: cf. Virg. *Ecl.* 3.30 [*uitula*] *bis uenit ad mulctram*. The fem. *mulctra* seems to be the normal word for 'milk pail', the neut. (first here and always plural) a metrical expedient (*ThLL* VIII 1565–6).

51 nec ... circumgemit ursus: either because there are no wild beasts, or because, as in many 'utopias', there is 'pax inter animalia' (Gatz (1967) 171–3, 229); cf. Virg. *Ecl.* 4.22 (33n.), Thomas on *G.* 3.537–8 (the Noric plague brings a 'reversion to a diseased golden age') *non lupus insidias explorat ouilia circum | nec gregibus nocturnus obambulat*. Between this theme and an *adynaton* (33n.) 'the boundary ... is very narrow' (Gatz (1967) 173). *circumgemo* (only here) may be yet another Horatian coinage (cf. *circummugio* (*C.* 2.16.33–4 (7.3n.)), *circumfremo*, Greek *peribremō, periklaiō, amphiachō*). Verbs compounded with *circum* are usually trans., but not always (*circumerro, circumsono*), which may make *ouili* (app. crit.) *lectio difficilior*.

uespertinus 'at evening' (adj. for adv.); cf. 1.18n., *S.* 1.6.113, 2.4.17 *uespertinus ... hospes*, *Ep.* 1.6.20, Brink on *Ars* 269 (*nocturnus*), Virg. *G.* 3.538 (above). Given the location of the 'happy fields' there may be a play on *uespertinus* in the sense 'western' (*S.* 1.4.30 *uespertina ... regio*, *OLD* s.v. 2).

52 nec intumescit ... uiperis: the verb (first here) may be 'transferred' from the vipers (Cic. *Vat.* 4 *tamquam serpens e latibulis ... inflato collo, tumidus ceruicibus*, Virg. *A.* 2.472, *OLD* s.v. *tumidus* 1a). Snakes are excluded from many 'utopias' (*C.* 1.17.8, 3.4.17–18 ('ideal landscapes'), Virg. *Ecl.* 4.24, Thomas on *G.* 2.153–4, 3.544–5). Their absence here might also make the place less attractive to Medea (58) and other witches (3.6, 5.15, 17.29nn.).

alta ... humus: possibly 'the deep ground', where vipers tend to nest (Plin. *Nat.* 8.139 *serpentium ... uipera sola terra dicitur condi*); cf. Lucr. 6.583–4 (a subterranean wind) *altam | diffindens terram*, Ov. Met. 4.239–40 (a burial) *alta | ... humo*, Plin. *Nat.* 18.175 *altum et graue solum*, *ThLL* I 1779. But H. could be glossing Greek *bathus* (lit. 'deep') in its sense 'fertile' (Orelli; cf. Hom. *Il.* 10.353, 18.547 *neioio batheiēs* ('deep fallow-land'), Hdt. 4.23.1 *gē ... bathugaios* ('deep-soiled soil'), Eur. *Andr.* 637 *batheian gēn*). It seems less likely that *alta* is predicate (*OLD* s.v. *altus* 1b), 'the ground is not a heaving mass of vipers' (Wickham).

53–6 The temperate climate (56n.) resembles that of Homer's Olympus, 'Elysian plain', and Phaeacia, Pindar's 'isle of the blest', and Sertorius' 'Atlantic islands' (41–60n.), as well as the idealized landscapes of Virgil's Italy (Thomas on *G.* 2.149) and H.'s own Sabine country (*C.* 1.17, 3.13, *Ep.* 1.10, 16) and Tarentum (*C.* 2.6; cf. Thomas (1982) 14–21).

53 felices mirabimur: for *felix* = *beatus*, cf. 12.25n. 'Utopias' and other strange places traditionally inspire 'wonder' (*C.* 3.25.14, Hom. *Od.* 7.45 (the city of the Phaeacians is) *thauma idesthai* ('a wonder to behold'), Virg. *G.* 1.38 *Elysios miretur Graecia campos*, Thomas (1982) 2, 23, 80).

largis: the adj. usually has a positive sense of 'generous' (e.g. Virg. *G.* 1.23 [*di*] *quique satis largum caelo demittitis imbrem*, *OLD* s.v. 3), but cf. Lucr. 1.282–3 (a destructive flood) *quam largis imbribus auget | montibus ex altis magnus decursus aquai.*

54 aquosus Eurus ... radat: cf. *S.* 2.6.25 *Aquilo radit terras*, Lucr. 5.256 *ripas radentia flumina rodunt. aquosus* and the other *-osus* forms in this poem (60, 62) are 'normal words' (3.18n.; cf. Ernout (1949) 13, 63, 73), although H. might be imitating Virg. *Ecl.* 10.66 *hiemis ... aquosae* (cf. *G.* 4.234, *A.* 4.52 *aquosus Orion*). Since it blows from the east (10.5n.) it seems unlikely that Eurus would even reach these western islands.

55 pinguia ... glaebis: another golden line (7n.) with both epithets possibly felt with both nouns, 'the seeds are not dried up in the rich soil' (Kenney). In agricultural contexts *pinguis* (a key word in Virgil's *Georgics* (Thomas on *G.* 1.8)) is normally used, not of seeds, but of their 'products' (e.g. 2.55) or the land in which they are planted (*C.* 3.4.15–16 *aruum | pingue*).

56 utrumque ... temperante 'moderating each of the two (extremes of climate)'. For *utrumque* (neut.) as a collective pronoun, cf. *S.* 2.4.7 *siue ... naturae ... siue artis, mirus utroque, Ars* 271, *OLD* s.v. *uterque* 2c. Jupiter (below) is often described as a 'moderator' of the natural world (N–H on *C.* 1.12.14–16, 3.4.45–8), but the verb here may also evoke ancient theories of *temperies* (*Ep.* 1.16.8) as the cause of fertility and absence of disease (Thomas (1982) 23; cf. 61–2n.).

rege ... caelitum: i.e. Jupiter (*C.* 4.4.2 *rex deorum*). In a number of 'utopias' past (e.g. Hes. *Op.* 111, Virg. *Ecl.* 4.6, 6.41, *G.* 2.536–8, *A.* 8.319–27) and present (West on Hes. (?) *Op.* 173a) the ruler is not Jupiter (Zeus) but his predecessor Saturn (Cronus; cf. Gatz (1967) 228–9). *caeles* (only here in H.) seems to be an archaism (*ThLL* III 66–7).

57–60 Not even the great seafarers of myth reached the islands. The absence of such 'intruders' indicates the remoteness of the place and perhaps 'raises the implicit question of how everyday Romans are to get there' (Romm (1992) 163). It probably also suggests the absence of corrupting influences (61–2n.), especially seafaring and warfare, which were unknown to the 'golden race' (64n.) and other 'happy' folk, but are the banes of succeeding ages (2.2n., N–H on *C.* 1.3, West on Hes. *Op.* 236–7, Virg. *Ecl.* 4.31–6, *G.* 1.136–8, 2.140–2, 539–40, Smith on Tib. 1.3.37–40, 47–8, Gatz (1967) 229). In Hesiod 'the isles of the blest' are reserved for (some of) the heroes (*Op.* 167–73; cf. 63n.), although not necessarily those mentioned here (58n.). H. seems to follow Virgil (*Ecl.* 4.31–6, but cf. *A.* 6.477–93) in seeing the heroes as no more 'pious' (63–6n.) than any other mortals.

57 non huc ... pinus: the *huc* seems to create the impression (cf. *ubi* 43, *illuc* 49), soon dispelled (*illa ... litora* 63), that H. has already reached the 'happy fields'. For *pinus* = ship made of pine (a kind of metonymy), cf. *C.* 1.14.11, Cat. 64.1–2 (of *Argo*), Virg. *Ecl.* 4.38–9 *nec nautica pinus | mutabit merces*, Tib. 1.3.37 (in the golden age) *nondum caeruleas pinus contempserat undas*.

Argoo ... remige: collective sing.; cf. Virg. *A.* 4.588, 5.116 *uelocem Mnestheus agit acri remige Pristim*. It is not clear if this use of *remex* is poetic or technical (cf. Liv. 26.36.12, 37.10.9). This seems to be the first instance of the epithet *Argous* in Latin (= Greek *Argōios*; cf.

Eur. *Med.* 477, *Andr.* 793, Ap. Rhod. 1.319 etc.). After the Argonauts obtained the Golden Fleece at Colchis (58n.), their return journey took them west, in some versions as far as the western Ocean (Diod. Sic. 4.56.3, *Orph. Argonaut.* 1030–1204). The *Argo* is sometimes considered the first ship (Pease on Cic. *Nat.* 2.89) and can be a symbol of seafaring and its evils (Virg. *Ecl.* 4.34–5, Romm (1992) 169).

58 impudica ... Colchis: the place was not contaminated by the sinister Medea (3.9–18, 5.61–6nn.). The substantive *Colchis* (first here in Latin; cf. Eur. *Med.* 132) may evoke the evil repute of her homeland (5.24n.), and the epithet (only here in H.) her crimes of treachery and kin-murder (AG (1971) 51–2). Yet there was a tradition that Medea married Achilles and ruled with him over the 'Elysian plain' or the 'isles of the blest' (Ibycus, fr. 291, Simonides, fr. 558 *PMG*, Ap. Rhod. 4.811–15 with scholia, Apollodorus, *Epit.* 5.5). *impudicus* occurs in comedy and Catullus (29.2, 10), but also in Senecan tragedy (*Phaed.* 704, 707, 735).

59 Sidonii ... nautae: possibly the followers of Dido and thus ancestors of Hannibal and the Carthaginians (8), or of Cadmus (Porph.), the founder of Thebes which, as the world's 'oldest city' (Var. *R.* 3.1.2–3, F. Vian, *Les origines de Thèbes* (Paris 1963) 76–87), could be a symbol of 'urban blight' (41–2n.). But H. might mean the Phoenicians in general, who were famous for voyages into the western Ocean (Romm (1992) 18–20, 126–7) as well as for greed and treachery (Hom. *Od.* 15.415–84 etc.). *cornua* here means the tips of the *antemnae*, the cross-pieces of the mast (N–H on *C.* 1.14.6, Williams on Virg. *A.* 3.549, 5.831–2). This sounds like a technical usage, but it is attested only in verse (*ThLL* IV 970) as are its Greek models or cognates *keraia* and (in this sense) *keros* (LSJ s.vv.).

60 laboriosa ... cohors: cf. 17.16. Among their *labores* was sailing west through Ocean to the land of the dead (41n.; cf. Romm (1992) 183–96). H. may imply that they, too, would have polluted the 'happy fields'; cf. *Ep.* 1.6.63 *remigium uitiosum Ithacensis Vlixei*, Hom. *Od.* 1.7 (their 'blind wickedness' (*atasthaliai*)).

Vlixei: scanned *Vlixeī* (17.14, 16, *C.* 1.6.7, 15.34, 2.19.14, 3.16.41), but cf. *Vlixeī* (v.ll. *Vlixi*, *-is*) at *Ep.* 1.6.63 (above), and *Lynceī* (v.l. *Lynceis*) at *S.* 1.2.90. This particular form of the gen. is first attested in H. and may have been invented by him for his lyric poetry (N–H on *C.* 1.15.34, M. Leumann, *Mus. Helv.* 2 (1945) 237–58).

61–2 H. may mean that with no outsiders (57–60) 'contaminating' the islands 'isolation protects their flocks and herds from disease as [in 63–6] it protects men from moral contagion' (Wickham). Yet it is not clear why, after eight lines on crops and humans (53–60), he should suddenly return to animals, or how, unless he refers to Medea's sorcery (5.45–6n.), outsiders could be responsible for 'astral violence'. It is possible that the couplet is interpolated (ed. Bipontina (1783); cf. 61n.), or that it belongs after line 52 (Heinze, Klingner) or 56 (Sh. Bailey), where it would fit the theme of 'moderate climate' (53–6n.; cf. H. Reynen, *Gymn. Beihefte* 4 (1964) 77–104, AG (1971) 49–51, Thomas (1982) 32). But none of the 'transposers' offers a convincing explanation as to how the dislocation occurred. The fact that Porph. does not comment on these lines is probably not significant, since he is also silent on 39–40, 43–4, and 51–2.

61 nulla ... contagia: cf. Virg. *Ecl.* 1.50 *nec mala uicini pecoris contagia laedent.* 'Contagions' can also be caused by climate (Thomas on Virg. *G.* 3.478–566 (the Noric plague)) or spread from humans (57–60) to animals (Lucr. 6.1215–24). *contagia* (only plural in Republican Latin) seems to be a poetic substitute, perhaps coined by Lucretius (Kenney on 3.345), for *contagio.* There was no disease in the 'golden age' (Hes. *Op.* 116, Gatz (1967) 229).

nullius astri: especially the 'Dog Star' Sirius (1.27n.); cf. Virg. *A.* 10.273–4 *Sirius ardor | ille sitim morbosque ferens mortalibus aegris.* The variant *Austri* (10.4) is possible, except that there is no reason why the south wind could not reach the islands (cf. 54n.). For the scansion *nullīus* (*nullīus* at *Ep.* 1.17.22, *Ars* 320, 324), cf. *Ep.* 1.1.14, Lucr. 1.224, 926, 4.1, LHS I 479. *nullius* is rare in elevated verse (once in Virgil (*G.* 4.453), Tibullus (1.9.31), 3× in Ovid (cf. McKeown on *Am.* 1.14.14), not in Propertius etc.), and this is the only instance in H.'s lyrics. It may be 'Lucretian' (cf. on *contagia*) or, perhaps, evidence that the couplet is interpolated (61–2n.).

62 torret impotentia: cf. *C.* 3.1.31–2 *torrentia agros | sidera*, *S.* 1.5.78, Virg. *G.* 4.425 *torrens sitientis Sirius Indos.* This seems to be the first instance of *impotentia* ('fury') used of natural forces, but cf. *C.* 3.30.3 *Aquilo impotens*, Cat. 4.18 *impotentia freta.* In ethics, if not in physics, *impotentia* can be an opposite of *temperantia* (56n.; cf. Cic. *Tusc.* 4.34). The word is attested in Latin tragedy (*inc. trag.* 66 *ROL* = Cic. *Tusc.* 4.35).

63-6 Jupiter reserved the islands for a 'pious race' when he 'stained the golden age with bronze' and 'hardened' it 'with iron'. H., as a *uates*, can provide escape for the 'pious'.

The emphasis on 'piety' as a requisite for inhabitants raises the question of whether Jupiter would accept even the 'better part' (37) of the Romans, since they still belong to an *impia ... deuoti sanguinis aetas* (19).

Jupiter's role in this recalls that of Zeus in the Hesiodic Prometheus myth (*Th.* 507–617, *Op.* 42–105) and especially the 'myth of the ages' (*Op.* 109–201). In the former, humans live a carefree existence until Zeus ruins it with hardship and suffering (cf. Virgil's 'theodicy' (*G.* 1.118–46)). In the latter, he replaces a happy 'golden race' (64n.) that died out of 'natural causes' first with disastrous 'silver' and 'bronze' (65n.) races, then with a 'juster and better' race of heroes (63n.), who are the ancestors (Clay (1989) 166–7) of the current 'iron race'. This last, although in many ways the worst of the lot, can still, if they listen to Hesiod, hope to recover some of the happiness of the golden and heroic races (*Op.* 225–37). Like many who adapt this myth (e.g. Arat. *Phaen.* 96–136 (= *HA* 427–67), Virg. *Ecl.* 4, Ov. *Met.* 1.89–150; cf. Gatz (1967) 52–103), H. 'simplifies' it by omitting the silver and heroic races (57–60n.). This results in a conception even more pessimistic than that of Hesiod, since the decline of humanity seems uninterrupted and, perhaps (64–5n.), irreversible. Cf. *C.* 3.6.45–6 *damnosa quid non imminuit dies?* | *aetas parentum peior auis tulit* | *nos nequiores, mox daturos* | *progeniem uitiosiorem.*

63 secreuit ... litora: cf. Hes. *Op.* 158–9, 166–71 (for the text, cf. West *ad loc.*) 'Zeus Cronides made a juster and better divine race of heroes ... some (of these) the end of death covered over, | but having granted others livelihood and dwelling apart from humans, | Zeus Cronides the father settled them at the edges of the earth | far from the immortal (gods). Cronus is their king, | and they dwell having hearts free of care | in the islands of the blest beside deep-eddying Ocean.' There are other places 'reserved' for deserving mortals, but most of them are in the land of the dead (N–H on *C.* 2.13.23, Cic. *Rep.* 6.16, Virg. *A.* 6.637–709, 8.670, Lattimore (1962) 32–43 (epitaphs), Gatz (1967) 232).

64-5 inquinauit ... durauit: taken in a metaphorical sense the verbs suggest moral 'corruption' (*C.* 3.6.18–19 *fecunda culpae saecula nuptias* | *primum inquinauere et genus et domos, OLD* s.v. *inquino* 3) and an existence made 'harsh' and 'cruel' (5.30, 11.21–2nn., *C.* 1.35.35 (9n.), s.v. *durus* 5, 8). But their literal meaning may offer a slight hope, since the 'gold', even though 'stained' and 'hardened' with baser metals, has not been eliminated and could perhaps be recovered.

Jupiter's 'metallurgy' is not entirely supernatural: gold was often alloyed with copper to make 'Corinthian bronze' (Plin. *Nat.* 34.8), and the ancients knew that gold (and silver) could be extracted from rock formations that also contained copper and iron ('chalcopyrites'; cf. J. Healy, *Mining and metallurgy in the Greek and Roman worlds* (London 1978) 37–8).

aere ... | aere: the repetition seems to emphasize the 'brazenness' of the age, perhaps because H.'s Romans are especially like the Hesiodic 'bronze race ... terrible and mighty, who cared only for the grievous works of Ares and for acts of violence ... and (who) having been destroyed at their own hands, went nameless into ... Hades' (*Op.* 143–55; cf. Arat. *Phaen.* 129–36, where Justice (Dike) abandons earth with the advent of the bronze race). There may be a play on *aes* in the sense 'money', which was often seen as a corruptor of humans in general and of Republican Rome in particular (e.g. *C.* 2.18, 3.6.29–36, 24.33–67, Sall. *Cat.* 10.3–4, Jal (1963) 384–9); cf. Virg. *A.* 8.326–7 (the end of Saturn's 'golden age' in Italy (56n.)) *deterior donec paulatim ac decolor aetas | et belli rabies et amor successit habendi.*

Some consider the repetition of *aere* 'unsuitable' (Brink (1982) 44) and prefer (in 65) the variant *aerea* (cf. Arat. *Phaen.* 130 *chalkeiē geneē* = Germ. *Arat.* 133 *aerea ... proles*). But H. does not use this adj. elsewhere (*aeneus* 7×) or, it seems, scan *dehinc* as a monosyllable (but cf. *S.* 1.5.97 (*dehinc* v.l. for *dein*), *S.* 1.6.39 *deicere*, *S.* 1.3.101 etc. (*dein, deinde, deinceps*)).

64 tempus aureum: cf. *C.* 4.2.39–40 *quamuis redeant in aurum | tempora priscum*, Thomas on Virg. *G.* 2.538 *aureus ... Saturnus* (56n.), *A.* 6.791–2, 8.324–5 *aurea ... saecula.* H.'s phrase, which casts the myth in 'temporal' rather than 'racial' terms (below), seems to connect the end of the poem with the opening 'chronology' of civil war (1n.). In Greek texts the usual phrase is 'golden race' (*genos, geneē*; cf. Gatz (1967) 228). There are some Latin parallels (Cic. *Nat.* 2.159 (based on Arat. *Phaen.* 114) *aureo genere*, Virg. *Ecl.* 4.9 *gens aurea*, Ov. *Met.* 1.89, 15.96 *aurea ... aetas* (but cf. 1n.)), but most Roman authors prefer temporal expressions. The difference may indicate that while the Greeks tended to view the myth as 'anthropology', it appealed to the Romans more as 'history' (Gatz (1967) 203–6).

65 quorum: probably objective gen. with *fuga*, 'escape from which' (*S.* 2.6.95 *leti fuga*, Virg. *A.* 9.538–9 *malorum | uelle fugam*), although it could be felt as possessive with *piis*, 'for the pious of which' (Cat. 14.23 *saecli incommoda, pessimi poetae*, Ov. *Met.* 8.97 (Scylla) *nostri infamia saecli*, Cic. *Quinct.* 7 *huiusce aetatis homines disertissimos*). But even if there are such folk in the world, they are unlikely to be Romans (63–6n.).

66 secunda ... datur fuga: cf. Virg. *A.* 67.23–4 (to prevent the 'pious' Trojans (21) from meeting Circe) *Neptunus uentis impleuit uela secundis | atque fugam dedit*. There seems to be no parallel for *secunda* (23n.) of *fuga*, a word whose epithets are usually pejorative (*ThLL* VI 1472).

66 uate me: H. will guide his followers as the 'seers' (*manteis*) Calchas, Proteus, and Tiresias respectively guided the Greeks to Troy (Hom. *Il.* 1.68–72), Menelaus home to Sparta (*Od.* 4.472–80), and Ulysses to Ithaca (11.100–37; cf. *S.* 2.5.5–6). For the term *uates* (17.44), cf. N–H on *C.* 1.1.35, Brink on *Ep.* 2.1.118–38, 2.94, *Ars* 400, Skutsch on Enn. *Ann.* 207, O'Hara (1990) 176–84. H.'s use of it here seems meant to explain how he has the knowledge (7.15–20n.) to find what Jupiter 'concealed'. But it may also cast doubt on the whole enterprise, since 'vatic' divination was often 'linked to deceit, charlatanry, and the propagation of harmful ... *ficta somnia*' (O'Hara (1990) 177, citing Lucr. 1.102–6). Cf. Enn. *Sc.* 319–22 Vahlen (= Cic. *Div.* 1.132) *superstitiosi uates impudentesque harioli, | aut inertes aut insani aut quibus egestas imperat | qui sibi semitam non sapiunt, alteri monstrant uiam; | quibus diuitias pollicentur* [42n.], *ab iis drachumam ipsi petunt*, Cic. *Div.* 1.113–17, 2.12 *num igitur ... quae tempestas impendeat, uates melius coniciet quam gubernator?*

EPODE 17

Introduction

H. pleads with Canidia to stop tormenting him: he is willing to admit the power of her magic and to lie about how wonderful she is.

Canidia's answer is that she will show no mercy: for the crimes he has committed he will be punished until he begs in vain for death.

The form of this poem, direct speech without any narrative 'frame', has been traced to a variety of sources, including lyric (cf. *C.* 1.28, 3.9, Sappho, fr. 1 L–P), mime, epigram (e.g. Cat. 67), bucolic, and satire (*S.* 2.3, 4, 5, 7), but it could be based on early Greek *iambus*. Although there seems to be no parallel in the surviving fragments, the connection of *iambus* with Greek drama (West (1974) 33–7) and the form of certain Hellenistic imitations (Call. *Iamb.* 9, Herondas, *Mimiamboi*) suggest that it, too, may have featured 'dialogue' of this sort. This is not to say that *iambus* is H.'s only source here: he seems to draw as well on magical texts (cf. 5 intro.), epic (e.g. 11–14n.), drama (12, 31–2nn.), and, especially, the lyric palinode of Stesichorus (42–4n.).

The 'palinode' section of H.'s speech is clearly meant to be humorous (37–52n.), but the overall tone of the poem may be more serious. H. seems to suffer the torments not only of the absurd Varus (16–36n.) but also of the innocent boy (1–18n.) who is in turn so similar to the 'primal victim' Remus (5 intro.). This suggests that Epode 17, like the other Canidia poems, is another symbolic representation of the curse afflicting both individual and city (App. 2). As the conclusion to a sequence of highly pessimistic poems (14 intro.) and, indeed, to the whole Epode book (81n.), the image of 'Canidia triumphant' could not be more disturbing and ominous (53–81n.).

1–18 The poet begs Canidia through her gods and the sources of her magic to stop her attacks. He appeals to mythic exempla: Telephus was healed by Achilles, Achilles returned Hector's corpse, Circe restored Ulysses' men to humanity.

The opening recalls the boy's prayer in 5.1–10, and H. may even intend his readers to think at first that the speaker is yet another innocent victim of Canidia's arts.

1 Iam iam ... do manus: as if 'already' (2.68n.) surrendering to an enemy (*OLD* s.v. *manus* 9d). This is the first of a series of military images (24, 25, 27, 36, 43, 56, 71, 73–5).

efficaci ... scientiae: for the epithet, cf. 3.17n. The term *scientia* (only here in H., otherwise mostly in prose) may be meant to flatter Canidia (cf. 5.72), since magic was usually referred to as an 'art' (e.g. 81, Virg. *A.* 4.493, Ov. *Am.* 1.8.5, 15.10) rather than a 'science' (Ingallina (1974) 153–6).

2 supplex: he is reduced to the condition of the wax puppet at *S.* 1.8.32–3 *cerea [effigies] suppliciter stabat, seruilibus ut quae | iam peritura modis.* The *et* here may be postponed (1.12n.) or co-ordinated with that in line 3.

regna per Proserpinae: a poetic euphemism; cf. N–H on *C.* 2.13.21, 3.4.46, Virg. *A.* 6.154 *regna inuia uiuis,* and Greek 'house of Persephone' (Theogn. 974, 1296 West etc.). For repeated *per* in prayer, cf. 5.5–8n. Proserpina figures more in literature than in cult at Rome (Wissowa (1912) 309–13, *RE* suppl. ix 1283–7), but her Greek counterpart Persephone-Kore is a goddess of witches (Tupet (1976) 14) and she is invoked in a first-century BC lead tablet cursing a certain Plotius (*CIL* i 2.2520 = *ROL* iv pp. 280–5): *bona pulchra Proserpina, Plutonis uxor ... eripias salutem, corpus, colorem* [21n.], *uires, uirtutes Ploti ... tradas illum febri quartenae, tertianae, cotidianae* [30] *... do tibi pectus, iocinera, cor, pulmones* [26], *ni possit sentire quid sibi doleat, intestina, uenter, umbilicus, latera, ni possit dormire* [24–6n.]

Dianae ... numina: cf. 5.51, 54nn. and, for poetic pl., *numina,* Virg. *G.* 1.30, [Tib.] 3.6.22, Ov. *Met.* 3.291 etc.

non mouenda: probably 'not to be provoked (rashly)' (*non lacessenda* Porph.); cf. 76, 15.3n., 13.6n., *C.* 3.21.6, *S.* 1.10.78 *men moueat cimex Pantilius,* 2.1.45–6 *qui me commorit ... | flebit.* But there may be a hint of *moueo* in the sense 'persuade', 'sway' (8, *C.* 1.21.16, 2.4.4–6, *Ars* 433), as if H. is acknowledging from the start that his prayer will be in vain.

4 libros: like the archetypes of the Greek magical papyri (*PGM*; cf. Betz's introduction) and certain scrolls burned at Rome in 13 BC (Suet. *Aug.* 31.1) and at Ephesus in the time of Paul (Acts 19:18–20). For *carmina,* 'incantations', cf. 5.72. *ualentium* governs *deuocare* (5.87, *C.* 3.25.15–16 *Baccharumque ualentium | proceras manibus uertere fraxinos*).

5 refixa: cf. Virg. *A.* 5.527–8 (of shooting stars) *caelo ... refixa ... sidera,* and, for the image, Enn. *Ann.* 27, 145 Skutsch *caelum prospexit stellis fulgentibus aptum,* Plin. *Nat.* 2.28 *sidera, quae adfixa diximus mundo.* Veia performs a *kathairesis* of the stars at 5.45–6; cf. 78n. below.

7 Spinning gadgets, the *iunx* ('magic wheel') and the *rhombus* or *rhombē* ('bull roarer') were often used in magic spells, either for hypnotism or as surrogates for the intended victims. Cf. Eupolis, *Baptai* (a play about the rites of Cotyto (56n.)) fr. 83 *PCG* 'O *rhombē* chewing me up!', Gow on Theocr. *Id.* 2.17 (= *HA* 590), Tupet (1976) 50–5. *turben* here could indicate either device (Schol.; cf. Serv. on *Ecl.* 8.21, who translates Theocritus' *iunx* as *turbo*), but the word usually means 'child's top', and H. may be mocking Canidia by implying that her apparatus is a 'toy'.

citumque: participial, 'set spinning'; cf. 9.20, Pl. *Ps.* 745 *turbo non aeque citust*, Tib. 1.5.3 *agor ut per plana citus sola uerbere turbo*, Virg. *A.* 7.378–80 *turbo*, | *quem pueri . . . exercent*.

retro solue: so as to 'reverse' the effect of the spell and 'unbind' H. (45; cf. 5.15, 71nn.). Since a top both spins on its axis and moves in a line, *retro* could go either with *citum* ('set spinning in reverse') or with *solue* ('release (to go) back').

8 nepotem ... Nereium: a poetic expression (9.7n.), perhaps emphasizing Achilles' relation to Nereus, the 'old man of the sea' famous for truth and kindness (Hes. *Th.* 233–6, N–H on *C.* 1.15.5). Cf. the familial resemblance implied at *C.* 1.10.1 *Mercuri, facunde nepos Atlantis* (M. Putnam, *C.P.* 69 (1974) 251–4). The form *Nereĭus* is not attested before H., but its use in Latin (Virg. *A.* 9.102, Ov. *Met.* 7.685, 13.162, *Ilias* 938) suggests that it may have originated in early Greek epic (cf. *C.* 1.17.22 *Semeleius*, Homeric *Capaneios*, *Neleios*, and E. Risch, *Wortbildung der homerischen Sprache* (Bern 1974) 127–8).

Telephus: the king of Mysia, wounded in a skirmish by Achilles and later healed with scrapings from the hero's spear. The story was told in the cyclic *Cypria* and was popular in Greek and Roman tragedy, where Telephus was often depicted as a ragged suppliant (Brink on *Ars* 96, *RE* IVA 366). It was also cited as an example of magic healing; cf. Prop. 2.1.63–4 *Mysus et Haemonia iuuenis qua cuspide uulnus* | *senserat, hac ipsa cuspide sensit opem*, Ov. *Am.* 2.9.7–8, *Rem.* 47–8, *Ib.* 253–4, *Tr.* 5.2.15–16, *Pont.* 2.2.26. Plin. *Nat.* 27.137 mentions a plant *telephion* used for healing skin ailments and wounds.

9 superbus 'in his arrogance' (2.7n.). *ordino* occurs in the *Odes* (2.1.11, 3.1.9, 4.11.20) but seems to be unpoetic (Axelson (1945) 101).

10 tela acuta: like H.'s own iambic 'darts' (K–H); cf. 6.12n., Cic. *De or.* 1.242 (an orator) *cum amentatas hastas acceperit, ipse eas oratoris lacertis uiribusque torquebit*, *Tusc.* 4.77, Cat. 116.3–4, 7–8. *torqueo* and *intorqueo* of missiles seem to refer 'to a rotating motion imparted by a thong (*amentum*)' (Harrison on Virg. *A.* 10.333–4; cf. N–H on *C.* 1.8.12).

11–14 The reference is to the end of the *Iliad*, especially 24.722–6 (the lament for Hector), 22.335–54, 23.182–3 (Achilles' threats against the corpse), and 24.469–570 (Priam's supplication). The story was popular in art and in later poetry (N–H on *C.* 1.10.13), including Ennius' tragedy *Hectoris Lytra* (12n.).

11 luxere: ritual lamentation, usually by women, was a crucial part of ancient Greek funerals (Burkert (1985) 192), and for a corpse to be 'unwept' (*aklautos*) was nearly as bad as for it to be 'unburied' (*athaptos*). Cf. Hom. *Il.* 22.386, 23.9 'let us mourn Patroclus, for that is the privilege of the dead', *Od.* 11.72 (5.83–102n.), Solon, fr. 21 West, Soph. *El.* 870, Eur. *Andr.* 1158–60, Virg. *A.* 11.372 *inhumata infletaque turba*. Most of these passages are cited by Lambinus, Bentley, and Brink (1982) 44–7 in support of *luxere*, but only Campbell and Sh. Bailey among recent editors accept it. The variant *unxere* not only limits the action to a less important aspect of the funeral, but contradicts *Il.* 24.582–90, where the servants of Achilles, not the Trojan women, 'anoint' Hector's corpse. It may be a palaeographical error (Brink) or the fault of an interpolator who knew such passages as *S.* 2.5.85–6, Enn. *Ann.* 147 Skutsch, Virg. *A.* 6.219, and Ov. *F.* 4.853 (Bentley).

matres: the mourners were not all mothers, but Hecuba and Andromache were prominent among them (*Il.* 24.710–59) and motherhood seems to be a special concern of Canidia (50–2, 5.5–6n.). *Ilius* is a rarer form (*Saec.* 37) than *Iliacus* (*C.* 1.15.36, *Ep.* 1.2.16, *Ars* 129) and, despite its occurrence in comedy (*OLD* s.v.), may be more elevated, as *Graius* is than *Graecus* (10.12, Brink in *Ars* 323).

11–12 feris | alitibus: an imitation of Homer's *oiōnoi ōmēstai*, 'flesh-eating birds' (*Il.* 11.453–4), later appropriated by Virg. *A.* 10.559 *alitibus linquere feris*.

12 With its three resolutions – more than in any other Horatian trimeter – this verse would be at home in early Roman drama (Soubiran (1988) 204), perhaps even Ennius' *Hectoris Lytra*. The initial dactyl may also provide an epic or mock-epic feel, or even recall the occasional 'intercalary' hexameter in Hipponax (fr. 23 West; cf. frr. 35, 128–9a, West (1974) 30).

homicidam: a prosaic word, but H. clearly imitates the Homeric formula *Hectoros androphonoio*, 'man-slaying Hector' (*Il.* 1.242 etc.; cf. 24.509, 724 (lamentations)). This is the closest thing in the *Epodes* to a 'compound epithet', and except for those involving numerical prefixes (e.g. *bimaris* (*C.* 1.7.2); 9 others (12 occurrences)), such forms are rare in H.'s other works as well (*C.* 2.19.4, 3.23.8, 4.7.11, 14.25, *Ars* 219). They are more common in earlier Latin poetry, especially epic and Lucretius (Skutsch on Enn. *Ann.* 198, 448, 554, Austin on Virg. *A.* 1.224, Norden on *A.* 6.141), but also in the less elevated verse of Laevius (*poet.* 7–8 *FPL*, Courtney (1993) 123–7) and Catullus (4.13, 11.6–7, 36.7, 58b, 3, 5; cf. Ross (1969) 17–22).

peruicacis ... Achillei: cf. *C.* 1.6.6 *Pelidae ... cedere nescii*, Brink on *Ars* 121 (Achilles) *impiger, iracundus, inexorabilis*, Acc. *trag.* 454–5 (Achilles of himself) *peruicacem dici me esse ... patior*. For the poetic forms *Achillei̯* and *Vlixei̯* (16), cf. 16.60n.

15–18 Cf. Hom. *Od.* 10.229–400. There the men kept their human mind while transformed (240); by having them lose even this (17), H. seems to make their case more like his own (45). Another apparent difference is that in Homer they are restored, not because Circe pities them, but because Odysseus, who has slept with her (333–47), asks it as a favour (383–7). But H. may be implying that he has slept with Canidia: this would make 19–20 more pointed, and be another hint that she is the addressee of Epodes 8 and 12 (App. 2).

15 saetosa: with *membra* (17). The hyperbaton, one of the largest in the *Epodes* (5.17, 9.11–13), may suggest that they only gradually 'stripped their bristly limbs of the harsh pelts'. Cf. Hom. *Od.* 10.393 'from their limbs the bristles receded' (*errheon*; cf. 18n.). The *-osus* adjectives here may contribute to the epic tone, although both belong to the third, 'normal', category of such forms (3.15n., Ernout (1949) 47, 63).

duris ... pellibus: abl. of separation; cf. *Ep.* 1.3.19–20 *cornicula ... | furtiuis nudata coloribus*, Virg. *A.* 2.153 *exutas uinclis ... palmas*.

16 laboriosi: despite 16.60 and the fact that the rowers are the ones who 'suffer', the epithet here probably goes with *Vlixei* to balance those of Hector (12) and Achilles (14) and as a gloss of Homeric *polytlas* ('much-suffering'). In common with other Latin authors, H. is fond of groups where 'the termination of the genitive noun and genitive epithet is the same' (Naylor (1922) xvii). Cf. 58, 1.24, 2.44, 12.21, 15.3.

17 Circa: like her niece Medea (3.9–14, 5.61–6), Circe was an archetype and model for witches (1.30, 5.76, Theocr. *Id.* 2.15–16 (5.61–6n.), Virg. *Ecl.* 8.70, Tupet (1976) 74–5, 120–2). The MSS are divided between *Circa* and the Greek-sounding *Circe* (cf. *C.* 3.12.8 *Bellerophonte*), but the former is supported by Probus, *GLK* IV 7.26.

mens et sonus 'sanity [5.75] and (human) voice'. The men keep the former in Homer (15–18n.); cf. *Od.* 10.239–40 'they had the heads and voice and bristles of pigs | and the shape, but their intelligence [*nous*] was intact as before'.

18 relapsus: sc. *est.* The image of something 'flowing back' is similar to that suggested by *errheon* at *Od.* 10.393 (15n.). *relapsus* is rarer and more poetic than the variant *relatus.*

honor 'beauty, dignity' (Wickham). Cf. 11.6, Hom. *Od.* 10.395–6 (restored by Circe) 'The men at once became younger than they were before | and much more handsome and better to look at.'

18–36 H. recites his sufferings, admits his fault in doubting Canidia's power, and asks how he can end his torment.

Most of his symptoms are conventional both for victims of magic and, not surprisingly, given the amatory purpose of so many spells, for people suffering from unrequited passion. If at the beginning he resembles the *puer*, he now seems more like the 'aged adulterer' Varus (5.81–2).

19 satis superque: a colloquialism (1.31) signalling a shift away from the (mock-) epic style of the opening.

20 'Instead of an honorific epithet [H. delivers] the first sharp blow' (K–H). It may be sharper because the line seems to parody Cat. 8.5 (=37.12) *amata nobis quantum amabitur nulla.* For the evil repute of sailors and pedlars, cf. *C.* 3.6.29–32, *Cat.* 13.23–4, Prop. 4.5.49–50, Ov. *Rem.* 306, Sen. fr. 52 Haase *institores gemmarum sericarumque uestium si intromiseris periculum pudicitiae est.*

21 fugit iuuentas: H. is now like the hags he found so disgusting (8.1–4, 12.7). For the 'flight of youth' cf. N–H on *C.* 2.5.13, 11.5–6 *fugit retro | leuis iuuentas et decor. iuuentas* was originally the name of a goddess (5.8n., N–H on *C.* 1.30.7) first 'metonymized' by Lucretius (5.888–9; cf. his treatment of *V(u)enus*). Cf. *C.* 2.11.6, 4.4.5, and Virg. *A.* 8.160, all of which verge on personification, which is rarely the case with the more prosaic *iuuenta* (e.g. *C.* 1.16.23, 3.14.27, *Ars* 115, Virg. *G.* 3.437).

uerecundus color: cf. Ter. *An.* 878 *uide num eius color pudoris signum usquam indicat*, the curse on Plotius (2n.) *eripias ... colorem*, and *CIL* x 8249 (a later curse table; cf. Audollent (1904) 248) *di inferi uobis commendo illius membra, colorem, figuram, caput, capillos*. Pallor is a common symptom of love (N–H on *C.* 1.13.5–6); cf. Theocr. *Id.* 2.88–9 (Simaitha) 'my colour often becomes like that of fustic [a source of yellow dye], | all of my hair flowed off my head, and only bones and skin are left [22n.]', Ov. *Ars* 1.729 *palleat omnis amans: hic est color aptus amanti*.

22 relinquor ossa 'I am left bones covered with sallow skin'. For the predicative construction, cf. 16.20, Cato, *Agr.* 32.1 *ne [rami] nimium crebri relinquantur*, LHS II 43. *relinquor* is Peerlkamp's conjecture based on the variant (or gloss) *amictus*. With *reliquit* (most editors) the subject has to be *uerecundus color*. This disrupts the natural reading of line 21 and seems to make little sense, since 'colour' can leave the skin but not the bones, which are already white (Bentley). Bentley's own *ora* for *ossa* (cf. 7.15) resolves the second difficulty, but eliminates the topos 'reduced to skin and bones' (Hom. *Od.* 16.145, Gow on Theocr. *Id.* 2.90, Pl. *Aul.* 564, *Capt.* 135, Lucr. 6.1270, Prop. 4.5.64).

23 odoribus: either an unguent (*C.* 1.5.2, *Ep.* 2.1.269) like that employed against Varus (5.59, 69), or the stench from Canidia's magic fires (35). H. mentions elsewhere that he was prematurely grey (N–H on *C.* 2.11.15, 3.14.25, *Ep.* 1.7.26, 20.24). For the prosaic *capillus*, cf. 5.16.

24–6 Cf. the curse on Plotius (2n.) and the formula *aufer illae [illi] somnum* in later tablets (Audollent (1904) 302, 341, 371; cf. *PGM* IV 356). Sleeplessness (*C.* 3.7.5–8, Smith on Tib. 1.2.76) and respiratory ailments (11.10) also afflict lovers.

24 nullum a labore ... otium 'no respite from suffering'. Cf. Ter. *Hau.* 75 *tantumne ab re tuast oti tibi*, Liv. 3.14.1 *ab externis armis otium*, 32.4 etc., *ThLL* I 13, Soph. *O.T.* 1280 *scholēi kakou* ('respite of ill') Eur. *Herc.* 725 *scholēn ... ponōn* ('of toils'). For *reclino*, 'lay to rest', cf. *C.* 2.3.7, Cic. *Arat.* 665, Sen. *Dial.* 1.3.9 *fatigatum corpus ... reclinauit*, *OLD* s.v. 1a.

25 urget: for the image, cf. N–H on *C.* 2.18.15 *truditur dies die*.

est = *licet*; cf. *S.* 1.2.79, 101, 5.87, 2.5.103, *Ep.* 1.1.32. The construction seems to be based on Greek *esti* and *exesti* and is rare in prose before the Empire (Austin on Virg. *A.* 6.596, LHS II 349).

26 leuare ... praecordia: a poetic way of saying *numquam possum respirare*. *spiritu* probably goes both with *leuare* ('ease [13.10] my innards [3.5] by breathing') and *tenta* ('innards distended [12.12, 16.50] with air').

27 ergo: a rare word in H.'s lyric (2.9n.). Since H. does not elsewhere 'deny' the efficacy of magic, *negatum* would seem to mean *id quod homines negauerunt* rather than, as most commentators take it, *id quod antea negaueram*.

uincor: continuing the military metaphor (1n.), although *uinco* can mean 'persuade' without any idea of force (43).

28 Sabella: pertaining to the Sabellic inhabitants of Samnium, including the Marsi (29, 5.76n.) and Paeligni (60n.). Cf. *C.* 3.6.38, *S.* 1.9.29-30 *instat fatum mihi triste, Sabella | quod puero cecinit diuina mota anus urna*, 2.1.36, *Ep.* 1.16.49, E. T. Salmon, *Samnium and the Samnites* (Cambridge 1967) 30-3, *EV* IV 626-7.

increpare: the meaning is either 'that incantations cause a (victim's) breast to roar (with pain)' (cf. Ov. *Ib.* 226 (the Furies) *cruentatas increpuere manus*, *OLD* s.v. *increpo* 2) or 'that incantations assail a (victim's) breast' (*C.* 4.15.1-2 *Phoebus ... me ... increpuit lyra*, s.v. 5). Attempts at emendation include *incremare* (Palmer), *et cremare* (Sh. Bailey), and *macerare* (Nisbet (1989) 95).

29 caputque: probably the head of a witch's human victim (cf. 5.74, *CIL* x 8249 (21n.)), although the Marsi were especially adept at smashing snakes (5.76, Lucil. 605-6 *ROL Marsus colubras | disrumpit cantu*, Virg. *Ecl.* 8.71, Fordyce on *A.* 7.750, Ov. *Am.* 2.1.35). *dissilio*, which may be a Lucretian coinage (1.385 etc.), seems to remain a poetic word (*Ep.* 1.18.42, *ThLL* VI 1.1469).

nenia: a repetitious chant and so, as here, a spell (cf. Ov. *Ars* 2.102 *mixta cum magicis nenia Marsa sonis*, *F.* 6.142), but also a dirge (N-H on *C.* 2.1.38, 20.21, 3.28.16), a child's jingle (*Ep.* 1.1.63), or doggerel (Petr. 46.4). Cf. J. Heller, *T.A.P.A.* 74 (1943) 215-68.

30 A line which would not be out of place in Roman comedy; cf. Ter. *Ph.* 1035 *ignosce: orat, confitetur, purgat: quid uis amplius?*, Pl. *Trin.* 1070 *mare, terra, caelum, di uostram fidem*, Ter. *Ad.* 790 *o caelum, o terra, o maria Neptuni*.

ardeo: fire consumes victims of magic (3.8, 5.24, 81-2), but also of desire (11.4, 13, 27, 14.9-10, 13-14).

31-2 atro ... | Nessi cruore: the blood was meant to be a love charm (3.17-18n.). It was 'black' because of contamination with the Hydra venom on Hercules' arrows. Cf. Soph. *Trach.* 572-5 (the dying Nessus to Deianira) 'If you take the coagulated blood from my wound, darkened by the Hydra's poison on Heracles' arrow, you will have a charm to win your husband back' (Easterling's paraphrase; the text is difficult), Thomas on Virg. *G.* 1.129, 2.130. For *delibutus* and *cruor*, cf. 3.6, 13nn. Canidia seems to take the reference to Hercules, who ended his torment by having himself cremated, as a hint that H. intends to commit suicide (6on.).

32-3 Sicana ... flamma: probably 'the Sicilian fire flourishing in boiling Aetna', although, as in a 'golden line' (e.g. 16.55n.), both epithets could be felt with both nouns (cf. *S.* 1.1.38 *feruidus aestus*, Ov. *Ib.* 596 *Sicanis Aetna*). *Sicanus* (only here in H.) as a poetic word for 'Sicilian' seems to have been introduced to Latin by Virgil (*Ecl.* 10.4). For Mt Etna, still an active volcano, as a symbol of intense heat, cf. Fordyce on Cat. 68.53 *cum tantum arderem quantum Trinacria rupes.*

33 uirens: lit. 'flourishing', an odd verb for a flame (hence the early conjectures *urens* and *furens*). But from Homer on (*Il.* 9.212) 'omnia, quae propria sunt herbis et floribus, tribuntur igni' (Peerlkamp). Cf. Lucr. 1.900 (tree branches) *flammai fulserunt flore coorto,* 4.450, Fordyce on Virg. *A.* 7.804 *florentis aere cateruas.* It is possible that *uirens* is an epithet (but cf. 1.26n.) indicating the 'greenish' colour of sulphur-fed volcanic fire (Orelli), but this might be better expressed by *lurens* (J. H. Onions, *C.R.* 1 (1887) 243-4, Sh. Bailey); cf. Ov. *Met.* 14.791 *lurida ... sulpura.*

donec: an archaic word occurring mostly in verse before Livy (Brink on *Ep.* 2.2.148, LHS II 629), although this is the only instance in the *Epodes* (5× in *Odes*, 12× in hexameters).

34 iniuriosis: to deny H.'s ashes burial would be a great *iniuria* (5.99n., 10.21-4, 16.13-14). Witches were thought to be able to control the winds and other meteoric phenomena; cf. Heubeck on Hom. *Od.* 10.1-79, Smith on Tib. 1.2.51-2, Ov. *Met.* 7.202 (Circe) *uentos abigoque uocoque,* Tupet (1976) 117-18. *iniuriosus* is not well-suited to verse (*C.* 1.35.13 seems to be the only other occurrence), but is otherwise a 'normal' *-osus* form (3.15n.).

35 cales: cf. *S.* 2.3.79–80 *quisquis luxuria tristiue superstitione | aut alio mentis morbo calet*, Brink on *Ep.* 2.1.108. The verb can also be used of amatory 'ardour' (11.13).

uenenis officina Colchicis: in apposition with *tu* (33), 'you ... the factory for Colchian [5.24n.] enchantments [5.22n.]'. This type of abuse is colloquial; cf. *Ep.* 1.15.31 (the glutton Maenius) *pernicies et tempestas barathrumque macelli*, Pl. *Truc.* 587 *ipsa quae sis stabulum flagiti*, *As.* 297 *gymnasium flagri, salueto*, Cat. 42.13 *o lutum, lupanar*, Hofmann (1951) 95–9. For the dat. of purpose instead of the more usual objective gen., cf. *C.* 1.2.10 (an elm tree) *quae sedes fuerat columbis*, LHS II 91, 95–6. Some take *uenenis ... Colchicis* as abl. of manner with *cales*, but this might suggest that Canidia has poisoned herself.

36 quae finis: feminine *finis* is rarer than masculine (*ThLL* VI 1.787), but occurs in both prose and verse and seems to be no different in meaning (N–H on *C.* 2.18.30). H. probably uses it here to avoid the jingle *qui finis*; cf. Virg. *A.* 2.554 *haec finis Priami fatorum* with Gell. 13.21.12.

stipendium 'tribute', like that paid to victors by the vanquished (*OLD* s.v. 3). The initial syllable, here at anceps, is normally short, although Ennius and Catullus lengthen it to fit their hexameters (Skutsch on Enn. *Ann.* 215 *Poeni stipendia pendunt*).

37–52 H. promises expiation either with sacrifice or with a song like that which rescued Stesichorus from blindness (42–4n.). But his palinode turns out to be 'a lampoon more bitter than that which it professes to retract' (Wickham).

37 effare: only here in H. 'The word belongs to poetical and solemn augural or quasi-augural language' (Skutsch on Enn. *Ann.* 46; cf. *ThLL* V 2.198).

cum fide: there may be a play on the other type of *fides* (13.9), as if H.'s lyre (39) will share in his punishment.

38 expiare: Canidia is addressed as if she were a goddess or deified mortal like Helen (42–4n.). *expio* can mean 'make amends (for a wrong done to a person)' (*OLD* s.v. 1b), but is primarily used in sacral contexts (5.90, *C.* 1.2.29, 2.1.5, Fugier (1963) 336–41). The phrase *seu poposceris ... siue* suggests prayer formula (*C.* 1.4.12 *seu* [Faunus] *poscat agna siue malit haedo*).

39 centum iuuencos: probably comic hyperbole. The offering of hecatombs, even to the great gods, was sometimes criticized as an excess of religion; cf. N–H on *C.* 2.14.5, Var. *Men.* 94–100 (*Heca-tombe*), Ov. *Tr.* 2.75–6 *ut fuso taurorum sanguine centum,* | *sic capitur minimo turis honore deus. iuuencus* seems to be a poetic word (1.25n.).

mendaci lyra: the phrase 'is ambiguous, meaning both that the instrument previously lied in defaming Canidia and that it will lie (again) in praising her' (Orelli). The Greek word *lyra* (9.5) may antici-pate the reference to Stesichorus, one of the nine canonical *lyrikoi* ('lyric poets'; cf. Gentili (1988) 243–4), but that instrument was also associated with Archilochus (13.9).

40 sonari: the passive is 'less muddling' (Brink (1982) 47) than the variant *sonare*, which would entail an ellipse of *me*, a colloquial-ism (*S.* 1.3.22, *Ep.* 1.2.11, 16.36, 18.106, 20.4) that seems inappropriate to the sacral language here (but cf. 41n.).

tu pudica, tu proba: possibly a reference to Cat. 42.24 *pudica et proba, redde codicillos,* itself a 'recantation' of 42.19 *moecha putida, redde codicillos.* But from Afran. *com.* 116 Ribbeck and Ov. *Am* 3.14.13–14 it seems that 'the alliterative phrase was probably conventional' (Fordyce on the Cat. passage).

40–1 H. here, as elsewhere (*C.* 3.25.3–7, 4.8.15–34; cf. Coleman on Virg. *Ecl.* 5.51–2)) combines two ancient ideas, that praise can lift its object (metaphorically) 'to the stars' (N–H on *C.* 1.12.47, 4.2.22–3, *S.* 1.7.23–6, 2.7.28–9), and that the gods can turn certain mortals (literally) into stars (*C.* 1.3.2, 12.25–8, N–H on *C.* 2.19.13). The Dios-curi are a leading example of the second phenomenon, and they are sometimes accompanied by a transformed Helen (N–H on *C.* 1.3.2, Plin. *Nat.* 2.101). A prediction of 'katasterism' for Canidia is espe-cially ironic in view of her power to pull stars down from the sky (5).

41 perambulabis: like *ambulo* (4.4), this seems to be a colloquial and unpoetic word (Bonfante (1936) 96), fittingly used elsewhere by H. of a wandering ox (*C.* 4.5.17) and of a play by the 'clumsy' early poet Atta (Brink, Rudd on *Ep.* 2.1.79). The pairing *astra sidus* may also undercut H.'s praise by implying that Canidia will be as out of place as the Latin word (*sidus*) is next to the Greek (*astra*).

42–4 Stesichorus of Himera (sixth century BC) composed a poem on the Trojan war in which, as in Homer, Helen eloped with Paris (frr. 187–92 *PGM*). He was struck blind and, after discovering that the Dioscuri, Helen's brothers, were the cause, recanted with two palinodes in which he apparently insisted that Helen was replaced

by a 'phantom' either before she got to Troy (the first palinode) or
before she boarded Paris' ship (the second). For the evidence, which
is confused and controversial, cf. Stes. frr. 192–3 *PGM*, Gentili (1988)
126–7, 274–5. The story and the idea of a 'palinode' became pro-
verbial (e.g. Cic. *Att.* 2.9.1, 4.5.1, 7.7.1; cf. M. Davies, *Q.U.C.C.* n.s.
12 (1982) 7–16), but H. probably knew Stesichorus' poetry at first
hand (cf. *C.* 4.9.8) and would later use the sequence 'Helen poem
followed by palinodes' in *C.* 1.15–17 (Santirocco (1986) 49–52).

42 infamis Helenae: it is not known exactly what Stesichorus
said, but 'defamation' of Helen was a frequent theme in Greek and
Latin literature. Cf. H.'s own *C.* 3.3.25 *Lacaenae ... adulterae* and *S.*
1.3.107–8 *nam fuit ante Helenam cunnus taeterrima belli | causa.*

offensus uice 'angered by the fate' of his sister. For this sense of
uicis, cf. Cic. *Att.* 8.2.2 *quoius ego uicem doleo*, Cat. 64.68–9 *neque tum
fluitantis amictus | illa uicem curans, OLD* s.v. 3. Some take *uice* here as
'in the place of' (cf. Schol. *propter Helenam laesus*) but that would be
more correctly expressed by the variant *uicem* (Brink (1982) 47–8).

43 fraterque ... Castoris: the temple of the Dioscuri in the
Forum was usually called *aedes Castoris* or *Castorum* (*OLD* s.v. *Castor*),
and Castor's name often has precedence in poetic references to the
pair (*C.* 4.5.35, *S.* 2.1.26–7, Fordyce on Cat. 4.27 *gemelle Castor et
gemelle Castoris*).

44 uati: H. may call him a 'prophet' (16.66n.) because he was
able to divine the cause of his blindness. Cf. Plato, *Phaedr.* 243a
(=Stes. fr. 192) 'For when he was deprived of his eyes because of
his slander of Helen he was not ignorant, as Homer had been, but
being a "musical man", knew the cause.' There is a different version
of Stesichorus' discovery in H.'s contemporary Conon the mytho-
grapher (*FGH* 1.26, F 1.18) and in Paus. 3.19.12; cf. Gentili (1988)
126–7.

lumina = *oculos*; cf. *C.* 4.3.2. H. otherwise avoids this usage, which
is common in Latin poets from Lucretius and Catullus on (*OLD* s.v.
lumen 3).

45 potes nam: prayer language; cf. N–H on *C.* 1.28.28, *S.*
2.3.283–4 *unum me surpite morti, | dis etenim facile est!*, West on Hes. *Th.*
420, Arch. fr. 130.1 West 'to the gods all things are easy', Virg. *A.* 6.117
potes namque omnia, Appel (1909) 153. For postponed *nam*, cf. 1.12n.

solue me dementia: cf. 7n. *dementia* (only here in H.) is often
used of the madness of love (Virg. *Ecl.* 2.69, 6.47, *G.* 4.488).

46–7 o nec ... | neque: the structure may echo the beginning of Stesichorus' second palinode (fr. 192 *PMG* (App. 1)) 'not a true story this, | neither did you board the well-decked ship, | nor did you come to the citadels of Troy'.

46 nec ... sordibus: *non es sordidi generis* (Porph.). Cf. *C.* 2.10.6–7, Cic. *Sest.* 60 [*uirtus*] *neque alienis umquam sordibus obsolescit.* H. parodies the references to noble ancestry that were conventional in ancient hymns and other praise poetry (e.g. *C.* 1.1.1, N–H on *C.* 1.10.1; cf. Arch. fr. 196a.10–12 West 'daughter of Amphimede, of a noble and sensible | woman whom now the mouldy earth covers').

47 in sepulcris pauperum: a spot unguarded except by the likes of the statue of Priapus in *S.* 1.8. It is not clear why Canidia would choose such a place to *scatter* human remains (48n.); in the satire, she and Sagana do the opposite, *collecting* bones for their magic (*S.* 1.8.22; cf. 5.23n.). Perhaps she was there to conceal what was left of the boy from Epode 5. Even when it did not involve murder, 'corpse-dumping' was a crime at Rome (Crook (1967) 135).

47–8 prudens ... dissipare: the only example in the *Epodes* of adj. with complementary inf., a poetic construction based on Greek usage. It is not uncommon elsewhere in H. (e.g. *C.* 1.10.7–8 *callidum ... | condere,* cf. Bo III 268) and in other late Republican poetry (LHS II 350–1).

48 nouendialis ... pulueres: apparently human remains (*OLD* s.v. *puluis* 3) fresh off the funeral pyre. Cf. Ov. *Ep.* 6.90 (Medea) *certaque de tepidis colligit ossa rogis,* Luc. 6.533–4 (the witch Erichtho) *fumantis iuuenum cineres ardentiaque ossa | e mediis rapit illa rogis.* The evidence is scanty (*RE* XVII 1181), but it appears that Romans were buried on the ninth day after death, when there would be a *cena nouendialis* (Petr. 65.10, [Quint.] *Decl.* 12.23, Porph., Schol. on this line, Serv. on Virg. *A.* 5.64) and, presumably (there is no parallel), the corpse would also be called *nouendialis.* There may be something similar in a poem of Hipponax (fr. 118E West = 130 Degani): 'they receive (?) the third-day (corpse?) from a herald'; the third day seems to have been the rule for Greek funerals (Degani *ad loc.*; cf. Plat. *Leg.* 959a).

This and Plin. *Nat.* 11.82 seem to be the only examples of the plural of *puluis* before the late Empire (N–W I 617–18).

49 hospitale ... purae: cf. 5.13–14, 59–60, where Canidia's *pectus* and *manus* are just the opposite. There may also be a sugges-

tion of her 'hospitality' to sailors and pedlars (20) and an allusion to
Helen, Paris' *hospita* (*C.* 1.15.2; cf. 3.3.25–6). Although not suited to
dactyls, *hospitalis* does not seem to be unpoetic (*C.* 2.3.10, *inc. trag.* 101
ROL).

50–2 H. concludes by pretending to retract the allegations that
Canidia's children are not her own (5.5–6n.).

50 tuusque uenter Pactumeius: the meaning of the epithet is
obscure. There was a *gens Pactumeia* in Campania (*RE* XVIII 2153–6),
but nothing is known about its members that would fit this con-
text. Perhaps they were noted for fecundity; the sense would then
be 'your womb (*OLD* s.v. *uenter* 4a) is as productive as that of a Pac-
tumeia' (cf. the weakly attested *partumeius*, 'giving birth [*partus*] as
easily as one urinates [*meio*]'). Other, more involved explanations are
(1) a child (s.v. *uenter* 4b) raised by a branch of that clan is actually
Canidia's (Porph., most commentators), or (2) her husband Varus
(5.73n.) is a Pactumeius, and their offspring, thought to be supposi-
titious, is genuine (Zielinski (1935) 448). This last is based on the idea
that Canidia and her crowd were from Campania (5.43n.).

50–1 tuo | cruore rubros ... pannos: the cloths with which
the midwife received the blood-covered placenta would be washed
for re-use, but also, perhaps (as Orelli suggests), to show a husband
that a birth had occurred (cf. V. French, *Helios* 13.2 (1986) 69–84).
H. implies that these *panni* may be 'red' with the blood, not of
Canidia, but of a 'surrogate' whose child she would pass off as her
own. Simulated pregnancies and births, usually intended to preserve
marriages or inheritances, were not uncommon at Rome. Cf. Pl.
Truc., *Cist.* (52n.), Courtney on Juv. 6.602, *RE* XVIII 2048–51. *obstetrix*
(*OLD* s.v.) and *pannus* (*C.* 1.35.22, *Ep.* 1.17.25, 32, *Ars* 16, *ThLL* x 1.232)
are prosaic words, but *lauit* as opposed to *lauat* seems to be poetic
(16.28n.).

52 fortis exsilis: a final hint that the offspring are false: women
who have just given birth are unlikely to be 'strong' and 'jumping
up'. Cf. Pl. *Cist.* 139–41 *postquam eam puellam a med accepit, ilico* | *eandem
puellam 'peperit' quam a me acceperat,* | *sine obstetricis opera et sine doloribus,*
Juv. 6.592–4. *puerpera* seems to be a technical term, but it does occur
in elevated poetry (*C.* 4.5.23, Cat. 34.14, Ov. *Met.* 6.337).

53–81 Canidia answers. Prayers will not move her: H. has spied
on her, mocked and defamed her, and must be punished. He cannot

escape his torment, even by suicide, any more than the great sinners of myth can escape theirs. Does he imagine that her mighty art will fail against him?

Touches of humour and parody do not diminish the ominous power of Canidia's words, which cast a shadow over the end of the Epode book like those cast by the plague over *De rerum natura* and the killing of Turnus over the *Aeneid*. Whatever dark force Canidia symbolizes (App. 2), the poet will never be free of her and the 'earth' – of Rome and Italy – will continue to yield to her arrogance.

53 obseratis auribus: cf. *C.* 3.11.7–8 (Lyde's) *obstinatas* | ... *auris* and, for the image of a bolted door, *S.* 2.6.46 *quae rimosa bene deponuntur in aure*, Cat. 55.21 *licet obseras palatum*.

fundis: cf. Virg. *A.* 6.55 *funditque preces rex pectore ab imo*. *fundo* is also used of 'streams' of abuse (Brink on *Ep.* 2.1.145–6 *Fescennina ... licentia ... | uersibus alternis opprobria rustica fudit*).

54–5 A common comparison; cf. *C.* 3.7.21 *scopulis surdior Icari*, Eur. *Med.* 28–9, *Andr.* 537–8 (Menelaus to Andromache) 'Why do you fall at my feet as one supplicating with prayers a salt-sea rock or wave?', Philodemus, *AP* 5.107, Ov. *Met.* 11.330.

54 nudis ... nauitis: dat. with *surdiora*; cf. Mart. 10.14.8 *lacrimis ianua surda tuis*. The sailors strip to swim unencumbered, as Odysseus does after Poseidon sinks his boat (Hom. *Od.* 5.321–2, 372). Cf. Hipp. fr. 115.5 West (App. 1). *nauita* is more poetic than *nauta* (10.15n.).

55 Neptunus = *mare* (7.3n.). But there may be a reference to Poseidon's anger against Odysseus (54n.).

alto ... salo: i.e. with 'his' own brine, a poetic pleonasm that 'virtually = *se*' (Kenney on *Mor.* 61); cf. Virg. *A.* 1.246 *mare ... pelago premit arua sonanti*, Housman (1972) 1200–1 and on Man. 1.539, Luc. 1.102. The epithet here probably means 'deep' (*OLD* s.v. 4a), as the 'high seas' (s.v. 4b) are usually those far from the shore with its rocks (N–H on *C.* 2.10.1, Fordyce on Virg. *A.* 7.6). *salum* occurs only here in H., but otherwise in both prose and verse.

56–9 inultus ut tu riseris ... impleris '(you think) you're going to get away with having mocked the rites of Cotyto ... and with having filled the city with my name?' For *ut* with the subj. of 'something not to be thought of, whether as improbable or as offensive' (Wickham), cf. *S.* 2.5.18 *utne tegam spurco Damae latus?*, *Ep.* 1.18.16–17, Cic. *Catil.* 1.22 *quamquam quid loquor? te ut ulla res frangat? tu* *ut umquam te corrigas?*, *OLD* s.v. *ut* 44. The construction, like the 'indignant infinitive' (8.1n.), seems to be colloquial (LHS II 631).

56 inultus: here 'unpunished' (*C.* 1.2.51, 3.3.42, *S.* 2.3.189) rather than 'unavenged' (6.16).

Cotytia: neut. pl. = *ta Kotytia* (cf. *ta Adōnia, ta Dionysia* etc.). 'Canidia gives this name to the dark rites described in Epod. 5, with their lustful purpose' (Wickham). As if to make certain that H. will understand her, she 'glosses' the word with an appositional phrase (57n.). Cotyto or Cotys was a Thracian goddess of love and war whose cult was brought to Greece in the fifth century (Roscher II 1398–1403). Except for this passage and *Cat.* 13.19–20, there seems to be no evidence for a cult at Rome (Wissowa (1912) 376; cf. Courtney on Juv. 2.92 *Cecropiam . . . Cotyton*). But she is an appropriate divinity for Canidia: she came from a barbarous land (5.14n.), her rites were orgiastic (57n.) and may have involved magic (7n.), and the Greeks connected her name with *kotos*, 'resentment' (*Etym. Magnum* 396.18, 599.55). Bendis, a Thracian goddess similar to Cotyto, is mentioned by Hipponax (fr. 127 West), but the context is unknown.

57 sacrum liberi Cupidinis: explaining *Cotytia*: 'the worship of Cotyto, a rite of licentious Cupid'. The cult was thought to involve uninhibited sexual acts (Eupolis, *Baptai* frr. 76–98 *PCG*, Juv. 2.91–2). *liberi Cupidinis* is metonymous (11.3n.); cf. Cic. *Tusc.* 4.70 *in Graecorum gymnasiis . . . isti liberi et concessi sunt amores*. Despite his role in poetry and philosophy, there were no real 'rites' of Cupid (Amor, Eros) at Rome (H. Fliedner, *Amor und Cupido* (Meisenheim am Glan 1974) 82–91).

58 pontifex: *pontificem nunc quasi censorem ac iudicem dicit* (Porph.). For the sarcastic use of the title, cf. Pl. *Rud.* 1377 *tun meo pontifex peiiurio es?*, Cic. *Sest.* 39 (of Clodius) *stuprorum sacerdotem*, Juv. 2.113–14 (the leader of an orgy) *senex fanaticus . . . sacrorum antistes*. There may also be a dig at the idea of poets as priests (16.66n.). The Esquiline, near Canidia's house (5.100n.), is the setting for her magic in *S.* 1.8.

59 impune: cf. *Ep.* 2.1.149–50 (fescennine mockery) *coepit . . . per honestas | ire domos impune minax*.

Vrbem nomine impleris: with his verses, as befits a blame poet (Intro. 3). Cf. 11.7–8, *S.* 2.1.45–6 *qui me commorit (melius non tangere, clamo), | flebit et insignis tota cantabitur urbe*, Arch. fr. 172.3–4 West (App. 1) 'now indeed you [Lycambes] appear as a source of much laughter for the townsfolk', Cat. 40.1–5 ('probably imitating Arch.' Kroll) *quaenam te mala mens, miselle Rauide, | agit praecipitem in meos iambos? | ... an ut peruenias in ora uulgi?* For the contracted form *impleris* (=*impleueris*), cf. *complesti* at 6.9.

60–1 'What will it avail to have enriched Paelignian hags or to have mixed faster-acting poison?' Porph. observes that either *mihi* or *tibi* can be supplied with *quid proderit*, but prefers *tibi*, as does Lambinus. Canidia assumes that H., like Varus (5.71–6), sought help from other witches (*ditasse ... anus*) or, like Hercules (31–2n.), is ready to kill himself (with the *toxicum*) rather than suffer further (cf. 63). If *mihi* is understood (Schol., Bentley, most commentators), she wonders why she herself employed the hags (evidently the coven of Epode 5, although nothing is said there about payment) or mixed poison, if H. can mock her with impunity (cf. 59). The variant *proderat* (Bentley, most edd.) was not known to Porph., and was probably meant to eliminate the ambiguity noted by him. The imperfect, referring back to the time of Epode 5 and *S.* 1.8, would make sense only with *mihi* (of Canidia), since H. was not involved in the events narrated in those poems.

60 Paelignas: the Paeligni were another Sabellic people (28n.), near neighbours of the Marsi (29, 5.76n.). There seems to be no other report of them as witches, but some features of their religion, such as the worship of bulls and a special role for priestesses, may have impressed Romans as akin to magic (*RE* XVIII 2242–3).

61 toxicum: a Greek word, lit. 'arrow poison' (cf. *toxon*, 'bow'), but already Latinized and used of other types of poison in Plautus (*Cist.* 298, *Mer.* 472).

62 sed 'however that may be' (N–H on *C.* 1.28.15, 2.1.37, 4.4.22, *S.* 1.1.27 etc.), resuming after the indignant questions (56–61) and also opposing *tardiora* to *uelocius* (61): 'but (despite the faster poison) death slower than you hope awaits'. The variant *si* was read by Porph. and makes sense if *tibi* is supplied in 61 (Lambinus punctuates *quid ... toxicum, si ... manent?*). But since, like *proderat*, it removes the ambiguity, it is probably *lectio facilior*.

uotis: cf. Ov. *Am.* 2.5.1–3 *nullus amor tanti est ... | ut mihi sint totiens maxima uota mori. | uota mori mea sunt.*

63 ingrata ... uita: possibly an ironic reference to 1.5–6 *uita ... | iucunda, si contra, grauis.* Despite his friendship with Maecenas

(Epodes 3, 14) and their survival of Actium (9), H.'s life will still be wretched. *misero* (sc. *tibi*) is dat. of agent with *ducenda est.*

in hoc 'for this purpose', the first instance of *in hoc* (*in id, in quid*) as the correlative for a final (or consecutive) *ut* clause. The construction, which occurs in Livy and later prose, may be colloquial in origin (LHS II 640). For the monosyllable at verse end, cf. 11.21, Intro. 6.

64 ut usque suppetas 'so that you may be continually available'. *suppeto* is a prosaic word which normally has as its subject not a person but 'money, resources, etc.' (*OLD* s.v. 1; cf. *Ep.* 1.12.4 *pauper enim non est, cui rerum suppetit usus*). Canidia speaks of H. as if he were nothing more than 'raw material' for torture.

laboribus: cf. 16, 24, 1.9. The variant *doloribus* probably arose as a gloss (Bentley); cf. the app. crit. at *Ep.* 1.1.44.

65–9 Tantalus, Prometheus, and Sisyphus all committed offences against the gods and were condemned by Zeus to eternal torment. The comparison suggests the magnitude both of H.'s crime, analogous to mythical acts of sacrilege, and of Canidia's power to punish, on a level with that of Jupiter. The topos of 'great sinners' had a long history from Homer on (*Od.* 11.572–600; cf. Norden, Austin on Virg. *A.* 6.580–627) and was a favourite of H. (*C.* 1.28.7–9, 2.13.33–40, 14.17–20, 18.29–40, 3.4.69–80, 11.17–24, 4.7.25–8, Oksala (1973) 173–8).

65 optat: the repetition at 67 and 68 may suggest an incantation (5.53n.).

Pelopis infidi pater: cf. *C.* 1.28.7, 2.13.37, 18.37–8 *Tantalum atque Tantali | genus* [Orcus] *coercet*, all, as here, reminders that Tantalus' crime doomed his descendants to commit further atrocities. Pelops treacherously killed Myrtilus, who had helped him win the hand of Hippodamia in a chariot race against her father. The story was familiar from Greek lyric and tragedy; cf. Cat. 64.346 *periuri Pelopis*, Thomas on Virg. *G.* 3.7–8 [*cui non dictus*] *Hippodameque umeroque Pelops insignis eburno, | acer equis?*

66 egens: cf. *S.* 1.1.59 *qui tantuli eget*, with its word play on Tantalus (1.1.68–9). *egeo* with the gen. rather than the abl. although preferred by H., seems to be colloquial (Ruckdeschel (1911) 25).

Tantalus: he cooked and served Pelops to the gods or stole their nectar and ambrosia to share with his friends (Pind. *Ol.* 1; cf. T.

Hubbard, *Helios* 14 (1987) 3–21). His punishment, to be 'tantalized' by food and drink he cannot reach (Hom. *Od.* 11.582–92, cf. *S.* 1.1.68–9) seems to be recalled in Canidia's starvation of the boy in Epode 5 (5.34n.). There was another version in which a stone hung over his head threatening to crush him (Arch. fr. 91.14–15 West, Kenney on Lucr. 3.980–3).

67 Prometheus: for trying to deceive Zeus and for stealing fire from Olympus he was chained to a pillar of rock and had his liver eaten by an eagle. In some versions Zeus allows Hercules to kill the eagle (Hes. *Th.* 507–616) or even release Prometheus in exchange for the dying Chiron (13.17n., Aesch. *Prom.*, Cat. 64.294–7). The tradition is also divided as to whether the pillar was in the underworld (N–H on *C.* 2.13.37, Aesch. *Prom.* 1040–93) or in the Caucasus mountains (e.g. Ap. Rhod. 2.1246–59, 3.851–3, Virg. *Ecl.* 6.42, Prop. 2.1.69–70). H. again refers to the myth at *C.* 1.3.27–8, 16.13–16, 2.13.37, and 18.34–6, and Maecenas wrote a prose (dialogue?) *Prometheus* (Sen. *Ep.* 19.9) which may have influenced these passages (K–H *ad locc.*; cf. N–H on *C.* 2.18).

obligatus aliti: not 'bound to the bird', which would make a strange picture, but 'bound [sc. to a pillar] for (the sake of) the bird' (Lambinus). With the variant *alite* the construction would be like that at *C.* 2.8.5–6 *obligasti | perfidum uotis caput* (cf. *OLD* s.v. *obligo* 4b). *ales* is a poetic word (3.14n.).

68 Sisyphus: he betrayed Zeus's secrets, tried to cheat death, and was condemned to try in vain to position a rock on top of a hill (Hom. *Od.* 11.593–60, Alcaeus, fr. 38A L–P). The story, like that of Tantalus, invited allegorical interpretation (Kenney on Lucr. 3.995–1002; cf. Virg. *A.* 6.616).

70–4 The three options for suicide, as Peerlkamp notes (*ad loc.* and on *C.* 3.27.58–64), are traditional. Cf. Schol. on Pind. *Ol.* 1.60 'the three ... suitable means of death are sword, hanging, cliff (*xiphos, anchōnē, krēmnos*)', Donatus on Ter. *An.* 605–6, Eur. *Hel.* 293–302, Ov. *Ep.* 2.131–44 (where Phyllis also mentions poison), Sen. *Phaed.* 258–60, Luc. 8.653–6, 9.106–7. Hanging is especially appropriate for H., since that is how victims of *iambus* kill themselves (6.13–14n.).

71 ense ... Norico: Noricum (modern Austria) produced a high grade of iron (Plin. *Nat.* 34.145). Since the region was not conquered until 15 BC, for H. 'The epithet is still novel and adventurous, a Roman substitute for the Greek "Scythian" or "Chalybian"' (N–H on *C.* 1.16.9 *Noricus* [*ensis*]). *ensis* is a poetic word (7.2n.).

recludere: cf. Virg. *A.* 10.601 *pectus mucrone recludit*, Sen. *Tro.* 1001 *reclude ferro pectus*.

72 nectes: cf. *Ep.* 1.19.31 (6.13–14n.) *nec sponsae* [i.e. Neobule] *laqueum famoso carmine nectit* and, for the construction, *C.* 1.26.8, 29.4–5, *Ep.* 2.2.96 *sibi nectat uterque coronam*. The variant *innectes* has its supporters (Lambinus, Borzsák), but that verb normally takes acc. of the part bound, abl. of the means of binding (e.g. Virg. *A.* 5.425 *et paribus palmas amborum innexuit armis*).

73 fastidiosa: both this and *curiosus* (77) are 'normal' *-osus* forms (3.16n., Ernout (1949) 16, 39–40). For *aegrimonia*, cf. 13.18n.

74 uectabor ... eques: an image that suggests the dominance of conqueror over vanquished (cf. Greek *kathippazomai*), master over slave (Pl. *As.* 699–703), and female over male lover (*S.* 2.7.47–50, Adams (1982) 165–6).

75 terra cedet insolentiae 'the earth will give way to my arrogance', as if she were a god. Cf. West on Hes. *Th.* 842–3 'great Olympus shook beneath the immortal feet | of lord (Zeus) as he stirred, and the earth groaned', Hom. *Il.* 13.18–19 'the tall mountains and woods shook | under the immortal feet of Poseidon as he came', and Ovid's parody at *Ars* 1.559–60 (Bacchus) *e curru ... | desilit* (*imposito cessit harena pede*). *insolentia* is not suited to hexameters, but does occur in Roman tragedy (Acc. fr. 259 *ROL*).

76–9 an quae ... possim: for *an* introducing an indignant question, cf. 6.15n. The rel. clause is either concessive (cf. *S.* 2.3.118–19), 'though I can (do all this)', or causal (*C.* 2.12.27, *S.* 1.5.68–9, 7.34, 2.3.40), 'seeing that I can (do all this)'.

76 mouere cereas imagines: as at *S.* 1.8.30–3. The use of 'voodoo dolls' was common in ancient, as in modern, magic. Cf. Gow on Theocr. *Id.* 2.28–9, Virg. *Ecl.* 8.80–1, Ov. *Am.* 3.7.29–30, *Ep.* 6.91–2, *PGM* IV 296–466, CXXIV 10–26, Audollent (1904) lxxviii, Tupet (1976) 49–50, C. Faraone, *C.P.* 84 (1989) 294–300.

77 curiosus: cf. Pl. *St.* 198–9, 208 *curiosi sunt hic complures mali, | alienas res qui curant studio maximo | ... nam curiosus nemo est quin sit maleuolus*, Cat. 7.11, *OLD* s.v. 3b. There may be a play on the sense 'careworn' (s.v. 4) with reference to H.'s suffering.

polo: here = *caelo* (*C.* 3.29.44, *OLD* s.v. 2) rather than anything more technical (*C.* 1.28.6). Porph. seems to have read *choro* (*stellarum scilicet*; cf. *C.* 4.14.21 *Pleiadum choro*), but most editors dismiss this as a gloss (cf. Schol. *polo: stellarum choro*).

78 deripere lunam: cf. 5n. Canidia seems to be taking credit for the moon's disappearance at *S.* 1.8.34–6 (*uideres* | ... *lunamque rubentem,* | *ne foret his testis, post magna latere sepulcra*). She cannot be referring to 5.46, where it is Veia who performs the *kathairesis*.

79 excitare mortuos: a reference to *S.* 1.8.28–9, 40–1. Necromancy is a well known practice of witches; cf. *Ep.* 2.2.209, Hom. *Od.* 10.504–40 (Circe instructs Odysseus in the art), Virg. *Ecl.* 8.98 *saepe animas imis excire sepulcris*, Pease on *A.* 4.490, *PGM* iv 1928–2005, 2140–44. *excito* seems to be a *uox propria*; cf. the tragic verses at Cic. *Tusc.* 1.37 (= *inc. trag.* 18–19 *ROL*) *unde animae excitantur obscura umbra opertae*.

80 desiderique ... pocula: potions like those mentioned at 5.37–8, 77–8. The variant *poculum* might specify the one made from the murdered boy (5.37–8), but the plural seems more appropriate where Canidia 'glories in her art and power' (Bentley).

81 plorem ... exitus 'am I to sob over the results of my art (since it is) accomplishing nothing against you?' The whole phrase is unpoetic. *ploro* occurs elsewhere in H. (5× in *Odes*, 6× in hexameters), but is rare in elevated verse (11.12n., Brink on *Ep.* 2.1.9, Axelson (1945) 28–9), while *nil ago* is colloquial (*S.* 1.9.15, 19, 2.3.103, Bonfante (1937) 38, *ThLL* i 1381).

exitus 'results', 'outcomes' (*C.* 3.6.6, 29.29, 4.14.38), plural because Canidia has tried and will try various means of afflicting her enemy. The word makes an appropriate 'exit' for the book; cf. *ibis* at the beginning (1.1).

APPENDICES

1. GREEK TEXTS

This appendix contains Greek texts of some of the fragments of Archilochus and other poets cited in the Commentary.

Archilochus (text of West (1989))

Fr. 4.6–9 West (9.35, 13.3–10nn.):

> ἀλλ' ἄγε σὺν κώ⌊θωνι θοῆς διὰ σέλματα νηὸς
> φοίτα καὶ κοίλ⌊ων πώματ' ἄφελκε κάδων,
> ἄγρει δ' οἶνον ⌊ἐρυθρὸν ἀπὸ τρυγός· οὐδὲ γὰρ ἡμεῖς
> νηφέμεν ⌊ἐν φυλακῆι τῆιδε δυνησόμεθα.

Fr. 8 West (16.35n.):

> πολλὰ δ' εὐπλοκάμου πολιῆς ἁλὸς ἐν πελάγεσσι
> θεσσάμενοι γλυκερὸν νόστον ∪ – ∪∪ –.

Fr. 13 West (5.22, 13.3–10, 16.39nn.):

> κήδεα μὲν στονόεντα Περίκλεες οὔτέ τις ἀστῶν
> μεμφόμενος θαλίηις τέρψεται οὐδὲ πόλις·
> τοίους γὰρ κατὰ κῦμα πολυφλοίσβοιο θαλάσσης
> ἔκλυσεν, οἰδαλέους δ' ἀμφ' ὀδύνηις ἔχομεν
> πλεύμονας. ἀλλὰ θεοὶ γὰρ ἀνηκέστοισι κακοῖσιν   5
> ὦ φίλ' ἐπὶ κρατερὴν τλημοσύνην ἔθεσαν
> φάρμακον. ἄλλοτε ἄλλος ἔχει τόδε· νῦν μὲν ἐς ἡμέας
> ἐτράπεθ', αἱματόεν δ' ἕλκος ἀναστένομεν,
> ἐξαῦτις δ' ἑτέρους ἐπαμείψεται. ἀλλὰ τάχιστα
> τλῆτε, γυναικεῖον πένθος ἀπωσάμενοι.   10

Fr. 15 West (1 intro.):

> Γλαῦκ', ἐπίκουρος ἀνὴρ τόσσον φίλος ἔσκε μάχηται.

Fr. 16 West (13.7n.):

> πάντα Τύχη καὶ Μοῖρα Περίκλεες ἀνδρὶ δίδωσιν.

Fr. 19 West (2 intro., 15.20n.):

οὔ μοι τὰ Γύγεω τοῦ πολυχρύσου μέλει,
οὐδ' εἷλέ πώ με ζῆλος, οὐδ' ἀγαίομαι
θεῶν ἔργα, μεγάλης δ' οὐκ ἐρέω τυραννίδος·
ἀπόπροθεν γάρ ἐστιν ὀφθαλμῶν ἐμῶν.

Fr. 22 West (16.41–60n.):

οὐ γάρ τι καλὸς χῶρος οὐδ' ἐφίμερος
οὐδ' ἐρατός, οἷος ἀμφὶ Σίριος ῥοάς.

Fr. 47 West (11.20–2n.):

                                    .]ε παρθένοι
θυρέων ἀπεστύ[παζ]ον.

Fr. 88 West (7.1–2n.):

'Ερξίη, πῆι δηῦτ' ἄνολβος ἀθροΐζεται στρατός;

Fr. 105 West (13.1–3n.):

Γλαῦχ', ὅρα· βαθὺς γὰρ ἤδη κύμασιν ταράσσεται
πόντος, ἀμφὶ δ' ἄκρα Γυρέων ὀρθὸν ἵσταται νέφος,
σῆμα χειμῶνος, κιχάνει δ' ἐξ ἀελπτίης φόβος.

Fr. 122 West (2 intro., 9.11, 16.34nn.):

χρημάτων ἄελπτον οὐδέν ἐστιν οὐδ' ἀπώμοτον
οὐδὲ θαυμάσιον, ἐπειδὴ Ζεὺς πατὴρ Ὀλυμπίων
ἐκ μεσαμβρίης ἔθηκε νύκτ', ἀποκρύψας φάος
ἡλίου †λάμποντος, λυγρὸν† δ' ἦλθ' ἐπ' ἀνθρώπους δέος.
ἐκ δὲ τοῦ καὶ πιστὰ πάντα κἀπίελπτα γίνεται   5
ἀνδράσιν· μηδεὶς ἔθ' ὑμέων εἰσορέων θαυμαζέτω
μηδ' ἐὰν δελφῖσι θῆρες ἀνταμείψωνται νομὸν
ἐνάλιον, καί σφιν θαλάσσης ἠχέεντα κύματα
φίλτερ' ἠπείρου γένηται, τοῖσι δ' ὑλέειν ὄρος.
                              Ἀρ]χηνακτίδης
                              ]ητου πάϊς[
                              ]τυθη γάμωι[

Fr. 124b West (11.13–14n.):

> πολλὸν δὲ πίνων καὶ χαλίκρητον μέθυ,
> οὔτε τῖμον εἰσενείκας ⟨ – ∪ – x – ∪ – ⟩
> οὐδὲ μὲν κληθεὶς ⟨ ∪ – x ⟩ ἦλθες οἷα δὴ φίλος.

Fr. 126 West (6.4n.):

> ἓν δ' ἐπίσταμαι μέγα,
> τὸν κακῶς ⟨μ'⟩ ἔρδοντα δεινοῖς ἀνταμείβεσθαι κακοῖς.

Fr. 130 West (17.45n.):

> τοῖς θεοῖς †τ' εἰθεῖάπαντα· πολλάκις μὲν ἐκ κακῶν
> ἄνδρας ὀρθοῦσιν μελαίνηι κειμένους ἐπὶ χθονί,
> πολλάκις δ' ἀνατρέπουσι καὶ μάλ' εὖ βεβηκότας
> ὑπτίους, κείνοις ⟨δ'⟩ ἔπειτα πολλὰ γίνεται κακά,
> καὶ βίου χρήμηι πλανᾶται καὶ νόου παρήορος.   5

Fr. 172 West (11.8, 17.59nn.):

> πάτερ Λυκάμβα, ποῖον ἐφράσω τόδε;
>   τίς σὰς παρήειρε φρένας
> ἧις τὸ πρὶν ἠρήρησθα; νῦν δὲ δὴ πολὺς
>   ἀστοῖσι φαίνεαι γέλως.

Fr. 177 West (5.2n.):

> ὦ Ζεῦ, πάτερ Ζεῦ, σὸν μὲν οὐρανοῦ κράτος,
>   σὺ δ' ἔργ' ἐπ' ἀνθρώπων ὁρᾶις
> λεωργὰ καὶ θεμιστά, σοὶ δὲ θηρίων
>   ὕβρις τε καὶ δίκη μέλει.

Fr. 188 West (8.3–4n.):

> οὐκέ|θ' ὁμῶς θάλλεις ἁπαλὸν χρόα· κάρφεται[ι γὰρ ἤδη
> ὄγμοι]ς, κακοῦ δὲ γήραος καθαιρεῖ.

Fr. 191 West (14.1–2n.):

> τοῖος γὰρ φιλότητος ἔρως ὑπὸ καρδίην ἐλυσθεὶς
>   πολλὴν κατ' ἀχλὺν ὀμμάτων ἔχευεν,
> κλέψας ἐκ στηθέων ἁπαλὰς φρένας.

Fr. 193 West (11.17, 14.1–2nn.):

> δύστηνος ἔγκειμαι πόθωι,
> ἄψυχος, χαλεπῆισι θεῶν ὀδύνηισιν ἕκητι
> πεπαρμένος δι' ὀστέων.

Fr. 196 West (11.1–2n.):

> ἀλλά μ' ὁ λυσιμελής
> ὦταῖρε δάμναται πόθος.

Fr. 201 West (5.27–8n.):

> πολλ' οἶδ' ἀλώπηξ, ἀλλ' ἐχῖνος ἓν μέγα.

Fr. 215 West (11.1–2n.):

> καί μ' οὔτ' ἰάμβων οὔτε τερπωλέων μέλει.

Fr. 234 West (11.16n.):

> χολὴν γὰρ οὐκ ἔχεις ἐφ' ἥπατι.

Fr. 254 West (12.15n.):

> οὔτοι τοῦτο δυνησόμεσθα.

Hipponax (*text of West (1989)*)

Frr. 5–10 West (10 intro.):

5   ὁ δὲ Ἱππῶναξ ἄριστα σύμπαν τὸ ἔθος λέγει·

> πόλιν καθαίρειν καὶ κράδηισι βάλλεσθαι.

6   καὶ ἀλλαχοῦ δὲ πού φησιν πρώτῳ ἰάμβῳ γράφων·

> βάλλοντες ἐν χειμῶνι καὶ ῥαπίζοντες
> κράδηισι καὶ σκίλλησιν ὥσπερ φαρμακόν.

7   καὶ πάλιν ἄλλοις τόποις δὲ ταῦτά φησι κατ' ἔπος·

> δεῖ δ' αὐτὸν ἐς φάρμακον ἐκποιήσασθαι.

8   κἀφῇ παρέξειν ἰσχάδας τε καὶ μᾶζαν
> καὶ τυρόν, οἷον ἐσθίουσι φαρμακοί.

9   πάλαι γὰρ αὐτοὺς προσδέκονται χάσκοντες
κράδας ἔχοντες ὡς ἔχουσι φαρμακοῖς.

10   καὶ ἀλλαχοῦ δέ πού φησιν ἐν τῷ αὐτῷ ἰάμβῳ·

λιμῶι γένηται ξηρός· ἐν δὲ τῶι θύμωι
φαρμακὸς ἀχθεὶς ἑπτάκις ῥαπισθείη.

Fr. 115 West (5.13–14n., 10 intro., 17.54n.):

    κύμ[ατι] πλα[ζόμ]ενος·
    κἀν Σαλμυδ[ησσ]ῷι γυμνὸν εὐφρονε̣.[5
    Θρήϊκες ἀκρό[κ]ομοι
    λάβοιεν – ἔνθα πόλλ' ἀναπλήσαι κακὰ
    δούλιον ἄρτον ἔδων –
    ῥίγει πεπηγότ' αὐτόν· ἐκ δὲ τοῦ χνόου
    φυκία πόλλ' ἐπέχοι,   10
    κροτέο̣ι δ' ὀδόντας, ὡς [κ]ύ̣ων ἐπὶ στόμα
    κείμενος ἀκρασίηι
    ἄκρον παρὰ ῥηγμῖνα κυμα.... δο̣υ·
    ταῦτ' ἐθέλοιμ' ἂν ἰδεῖν,
    ὅς μ' ἠδίκησε, λ[ὰ]ξ δ' ἐπ' ὁρκίοις ἔβη,   15
    τὸ πρὶν ἑταῖρος [ἐ]ών.

Fr. 128 West (10.21n.):

Μοῦσά μοι Εὐρυμεδοντιάδε̣α τὴν ποντοχάρυβδιν,
τὴν ἐν γαστρὶ μάχαιραν, ὃς ἐσθίει οὐ κατὰ κόσμον,
ἔννεφ', ὅπως ψηφῖδι ⟨   ⟩ κακὸν οἶτον ὀλεῖται
βουλῆι δημοσίηι παρὰ θῖν' ἁλὸς ἀτρυγέτοιο.

Stesichorus (*text of Page*, PMG)

Fr. 192 PMG (17.46–7n.):

    οὐκ ἔστ' ἔτυμος λόγος οὗτος,
    οὐδ' ἔβας ἐν νηυσὶν εὐσέλμοις
    οὐδ' ἵκεο πέργαμα Τροίας.

Callimachus (text of Pfeiffer)

Fr. 202(= *Iamb.* 12).68–70 Pfeiffer (15.7–9n.):

ἡ δ' ἐμὴ τῇ παιδὶ καλλίστη δόσις,
ἔστ' ἐμὸν γένειον ἀγνεύῃ τριχός
καὶ ἐρίφοις χαίρωσιν ἁρπαγ[ες λ]ύκ[ο]ι.

2. CANIDIA

Canidia, who appears only in H., is featured or mentioned in six poems (Epodes 3, 5, 17, *S.* 1.8, 2.1.48, 8.95) and may figure in three others (Epodes 8, 12 (cf. 8 intro.), *C.* 1.16 (scholia ad loc., E. A. Hahn, *T.A.P.A.* 70 (1939) 213–30). The relative or dramatic chronology is not certain, but *S.* 1.8 seems to be the 'earliest', followed by the Epodes in sequence, the Satires from book 2, and, as an end to the whole business, the Ode.

Various 'facts' can be assembled: Canidia lives somewhere near and frequents the Esquiline (5.100, 17.58, *S.* 1.8); her appearance, although strange (5.15–16, 17.46, *S.* 1.8.24), suggests that of a Roman matron (5.5–6n.), and she may have a husband (5.73n.; cf. *S.* 2.1.48) and children, whether genuine or not (5.5–6, 17.50–2nn.). She is not young (5.47; cf. 8.1–4, *S.* 1.8.48), is horribly ugly (8, 12), with poisonous breath (*S.* 2.8.95), but seems to have lovers, including, perhaps, H. himself (17.15–18n.; cf. 12 intro.). With the aid of her weird followers (5.25, 29, 41–4nn., *S.* 1.8.24–5) she practises both poisoning (3.7–8, 17.61, *S.* 2.1.48, 8.95) and love magic (5.37–8 etc., 17.19–36n., *S.* 1.8.30–3). She seems to be skilled in every magical art, but most of her acts involve 'necromancy' (raising ghosts, stealing parts from dead humans and animals, using plants etc. associated with funerals). Her spells are not always successful (5.61–72, 17.60–1, *S.* 1.8.44–50), and can have sinister 'side effects' (5 intro.).

The meaning of all this, if there is a meaning, depends on how the figure of Canidia is interpreted. There are basically two possibilities (cf. Rudd (1966) 148–9, Setaioli (1981) 1704–7): (1) she is a historical person whom H. ridicules for amusement or attacks because he considers her a threat; (2) she is a fictional character, a stock figure with, perhaps, a symbolic significance.

The first view is that of H.'s scholiasts: *sub hoc Canidiae nomine Gra-*
tidiam Neopolitanam unguentariam intellegi uult, quam ut ueneficam Horatius
semper insectatur. sed quia non licet probrosum carmen in quemquam scribere,
idcirco fere poetae similia adfingunt. sic et Vergilius in bucolicis [*Ecl.* 10] *pro*
Cytheride Lycoridem appellat (Porph. on 3.7–8; cf. on 5.43, *S.* 1.8.23–4,
25, Schol. on 3.8, 5.25, 17.50). This has convinced some modern
commentators, but nearly all of it can be traced to H.'s text (cf. 5.25,
41–4, 43, 59, 17.50nn., *S.* 2.1.82–3, *Ep.* 2.1.152–4 (the prohibition
against a 'libellous song'), Fraenkel (1957) 62–3). The exception is
the mention of 'Gratidia', but H.'s scholia and other ancient critics
play this 'name game' elsewhere (e.g. Schol. on *C.* 2.12.13, Porph.,
Schol. on *S.* 1.2.25, 64, 10.36; cf. Apul. *Apol.* 10, Rudd (1966) 147–9),
and it is possible that someone 'invented Gratidia as a prototype of
Canidia: the one name points as clearly to attractive youth as the
other points to old age' (Fraenkel (1957) 62; see below).

This is not to say that the figure of Canidia is wholly incredible:
there were real witches in Rome (5 intro.), and many in H.'s audi-
ence would probably have accepted the Canidia poems in the most
literal way. But most modern commentators have felt that, as with
the 'exemplary enemies' in early Greek *iambus* (Intro. 3), there is
something more to Canidia. Her name, like so many in H. (Intro. 3),
including those of the creatures associated with her (5.25, 29, 41–4,
73nn.), may provide a clue. It could suggest a 'goose' (Greek *chēn*,
chān; cf. *chēnideus* (Ael. *N.A.* 7.47), 'gosling', and, for witches as birds,
5.20n., Prop. 4.5 ('Acanthis')), a rapacious, sexually promiscuous,
and ill-omened bird, but also, in its 'service' to Juno and Mars, a pro-
tector of Rome (*RE* VII 721–35). Or there might be a play on Greek
kenon (Ionic *keinon*) *eidos*, 'empty (false) shape', hinting at deception
and the 'false Helen' in the palinode of Stesichorus (17.42–4n.).
Others see a connection with dogs (*canis*), with Canidia a kind of
'alter ego' for the doglike iambist (6.1, 15nn.), or a perverse 'Muse'
of *iambus*, or an 'avatar' of the 'dog-star' Canicula, which weakens
men and saps their virility (E. Oliensis, *Arethusa* 24 (1991) 107–38,
Gowers (1993) 188–9; cf. 1.27n.).

But the most compelling theory (Düntzer (1892), W. S. Anderson,
A.J.Ph. 93 (1972) 4–13) associates Canidia with *canities*, 'old age', and
sees in her a symbol of Rome's 'senescence' and especially of its
ancient curse (7.17–20n.) which, like the corpses on the Esquiline (*S.*

1.8) and the shade of the murdered boy (Epode 5), refuses to stay 'buried'. It is even possible that Canidia somehow represents Rome 'herself', a 'woman' (cf. Cic. *Catil.* 1.27–9) who allures and seduces her 'lovers' (=*patriae amatores*; cf. N–H on *C.* 1.14) yet also 'poisons' them with disgust and hatred for their fellow citizens and finally for her.[1] The *Epodes* and *Satires* (*S.* 2.8.95) end with the effects of this 'poison' unabated, and it is not until the *Odes* that H. can replace his hatred of Rome with *desiderium* (*C.* 1.14.17–18) and sing a 'palinode' that has a chance of being heard (*C.* 1.16).

3. CRETIC-SHAPED WORDS

The iambic metres of the *Epodes* (Intro. 6) allow 'cretic-shaped words' (CS), words which contain or end in a sequence of syllables forming a 'cretic' ($-\cup-$). Since words of this shape usually cannot be accommodated to dactylic verse, the vehicle for most surviving 'elevated' Latin poetry, it might be expected that an original audience would perceive many of them as somehow 'unpoetic' (Intro. 5).[2] This would be especially likely in the case of CS that are 'cretic-containing' (CC), in which the cretic is part of the word itself, rather than 'cretic-ending' (CE), in which it is a result of the termination, since the former are nearly always excluded from dactylic poetry, while the latter can be accommodated in other grammatical forms.[3]

---

[1] For cities and countries personified as women, cf. *C.* 1.14 and Alcaeus, fr. 306 L–P ('ships of state' that also resemble ageing prostitutes (cf. Gentili (1988) 210)), N–H on *C.* 1.22.16, 4.5.26, Arch. frr. 22 (App. 1), 113 West (a man 'raping' a place (?)), Solon, fr. 36 West, Pind. *Ol.* 6.100 etc., *Rhet. Her.* 4.66, Cic. *Catil.* 1.27, Luc. 1.185–92, Hense (1868) 157–8, 216.

[2] The 'problem' of CS is discussed in various works on Latin poetic language (e.g. F. Hultgren, *N. Jahrb.* 107 (1873) 754–6, E. Bednara, *A.L.L.* 14 (1905–6) 319–23, Axelson (1945), M. Leumann, *Kleine Schriften* (Zurich 1959) 146–7), but most of these focus on how dactylic verse 'compensates' for having to avoid CS, and there seems to be no detailed account of their role in verse that allows them. This appendix is not intended to be such an account, since it is concerned chiefly with the CS and especially the CC in the *Epodes* and omits, among other things, statistical analysis (cf. N. Greenberg, *T.A.P.A.* 121 (1991) 319–20) as well as any consideration of CS and CC in verse later than H.

[3] In what follows plural nouns and participial and adverbial forms are counted as CC only when they are not attested in non-CS forms (e.g. *nuptiae*, *immerens*, *longule*, but not *arbitrae*, *assidens*, and *optime*).

In the *Epodes* the majority of CS (170 of 243 = 70%) are CE which can and usually do occur in dactylic verse and would thus seem to be 'poetic'.[4] It is more difficult to establish the stylistic level of the remaining CS, those that are CC, since the main 'elevated' genre which allowed such forms, Republican Latin tragedy, survives only in fragments. But a survey of those fragments and of samples of other CS-allowing Republican verse suggests that, when H. wrote the *Epodes*, CC were not felt *per se* to be inappropriate to any level of poetry. From Livius Andronicus to H. the percentage of verses containing CS of any sort remains fairly constant (Table 1). There is more variation in the frequencies of CC, and thus of the percentage of CS made up of CC,[5] but there seems to be no marked difference between tragedy and comedy in this regard, and the frequencies in the sample of Terence and in the tragic fragments of Pacuvius are very close to that in the *Epodes*.

The loss of most tragedy also precludes accurate histories of individual CC, but some observations are possible. Of the 61 different CC in the *Epodes* (below), 54 (89%) can be found in Republican prose as well as verse,[6] 18 (30%) are attested in Republican comedy but not tragedy, 3 (5%) in tragedy but not comedy, 15 (25%) in both genres, while 22 (36%) are not attested in verse earlier than the

It should be noted that words which are CC 'by nature' are sometimes scanned as 'dactyls' ($-\cup\cup$) not only in drama but in Republican and especially Imperial hexameter verse (Austin on Virg. *A.* 2.735). In H. there are 8 examples of this, 3 involving the intractable name 'Pollio' (*C.* 2.1.14 (Alcaic), *S.* 1.10.42, 85; cf. Coleman on Virg. *Ecl.* 3.84), another 3 forms of *nescioquis* (*S.* 1.9.2, 67, *Ep.* 2.2.35), with the remaining two occurring in the highly colloquial *S.* 1.4 (*mentio* (93), *dixero* (104)). For elision with correption (3.22n.) of CS and CC, cf. *S.* 1.1.59, 9.6, 2.7.53, 8.83, *Ep.* 1.7.95, and Soubiran (1966) 207–18.

[4] Of the CE in the *Epodes*, 84% are attested in non-CS forms in Republican dactylic verse. Most of the rest eventually turn up in Ovid or later hexameters; the exceptions are *Bupalo* (6.14), *Colchicis* (5.24, 17.35), *emancipatus* (9.12), *exercitatas* (9.31), *Hibericis* (4.3), *illigata, illigaturum* (1.25, 3.11; cf. Virg. *A.* 10.794 (tmesis)), *inemori* (5.34), *interminato* (5.39), *intueris* (5.9; cf. Lucr. 4.713 (tmesis)), *ordinarat* (17.9), *scientiae* (17.1), and *scientioris* (5.72).

[5] The relative infrequency of CC in the earliest dramatic verse (Andr., Naev., Enn.) is hard to explain. It may be a consequence of small sample size, or of the 'poverty' of the early language in respect of certain word types that are likely to be CC (cf. Table 3).

[6] The CC which are not in Republican prose include H.'s coinages (n. 7 below) as well as *inquietus, peruicax, siticulosus,* and *uiperinus.*

Table 1. *Frequencies of CS and CC in Republican verse*

	No. of verses	Percentage with CS	Percentage with CC	Percentage of CS consisting of CC
H. *Epodes*	537	45	14	30
Cat. iambs	194	62	20	32
Tragedy (total)	1,628	36	8	21
Andr.	41	37	2	7
Naev.	59	24	5	21
Enn.	373	37	5	14
Pac.	380	38	11	28
Acc.	660	35	8	23
Cic.	115	47	9	19
Comedy (total)	2,524	34	8	24
Naev.	107	36	4	10
Pl. *Men.*	1,162	32	7	22
Caecil.	274	34	7	20
Ter. *An.*	981	37	11	29

Epodes. The first three figures seem to suggest a 'low' stylistic level (Intro. 5), but the fourth may indicate that in this respect there was at least some overlap between comic and tragic diction,[7] and the fifth could be taken as evidence that, far from being 'biased' against CC, H. was willing to introduce new ones to the poetic language.[8]

On the other hand, there do seem to be differences both between H. and his predecessors and among those predecessors in regard to preferred types of CC (Table 3). In the *Epodes*, the largest groups are

[7] On the other hand, of the 90 different CC in the tragic fragments, nearly half (43 = 48%) are not attested in Republican comedy, and of these another half (22 = 24% of the total) do not occur in any other Classical Latin. But this suggestion of a vocabulary unique to tragedy may result from the fact that many of these particular words (26 = 60% of those not in comedy) are extant precisely because they are cited by grammarians as unique or unusual.

[8] Of these, four may be Horatian coinages (Intro. 5; cf. 3.16, 5.47, 8.20, 16.38nn.), while the rest occur in prose earlier than H. and may be 'prosaic' (Intro. 5). There is little 'overlap' between the CC in the *Epodes* and those in the 'Neoterics' (Intro. 5, n. 54). For the *Odes*, cf. n. 11 below.

Table 2. *Frequencies of CS and CC in H.* Epodes *and* Odes

	No. of places allowing CS and CC	Percentage with CS	Percentage with CC	Percentage of CS consisting of CC
H. *Epodes*	1,922	13	4	30
H. *Odes* (total)	4,284	16	2	13
Odes 1	1,102	17	3	16
Odes 2	990	13	2	15
Odes 3	1,446	16	2	14
Odes 4	746	18	1	8

made up of compound words (36%) and of adjectives in *-osus* (15%).[9] Compounds are also a major group in the CC of tragedy (22%), Plautus (22%), Terence (31%), and Catullus (22%), but in tragedy they vie with forms in *-itas* (23%) and *-tudo* (23%), in Plautus with forms in *-io* (11%), in Terence with forms in *-atio* (11%) and *-itas* (14%), and in Catullus with forms in *-atio* (14%) as well as in *-osus* (13%).

It also appears that H. changed his view of CC when he moved from the *Epodes* to the *Odes*. Since lyric metres are much less receptive to CS than iambic, it is necessary to compare frequency in terms of number of places allowing CS rather than number of verses (Table 2).[10] Such a comparison reveals that although the frequency of CS in the *Odes* resembles that in the *Epodes*, the frequency of CC, and thus of CS made up of CC, is greatly diminished, especially in

---

[9] 'Compound words' include both those formed with prefixes (the vast majority and the only type in the *Epodes* (17.12n.)) and those made up of separate lexical words (e.g. *noctiluca* (*C.* 4.6.38), *tauriformis* (*C.* 4.14.25)). For words in *-osus*, cf. 3.16n.

[10] The difference between iambic and lyric can be illustrated by comparing four lines of epodic 'System 1' (Intro. 6), which contain 14 places allowing CS, with the Alcaic stanza, containing only 7, and the Sapphic, containing only 6 such places. The differences between the various lengths of iambic and trochaic verse are less extreme (e.g. 4 places in an iambic trimeter (senarius), 6 places in a trochaic septenarius).

Table 3. *Types of CC in Republican verse*

	Epodes	*Odes*	Trag.	Pl.	Ter.	Cat.
Number of different CC	61	66	90	330	167	85
Compounds (%)	36	39	22	22	31	22
CC in *-alis* (%)	5	8	3	4	3	2
in *-atio* (%)	5	—	4	9	11	14
in *-atus* (%)	5	5	2	7	2	—
in *-illus* (%)	—	—	—	1	—	7
in *-io* (%)	5	1	8	11	6	6
in *-itas* (%)	3	11	23	8	14	1
in *-osus* (%)	15	23	3	7	5	13
in *-tudo* (%)	—	—	23	4	4	—
Foreign CC (%)	7	9	—	5	6	7
Other types (%)	19	4	12	22	18	28
Total number of different types of CC	17	10	15	34	22	19

the fourth book.[11] Analysis of the *Odes'* 67 different CC shows distribution similar to that in the *Epodes* of words attested in comedy, tragedy, and in H. for the first time, but there are fewer words that also occur in Republican prose.[12] Finally, there is less variety in the

[11] Catullus also has a lower frequency of CC in his lyrics (4% of places) than in his iambics (6% of places), but the difference is not as great as that between *Odes* and *Epodes*, and there is much less of a 'decline' in the percentage of CS made up of CC (32% for the iambs, 27% for the lyric).

[12] The figures for the *Odes* are 53 (79%) in Republican prose, 18 (27%) in comedy only, 4 (6%) in tragedy only, 12 (18%) in both genres, and 22 (33%) not in verse before the *Odes*. Of the last, 9 are either foreign (*Achaemenes* (2.12.21), *Daedaleus* (2.20.13, 4.2.2), *Phidyle* (3.23.2)) or what appear to be Horatian coinages (*fabulosus* (1.22.7, 3.4.9), *faustitas* (4.5.18), *intaminatus* (3.2.18), *irrepertus* (3.3.49), *irretortus* (2.2.23), *tauriformis* (4.14.25); cf. Bo III 391–5), while the rest occur in Republican prose. There are 18 'repeats' from the *Epodes* (cf. the list below). As with the *Epodes* (above, n. 8), there is little 'overlap' with the 'Neoterics': 13 words (19%) in common, but only 2 (*Dindymene* (1.16.5; cf. Cat. 63.13), *Formianus* (1.20.11; cf. Cat. 41.4, 43.5; also in prose) not attested in verse earlier than the Neoterics.

types of CC (Table 3), and although compound words (39%) and forms in *-osus* (23%) are still the largest groups, there is a suggestion of what may be a 'tragic' (but also Terentian) predilection for forms in *-itas* (10%).

The following list of the CC in the *Epodes* is meant to suggest the history of each word in Latin literature up to and including H. In the annotations, 'com.' refers to fragments of comedy outside of Plautus (Pl.) and Terence (Ter.), 'prose' to Republican Latin prose earlier than Livy. Tragedy is cited according to *ROL*, other fragments according to *FPL*.

aegrimonia: 13.18, 17. 73 (Pl., prose)

aestuosus: 3.18, 16.62 (*C.* 1.22.5, 31.5, 2.7.16, Pl., Pac. *trag.* 103, Cat., prose)

Africanus: 9.25 (Pl., prose)

allaboro: 8.20 (*C.* 1.38.5; Horatian coinage?)

Anacreon: 14.10 (prose)

antea: 11.1 (Ter., Cat., prose)

Argonautae: 3.9 (prose)

Ariminensis: 5.42 (prose)

attagen: 2.54 (cf. Var. *Men.* 403 *attagena*)

benignitas: 1.31 (Pl., Ter., com., prose)

ciuitas: 16.18, 36 (*C.* 3.29.25, 4.2.51, Pl., Ter., com., Pac. *trag.* 53, Enn. *trag.* 291, prose)

conscientia: 5.29 (prose)

contumelia: 11.26 (Pl., Ter., com., Pac. *trag.* 182, 280, prose)

curiosus: 17.77 (Pl., Ter., com., Cat., prose)

delibutus: 3.13, 17.31 (Pl., Ter., Pac. *trag.* 201, prose)

detestatio: 5.89 (prose)

efficax: 3.17, 17.1 (*C.* 4.12.20, prose)

eiulatio: 10.17 (Pl., prose)

elaboro: 14.12 (*C.* 3.1.18, prose)

Esquilinus: 5.100, 17.58 (prose)

fastidiosus: 17.73 (*C.* 3.1.27, 29.9, Pl., prose)

fenerator: 2.67 (prose)

formidulosus: 5.55 (*C.* 2.17.18, Pl. Ter., com., prose)

hospitalis: 17.49 (*C.* 2.3.10, Pl., *inc. trag.* 41, prose)

illiteratus: 8.17 (com., prose)

immerens: 6.1, 7.19 (*C.* 2.13.12, Pl., Cat., prose)

impotentia: 16.62 (*inc. trag.* 110, prose)

impudicus: 16.58 (Pl., com., Cat., prose)

imputatus: 16.44 (prose? cf. Paul. *Fest.* 108M)

indignatio: 4.10 (com., prose)

infidelis: 5.50, 16.6 (Pl., Acc. *trag.* 651, prose)

inhospitalis: 1.12 (*C.* 1.22.6, Var. *Men.* 426, prose)

iniuriosus: 17.34 (*C.* 1.35.13, prose)

inominatus: 16.38 (Horatian coinage?)

inquietus: 5.95 (com.)

insepultus: 5.99 (Pl., Naev. *pr.* 2, prose)

insitiuus: 2.19 (prose)

insolens: 16.14 (*C.* 1.16.21, 2.3.3, 4.2, Ter., Pac. *trag.* 60, *inc. trag.* 67, prose)

insolentia: 17.75 (com., Acc. *trag.* 259, prose)

inuerecundus: 11.13 (Pl., *fab. inc.* 179, prose)

irresectus: 5.47 (Horatian coinage?)

laboriosus: 16.60, 17.16 (Pl., Ter., Cat., Calv. *poet.* 2, prose)

liberi: 2.40, 5.5, 17.57 (Pl., Ter., Enn. *trag.* 307, Acc. *trag.* 427, Cic. *poet.* 42.2, prose)

libidinosus: 10.23 (prose)

militaris: 9.15 (*C.* 1.8.5, 22.13, Pl., prose)

nouendialis: 17.48 (prose)

obliuio: 5.70, 14.2 (*C.* 4.9.34, com., Acc.(?) fr. 697 Ribbeck, Bibac. *poet.* 3, prose)

obsoletus: 17.46 (*C.* 2.10.6, prose)

obstetrix: 17.53 (Pl., Ter., prose)

occasio: 13.4 (Pl., Ter., com., Acc. *trag.* 106, prose)

officina: 17.35 (*C.* 1.4.8, prose)

otiosus: 5.43 (*C.* 3.18.13, Pl., Ter., Enn. *inc. scen.* 238 Vahlen, Cat., prose)

Pactumeius: 17.50 (cf. *CIL* x 3778 etc.)

peruicax: 17.14 (*C.* 2.19.9, 3.3.70, Ter., Acc. *trag.* 8)

potio: 5.73 (Pl., prose)

siticulosus: 3.16 (prose?; cf. 3.16n.)

Terminalia: 2.59 (prose)

triumuiralis: 4.11 (prose)

uiperinus: 3.6 (*C.* 1.8.9, 2.19.19, Acc. *trag.* 552)

umbilicus: 14.8 (*inc. fab.* 18, Cat., prose)

usitatus: 5.73 (prose)

BIBLIOGRAPHY

This list includes works cited in the Introduction and Commentary by abbreviation (1), by name of editor or author (2), or by name of author and date (3). With a few exceptions, it does not include standard editions and commentaries referred to by the name of the editor (e.g. 'Enn. *Sc.* 5 Vahlen') or commentator ('Skutsch on Enn. *Ann.* 5') unless these are abbreviated (L–P etc.). For other abbreviations, see *OLD* (Latin texts), LSJ (Greek texts), and *L'année philologique* (periodicals); for additional bibliography on the *Epodes*, see Setaioli (1981).

I. ABBREVIATIONS

AG   Ableitinger-Gruenberger (see 3).
CE   (ed.) F. Buecheler, *Carmina epigraphica*. Leipzig 1895–7.
CIL   *Corpus inscriptionum latinarum*. Berlin 1863– .
D–S   (edd.) C. Daremberg, E. Saglio, *Dictionnaire des antiquités grecques et romaines*. Paris 1877–1919.
EG   (ed.) D. L. Page, *Epigrammata graeca*. Oxford 1975.
E–M   A. Ernout, A. Meillet, *Dictionnaire étymologique de la langue latine*. Paris 1959.
EV   *Enciclopedia Virgiliana*. Rome 1984– .
FPL   (edd.) W. Morel, K. Buechner, *Fragmenta poetarum latinorum*. Leipzig 1982.
GLK   (ed.) H. Keil, *Grammatici latini*. Leipzig 1857–70.
HA   (ed.) N. Hopkinson, *A Hellenistic anthology*. Cambridge 1988.
ILS   H. Dessau, *Inscriptiones latinae selectae*. Berlin 1892–1916.
K–G   R. Kühner, B. Gerth, *Ausführliche Grammatik der griechischen Sprache*. Hanover 1904.
K–H   Kiessling, Heinze (see 2).
K–S   R. Kühner, C. Stegmann, *Ausführliche Grammatik der lateinischen Sprache*. Darmstadt 1955.
LHS   M. Leumann, J. Hofmann, A. Szantyr, *Lateinische Grammatik* I–II. Munich 1965–77.

LIMC   *Lexicon iconographicum mythologiae classicae.* Zurich 1981– .

L–P   (edd.) E. Lobel, D. L. Page, *Poetarum Lesbiorum fragmenta.* Oxford 1952.

LSJ   (edd.) H. Liddell, R. Scott, H. Stuart Jones, *A Greek–English lexicon.* Oxford 1968.

MRR   T. R. S. Broughton, *The magistrates of the Roman republic.* New York 1951–60.

M–W   (edd.) R. Merkelbach, M. L. West, *Fragmenta Hesiodea.* Oxford 1967.

N–H   Nisbet, Hubbard (see 2).

N–W   F. Neue, C. Wagener, *Formenlehre der lateinischen Sprache.* Berlin 1892–1905.

OCD   *Oxford classical dictionary.* Oxford 1970.

OLD   *Oxford Latin dictionary.* Oxford 1982.

PCG   (edd.) R. Kassel, C. Austin, *Poetae comici graeci.* Berlin 1983– .

PEG   (ed.) A. Bernabé, *Poetae epici graeci.* Leipzig 1987.

PGM   (ed.) K. Preisendanz, *Papyri graecae magicae.* Stuttgart 1973–4. See also (ed.) H. Betz, *The Greek magical papyri in translation.* Chicago 1986.

PLM   E. Baehrens, *Poetae latini minores.* Leipzig 1879–93. Rev. F. Vollmer (incomplete) 1911–35.

PMG   (ed.) D. L. Page, *Poetae melici graeci.* Oxford 1962.

RE   *Real-Encyclopädie der classischen Altertumswissenschaft.* Stuttgart 1893– .

ROL   (ed.) E. H. Warmington, *Remains of old Latin* I–IV. London 1956–67.

Roscher   (ed.) W. Roscher, *Ausführliches Lexicon der griechischen und römischen Mythologie.* Leipzig 1884–1937.

SLG   (ed.) D. L. Page, *Supplementum lyricis graecis.* Oxford 1974.

ThLL   *Thesaurus linguae latinae.* Leipzig 1900– .

2. HORACE: EDITIONS AND COMMENTARIES

Bentley, R., *Q.H.F. Opera* I–II. Amsterdam 1728 (repr. New York 1978).

Bo, D., *Q.H.F. Opera* I–III. Turin 1957–60.

Borszák, S., *H. Opera.* Leipzig 1984.

Brink, C. O., *H. on poetry* i–iii. Cambridge 1963–82.

Campbell, A. Y., *H. Carmina et Epodi.* Liverpool 1953.

Giarratano, C., *Il libro degli epodi.* Turin 1930.

Ingallina, S., *Orazio e la magia.* Palermo 1974.

Keller, O., *Epilegomena zur Horaz.* Leipzig 1879.

Keller, O., Holder, A., *Q.H.F. Opera* i–ii. Leipzig 1899.

Kiessling, A., Heinze, R., *Q.H.F.* i–iii. Berlin 1930.

Klingner, F., *H. Opera.* Leipzig 1959.

Lambinus, D., *Q.H.F. Opera.* Lyons 1561.

Miles, R., *The Epodes of Horace.* Newcastle upon Tyne 1980.

Mueller, L., *H. Oden und Epoden.* Leipzig 1900.

Naylor, J., *H. Odes and Epodes.* Cambridge 1922.

Nisbet, R. G. M., Hubbard, M., *A commentary on H. Odes* i–ii. Oxford 1970–8.

Orelli, J. *et al., Q.H.F. Opera.* Berlin 1886.

Page, T. E., *H. Odes and Epodes.* London 1895.

Peerlkamp, P. H., *Q.H.F. Carmina.* Amsterdam 1862.

Plessis, F., *Q.H.F. Odes, épodes, chant séculaire.* Paris 1924.

Rudd, N., *H.: Epistles Book II and 'Ars Poetica'.* Cambridge 1989.

Shackleton Bailey, D. R., *H. Opera.* Stuttgart 1985.

Turolla, E., *Q.H.F. Giambi.* Turin 1957.

Vollmer, F., *H. Opera.* Leipzig 1912.

Wickham, E., *H. Odes and Epodes.* Oxford 1896.

3. OTHER WORKS

Ableitinger-Gruenberger, D. (1968). 'Die neunte Epode des Horaz', *W.S.* 2: 74–91.

(1971). *Der junge Horaz und die Politik.* Heidelberg.

Adams, J. N. (1982). *The Latin sexual vocabulary.* Baltimore.

Ahl, F. M. (1985). *Metaformations.* Ithaca.

André, J. (1949). *Les termes de couleur dans la langue latine.* Paris.

(1961). *L'alimentation et la cuisine à Rome.* Paris.

Appel, G. (1909). *De Romanorum precationibus.* Giessen.

Armstrong, D. (1986). 'Horatius eques et scriba: Satires 1.6 and 2.7', *T.A.P.A.* 116: 255–88.

(1989). *Horace.* New Haven.

Audollent, A. (1904). *Defixionum tabellae.* Paris.

Axelson, B. (1945). *Unpoetische Wörter.* Lund.

Babcock, C. (1966). 'A reconsideration of Horace's 15th Epode', *A.J.Ph.* 87: 400–19.

(1974). 'The language of commitment in Epode 1', *C.J.* 70: 14–31.

(1978). 'Horace, Epode 13', in (ed.) D. Reichel, *Wege der Wort.* Cologne.

Barber, P. (1988). *Vampires, burial, and death.* New Haven.

Bartels, C. (1973). 'Die neunte Epode des Horaz als sympotisches Gedicht', *Hermes* 101: 282–313.

Benveniste, E. (1969). *Le vocabulaire des institutions indo-européennes.* Paris.

Blok, W. (1961). *Woortkreus en stijlniveau van de 1e, 3e, 4e, en 13e Epode van Horatius.* Leiden.

Bonfante, G. (1936–7). 'Los elementos populares en la lengua de Horacio', *Emerita* 4–5: 86–247, 17–88.

Bremer, J. *et al.* (1987). *Some recently found Greek poems.* Leiden.

Brink, C. O. (1982). 'Horatian notes III', *P.C.P.S.* 28: 30–56.

Brown, R. (1987). *Lucretius on love and sex.* Leiden.

Brunt, P. A. (1988). *The fall of the Roman Republic.* Oxford.

Buchheit, V. (1961). 'Horazens programmatische Epode', *Gymn.* 68: 520–6.

Buechner, K. (1970). *Studien zur römischen Literatur* VII. Wiesbaden.

Burkert, W. (1985). *Greek religion.* Cambridge Mass.

Cairns, F. (1972). *Generic composition in Greek and Roman poetry.* Edinburgh.

(1978). 'Horace, Epode 2, Tibullus 1.1 and the rhetorical praise of the countryside', *M.Ph.L.* 17: 79–91.

(1983). 'Horace Epode 9: some new interpretations', *I.C.S.* 8: 80–93.

Campbell, D. (1982–92). *Greek lyric* I–IV. London.

(1983). *The golden lyre.* London.

Carrubba, R. W. (1966). 'The curse on the Romans', *T.A.P.A.* 97: 29–34.

(1969). *The Epodes of Horace.* The Hague.

Carter, J. M. (1970). *The battle of Actium.* New York.

Christes, J. (1990). 'Die 14. Epode des Horaz', *Gymn.* 97: 341–56.

Clay, J. S. (1983). *The wrath of Athene.* Princeton.

(1986). 'Archilochus and Gyges', *Q.U.C.C.* 24: 7–17.

(1989). *The politics of Olympus.* Princeton.

Commager, S. (1962). *The Odes of Horace.* New Haven.

Comotti, G. (1989). *Music in Greek and Roman culture.* Baltimore.

Copley, F. (1956). *Exclusus amator*. Madison.

Courtney, E. (1993). *The fragmentary Latin poets*. Oxford.

Cremona, V. (1982). *La poesia civile di Orazio*. Milan.

Crook, J. (1967). *Law and life of Rome*. Ithaca.

Davis, G. (1991). *Polyhymnia: the rhetoric of Horatian lyric discourse*. Berkeley.

Degani, E. (1983). *Hipponax*. Leipzig.

Düntzer, H. (1892). 'Des Horatius Canidia-Gedichte', *N. Jahrb.* 145: 597–613.

Ernout, A. (1949). *Les adjectives latins en -osus et en -ulentus*. Paris.

Fantham, E. (1992). *Lucan: De bello ciuili* II. Cambridge.

Fedeli, P. (1978). 'Il v epodo e i giambi d'Orazio come espressione d'arte alessandrina', *M.Ph.L.* 3: 67–138.

Fitzgerald, W. (1988). 'Power and impotence in Horace's Epodes', *Arethusa* 17: 176–91.

Fraenkel, E. (1957). *Horace*. Oxford.

Fugier, H. (1963). *Recherches sur l'expression du sacré dans la langue latine*. Strassburg.

Gatz, B. (1967). *Weltalter, goldene Zeit und sinnverwandte Vorstellungen*. Spudasmata 16.

Gelzer, M. (1968). *Caesar*. Cambridge Mass.

Gentili, B. (1988). *Poetry and its public in ancient Greece*. Baltimore.

Gowers, E. (1993). *The loaded table*. Oxford.

Grassman, V. (1966). *Die erotischen Epoden des Horaz*. Munich.

Gratwick, A. (1993). *Plautus: Menaechmi*. Cambridge.

Griffin, J. (1986). *Latin poets and Roman life*. Chapel Hill.

Hanslik, R. (1962). 'Horaz und Aktium', *Serta Phil. Aenipontana*: 335–42.

Hellegouarc'h, J. (1972). *Le vocabulaire latin des relations et de parties politiques sous la République*. Paris.

Henderson, J. (1991). *The maculate Muse*. Oxford.

Henderson, J. (1987). 'Suck it and see (Horace Epode 8)', in *Homo Viator: classical essays for J. Bramble*. Bristol.

Hense, C. (1868). *Poetische Personification in griechischen Dichtungen*. Halle.

Heyworth, S. J. (1993). 'Horace's Ibis: on the titles, unity, and contents of the Epodes', *Proceedings of the Leeds International Seminar* VII: 85–96.

Hierche, H. (1974). *Les épodes d'Horace.* Brussels.

Hofmann, J. B. (1951). *Lateinische Umgangsprache.* Heidelberg.

Horsfall, N. (1973). 'Three notes on Horace's Epodes', *Phil.* 117: 136–8.

Housman, A. E. (1972). *Collected classical papers.* 3 vols. Cambridge.

Huzar, E. (1978). *Mark Antony.* Minneapolis.

Jacoby, F. (1914). 'Eine vergessene Horazemendation (Epod. IV. 10)', *Hermes* 49: 454–63.

Jal, P. (1962). 'Les dieux et les guerres civiles dans la Rome de la fin de la République', *R.E.L.* 40: 170–200.

(1963). *La guerre civile à Rome.* Paris.

Kenney, E. J. (1971). *Lucretius: De Rerum Natura Book III.* Cambridge.

(1982). 'Books and readers in the Roman world', in *The Cambridge history of Classical literature* II. Cambridge.

(1984). *The ploughman's lunch. Moretum: a poem ascribed to Virgil.* Bristol.

(1990). *Apuleius: Cupid and Psyche.* Cambridge.

Kienast, D. (1982). *Augustus.* Darmstadt.

Kilpatrick, R. (1970). 'An interpretation of Horace's Epode 13', *C.Q.* 20: 135–41.

Kirn, B. (1935). *Zur literarischen Stellung von Horazens Jambenbuch.* Tübingen.

Klingner, F. (1961). *Römische Geisteswelt.* Hamburg.

Kraggerud, E. (1984). *Horaz und Aktium.* Oslo.

Kuhn, F. (1973). *Illusion und Disillusionierung in den erotischen Gedichten des Horaz.* Heidelberg.

Kukula, R. C. (1911). *Römische Säkularpoesie.* Leipzig.

Kurfess, A. (1951). *Sibyllinische Weissungen.* Berlin.

Lattimore, R. (1962). *Themes in Greek and Latin epitaphs.* Urbana.

Leo, F. (1900). *De Horatio et Archilocho.* Göttingen.

Liebeschuetz, J. (1979). *Continuity and change in Roman religion.* Oxford.

Lilja, S. (1972). *The treatment of odours in the poetry of antiquity.* Helsinki.

(1983). *Homosexuality in Republican and Augustan Rome.* Helsinki.

Löfstedt, E. (1956). *Syntactica* I. Lund.

Luck, G. (1985). *Arcana mundi.* Baltimore.

Mankin, D. (1988a). 'The addressee of Virgil's 8th Eclogue', *Hermes* 116: 63–76.

(1988b). Review of Borszak, *Horatius Opera*, Shackleton Bailey, *Horatius Opera*, *A.J.Ph.* 109: 270–4.

314 BIBLIOGRAPHY

(1989). 'Achilles in Horace's 13th Epode', *W.S.* 102: 133–40.

(1992). '*C.* 3.14: how 'private' is Horace's party?', *Rh.M.* 135: 378–81.

Marouzeau, J. (1949). *L'ordre des mots dans la phrase latine* III. Paris.

Martina, M. (1989). 'A proposito di Hor. Epod. 1.29', *B. Stud. Lat.* 19: 49–53.

Nagy, G. (1979). *The best of the Achaeans*. Baltimore.

Newman, J. K. (1967). *Augustus and the new poetry*. Brussels.

Nisbet, R. G. M. (1984). 'Horace's Epodes and history', in (edd.) T. Woodman, D. West, *Poetry and politics in the age of Augustus*. Cambridge.

(1989). 'Footnotes on Horace', in *Studies in Latin literature and its tradition in honour of C. O. Brink*. Cambridge.

Norden. E. (1926). *P. Vergilius Maro Aeneis Buch VI*. Berlin.

O'Hara, J. (1990). *Death and the optimistic prophecy in Virgil's Aeneid*. Princeton.

Oksala, T. (1973). *Religion und Mythos bei Horaz*. Helsinki.

Onians, R. (1954). *The origins of European thought*. Cambridge.

Opelt, I. (1965). *Die lateinischen Schimpfwörter*. Heidelberg.

Otto, A. (1890). *Die Sprichwörter und sprichwörtlichen Redensarten der Römer*. Leipzig.

Page, D. L. (1971). *Euripides: Medea*. Oxford.

Parker, R. (1983). *Miasma*. Oxford.

Pelling, C. (1988). *Plutarch: Life of Antony*. Cambridge.

Perret, J. (1964). *Horace*. New York.

Pfeiffer, R. (1968). *History of classical scholarship*. Oxford.

Pichon, R. (1902). *De sermone amatorio apud Latinos elegiarum scriptores*. Paris.

Plüsz, T. (1881). *Horazstudien*. Leipzig.

(1904). *Das Jambenbuch des Horaz*. Leipzig.

Porter, D. (1987). *Horace's poetic journey*. Princeton.

Putnam, M. (1986). *Artifices of eternity: Horace's fourth book of Odes*. Ithaca.

Reinhold, M. (1988). *A historical commentary on Dio's Roman History books 49–52*. Atlanta.

Richardson, L. (1992). *A new topographical dictionary of ancient Rome*. Baltimore.

Richlin, A. (1992). *The garden of Priapus*. Oxford.

Romm, J. (1992). *The edges of the earth in ancient thought*. Princeton.

Ross, D. O. (1969). *Style and tradition in Catullus*. Cambridge Mass.

(1979). 'Old logs and ancient saws (Epode 2.43)', *A.J.Ph.* 100: 241–4.

Rossi, L. E. (1976). 'Asynarteta from the Archaic to the Alexandrian poets', *Arethusa* 9: 207–29.

Ruckdeschel, F. (1910–11). *Archaism und Vulgarismen in der Sprache des Horaz* I–II. Erlangen.

Rudd, N. (1966). *The Satires of Horace*. Berkeley.

Santirocco, M. (1986). *Unity and design in Horace's Odes*. Chapel Hill.

Schein, S. (1984). *The mortal hero*. Berkeley.

Schmidt, E. A. (1977). '*Amica uis pastoribus*: der Jambiker Horaz in seinem Epodenbuch', *Gymn.* 84: 401–23.

Scullard, H. (1981). *Festivals and ceremonies of the Roman Republic*. Ithaca.

(1982). *From the Gracchi to Nero*. London.

Setaioli, A. (1981). 'Gli Epodi di Orazio nella critica dal 1937–72 (con un'appendice fine al 1978)', *ANRW* II 31.3: 1674–1788.

Shackleton Bailey, D. R. (1956). *Propertiana*. Cambridge.

Soubiran, J. (1966). *L'élision dans la poésie latine*. Paris.

(1988). *Essai sur la versification dramatique des Romains*. Paris.

Syme, R. (1939). *The Roman revolution*. Oxford.

Tarditi, G. (1968). *Arciloco*. Rome.

Tarrant, R. (1983). 'Horace', in (ed.) L. D. Reynolds, *Texts and transmissions*. Oxford.

Taylor, L. R. (1966). *Roman voting assemblies*. Ann Arbor.

Thomas, R. F. (1982). *Lands and peoples in Roman poetry*. Cambridge.

Tränkle, H. (1960). *Die Sprachkunst des Properz*. Wiesbaden.

(1990). *Appendix Tibulliana*. Berlin.

Treu, M. (1959). *Archilochos*. Göttingen.

Tupet, A.-M. (1976). *La magie dans la poésie latine*. Paris.

Van Raalte, M. (1986). *Rhythm and metre*. Assen.

Watson, L. C. (1983a). 'Problems in Epode 11', *C.Q.* 33: 229–38.

(1983b). 'Two problems in Horace Epode 3', *Phil.* 127: 80–6.

(1987). 'Epode 9, or the art of falsehood', in *Homo Viator: classical essays for J. Bramble*. Bristol.

Watson, P. (1985). 'Axelson reconsidered: the selection of vocabulary in Latin poetry', *C.Q.* 35: 430–48.

West, M. L. (1974). *Studies in Greek elegy and iambus.* Berlin.

(1980). *Delectus ex iambis et elegis Graecis.* Oxford.

(1982). *Greek metre.* Oxford.

(1989–92). *Iambi et elegi Graeci* i–ii. Oxford.

White, K. D. (1970). *Roman farming.* Ithaca.

Wili, W. (1948). *Horaz.* Basel.

Wilkinson, L. P. (1951). *Horace and his lyric poetry.* Cambridge.

Williams, G. (1968). *Tradition and originality in Roman poetry.* Oxford.

Wissowa, G. (1912). *Religion und Kultus der Römer.* Munich.

Wistrand, E. (1958). *Horace's ninth Epode and its historical background.* Göteborg.

Wurzel, F. (1938). 'Der Ausgang der Schlacht von Aktium und die 9. Epode des Horaz', *Hermes* 73: 361–79.

Zanker, P. (1990). *The power of images in the age of Augustus.* Ann Arbor.

Zielinski, T. (1935). 'L'envoûment de la sorcière chez Horace', in *Mélanges O. Navarre.* Tolosa.

INDEXES TO THE COMMENTARY

References are to the introductions to individual poems (e.g. 2 intro.) and to lines of the text (e.g. 2.2 = note on Epode 2.2).

1 Latin words

317

2 General

Printed in the United States
65148LVS00007B/1